USING LOTUS 1-2-3

RELEASE 2.2

USING LOTUS 1-2-3
RELEASE 2.2

Keiko Pitter
Truckee Meadows Community College

Richard Pitter
Desert Research Institute

Mitchell **McGRAW-HILL**
New York St. Louis San Francisco Auckland Bogotá Caracas
Hamburg Lisbon London Madrid Mexico Milan Montreal
New Delhi Oklahoma City Paris San Juan Sao Paulo Singapore
Sydney Tokyo Toronto Watsonville

Mitchell **McGraw-Hill**
55 Penny Lane
Watsonville, CA 95076

USING LOTUS 1–2–3 RELEASE 2.2

Copyright © 1990 by McGraw-Hill, Inc. All rights reserved. Printed in the United States of America. Except as permitted under the United States Copyright Act of 1976, no part of this publication may be reproduced or distributed in any form or by any means, or stored in a database or retrieval system, without the prior written permission of the publisher.

1 2 3 4 5 6 7 8 9 0 DOH DOH 9 5 4 3 2 1 0

ISBN 0-07-050258-7

Sponsoring Editor: Roger L. Howell
Production Manager: Betty Drury
Production Services by BMR
    Copy Edit: Chris Bernard
    Cover and Text Design: Randall Goodall, Seventeenth Street Studios
    Desktop Production: Curtis Philips
    Project Management: Melanie Field
Printer: R.R. Donnelley & Sons

Library of Congress Card Catalog No.: 89-62077

LOTUS and 1–2–3 are trademarks of Lotus Development Corporation.

IBM, IBM PC, and PC DOS are registered trademarks of International Business Machines Corporation.

MS DOS is a registered trademark of Microsoft, Inc.

Allways is a registered trademark of Funk Software, Inc.

VP-Planner is a registered trademark of Paperback Software International.

CONTENTS

Preface, xiii

**LESSON 1
COMPONENTS
OF IBM
MICROS AND
COMPATIBLES**

Function of a Computer, 3
Processing Components, 5
    MPU, 5
    Main Memory, 6
Output Components, 8
    Monitor and Printer, 8
    Disk Drive and Modem, 10
Input Components, 11
    Keyboard, 11
    Mouse, 11
    Disk Drive and Modem, 12
Starting the Computer, 12
The Keyboard, 15
Keyboard Features, 16
    Characters, 16
    Space Bar, 16
    Enter, 17
    Control Characters, 17
    Function Keys, 17
    Alt, 17
    Numeric Keyboard, 17
    Esc, 18
    Tab, 18
    PrtSc, 18
    Backspace, 19
    Ins and Del, 19
    Keys to Keep Distinct, 19
    Auto-Repeat, 19
Learn to Use the Software, 20
Function of a Disk, 20
Disks, 20

Care and Handling of 5 1/4-inch Disks, 23
Care and Handling of 3 1/2-inch Disks, 24
Hard Disks, 25
Care of Disk Drives, 25
Identifying Disk Drives, 26
End of Lesson 1, 26
Summary, 27
Review Questions, 27
Configuration of My Computer, 28

LESSON 2
THE DISK OPERATING SYSTEM

Orientation, 31
Starting Off, 32
Default Disk Drive, 32
Changing the Default Drive, 32
DOS Commands, 33
   VER, 34
   FORMAT, 34
   CHKDSK, 36
   DIR, 37
   COPY, 39
   RENAME, 41
   ERASE, 41
   TYPE, 42
   COMP, 42
   DISKCOPY, 42
   DISKCOMP, 43
   MKDIR, 44
   CHDIR, 45
   TREE, 47
   RMDIR, 47
   Executing Programs, 48
End of Lesson 2, 48
Summary, 48
Review Questions, 49

LESSON 3
SOME ADVANCED DOS FEATURES

Orientation, 53
Starting Off, 53
Batch Files, 54
Path Command, 56
AUTOEXEC.BAT, 57

CONFIG.SYS, 60
End of Lesson 3, 61
Summary, 61
Review Questions, 62

LESSON 4 CREATING A SIMPLE SPREADSHEET

Introduction, 65
Lotus 1-2-3 Releases, 67
Starting Lotus, 69
   Using a Floppy Drive System, 69
   Using a Hard-Drive or Networked System, 70
Using a Printer, 71
Starting Off, 72
The 1-2-3 Access System, 72
Entering 1-2-3, 73
   The Control Panel, 74
   The Worksheet Area, 75
   The Status Line, 75
Moving the Cell Pointer, 76
Sizing the Worksheet, 76
The Goto Key (5), 77
The Command Structure, 78
Erasing An Entry (/RE), 80
Erasing the Worksheet (/WEY), 82
Labels and Values, 82
   Characters Designating Values, 82
   Characters Designating Labels, 83
Entering Labels, 83
   Uppercase, 83
   Correcting Errors, 84
Entering Values, 84
Preparing the Worksheet, 84
Entering Formulas (Mathematical Expressions), 86
File Commands (/F), 89
Specifying a Directory (/FD), 90
Saving a File (/FS), 90
Printing Files (/PP), 91
End of Lesson 4, 94
Summary, 94
Review Questions, 96
Exercises, 97

LESSON 5 ENHANCING THE SIMPLE SPREADSHEET

Starting Off, 99
The Help System (F1), 99
The Undo Command (ALT-F4), 100
Retrieving a File (/FR), 101
Inserting Rows (/WIR), 103
   The Copy Command (/C), 105
Repeating Labels (\), 107
Setting the Width of a Column (/WC), 108
The Sum Function (@SUM), 113
The Global Display Format (/WGF), 114
The Range Format Command (/RF), 117
Zero Suppression, 118
Saving a File that Already Exists on Disk, 118
Printing the Spreadsheet in Sections, 119
End of Lesson 5, 121
Summary, 121
Review Questions, 123
Exercises, 123

LESSON 6 MODIFYING THE DISPLAY FORMAT

Starting Off, 127
Freeze Titles Command (/WT), 128
   Window Command (/WW), 130
   Jumping Between Windows (F6), 131
Hiding a Column (/WCH), 133
Move Command (/M), 135
Deleting Rows (/WDR), 136
Deleting Columns (/WDC), 137
   Edit Key (F2), 138
Text Display, 138
Formula Printout, 140
Search and Replace (/RS), 142
End of Lesson 6, 144
Summary, 144
Review Questions, 146
Exercises, 146

LESSON 7
CREATING PRESENTATION GRAPHICS

Starting Off, 149
Graphics, 149
Pie Charts, 151
   Crosshatching a Graph, 156
   Exploding a Pie Chart, 157
   Naming a Graph, 158
   Saving a Graph, 159
Bar Graph, 160
Stacked-Bar Graphs, 166
Line Graph, 167
Xy Graph, 172
Manual Scaling, 175
Grids, 178
Printing Graphs, 178
End of Lesson 7, 182
Summary, 183
Review Questions, 184
Exercises, 185

LESSON 8
USING A SPREADSHEET AS A DATABASE

Starting Off, 187
Data Management, 187
An Inventory Application, 188
Sorting, 189
Data Query, 193
   Other Text-Selection Criteria, 199
   Formula Conditions, 200
   Multiple Selection Criteria, 203
   Unique Option, 205
   Delete Option, 206
End of Lesson 8, 206
Summary, 206
Review Questions, 207
Exercises, 208

LESSON 9
USING OTHER DATA FEATURES

Starting Off, 211
Data Distribution, 211
   Data Fill, 212
   Distribution Table, 213
Range Names, 214
   Range Name Label Command (/RNL), 216
   Range Name Table Command (/RNT), 217

Data Table, 220
One-way Data Table (/DT1), 221
Two-way Data Table (/DT2), 224
End of Lesson 9, 229
Summary, 229
Review Questions, 230
Exercises, 231

LESSON 10 USING BUILT-IN FUNCTIONS

Starting Off, 235
Functions, 235
   Mathematical Functions, 237
   Statistical Functions, 239
   Logical Functions, 242
   Financial Functions, 246
   Date/time Functions, 248
   Database Functions, 250
   String Functions, 251
   Special Functions, 253
End of Lesson 10, 259
Summary, 259
Review Questions, 261
Exercises, 262

LESSON 11 PRINTING REPORTS

Starting Off, 265
Printer Default Settings, 265
   Printer Settings, 266
Print Command Options, 267
   Margin Settings, 269
   Setup String, 270
   Header and Footer, 271
   Page Numbers and Date, 272
   Border, 272
   Other, 273
End of Lesson 11, 274
Summary, 274
Review Questions, 275
Exercises, 275

LESSON 12 MULTIPLE FILES

Starting Off, 279
Combining Files, 281
Modular Spreadsheets, 284
Adding Values from Several Spreadsheets, 287
Linking Data Between Files, 289
Exporting ASCII Files, 293
Importing ASCII Files, 293
    Data Parsing, 297
The Lotus Translate Utility, 300
End of Lesson 12, 304
Summary, 304
Review Questions, 305
Exercises, 306

LESSON 13 INTRODUCING MACROS

Starting Off, 309
Macros, 309
Creating and Using Macros, 310
The Lotus Learn Feature, 315
Multiple-Line Macros, 321
Learn Feature vs. Direct Entry of Macros, 323
End of Lesson 13, 324
Summary, 324
Review Questions, 325
Exercises, 326

LESSON 14 ADVANCED MACRO COMMANDS

Starting Off, 329
Advanced Macro Commands, 329
Data-Manipulation Commands, 331
    {LET Location, Entry}, 331
    {BLANK Location}, 331
Flow-of-Control Commands, 331
    {BRANCH Location}, 331
    {IF Condition}, 334
    {QUIT}, 335
    {RETURN}, 335
Interactive Commands, 337
    {?}, 337
    {GETNUMBER Prompt,Location}, 337
    {GETLABEL Prompt,Location}, 337
    {MENUBRANCH Location} and {MENUCALL Location}, 338
    {WAIT Time-Number}, 338

Macro example, 338
    MENUBRANCH example, 340
    MENUCALL example, 345
Autoexecute Macros, 350
End of Lesson 14, 351
Summary, 351
Review Questions, 353
Exercises, 354

LESSON 15 ADD-IN PROGRAMS

Starting Off, 357
Add-in Programs, 357
Add-in Command (/A), 358
Macro Library Manager, 359
    Editing Macro Libraries, 363
Allways, 365
    Invoking and Using Allways, 366
    Fonts and Boldface, 369
    Shading and Lines, 373
    Printing, 375
    Margins, 375
    Graphs, 377
    Editing Graphs, 379
End of Lesson 15, 381
Summary, 381
Review Questions, 382
Exercises, 383

Glossary, 385

Lotus 1-2-3 Command Summary, 395
    Lotus Access System Menu, 395
    Control Panel, 395
    Cell Pointer Movement, 396
    Correcting Mistakes, 396
    1-2-3 Function Keys, 396
    1-2-3 Menu Commands, 397
    Printer Setup Strings, 404
    Printgraph Menu Commands, 404
    Allways Menu Commands, 405
    Allways Function Keys, 407
    Macro Library Manager Commands, 408

Index, 409

PREFACE

Using Lotus 1–2–3 Release 2.2 is a hands-on tutorial that presents both basic introductory material on how to use spreadsheets and several more advanced topics that are applied in many types of spreadsheet use. This book is the result of an evolutionary process, with regard to both electronic spreadsheets and my previous modules and books on using spreadsheets.

CHANGING STUDENT NEEDS

Several years ago, I began writing books introducing students to microcomputer applications. At that time, microcomputers were new to most students and students knew little of the productivity gains possible with their use. Things have changed since then! Today, many students know what computers can do. In fact, most students have access to computers at work or at home. Many even have a passing knowledge of various application software packages, but they want more.

At Truckee Meadows Community College, we initially offered general computer literacy classes that covered the fundamentals of word processing, spreadsheets, and file management. Then we noticed the growing number of students who knew one or two application areas and wanted to learn others. Therefore, we offered a series of one-credit courses in different application areas.

Today, students want to learn not only the fundamentals of an application software package, but its advanced features, too. We now offer fifteen-week courses in each application area. This book was designed as the lab manual for a semester-long course in spreadsheets, using Lotus 1–2–3 Release 2.2.

In 1984, my first IBM computer manual, *Using Microcomputers: An IBM PC Lab Manual*, was published. The publishers also released a shortened version, *Using Microcomputers: Lotus 1–2–3 for the IBM PC*, which covered just the Lotus 1–2–3 portion of that manual. In response to the need for a manual for a semester-long course in spreadsheets, I published a manual on VP-Planner in 1988. In the Lotus *Using Microcomputers* and two subsequent editions of the IBM *Using Microcomputers*, I covered Releases 1A, 2, and 2.01 of Lotus 1–2–3. This manual is my first to cover Release 2.2. It describes not only the use of many new features, such as add-ins and the Learn and Undo features, but also how to use other advanced features, such as macros and data parsing.

BOOK ORGANIZATION

This book answers questions users most often ask about Lotus 1–2–3, using language that is neither too technical nor too elementary. It contains fifteen lessons: The first three lessons introduce the student to the operation of an IBM micro or compatible and its disk operating system (DOS). The next six lessons cover basic concepts, and the last six lessons present advanced topics of Lotus 1–2–3.

Throughout the book, the student is told or shown what entries to make and what responses to expect from the computer at each stage of an application. Whenever possible, the reason for each entry is given. "Practice Times" appear throughout the text to test the student's understanding of the material. Although solutions are not given, the student should complete each Practice Time. If a student cannot perform a Practice Time, he or she should review the relevant material. In addition, there are review questions and two or more exercises. These help the instructor keep track of student progress.

SUPPLEMENTARY MATERIAL

Although the book does not contain solutions to practice time problems or end-of-lesson exercises, disks containing solutions are available to instructors upon request. These disks contain worksheets for all the files saved during the lessons and all the end-of-lesson exercises.

Note, however, that there may be more than one solution to a spreadsheet problem. A student's spreadsheet is not necessarily wrong because it differs from the one on the solution disk.

SOFTWARE REQUIREMENTS

For this book, the student needs a floppy data disk (a blank diskette or one that may be erased) and Lotus 1–2–3 Release 2.2. Lotus 1–2–3 may be operated from a hard-disk system, from a network, or from floppy diskettes. If it is operated from floppy diskettes, the student also needs **PC DOS** or **MS DOS** (version 2.11 or higher) when turning on the computer. In Lessons 2 and 3, the student needs a floppy disk which contains **DOS**.

In Lesson 15, the Lotus Macro Library Manager and Allways, two add-in programs, are presented. Both add-ins are included in the Lotus 1–2–3 Release 2.2 software package. Allways cannot be used if you are operating Lotus 1–2–3 from floppy diskettes.

HARDWARE REQUIREMENTS

The student needs access to an IBM PC or compatible with at least 512 kilobytes of RAM, a monitor with graphics capability, two floppy disk drives or a floppy drive with either a hard drive or a network, and either a printer or access to a computer with a printer. For the Allways section in Lesson 15, a hard drive or network is required and 640 kilobytes of RAM is recommended.

ACKNOWLEDGMENTS

I extend my gratitude to the staff at Mitchell Publishing, Incorporated, particularly to Roger Howell, for understanding my busy schedule and having so much confidence in my work. Bill Barth of Cayuga Community College and Thomas Lightner of the University of Colorado provided excellent reviews, and Christopher Bernard of Business Media Resources edited the material.

Finally, I thank my children, Greg and Jackie, for helping me in so many ways and thereby continuing their support of my projects.

Keiko Pitter
Reno, Nevada
December, 1989

**USING
LOTUS
1-2-3
RELEASE 2.2**

LESSON 1
COMPONENTS OF IBM MICROS AND COMPATIBLES

SUPPLIES NEEDED

For this part of the manual, you will need:

- The DOS disk: A DOS disk accompanies the computer at the time of purchase.

OBJECTIVES

Upon completion of the material presented in this lesson, you should be able to understand the following features and processes:

- The function of a computer
- The identity and function of the various components of a computer
- How to turn the computer on and off
- How to use the keyboard

FUNCTION OF A COMPUTER

The function of a computer is to process data and produce a result. **Data** include any raw facts you enter into the computer for processing. The end-result of processing is the processed data, or **information**, presented in a format (or medium) that people, computers, or other machines can use.

This means that a computer system not only processes data, but also must provide ways for data to be entered (the **input**) and for the results to be produced (the **output**).

The components discussed here are as follows:

Processing Components
   Microprocessor (MPU)
   Random Access Memory (RAM)

COMPONENTS OF IBM MICROS AND COMPATIBLES

Read Only Memory (ROM)
Peripheral interfaces and expansion boards

Output Components
Printer
Monitor
Disk Drive(s)
Modem

Input Components
Keyboard
Mouse
Disk Drive(s)
Modem

Figure 1–1   An IBM PS/2 computer.

Figure 1–2   Inside of an IBM PS/2 computer.

PROCESSING COMPONENTS

A number of options are available for IBM micros and compatibles, so the way your computer is configured may be slightly different from the configuration of the system illustrated in Figure 1–2.

MPU

The large board on the bottom of the computer (partially covered in Figure 1–2) is the **motherboard**, which connects all the individual pieces electronically. The black rectangular boxes on the motherboard are called **integrated circuits**, or **chips**.

One of the larger chips on the motherboard is the **microprocessing unit**, or the **MPU**. Inside the MPU is the circuitry needed to do addition, subtraction, and comparison—functions that a computer performs. In IBM micros and compatibles, the MPU is an Intel 8088, 80286, or 80386 chip. The numbers refer to the design of a specific model of chip. Other microcomputers use different chips: for example, Apple IIGS uses 65C816 and Apple Macintosh uses a Motorola 68000.

The Intel 80286 and 80386 are newer generations of the 8088 chip. A machine with an 80286 chip can process information faster than a machine with 8088 chip, and a 80386 machine can process information much faster than a 80286 machine.

■ MAIN MEMORY

A computer also must store information while data are being processed. That place is called main memory. The main memory is on the chips. There are two types of main memory—**Random Access Memory (RAM)** and **Read Only Memory (ROM)**.

RANDOM ACCESS MEMORY (RAM)

Random Access Memory, or RAM, stores what you enter into the computer as well as the intermediate results from the computer's calculations. What you enter may be a program or data.

Information on RAM is volatile, meaning its contents are erased when the power is interrupted, or turned off. Thus, it is important when you are using the computer to make sure you save the data on another medium from time to time. Otherwise, you can lose all the data you have just entered or processed.

The RAM capacity of IBM micros and compatibles holds approximately 128,000 characters, or 128K bytes, to 640K bytes or more. A **character** is a single letter, digit, or special symbol. This amount is **expandable**, or can be increased to several megabytes (million bytes). (A byte is a computer-system format for encoding characters.)

For a program to be used on a computer—that is, for its instructions to be carried out—it must first be brought into RAM. That means the computer must have enough RAM capacity to hold the program.

Each software package has its memory requirements. Lotus 1–2–3 Release 2.2, covered in this manual, requires a minimum of 320K of RAM. To use the Allways add-in, described in Lesson 15, you need at least 512K of RAM, called conventional memory. (Lotus can use up to 4 megabytes of expanded memory RAM.) You

6 USING LOTUS 1-2-3

will need a computer with 640K of RAM to do all the lessons in this manual.

Buying Tip: Before purchasing software, check the memory requirement and make sure you have enough RAM on your computer to support it.

READ ONLY MEMORY (ROM)

Read Only Memory, or ROM, comes already loaded with the information that the computer needs to process what you enter. The information on ROM is not volatile; you can use the information, but you cannot erase or change it. The information that comes on ROM is called firmware.

EXPANSION SLOTS

At the back, left side of the motherboard are expansion slots. Your monitor and your printer, if you have one, may be connected to a board in one of these slots. These boards are called **interface boards** or **adaptor cards**. They allow IBM micros and compatibles to be connected to, or interfaced with, **peripherals** (devices that perform support functions). Sometimes also in the expansion slots are memory boards that let you expand the RAM of the computer.

Buying Tip: In the past, the number of slots that were available dictated how much peripheral equipment could be attached to a computer. Although this is still true to some extent, many of today's micros already have various connectors (such as one to connect the printer) built-in, thus eliminating the need for you to purchase interface boards.

PRACTICE TIME

Enter the following information on your computer. You may need to consult with your instructor to find out the answers.

My computer is a(n) _____.

My computer has an 80286 or 80386 chip (Y/N) _____.
If Yes, which?_____

The RAM capacity of my computer is _____.

OUTPUT COMPONENTS

The information a computer produces (the output) must be in a form (a medium) that a person, a computer, or other machines can use. The medium that can be used by noncomputer machines will not be discussed here.

MONITOR AND PRINTER

When a person uses the output, it must be in a readable format. The output can be printed on paper or on screen). The output devices, then, are the monitor and the printer.

MONITOR

The monitor has a screen that can display either 80 or 40 columns by 24 or more lines. Most programs use the 80 column display. Monitors that display in two tones (green and black, amber and black, or black and white) are called **monochrome**. Monochrome monitors, in general, will not display graphics unless a special graphics card (such as the Hercules graphics card) is installed. However, they are easy to read for text displays.

There are three kinds of color monitors: CGA, EGA, and VGA. Technical differences between the three types will not be discussed here. The clarity and crispness of output, by which these can be compared, is referred to as **resolution**. **CGA (Color Graphics Adaptor)** monitors are good for displaying graphics or playing games. They are mediocre for working with text processing because of their low resolution. **EGA (Enhanced Graphics Adaptor)** monitors have higher resolution than CGA monitors. They are capable of showing sixty-four or more different colors. The problem is that some equipment (such as monitor projection devices) that work with CGA signals will not work with EGA signals, and vice versa. The newest, **VGA (Video Graphics Array)** monitors can receive both CGA and EGA signals, and in addition, have higher resolution and more colors.

Buying Tip: The type of monitor you purchase depends on the use. In the past, if your usage was primarily text processing (such as word processing and spreadsheets), a monochrome monitor was recommended. This was because the low resolution on a CGA monitor could cause eye strain. Today, many software take advantage of color display to distinguish commands, and the use of graphics (again, in various colors) is ever-increasing. Thus, the high resolution EGA and VGA monitors are easy to read and make software easy to use because of the use of color. You will have to weigh these factors (colors and resolution) against the cost to make your selection.

PRACTICE TIME

Enter the following information on your computer. You may need to consult with your instructor to find out the answer.

My monitor is a (monochrome, CGA, EGA, VGA) _____ monitor.

PRINTERS

In general, there are three types of printers used today. They are dot matrix, letter quality, and laser printers. **Dot matrix** printers form characters as a combination of dots. The number of dots used to form characters determines how good the resolution of the output is. Some of the better dot matrix printers use 24 pins to make dots. Dot matrix printers can print characters in different styles or sizes and are controlled by special codes. They can also print graphics.

Letter quality printers are like typewriters. They produce documents of legal quality. They cannot produce graphics. They are slower than the dot matrix printer and generally cost a little more. To change the character style or size in most such printers, the print head must be changed, as in an electric typewriter.

Laser printers produce high-resolution output using laser technology. The result is almost of publication quality. They can also produce graphics with smooth lines instead of the broken lines common in output produced by the printers previously discussed. The popularity of their use with microcomputers is increasing. They are the most expensive of the three and are slow in producing output.

There is one additional item to note about printers. That is, all printers are either parallel or serial printers. Again, the technical discussion on the difference is not given here. A parallel printer is connected to a parallel port at the back of the computer, and a serial printer is connected to a serial port at the back of the computer. (They use different interface boards.) A parallel port on a computer is referred to as LPT1 (a second parallel port is called LPT2, the third, LPT3, and so on). A serial port on a computer is referred to as COM1 (then COM2, COM3, and so on). This information is needed because some software is written to work with just parallel printers, while others are written to work with serial printers. In most cases, you need to specify the port where the printer is connected (so the program knows where to send the output).

Buying Tip: For most general purpose printing, a dot matrix printer is adequate. Today's better dot matrix printers have near letter quality resolution and their output is very difficult to distinguish from that of a letter quality printer (at least to the naked eye).

A laser printer is nice to have if you require high-quality output. The price has dropped to the level that most businesses can afford. You will have to weigh cost, software compatibility, speed, resolution, and ease of use in making selection.

PRACTICE TIME

Enter the following information on your computer. You may need to consult with your instructor to find out the answers.

The printer attached to my computer is a _____ (give brand name and model).

It is a _____ (dot matrix, letter quality, laser) printer and is connected to _____ (LPT1 or COM1).

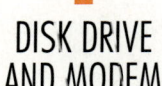

DISK DRIVE AND MODEM

When output is to be used by a computer, data must be in a computer-readable format. The medium most commonly used to store information to be passed onto another computer is a disk, either a floppy diskette or a hard disk. Disks are discussed in more detail in the next lesson.

If the output is sent directly to another computer, a **modem** might be used. A modem (*mo*dulator-*dem*odulator) is a device that connects the computer to another by a communication line, such as a telephone, through which information can be transmitted.

10 USING LOTUS 1-2-3

INPUT COMPONENTS

Input is the information a computer receives. There must be a way to input data.

KEYBOARD

Data are normally entered by typing on the keyboard. As you type, the corresponding characters are echoed (displayed) on the monitor. After entering certain kinds of information, you must press the (ENTER) (or RETURN) key before the computer can process the typed data. In other cases, the typed information is processed directly. The entry method depends on the software you are using.

There are two types of keyboards used with IBM micros and compatibles. These will be discussed later.

MOUSE

A mouse is a small, hand-held device with a roller ball on the bottom. It allows you to send instructions to the computer by moving the mouse across the desk, causing the cursor on the screen to move likewise, pointing at the options displayed on the screen. A mouse can be used with a program only if the application program recognizes its use. The usage of a mouse with IBM software is increasing.

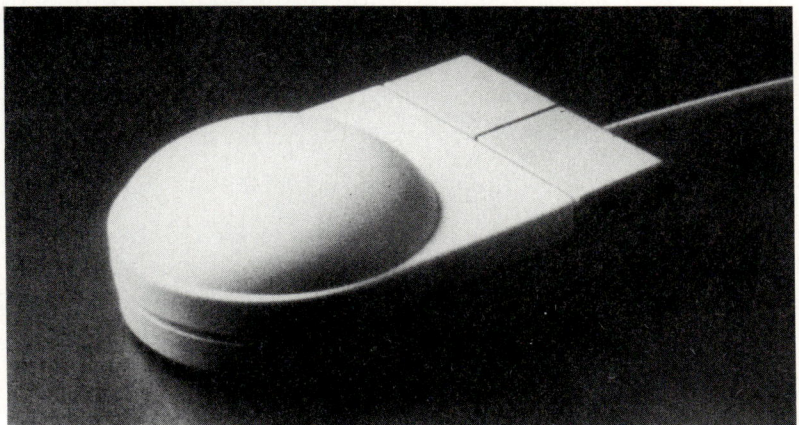

Figure 1–3   A mouse for an IBM microcomputer and compatible.

COMPONENTS OF IBM MICROS AND COMPATIBLES   11

DISK DRIVE AND MODEM

If the information you want to process is on a disk, you use a disk drive as an input device. The use of disks and disk drive is explained in the next lesson. If the information is coming from another computer via a communication line, you may use a modem.

STARTING THE COMPUTER

So that you can see how the keyboard works, you will now turn your IBM micro or compatible on. This way, you can see that the characters you type on the keyboard are displayed on the screen.

Note: If you are working on a computer with a hard disk, all you have to do to start a computer is to turn it on. All the information that a computer needs is on the hard disk. For practice, however, you will go through the procedure given here.

Make sure that you have a **DOS** disk, and just follow the steps given below. (A **DOS** disk is either the IBM Disk Operating System disk [DOS System disk] or a disk that has **DOS** placed on it. Your **DOS** disk may be a 5 1/4-inch disk or a 3 1/2-inch disk. A 3 1/2-inch disk is smaller than a 5 1/4-inch, and is in a solid metal and plastic casing [whereas the 5 1/4-inch disk is in an envelope]. The differences between the two are discussed further in a later section.)

- Turn the monitor switch on. On some models, the monitor is turned on with the computer.
- Make sure the computer is off.
- Lift the door for drive A (the drive on your left or on top). If there is a disk in the slot, carefully remove it.

If you are using a 5 1/4-inch disk:

- Remove the **DOS** disk from its envelope and insert it into drive A, oval cutout end first, label side up. Be careful not to bend or force the disk. If you feel any resistance, pull the disk back out slowly and try again.
- Close the door to the disk drive.

If you are using a 3 1/2-inch disk:

- Insert the DOS disk into drive A, metal end first, label side up. When inserted properly, the disk will lock in place.

Now, to continue with the rest of start-up:

- Turn the computer switch on.
  - ➤ It may take 15 seconds or more for the computer to react. The IBM micro or compatible goes through a diagnostic routine each time it is turned on. Be patient.
  - ➤ The red light on the disk drive lights up, and the disk drive starts to operate.
  - ➤ The following message appears on the screen.

    ```
    Current date is Tue 1-01-1980
    Enter new date (mm-dd-yy):
    ```

The computer offers you a chance to reset its internal calendar, which begins at 1-01-80 when the computer is booted up. Your computer may be equipped with a clock, or a battery-run device that keeps track of date and time even when the computer is turned off. Once you activate this clock, the correct date and time will be displayed when you turn the computer on. If that is the case, there is really no need to change the time or date, unless that is what you specifically want to do. (To activate the clock, see the instruction for the clock installed on your machine.)

The calendar format is month-day-year, with the number separated by hyphens. On September 29, 1991, for example, you can enter 9-29-91.

- Enter the date, as shown above. Then press the (ENTER) key. The (ENTER) key is the down-left-arrow key between the main keyboard and the numeric keyboard on the right. The (ENTER) key is referred to as the RETURN key in some software.
  - ➤ A message similar to the following appears on the screen:

    ```
    Current time is 0:00:41.24
    Enter new time:
    ```

> The computer offers you a chance to reset its internal time, which started when it was booted up. The format, using a 24-hour clock, is hours:minutes:seconds with the numbers separated by colons. If you want to enter 2:35 p.m., you enter 14:35.

- Enter the time, as shown above. Then press the (ENTER) key.

> The screen displays a message similar to the following:

```
The IBM Personal Computer DOS
Version 3.30 (C)Copyright International
      Business Machines Corp 1981, 1987
      (C)Copyright Microsoft Corp 1981, 1986

A>
```

(You may have a slightly different message, depending on the version of DOS you are using.)

This is the IBM PC DOS copyright notice. A> is the DOS prompt. A **prompt** is a message from computer to operator that requests a response or entry. This prompt indicates that drive A is the default drive. More information about disk drives is presented later in this manual.

> The flashing underscore character to the right of the prompt is the cursor. The cursor shows the position on the screen where your entries are made.

- Remove the disk from the drive and store it.

You have just completed a **cold start** of the computer. A cold start involves turning the computer on to let it start automatically.

You can restart the computer when it is on without turning the power switch off. This is done by simultaneously holding down keys marked (CTRL) and (ALT) while you press the key marked (DEL). This is called a **warm start**, since the computer is already on and, thus, warmed up.

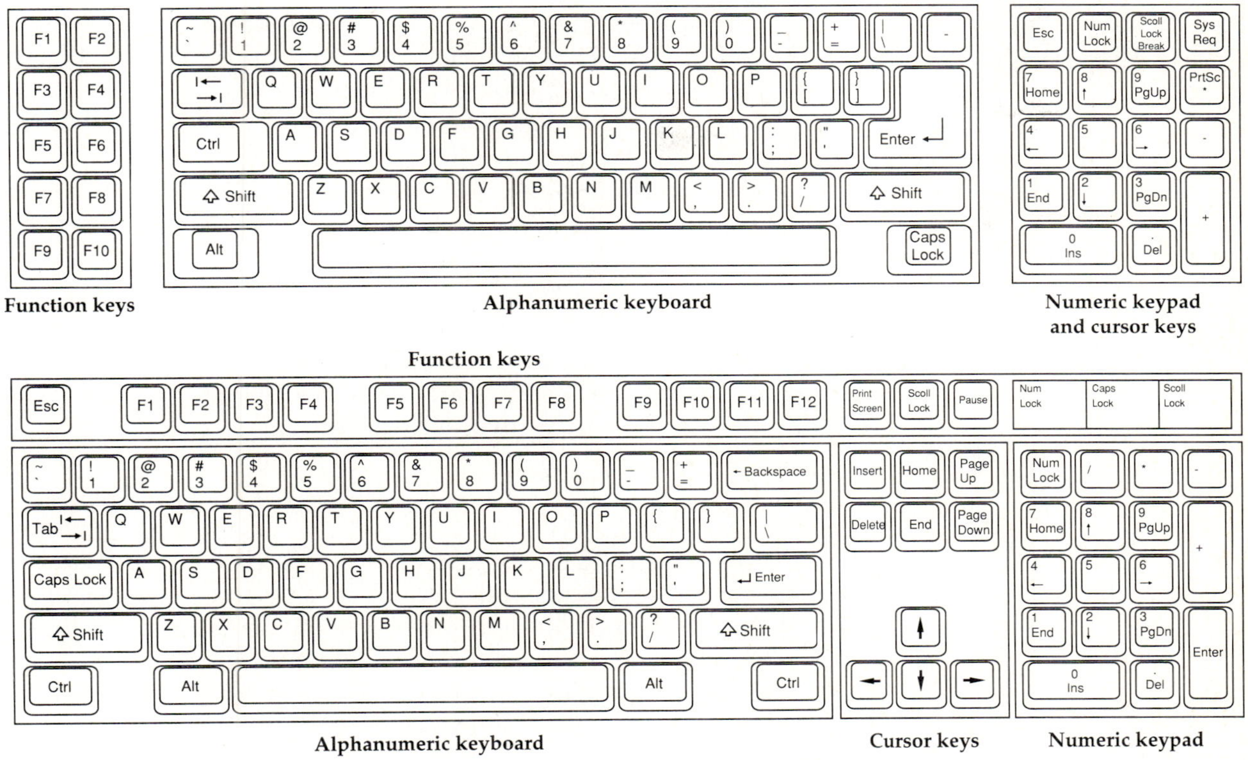

Figure 1–4 The top illustration is of an IBM PC keyboard. The bottom illustration is an IBM PS/2 keyboard.

THE KEYBOARD

The IBM micro or compatible you are using has one of two different types of keyboards, depending on when it was purchased. It may have the standard keyboard found on earlier models, or an enhanced keyboard which comes with newer models. Although they both have the same keys, they are not in the same locations on the keyboard, most obvious being the location and number of function keys and the presence of a second set of arrow keys. If you are using one of the IBM compatibles, your keyboard may also be slightly different.

This manual describes a standard keyboard. If you have one of the others, you may have to check for the placement of some keys.

COMPONENTS OF IBM MICROS AND COMPATIBLES **15**

KEYBOARD FEATURES

You might notice how similar the computer keyboard is to a typewriter keyboard. The purpose of the keyboard is to send characters to the computer. Which of these characters are recognized or what each is used for depends on the software being used at the time.

As different features of the keyboard are explained in this section, take time and try the features yourself. As you type the keys, the computer might respond with

> `Bad command or file name`

The computer is indicating that **DOS**, the software that is running in the computer right now, does not recognize what you typed. Ignore this message for the time being.

CHARACTERS

The keyboard can generate 256 characters. Not all of them are visible, and many have special meanings. The character set of an IBM micro or compatible includes 26 lowercase letters, 26 uppercase letters, 10 numerals, and 34 special characters. The uppercase letters can be obtained by holding down one of the keys with the broad up arrows (a (SHIFT) key) while you press the key or by pressing the key marked Caps Lock (the (CAPS LOCK) key) once before pressing the keys.

Some special characters require that you hold down the (SHIFT) key even if the (CAPS LOCK) key has been pressed: These are the characters that appear on the upper half of a key. For example, the key with a semicolon, ;, has a colon, :, on the upper half. To type a semicolon, you just press the key; but to type a colon, you must hold the (SHIFT) key down while pressing the key. The (CAPS LOCK) key is a toggle key. The first time you press it, it shifts the keyboard into uppercase mode. The second time, all letters are lowercase (unless the (SHIFT) key is pressed).

SPACE BAR

The long bar at the bottom of the keyboard is the space bar. Press it to generate blank spaces between characters. Unlike a blank

16 USING LOTUS 1-2-3

space on a typed sheet, pressing the space bar actually inserts a space character into the data being typed.

ENTER

The (ENTER) key is the down-left-arrow key between the main keyboard and the numeric keyboard. It does not have the same function as on a typewriter keyboard. In Lotus 1–2–3, pressing (ENTER) indicates the end of an entry or selection of the highlighted menu option.

CONTROL CHARACTERS

You can enter 32 control characters in the computer. These are generated by holding down the key marked Ctrl (the (CTRL) key) and pressing a character key. This sequence is indicated in the text as (CTRL)-character. Such a sequence of keypresses may or may not cause characters or a message to appear on the screen, and they have variable functions as defined by each software package.

FUNCTION KEYS

To the left of the main keyboard are 10 function keys, marked (F1) to (F10). (On the enhanced keyboard, there are 12 function keys, found across the top of the keyboard.) Lotus 1–2–3 uses the function keys as shortcuts for entering some commands and as the only way a few commands are entered.

ALT

The key marked Alt, located to the left of the space bar, is the (ALT) key. In Lotus 1–2–3, it is used with an alphabetic keystroke to run a macro, or with a function key as a shortcut for entering some commands.

NUMERIC KEYBOARD

To the right of the main keyboard is the numeric keyboard. You need to know several important things about it. Before you can enter numerals or the period from the keypad, you must either hold down the (SHIFT) key or press the (NUM LOCK) key. Like (CAPS LOCK), (NUM LOCK) is a toggle key. After pressing (NUM LOCK) once, you generate the characters that appear on the upper half of the keys on the keypad. Press it again to generate the cursor moves on the bottom half of the keys. (NUM LOCK) has no effect on the number keys of the main keyboard, just on the keys in the numeric keypad.

On the lower half of the 8, 6, 4, and 2 keys are short arrows. In lowercase mode, these may be used for cursor movement. That is, when you press one of the arrow keys, the cursor moves one position in the direction of the arrow.

On the lower half of the 7 key is inscribed Home. The (HOME) key also may be a cursor movement key. When you use Lotus 1–2–3, pressing the (HOME) key causes the cursor to move to the top left-hand corner of the screen.

The 1, 3, and 9 keys have the labels END, PgDn, and PgUp, respectively. These keys have special cursor movements defined in the software.

Note: The enhanced keyboard has a second set of cursor movement keys between the main keyboard and the numeric keyboard. This way, you can leave the numeric keyboard in numeric mode all the time.

■ ESC

At the upper left-hand corner of the main keyboard is the escape key, marked Esc (the (ESC) key). Its function depends on what you are doing in Lotus 1–2–3.

■ TAB

The (TAB) key has two arrows pointing in opposite directions. It is just below the (ESC) key. The (TAB) key has several functions in Lotus 1–2–3, depending on what you are doing.

■ PRTSC

The key marked PrtSc (PRINT SCREEN) on its upper half is found just below the (ENTER) key. (There is a second PrtSc key on the enhanced keyboard.) To get a printout of the current screen display, you hold down the (SHIFT) key and press PrtSc. Of course, you must have a printer attached to your computer.

BACKSPACE

The key with the arrow pointing left, found just above the (ENTER) key, is the (BACKSPACE) key (BKSP). It may be used to move the cursor to the left one or more character spaces, or to erase the character to the left of the cursor.

INS AND DEL

Two wide keys found below the numeric keyboard are the (INS) and (DEL) keys. (INS), or Insert, is a toggle key. Sometimes, as you insert characters in the middle of a pre-typed line, the characters to the right of the cursor move over to let you insert the new characters. If you were to press the (INS) key, the characters you type will replace the characters already there. If you were to press the (INS) key for the second time, the characters you type are inserted once more. The third time, they overstrike; and so on.

The (DEL) key is used to delete the character at the cursor position.

KEYS TO KEEP DISTINCT

Some characters must be used carefully. On a typewriter, you can use one character for another if they look similar as typed; on a computer, you must type the exact key, since each key generates a unique signal to the computer. Examples are:

- Lowercase letter L and number 1
- Letter O (oh) and number 0 (zero)

AUTO-REPEAT

When you hold down a key on the keyboard, the character will repeat itself.

LEARN TO USE THE SOFTWARE

Each key generates a unique signal to the computer. The function of each key and its recognition by the computer depend on the software being used. Even the method used to correct your typing errors depends on the software being used. You should be getting the idea that, beyond turning it on, learning how to use a computer means learning how to use specific software.

Don't be frustrated or intimidated. If you type in the command for the wrong software, the computer usually just responds with an error message indicating that it doesn't recognize what you typed. These errors do not harm the computer. And, most often, they do not affect whatever it is you are trying to accomplish by using the computer. The worst that can happen is that you might have to turn the computer off and start all over again.

FUNCTION OF A DISK

A disk is an external storage medium. It is used to store information that is needed at a later time. If you recall, there are two types of internal storage: RAM and ROM. RAM is storage where you can read and write information but it is volatile. The moment the computer is turned off or power is interrupted, the information is lost. ROM is read-only memory, meaning, you can only read information from it, although it is not volatile. You cannot put any new information or change information currently on it. External storage is permanent storage, where you can read and write information.

When information is written to a disk, each group of information is stored as a file. That is, if you prepare a letter using a word processor, the letter is stored on a disk as a file with a filename to identify it. A computer program is stored on a disk as a file, again with a proper filename to identify it. Most application software has commands to let you store and retrieve files from a disk.

DISKS

There are two types of disks that are used with a PC: floppy disks and hard disks. Although they both operate in a similar manner, floppy disks are a flexible, portable medium, whereas hard disks are rigid metallic platters. Floppy disks are used with floppy disk

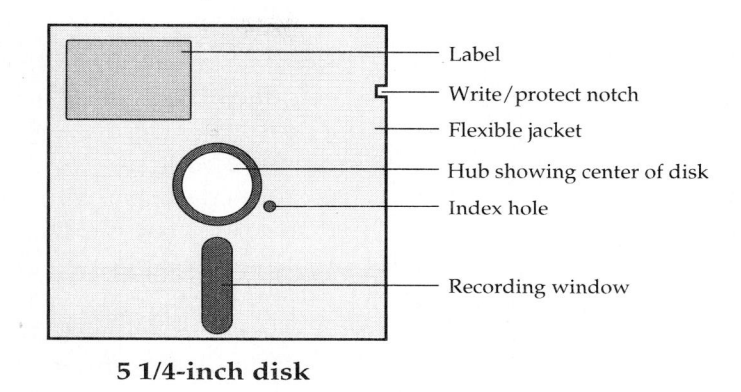

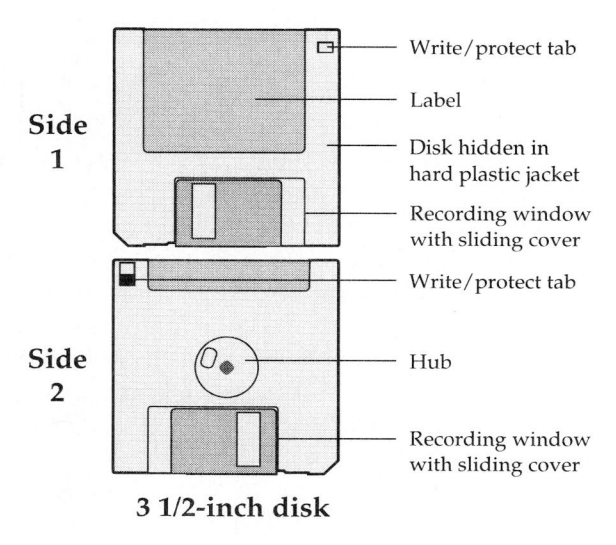

Figure 1–5 The top illustration is of a 5 1/4-inch disk and the bottom illustration is of a 3 1/2-inch disk.

COMPONENTS OF IBM MICROS AND COMPATIBLES

drives (referred to simply as disk drives in this manual) and hard disks are housed in a hard-disk-drive unit. Hard disks are explained in little more detail at the end of this section.

The disks used more often on IBM micros and compatibles are 5 1/4-inch floppy disks. There are newer models of PC's, the IBM PS/2's in particular, that use 3 1/2-inch disks. (Both 5 1/4-inch and 3 1/2-inch disks are referred to simply as disks in this manual.) The 5 1/4-inch disks and 3 1/2-inch disks are very similar in function and operation. There are some subtle differences, however, and they are pointed out.

A disk stores data as magnetic spots on a circular piece of mylar that has an oxide coating. The disk is inside a protective jacket (for 5 1/4-inch disks) or plastic cartridge (for 3 1/2-inch disks). It was called a floppy disk because the mylar material is pliant, and in its protective jacket, 5 1/4-inch disks can "flop" (flex) back and forth. The 3 1/2-inch disks come in rigid, plastic cartridges, so the term floppy does not apply to them. The cartridge on a 3 1/2-inch disk protects the diskette inside much better than the jacket on 5 1/4-inch disk.

The information on a disk is stored along concentric recording positions on the disk, known as tracks. Information may be stored on both sides of the disk. There are 40 tracks per side on each 5 1/4-inch disk and 80 per side on each 3 1/2-inch disk. A 5 1/4-inch, although bigger, can store less information than the 3 1/2-inch disk. The storage capacity on a 5 1/4-inch disk is approximately 360K and on a 3 1/2-inch disk is approximately 720K. The information is written onto and read from the disk through an opening in the jacket or cartridge. The circular mylar disk inside spins like a phonograph record, and a **read-write head** accesses information.

Note: Newer disk drives permit the use of higher capacity disks. Now, 5 1/4-inch disks which can hold up to 1.2M (M stands for megabyte, and represents 1000K) and 3 1/2-inch disks which can hold up to 1.44M are available.

In the case of 5 1/4-inch disks, the opening is visible and is called the access window. A 3 1/2-inch disk has a mechanical shutter that opens automatically to reveal the access window when the disk is inserted in the disk drive and closes automatically when taken out.

Most 5 1/4-inch disks have a small notch on the side. This is the write-protect notch. If you cover the write-protect notch, the disk is protected from being written over or changed. When you purchase disks, gummed tabs are provided for this purpose.

Note: If you have covered the write-protect notch with a gummed tab, check periodically to make sure that it is securely in place. Many disk drive problems occur when gummed tabs come off and get stuck inside the drive. This is also true of labels you might have attached on the disk.

A 3 1/2-inch disk can be write-protected using the write-protect tab. It is write-protected (you cannot change the information on it) when the tab is moved to reveal the hollow opening. When the opening is closed, the disk is not write-protected (and you can read or write information).

When you purchase a disk, it does not contain any information on it. The disk must be prepared so that it is able to store and retrieve data. The process of preparing a disk to accept data is called formatting a disk. If you need to format a disk, the process is explained in the next lesson.

CARE AND HANDLING OF 5 1/4-INCH DISKS

You must use proper care in handling 5 1/4-inch disks. They are very fragile. Here are some suggestions for their care and handling:

- Always handle disk by its plastic jacket only.
- Insert the disk in disk drive, access window end first, label side up.
- Always keep the disk in its envelope when not in use.
- Do not touch the surface of the disk or wipe the surface with rags or tissue paper.
- Do not let disks collect dust.
- Keep disks out of the sun and away from other sources of heat, which can cause them to warp or lose data.
- Keep disks at least 2 feet away from magnetic fields, such as those generated by electrical motors, radios, televisions, tape recorders, and other devices. A strong magnetic field will erase information on a disk.

- When writing on a disk label already attached to the disk, use only a felt-tipped pen. Never use any sort of instrument with a sharp point. Also, never use an eraser. Eraser dust is abrasive and may get on the mylar surface.

- Store disks in a vertical position. Never bend them or attach paper clips to them.

- Never open the drive door or remove a disk while the drive is running—that is, while the IN USE light on the front of the disk drive is on. If you do, you can damage the data on your disk.

- Check to make sure that the gummed tab and external labels are on securely.

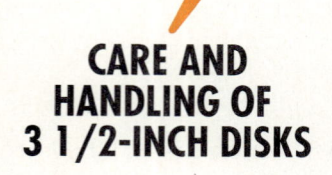

CARE AND HANDLING OF 3 1/2-INCH DISKS

A 3 1/2-inch disk is well protected and is quite sturdy. However, there are some general rules you should follow in handling it.

- Insert the disk in the disk drive metal end first, label side up.

- Never open the mechanical shutter while a disk is out of the drive. Doing this exposes the surface to dirt, dust, fingerprints, etc.

- Do not let disks collect dust.

- Keep disks out of the sun and away from other sources of heat, which can cause them to warp or lose data.

- Keep disks at least 2 feet away from magnetic fields, such as those generated by electrical motors, radios, televisions, tape recorders, and other devices. A strong magnetic field will erase information on a disk.

- When writing on a disk label already attached to the disk, use only a felt-tipped pen. Also, never use an eraser. Eraser dust is abrasive and may get on the mylar surface.

- Never remove a disk while the drive is running—that is, while the IN USE light on the front of the disk drive is on. If you do, you can damage the data on your disk.

- Check to make sure that the external labels are on securely.

HARD DISKS

A hard disk unit is a sealed enclosure containing one or more rigid metallic platters (usually an aluminum platter covered with a thin iron-oxide coating). This enclosure may be installed in the same cabinet as the processing unit (internal hard disk) or in a separate cabinet (external hard disk). A hard disk is sometimes called a **fixed disk** or **Winchester drive**.

Note: There are hard disks available on (interface) boards that are inserted in an unused expansion slot in the computer. These are called **hard cards**.

Hard and floppy disks use similar principles. Both record data in tracks. The advantage of a hard disk is greater storage capacity and speed. When expressing the storage capacity of a hard drive, the term megabyte, or million bytes, is used instead of K, kilobyte, or a thousand, for floppy disks. You can install 20, 30, or even 200-megabyte hard disks on a computer. The access speed of a hard drive is 2 to 10 times faster than that of a floppy disk.

CARE OF DISK DRIVES

A disk drive is a sensitive mechanical device and should be treated as such. Because it has moving parts, it is even more sensitive than the computer. You should not drop it, jar it sharply, or plug it in or unplug it when the computer is on.

The read-write head on the disk drive should be cleaned periodically. It only takes a minute amount of dust, dirt, oils or magnetic oxide particles on the disk drive head to cause problems.

When you transport the disk drive, insert the cardboard packing disk (which accompanied the drive when it was purchased) or a blank disk to protect the drive's internal mechanism. A hard disk is even more susceptible to physical damage because of its design. You must be careful not to move the unit without first properly positioning (parking) its read-write head. You must also use extreme caution when shutting down the system as well to avoid turning off power when the hard disk is writing data.

IDENTIFYING DISK DRIVES

IBM micros and compatibles come with one or more installed floppy disk drives. Some have a hard disk drive installed. Each disk drive must be connected to a disk interface board, or disk controller card. The disk controller card, in turn, is inserted into one of the expansion slots in the computer. If there is only one drive, it is known as drive A. If there are two drives, they are drives A and B. If there is a hard drive, it is usually drive C.

PRACTICE TIME

Enter the following information on your computer. You may need to consult with your instructor to find out the answers.

There are _____ (how many) 3 1/2-inch disk drives on my computer. Their capacity is _____.

There are _____ (how many) 5 1/4-inch disk drives on my computer. Their capacity is _____.

There is a hard disk on my computer._____ (Y/N) Its capacity is _____.

Visually identify which drive is drive A.

END OF LESSON 1

At this time, you will end your session.

- If you have not already done so, remove the disk from the drive.
- Turn off two switches: one for the computer and one for the monitor. The order in which you turn off the computer and monitor is not important.

26 USING LOTUS 1-2-3

SUMMARY

In this lesson, various components of a computer are presented.

- The function of a computer is to process data and produce a result.
- The microprocessor unit (MPU) is the brain of the computer.
- Random Access Memory (RAM) is where both the program and data are temporarily stored during processing. It is a volatile memory.
- Read Only Memory (ROM) contains firmware.
- Expansion slots are where peripheral devices are connected.
- Two-tone monitors are called monochrome monitors.
- There are three kinds of color monitors: Color Graphics Adaptor (CGA), Enhanced Graphics Adaptor (EGA), and Video Graphics Array (VGA).
- Computer output can be passed onto a computer via disk or modem.
- Input components include keyboard, mouse, disk drive, and modem.
- In general, there are two types of disks: floppy and hard. There are two types of floppy disks: 3 1/2-inch and 5 1/4-inch.
- Information on a disk is accessed through an access window. On a 3 1/2-inch disk, the access window is protected by a mechanical shutter.
- A disk can be write-protected.

REVIEW QUESTIONS

1. What is the function of a computer?

2. Why do different computers have different microprocessor chips?

3. What does *volatile* mean?

4. Is a blank space a byte? Explain.

5. Name three types of printers and an advantage/disadvantage of each.

6. Why is a disk drive both an input and an output component?

7. Why do you need an external storage device?

8. How is information stored on a disk?

9. What does it mean when a disk is "write-protected"? How is it done?

10. What is the advantage of having a hard disk on a computer?

CONFIGURATION OF MY COMPUTER

Transfer the information you entered in Practice Time to this page for future reference.

My computer is a(n) _____.

My computer has an 80286 or 80386 chip (Y/N) _____.
If Yes, which?_____

The RAM capacity of my computer is _____.

The printer attached to my computer is a _____ (give brand name and model).

It is a _____ (dot matrix, letter quality, laser) printer and is connected to _____ (LPT1 or COM1).

My monitor is a _____ (monochrome, CGA, EGA, VGA) monitor.

There are _____ (how many) 3 1/2-inch disk drives on my computer. Their capacity is _____.

There are _____ (how many) 5 1/4-inch disk drives on my computer. Their capacity is _____.

There is a hard disk on my computer._____ (Y/N). Its capacity is _____.

LESSON 2
THE DISK OPERATING SYSTEM

SUPPLIES NEEDED

For this part of the manual, you need the following:

- The DOS disk: A DOS disk accompanied the computer at the time of purchase
- A scratch disk: A scratch disk is a blank disk or one whose content you no longer need

OBJECTIVES

Upon completion of the material presented in this lesson, you should be able to understand the following:

- What a default drive is and how to change it
- The purpose of the Disk Operating System (DOS)
- Difference between internal and external DOS commands
- How to format a disk
- How to manage files on a disk

ORIENTATION

The **disk operating system**, or **DOS**, is a computer program which controls the information transfer between the computer and the disk drives. It allows files of information to be easily saved, copied, listed, and deleted. Anyone who wishes to make serious use of a microcomputer should become familiar with the DOS commands.

The IBM version of DOS is available on a disk which is provided with IBM microcomputers. Some software provides its own set of DOS instructions, thus there is no need for you to know DOS. Still, much of the software for IBM micros and compatibles uses some of the DOS commands.

STARTING OFF

Start up your IBM micro or compatible using the DOS disk. You did this in the last lesson.

DEFAULT DISK DRIVE

The prompt on the screen consists of two characters. Right now, the first character is an A. The second character is always a >. The purpose of the first character is to indicate the default disk drive—the drive the computer will use, unless instructed otherwise. When you give a command, the command may require the computer to get a file from the disk. If you want the computer to get a file from a disk in a drive other than the default drive, you must indicate the drive to be used. This will become clearer in the next section.

CHANGING THE DEFAULT DRIVE

To change the default drive, you simply type the drive name, A or B, followed by the colon (:). That is, if your default is currently drive A and you want to change to B, you type **B:** and press (ENTER). The prompt will then read B>. To change it back to A, you type **A:** and press (ENTER).

One word of advice: there must be a disk in the new drive before you can change the default. If you try to change the default without a disk in the new drive, you get the message

 `Abort, Retry, or Ignore?`

If that happens, you can insert a disk in the new drive and type **R** for Retry and press (ENTER). If you changed your mind about changing the default, type **I** for Ignore and press (ENTER). You will get the message

 `Current drive is no longer valid>`

Then enter the drive you would like to have as the default.

DOS COMMANDS

As mentioned earlier, you should become familiar with **DOS** commands, because they give an efficient way to manage your data. There are times when you want to prepare a disk to store data, examine the contents of a disk, or transfer files (for creating backup, for example), without going into any application software.

Some DOS commands are **internal** and others are **external** (sometimes called resident and transient commands.) Internal commands are transferred to memory when the computer is started. This means that, once you load DOS by starting up the computer, you do not need to have the DOS disk in a drive to carry out these commands.

External, or transient, commands are on a disk as files. Therefore, the disk containing the command files (generally the DOS disk) must be in a disk drive for the command to be carried out.

An internal, or resident, command can be issued by simply typing the proper entry. For an external command, you must specify which drive contains the DOS disk. If the drive that contains the DOS disk is the default drive, you may omit the drive specification. For example, you can use the (internal) DIR command simply by typing **DIR**. However, if the DOS disk is in drive B and the default drive is A, you must type **B:FORMAT** to issue the (external) FORMAT command.

The following commands are discussed briefly in this manual. You should consult the DOS manual for details.

VER	Displays the DOS version under which you are operating.

Commands Used with Disks:

FORMAT	Formats a disk.
CHKDSK	Checks the status of a disk.

Commands for Using and Moving Files:

DIR	Displays the names of all the files on the disk in the disk drive.
COPY	Copies a file.
RENAME	Renames the file.
ERASE	Erases the specified file from disk.
TYPE	Displays the contents of a file on the screen.

THE DISK OPERATING SYSTEM

Commands Used to Safeguard Your Files:

COMP	Compares the contents of two files.
DISKCOPY	Creates a copy of one disk on another. Formats the target disk, if necessary.
DISKCOMP	Compares the contents of two disks.

Commands Most Often Used with a Hard Disk:

MKDIR	Creates a new subdirectory.
CHDIR	Changes the current directory of a specified drive.
RMDIR	Deletes a specified subdirectory.
TREE	Displays all the directory paths of a specified drive.

When a DOS command is entered, the command may or may not be preceded by the name of the drive where the disk containing the command file is found, depending on whether the command is internal or external and which drive is set as the default. Also, the command may require that you specify one or more drives or a drive and filename. In addition, the command may allow for a number of options. Options are usually a slash followed by a character, such as /S. These options expand the versatility of DOS commands, allowing you to have a command do things certain way.

VER

This internal command displays the DOS version number that you are working with. There are many versions of DOS. Sometimes you need to know the version since certain software is supported by a particular version of DOS. Just type **VER** and press (ENTER) and see what is displayed.

FORMAT

Next, you need to know how to prepare a disk for use. When you buy blank disks, there is nothing on them. A disk must be formatted before you can put information on it. This applies to a hard disk as well. To format a disk means to prepare it to store information.

Some software provides instructions on how to format a disk from within the command set for that package. Other software packages require that your data disk already be formatted. A hard disk must be formatted with DOS, not from an application package.

The following is the procedure for formatting a disk in DOS using the FORMAT command.

- Insert the DOS System disk in drive A. Make sure that the default drive is A.

The FORMAT command is an external command. You must specify the drive on which the file that contains the FORMAT command can be found. Since the DOS disk is in drive A and the default drive is A, you can just type **FORMAT**. Had the DOS disk been in drive B (with default still being A), you would have had to type **B:FORMAT**. On the other hand, if the default was B and the DOS disk was A, you would have had to type **A:FORMAT**. As part of the FORMAT command, you also have to specify the disk drive in which you intend to insert the disk to be formatted. If it is to be in drive A, you type **FORMAT A:**, and if it is to be found in drive B, you type **FORMAT B:**. If you do not specify this, the computer assumes that the new disk is in the default drive.

- Type **FORMAT B:** and press the (ENTER) (or RETURN) key. The command can be typed in uppercase or lowercase, but *there must be a space before the B:*.

    ➤ The screen displays the message

    ```
    Insert new diskette for drive B
    and strike ENTER when ready
    ```

Insert a scratch disk in drive B. A scratch disk is either a blank disk or one whose contents you no longer need. You can reformat a disk that already contains information. However, when you do, the existing information is lost. Therefore, you must make sure that you no longer need the information on a disk before you reformat it.

- Press (ENTER) to begin formatting.

    ➤ When the formatting is complete, the screen message shown may look as follows:

```
Formatting..Format complete
362496 bytes total disk space
362496 bytes available on disk
Format another (Y/N)?
```

DOS specifies that the disk is formatted for a total of 362496 bytes, or characters, and that all 362496 bytes are available for storing information. The program is ready to format another disk, if instructed to do so. You are to enter **Y** or **N**, depending on whether you want another disk formatted.

- Enter **N** if you do not want to format any more disks, and press (ENTER).
- Leave the newly formatted disk in drive B.

The disk in drive B is now formatted and ready for use. That is, it is ready to hold your data. However, it cannot be used to start the computer.

In order for a disk to be a system disk (one with which to start a computer), it must contain the following files: IBMBIO.COM, IBMDOS.COM, and COMMAND.COM. That is, aside from being formatted, these three files must be transferred (from the DOS disk in drive A, in this case, to the formatted disk in drive B).

Note that two of these files (IBMBIO.COM and IBMDOS.COM) are "hidden" files. This will be explained later. To create a disk that can be used to start the computer, you include an option, or a system parameter, (/S) with the format command. That is, you type **FORMAT B: /S**.

Do not confuse the "system" disk formatted with /S option with the "DOS" disk used to start up the computer at the beginning of the lesson. A system disk will let you start up the computer. A DOS disk will not only let you start up the computer, but it contains all the external DOS commands. Consult the DOS manual for details.

CHKDSK

CHKDSK command is used to analyze directories and the way files are stored on a disk found in a designated drive or an individual file on the disk specified. It can also optionally correct damage (/F). Here, you will use the command to check the status of the recently formatted disk.

- Enter **B:** and press (ENTER) to change the logged disk drive from A to B.
    ➤ The prompt now reads **B>.**

You will now use the CHKDSK command to check the disk in drive B. However, CHKDSK is an external command and the DOS disk is in drive A. Since drive A is not the default drive, you need to specify that the DOS disk is in drive A and that the disk to be checked is in drive B.

- Enter **A:CHKDSK B:** and press (ENTER).
    ➤ The screen message shown may look as follows:

    ```
    362496 bytes total disk space
    362496 bytes available on disk
    655360 bytes total memory
    618496 bytes free
    ```

Had there been files on the disk, CHKDSK would have reported the number of files and how much space they take up on the disk. The second set of numbers tells the status of memory on the computer you are using.

PRACTICE TIME

Try the CHKDSK command on the DOS disk in drive A.

DIR

To see what files are on a disk, use the DIR command. DIR is an internal command. You can issue it at any time after you have started the computer. You can specify the drive in which the disk to be examined is located. If none is specified, the default is assumed.

- With drive A as the default, type **DIR** and press (ENTER).
    ➤ The directory for the disk in drive A is displayed, scrolling by rather quickly. **Scrolling** means that after the screen fills up, as each new line appears at the bottom, the line at the top disappears.

Let's try this again using the /P option.

THE DISK OPERATING SYSTEM

```
FC       EXE     15807 10-06-88  12:00a
GRAPHICS COM     16693 10-06-88  12:00a
FASTOPEN EXE     16702 10-06-88  12:00a
XCOPY    EXE     17055 10-06-88  12:00a
CHKDSK   COM     17787 10-06-88  12:00a
JOIN     EXE     17813 10-06-88  12:00a
ATTRIB   EXE     18263 10-06-88  12:00a
SUBST    EXE     18467 10-06-88  12:00a
PRINTER  SYS     18914 10-06-88  12:00a
REPLACE  EXE     19415 10-06-88  12:00a
MEM      EXE     20005 10-06-88  12:00a
DEBUG    COM     21574 10-06-88  12:00a
IFSFUNC  EXE     21739 10-06-88  12:00a
FORMAT   COM     22859 11-30-88  12:00a
MODE     COM     22960 10-06-88  12:00a
SELECT   DAT     22999 11-30-88  12:00a
KEYBOARD SYS     23328 10-06-88  12:00a
SELECT   HLP     28695 10-06-88  12:00a
XMA2EMS  SYS     29211 10-06-88  12:00a
BACKUP   COM     36880 11-30-88  12:00a
RESTORE  COM     36946 11-30-88  12:00a
EGA      CPI     49068 11-30-88  12:00a
FDISK    EXE     60935 10-06-88  12:00a
Press any key to continue . . .
```

Screen Display 2–1

- Type **DIR /P** and press (ENTER).

    ➤ A screen similar to that in Screen Display 2–1 is displayed.

This display will not be explained in detail in this manual. The things to note are that **filenames** appear in the first column and their **extensions** appear in the second column. The third column displays the **file size** and the fourth column displays the **date** the file was created.

The name on the first column often is the one used to store or retrieve a file for use by an application program. The extension on the second column often is assigned by the application program to distinguish the data file according to its use. When a complete filename is requested, you must give both the filename and extension, separated by a period (.). For example, if the filename is MYFILE and the extension is DAT, the complete filename is MYFILE.DAT. A filename is between one and eight characters in length, and an extension is between one and three characters in length. Almost any character can be used in a filename and extension, except the following set of characters:

. , " / \ [ ] : ; | < > + = * ?

At this point, you are probably still pretty hazy about terms like *file* and *filename*. Don't worry, for the time being. These will become clearer to you as you go through the rest of this manual.

- ■ Press any key to see the rest of the directory. Repeat as needed to finish.

You can also look at the directory of a disk in another drive (non-default).

- ■ Type **DIR B:** (or **DIR B: /P**) and press (ENTER).
  - ➤ You see the directory of the disk in drive B, which should be empty.

If you want to look at just those files on drive A with, say EXE as extension, you can use the "wild card" character to specify this. This special wild card character is the asterisk (*). When it is used, it is the place holder for any possible characters.

- ■ Type **DIR A: *.EXE** and press (ENTER).
  - ➤ Only those files with extension EXE are listed.

PRACTICE TIME

Try **DIR A: *.*.** What do you think happened?

Earlier, it was mentioned that IBMBIO.COM and IBMDOS.COM are hidden files. That means, they do not appear on any directory. Hence, the only way those files can be transferred is by using the /S option with the FORMAT command.

COPY

To copy some files from one disk to another, you use the COPY command, which is another internal command. Although there are

THE DISK OPERATING SYSTEM 39

many options in copying files, only the procedures needed for making backup copies of a file are discussed here. That is, you will learn how to (1) copy a file from one disk to another and to use either the same name or a different name, and (2) copy all files from one disk to another.

The idea is that you have a disk that contains data files from which you want to make backup copies. You want to copy these data files onto the disk you formatted earlier. Since you do not yet have any data files, you will copy a command file on the DOS disk in drive A onto your disk in drive B. Since you do not want to accidentally erase a file on the DOS disk, it is suggested that you write protect the DOS disk before you start. (See Lesson 1.)

The file you will copy is FORMAT.COM. For this procedure, you have to use the complete name (both the filename and the extension).

- Type **COPY A:FORMAT.COM B:** and press (ENTER).

    ► The following message appears on the screen:

    ```
    1 File(s) copied
    ```

DOS creates a file by the same name on the disk in drive B and copies the contents of A:FORMAT.COM to it. The original file stays intact. If there is a file by the same name on the disk in drive B, it is overwritten; that is, the new information replaces the old.

■
PRACTICE TIME

Use DIR to check the contents of the disk in Drive B.

If you want to copy a file on a disk in drive A (filename1) onto a file with a different name (filename2) on drive B, do the following: type **COPY A:filename1 B:filename2** and press (ENTER). If filename2 is specified, the file from drive A is copied to the file with filename2 on drive B. If it is not specified, then the same name as used in drive A is assumed.

PRACTICE TIME

Copy the file FORMAT.COM from drive A again, this time onto a file name MYOWN.COM in drive B. Use DIR to make sure that the file MYOWN.COM exists in drive B.

If you want to copy all the files from the disk in drive A to the disk in drive B, you can use the wild card. That is, enter **COPY A:*.* B:** and press (ENTER).

RENAME

The RENAME command is used to rename a file on a disk. It is an internal command, and its format is RENAME filename1 filename2, where filename1 is the old name and filename2 is the new name. Again, these names must be complete names and may include the drive specification (for filename1). Otherwise, the file is assumed to be on the disk in the default drive.

It is best not to depend on the default drive setting. Get into the habit of specifying the drive with the filename. This will reduce accidental erasure of files and may eliminate many hours of frustration.

- Type **RENAME B:MYOWN.COM YOURS.COM** and press (ENTER).
  ➤ The light in front of drive B goes on for a while. When it goes out, the file has been renamed.
- Use the DIR command to verify.

ERASE

To remove an unwanted file from a disk, you use the ERASE command (internal). The format is ERASE filename, where filename is the complete name of the file to be removed. As part of the filename, you also can specify the drive that holds the source file. You will remove the file YOURS.COM is drive B.

- Type **ERASE B:YOURS.COM** and press (ENTER).

> ➤ The light in front of drive B goes on for a while. When it goes off, the file YOURS.COM has been erased.

> ■ Use DIR command to verify.

Note: Care must be taken when you issue this command so that you don't inadvertently remove a file you want to keep.

■ TYPE

The TYPE command (internal) is used to display the contents of a file on the screen. Certain types of files can be displayed in a legible format. Other files, however, may appear unreadable. This command will be explained in the next lesson when discussing the AUTOEXEC.BAT file.

■ COMP

The COMP command (external) is used to compare the contents of two specified files. You will compare the FORMAT.COM file in drive A with the FORMAT.COM file in drive B. Remember, this is an external command. You have to be sure that the disk containing the command file is either the default or is specified.

> ■ Type **A:COMP A:FORMAT.COM B:FORMAT.COM** and press (ENTER).

> ➤ A message similar to the following is displayed:

```
Files compares OK
Compare more files (Y/N)?
```

If there is a mismatch, a message indicating the nature of the mismatch is displayed. For specific messages, see the DOS manual.

■ DISKCOPY

The DISKCOPY command (external) creates a track-by-track copy of one disk on another disk. If necessary, it formats the target disk. Its format is DISKCOPY d1: d2: where d1 is the drive where the source disk is found and d2 is the drive where the target disk is found. If the same disk is specified for both d1 and d2, you will have to do disk swapping to accomplish the process.

You will copy the DOS disk in drive A onto the disk in drive B.

- With A as the default drive, type DISKCOPY A: B: and press (ENTER).

  ► The following message appears:

  ```
  Insert SOURCE diskette in drive A:
  Insert TARGET diskette in drive B:
  Press any key when ready
  ```

- At this point, verify that the DOS disk is in drive A and your formatted (scratch) disk is in drive B. When satisfied, press any key.

  ► The lights on drives A and B go on intermittently as messages appear on the screen indicating sectors and tracks being copied.
  ► When copying is done, the following message appears on the screen:

  ```
  Copy another diskette (Y/N)?
  ```

- Type **N** and press (ENTER), since you do not want to copy any more disks.

- Use the DIR command on both disks to check the contents.

DISKCOMP

This external command lets you compare the contents of two disks, sector by sector. You will compare the two disks from the DISKCOPY operation.

- Type **A:DISKCOMP A: B:** and press (ENTER).

  ► The following message appears on the screen:

  ```
  Insert FIRST diskette in drive A:
  Insert SECOND diskette in drive B:
  Press any key when ready ...
  ```

The first disk is the original. In your case, it is the **DOS** disk in drive A. The second disk is the one you are comparing with the first to see if it is the same. In your case, the one in drive B is the SECOND disk.

- Verify that the appropriate disks are in drives **A** and **B** and press any key.
  - ➤ Messages appear on the screen indicating the tracks being compared.
  - ➤ After a while, the following message appears on the screen:

    ```
    Compares OK
    Compare another diskette (Y/N)?
    ```

If some other message appears on the screen, see the **DOS** manual.

- Type **N** and press (ENTER), since you do not want to compare any more disks at this time.

PRACTICE TIME

Erase all files in the disk in drive B. First of all, remove the DOS disk in drive A so that you don't accidentally erase its information. You can now find out names of all files in the disk (using DIR) and erase them individually, or you can use the wild card, or * symbol. Simply type **ERASE B:*.*** and press (ENTER).

MKDIR

As the number of files on each disk increases, so does the need to have the disk well organized. This is especially true of hard disks with large capacity. DOS allows you to create tree-structured directories. The original directory, or the root directory, can have a number of subdivisions, or subdirectories, each containing files with a common subject matter. The subdirectories in turn can have more specific subdirectories of their own.

Let's say, for example, that you still had all kinds of files in the disk in drive B. If you were to add data files from an application, such as Lotus 1–2–3, onto the disk, it would be very difficult to selectively identify these data files at a later time. If you were to

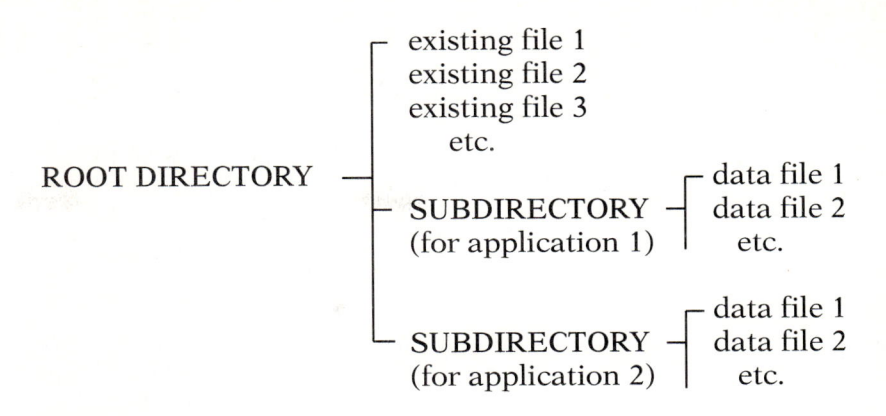

```
                        ┌─ existing file 1
                        │  existing file 2
                        │  existing file 3
                        │     etc.
ROOT DIRECTORY ─┼─                          ┌─ data file 1
                        ├─ SUBDIRECTORY   ─┤   data file 2
                        │  (for application 1)  │     etc.
                        │                        ┌─ data file 1
                        └─ SUBDIRECTORY   ─┤   data file 2
                           (for application 2)     etc.
```

create a subdirectory and place all your data files in the subdirectory, they would be easier to access.

To create a subdirectory, you use the MKDIR command (internal). MKDIR stands for Make Directory. Its format is MKDIR d:*name*, where d: is the drive on which a subdirectory is to be created and *name* is the name you want to call this subdirectory. The subdirectory name follows the same rules as the filename.

- Type **MKDIR B:MYSUB** and press (ENTER). If B was already the default drive, there is no need to specify. Also, MKDIR can be abbreviated as MD.

- Now, type **DIR B:** to look at the directory for the disk in drive B.

  ➤ You see the entry

     `MYSUB <DIR>`

  You have created a subdirectory.

■ CHDIR

You are still in the root directory. That is, if you were to copy a file onto the disk in drive B, it is placed in the root directory along with other existing files. It is like having a little pointer. The location of the pointer tells which directory or subdirectory is currently being utilized. To move the pointer to the newly created subdirectory, you use the CHDIR command (internal), which stands for Change Directory.

- With B as the default drive, type **CHDIR MYSUB** and press (ENTER). You can type **CD** as an abbreviation for CHDIR.
- Use DIR on drive B again.
  - ➤ The following message indicates that you are now in MYSUB subdirectory:

  `Directory of B:\MYSUB`

You can create another level of subdirectory within MYSUB. At this point, if you were to copy a file onto the disk in drive B, that file is placed in the MYSUB subdirectory.

You can get back to the root directory no matter where you are by typing **CD**. If you want to get back to the subdirectory just above the current one, you type **CD ..** (two periods). The space between CD and either \ or .. is optional.

PRACTICE TIME

1. Create another subdirectory NEXTSUB within MYSUB.

2. Create subdirectory YOURSUB in the root directory (the same level as MYSUB).

3. Try moving from one subdirectory to another.

Once you create subdirectories on a disk, it is very important that you keep track of which subdirectory a particular file was placed in. The complete name of a file will now include the subdirectory, or the path, it is placed in. The name now starts with the root directory, which is the drive name such as B:, followed by a backslash (\) and the subdirectory name. The backslash with subdirectory name is repeated as many times as needed to go down different levels of subdirectory. When the subdirectory where the file is located is reached, place a backslash followed by the filename. For example, to refer to the data file called ADATA.DAT in subdirectory MYSUB, you use B:\MYSUB\ADATA.DAT. To refer to the data file called BDATA.DAT in subdirectory NEXTSUB, which is in subdirectory MYSUB, you will want to use the path and filename B:\MYSUB\NEXTSUB\BDATA.DAT.

TREE

If you wonder what your tree structure looks like right now, you can use the external command TREE.

- Make sure that you are in the root directory of drive B by entering **CD**.

- Insert the DOS disk in drive A (Remember, TREE is an external command), and type **A:TREE B:** and press (ENTER).

    ➤ You will see the following:

    ```
    DIRECTORY PATH LISTING FOR VOLUME XXXXX
    Path: \MYSUB
    Sub-directories: NEXTSUB

    Path: \MYSUB\NEXTSUB
    Sub-directories: None

    Path: \YOURSUB
    Sub-directories: None
    ```

Remember, the path is the same as the subdirectory name. If you were to use the /F option with the TREE command, for example, TREE B: /F, the files in each subdirectory are listed as well.

RMDIR

The Remove Directory command, RMDIR, is an internal command that lets you remove a subdirectory. Before a subdirectory can be removed, it must be empty: the subdirectory must not contain any files or other subdirectories. Once it is empty, place yourself in the subdirectory just above the one you want to remove, then issue the command.

- Make sure that the subdirectory NEXTSUB is empty.

- Change directory to the subdirectory above NEXTSUB, which is MYSUB.

THE DISK OPERATING SYSTEM **47**

- Type **RMDIR NEXTSUB** and press (ENTER). You can abbreviate RMDIR as RD.
- Use DIR on MYSUB (DIR: B:\MYSUB) to verify that NEXTSUB has been removed.

PRACTICE TIME

Remove the MYSUB subdirectory.

EXECUTING PROGRAMS

Usually, when an application program is to be executed from floppy disks, you start up the computer with a disk containing DOS, replace the DOS disk with the program disk, and type the program name. You can find the program name in the user manual.

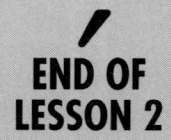

END OF LESSON 2

- Remove disks from the disk drives and store them.
- Turn off the computer and monitor.

SUMMARY

In this lesson, various DOS commands are presented.

- The default drive is the drive the computer will use unless instructed otherwise.
- To change the default drive, simply press the drive name, A or B, followed by a colon (:).
- Some DOS commands are internal and others are external. In order to use external commands, the DOS disk must be in the computer.

- Directories are used to organize files kept on a disk.
- The following commands are discussed:

    VER　　　　　Displays the DOS version under which you are operating.

    Commands Used with Disks:

    FORMAT　　Formats a disk.
    CHKDSK　　Checks the status of a disk.

    Commands for Using and Moving Files:

    DIR　　　　　Displays the names of all the files on the disk in the disk drive.
    COPY　　　　Copies a file.
    RENAME　　Renames the file.
    ERASE　　　Erases the specified file from disk.
    TYPE　　　　Displays the contents of a file on the screen.

    Commands Used to Safeguard Your Files:

    COMP　　　　Compares the contents of two files.
    DISKCOPY　Creates a copy of one disk on another. Formats the target disk, if necessary.
    DISKCOMP　Compares the contents of two disks.

    Commands Most Often Used with a Hard Disk:

    MKDIR　　　Creates a new subdirectory.
    CHDIR　　　Changes the current directory of a specified drive.
    RMDIR　　　Deletes a specified subdirectory.
    TREE　　　　Displays all the directory paths of a specified drive.

REVIEW QUESTIONS

1. Explain what is meant by the default disk drive. How do you know what it is at any time, and how do you change it?

2. What does the FORMAT command do?

3. When you have 30 or more files on a disk, how do you get a listing of the filenames on screen without some scrolling off the top before they can be read?

4. What is a wild card character? How do you use it?

5. How does DISKCOPY A: B: differ from COPY A:*.* B:?

6. How do you move to a subdirectory named SUBA? How do you move back to the root directory?

7. How do you verify that a file, once copied, is an exact duplicate of the original file?

8. If you've created a maze of subdirectories on a disk over time, how can you locate the path to one particular subdirectory?

9. Why might a disk be organized with several subdirectories?

LESSON 3
SOME ADVANCED DOS FEATURES

SUPPLIES NEEDED

For this part of the manual, you need:

- The DOS disk
- A scratch disk

OBJECTIVES

Upon completion of material presented in this lesson, you should be able to understand the following:

- How to create and execute batch files
- The purpose of the AUTOEXEC.BAT file
- The purpose of the CONFIG.SYS file

ORIENTATION

There are a many things to learn in using DOS. In the previous section, the basic commands of DOS were mentioned so that you might make use of them while working with Lotus 1–2–3 in this manual. In this section, some advanced features and commands are presented. These commands and features are advanced only in terms of the extra capabilities they provide.

STARTING OFF

Start up your computer using the DOS disk. You will make a system disk (not a DOS disk), that is, a data disk with which you can start the computer.

SOME ADVANCED DOS FEATURES

PRACTICE TIME

Format a disk in drive B (it can be the disk you used during the last lesson) with the systems option (/S).

BATCH FILES

Most of the time, you enter DOS commands one by one from the keyboard. Sometimes, however, it is necessary to enter the same sequence of DOS commands repeatedly. For example, let's say that at the end of the computer session every day, you have to copy four data files in different subdirectories onto a backup disk. You may have to type the following four commands:

COPY A:\MYSUB\ADATA.DAT B:
COPY A:\MYSUB\NEXTSUB\BDATA.DAT B:
COPY A:\YOURSUB\CDATA.DAT B:
COPY A:\YOURSUB\ANSUB\DDATA.DAT B:

With the names being so long, it is very easy to make typing errors. There is a much better way to do this chore, and that is to use a batch file.

A **batch file** is a disk file consisting of a list of DOS COMMANDS. That is, a series of DOS commands is stored in a text file, which is given a filename with the extension BAT. You can create this file by using the COPY command.

Earlier, the COPY command was discussed in terms of making backup copies of a file. The COPY command can be used to create a text file from keyboard input as well. There are two things that need to be specified with a COPY command: where to copy from (**source**) and where to copy to (**target**). To create a batch file, the source is keyboard input, or CON:, and the target is the batch file.

- Make sure that your formatted disk is still in drive B.

- Type **COPY CON: B:MY.BAT** and press (ENTER).

    ➤ The cursor just moves to the next line down.

- Type the four lines shown below, making sure to press (ENTER) after each line, except the last line. After you finish typing the fourth line, wait. Be sure to verify what you type on each line before you press

(ENTER). You cannot make any typing errors. (If you do, you need to start over.)

>   COPY A:\MYSUB\ADATA.DAT B:
>   COPY A:\MYSUB\NEXTSUB\BDATA.DAT B:
>   COPY A:\YOURSUB\CDATA.DAT B:
>   COPY A:\YOURSUB\ANSUB\DDATA.DAT B:

- Press the (F6) function key and then press (ENTER).

  ➤ The following message appears on the screen:

  `1 file(s) copied`

The batch file MY.BAT has been created. To make sure that you did not make any typing errors, you will look at the content of the MY.BAT file using the TYPE command.

- Type **TYPE B:MY.BAT** and press (ENTER).

  ➤ The content of B:MY.BAT is displayed.

In order to have the computer carry out the series of DOS command in the batch file, you just type the batch filename, in this case MY (leave out the extension). DOS will then search the default drive, find the batch file, and carry out the various commands in the order specified. Since you used some nonexistent file names in this batch file, you cannot test it right now.

PRACTICE TIME

1. Create a batch file, B:TEST.BAT, that contains the following DOS commands:

   DIR A:
   DIR B:

2. Test the batch file by entering TEST.

3. From the root directory, create a subdirectory TESTSUB.

4. Copy the batch file, TEST.BAT, to the subdirectory TESTSUB. That is, give the command

   COPY B:TEST.BAT B:\TESTSUB\TEST.BAT

5. Then erase the batch file TEST.BAT from the root directory.

6. With the DOS disk in drive A, enter the TREE command. That is, type **A:TREE B: /F** and press (ENTER).

PATH COMMAND

When the execution of batch file was mentioned above, it was noted that DOS searched for the batch file in the current directory. What if the batch file was not there? In your case, the TEST.BAT file is in the TESTSUB subdirectory. What happens if you try to execute it from the root directory?

- Make sure you are in the root directory.
- Execute the batch file TEST.

    ➤ You get an error message:

    ```
    Bad command or file name.
    ```

    That means, the batch file was not found in the current directory.

The PATH command (internal) defines the search sequence for batch files and DOS commands. The format for the PATH command is PATH d:path;d:path;... where d: is the drive and path is the subdirectory name. You can specify as many drive and subdirectory names as you wish, separated by semicolons (;). When you enter a command that is not found in the current directory of the default drive, DOS searches the named paths in the sequence you specified.

Typing **PATH** with no parameters displays the current path, or what you specified the last time you entered PATH. If you were to type **PATH** and press (ENTER) right now, you would get the message:

```
No Path
```

(since you haven't entered any yet). When you create many batch files, you may want to place such files in one subdirectory (for organization). Then, each time you use the computer, you would enter the PATH command specifying that subdirectory. Then, you could use the batch files from any directory.

56 USING LOTUS 1-2-3

- Type **PATH B:\;B:\TESTSUB** and press ENTER.
- Now, execute the batch file TEST.
    ➤ The batch file commands are executed.

First, the computer searched the root directory for the batch file TEST.BAT. When it could not be found, the computer searched the B:\TESTSUB subdirectory and carried out the commands.

AUTOEXEC.BAT

The AUTOEXEC.BAT file is a special batch file that is automatically executed whenever the computer is started up. If your startup disk contains a file with the name AUTOEXEC.BAT, then it is executed on DOS startup without any action on your part.

What that means is, the PATH command that was mentioned in the previous section can be placed in the AUTOEXEC.BAT file. That way, every time you start the computer, the AUTOEXEC.BAT file is executed and hence the PATH command is executed.

If you do include an AUTOEXEC.BAT file, when the computer is started, only the commands that are in AUTOEXEC.BAT file are executed. Two commands that you see when you start the computer from the DOS System disk are DATE and TIME commands. These are the commands that let you specify date and time. You can include these in your AUTOEXEC.BAT as well. If you have a clock/calendar installed in your system, you would place the command to activate the clock in the AUTOEXEC.BAT file instead.

So, let's say that you want to create an AUTOEXEC.BAT file that contains the TIME, DATE, and PATH commands.

- Remove the DOS disk from drive A.
- Move the disk in drive B to drive A.

You will create an AUTOEXEC.BAT file on the system disk.

- Enter **COPY CON: AUTOEXEC.BAT**.
- Enter the following commands in AUTOEXEC.BAT file:

    TIME
    DATE
    PATH B:\;B:\TESTSUB\

SOME ADVANCED DOS FEATURES **57**

- Press the (F6) function key followed by (ENTER).
- Now, warm start the computer. Do you remember how? Hold down the keys marked (CTRL) and (ALT), and press the key marked (DEL).
  ➤ The computer starts up, asking for the time and date, then the PATH is set.

There are several other commands a batch file might contain. However, the use of these commands is not limited to batch files. That is, these commands can be issued at any time that you are in DOS mode.

One is ECHO OFF. It prevents the screen display of DOS commands executed from a batch file. Usually, as commands are executed from a batch file, they are displayed, or echoed, on the screen. Once ECHO OFF is executed, these commands are not echoed. The ECHO ON command will reactivate echoing. A reason for including an ECHO OFF command might be to keep the screen from becoming cluttered.

- Type **ECHO OFF** and press (ENTER).
  ➤ The prompt disappears from the screen.
- Type **ECHO ON** and press (ENTER).
  ➤ The prompt reappears.

Another command that "cleans up" the screen is the CLS command. This command clears the screen and sends the cursor to "home," which is the top left-hand corner of the screen.

- Type **CLS** and press (ENTER).
  ➤ The screen clears and the cursor goes "home."

A useful command to include in a batch file, particularly in an AUTOEXEC.BAT file, is the PROMPT command. The PROMPT command lets you set a new DOS prompt. Right now your prompt is the default drive, followed by >. When you have many subdirectories, it is helpful to see which subdirectory you are located in.

- Type **PROMPT pg** and press (ENTER).

- Change to the TESTSUB subdirectory using CD TESTSUB.
  ➤ The prompt now reads B:\TESTSUB>.

The pg that followed the word PROMPT are special options. These options are each in the form of $c, where c can be one of many options. $p means you want to show the current directory as the prompt. $g means you want to show the symbol >. Consult your DOS manual for other options. You can even set the colors of your screen's background and text through the PROMPT command.

- Type **PROMPT** and press (ENTER) to get back to the way it was.

If you want a message displayed on the screen, you can create a file containing text using the COPY CON: (copy from keyboard to a specified file) and TYPE it.

- Enter **COPY CON: MESSAGE** to create a text file named MESSAGE.
- Type the following. At end, press the (F6) function key, followed by (ENTER).

This disk was prepared for your use.

- Enter **TYPE MESSAGE**.

You will now recreate the AUTOEXEC.BAT file utilizing all the above-mentioned commands.

- Enter the following in the AUTOEXEC.BAT file. (When you COPY CON: to AUTOEXEC.BAT file, it will replace the previous one.)

  ECHO OFF
  PATH A:\;A:\TESTSUB
  PROMPT pg
  CLS
  TYPE MESSAGE
  DIR A:

- Check and make sure that your AUTOEXEC.BAT file is correct.

SOME ADVANCED DOS FEATURES

■ Warm start the computer.

You can change the content of MESSAGE file to display whatever other message you want to see.

PRACTICE TIME

1. Experiment with the AUTOEXEC.BAT file by taking out some commands or inserting other commands.

2. Create other batch files in TESTSUB subdirectory that:

   a. Clear the screen, change directory to TESTSUB, then display the content of the current directory (DIR).

   b. Clear the screen, change directory to the root directory, then display the content of the current directory.

   c. Turn off echoing, clear the screen, and execute the TEST batch file.

The MODE command is often included in the AUTOEXEC.BAT file, but its use requires some knowledge of the peripheral units that you are using, and hence will not be discussed in detail here. In general, the MODE command is used to set the way a printer, a monitor, or a communication port operates. For example, most software is designed to be used with a parallel printer. If you have a serial printer, then you can use the MODE command to redirect all output intended for a parallel port (where a parallel printer is connected) to a serial port (where a serial printer is connected) instead. This allows you to use the serial printer.

CONFIG.SYS

One feature that is worth mentioning is the CONFIG.SYS file. Whenever you start up your computer, DOS files are loaded and the computer searches for an AUTOEXEC.BAT file in the root directory (and if it's there, its commands are carried out). One other step that is carried out is that DOS searches for a file called

CONFIG.SYS. If it is found, its commands are executed just like the AUTOEXEC.BAT file. The difference between these two files is that CONFIG.SYS contains a very limited set of commands that can only be executed from the CONFIG.SYS file. These commands are BREAK, BUFFERS, COUNTRY, DEVICES, FCBS, FILES, LASTDRIVE, and SHELL. Some software requires that some of these be set to certain values. Consult your software manual for specific requirements. CONFIG.SYS can be created using COPY CON: CONFIG.SYS.

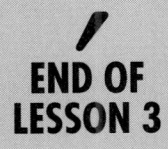

END OF LESSON 3

- Remove disks from the disk drives and store them.
- Turn off the computer and monitor.

SUMMARY

In this lesson, various advanced DOS commands are presented.

- A batch file is a file containing a list of DOS commands.
- An AUTOEXEC.BAT file is a batch file that is automatically executed when the computer is started up.
- The CONFIG.SYS file contains other commands that a software needs to set specific parameters.
- The following commands are discussed:

PATH	Defines the search sequence for **batch files** and **DOS** commands.
ECHO OFF	Disables the screen display of DOS commands.
ECHO ON	Enables the screen display of DOS commands.
CLS	Clears the screen and sends the cursor to the top left corner of the screen.
PROMPT	Changes the prompt on the screen.

REVIEW QUESTIONS

1. What does the PATH command do?

2. What is a batch file?

3. How is a batch file made to execute?

4. How do you create a batch file? How do you terminate keyboard entry for a batch file?

5. What is special about the file AUTOEXEC.BAT?

6. What is the purpose of the CLS command?

LESSON 4
CREATING A SIMPLE SPREADSHEET

OBJECTIVES

Upon completion of the material presented in this lesson, you should be able to:

- Know the terminology used with spreadsheets
- Move the cell pointer in a spreadsheet
- Enter spreadsheet commands
- Enter data into a spreadsheet file
- Understand the difference between labels and values
- Enter simple formulas
- Save a file on a disk
- Print a spreadsheet

INTRODUCTION

Spreadsheets made up of rows and columns (also called worksheets) have been used in business for over a century. Much information used in running a business is kept on a spreadsheet. Information is entered with a pen or pencil, and calculations are done using calculators. This work, however, usually takes many hours of tedious calculations and recalculations—precisely the kind of job best done on a computer.

This is where an *electronic spreadsheet* comes in. It lets the computer be pencil, spreadsheet, and calculator. The main memory of the computer is the spreadsheet, the monitor (the screen) is the window through which you view your work, and the keyboard is the pencil. You store in the computer's memory the formulas and values used in the calculations, and instruct the computer to perform calculations as needed. If you need to change a formula or value, you only enter the changes; the electronic spreadsheet updates the rest of the worksheet.

Because the computer can calculate and recalculate rapidly, the electronic spreadsheet is the best tool to answer such "what-if" questions that arise in business as: What if we increase the interest rate? What if we increase the markup percentage? What if we give our employees a 10% wage increase? Spreadsheets can be used for financial forecasting, budgeting, stock portfolio analysis, cost analysis, and more.

Impressed? Maybe not. You might wonder what good it would do you to learn how to use a spreadsheet program. After all, you might not work for a business. You can, however, use spreadsheets in other activities as well.

- Using a spreadsheet, teachers can keep track of students' grades on exams and homework. The computer can be instructed to figure the class average for a test, each student's total score and grade average for several tests, and so on.

- An electronic spreadsheet can be used to do the household budget. Did you ever wonder if you could afford to buy a new car? If you save $20 a month this year and increase the amount by 5 percent each year, how much can you save in five years? What if you increase the amount by 8 percent instead? Using a spreadsheet program, you can answer these questions very quickly.

An electronic spreadsheet makes working with numbers flexible and convenient. Without an electronic spreadsheet, one can get bogged down in the mechanical process of calculations and fail to make the proper analysis of the results.

It was the introduction of spreadsheets that led businesspeople to view the microcomputer as a potentially useful tool for business rather than as a toy for hobbyists. Today there are many spreadsheet software packages on the market, such as Lotus 1–2–3, SuperCalc, VP Planner Plus, Quattro, MultiPlan, and Excel. They all perform basic spreadsheet functions in a similar manner. In fact, if you can use one, adapting to another is not difficult.

The spreadsheet program used here is Lotus 1–2–3 Release 2.2. Although Lotus 1–2–3 was not the first spreadsheet program, it is the best selling one today. The name 1–2–3 originated because the earliest release of the program contained three integrated parts;

that is, in addition to a spreadsheet (ability to manipulate rows and columns of numbers), it also featured capabilities for data management and graphics. The data-management part allows you to arrange data and extract a certain portion of the spreadsheet for use. The graphics part allows you to create graphs out of the spreadsheet data.

Lotus 1–2–3 offers many options and powerful features. Release 2.2 has several useful improvements over the earlier version, Release 2.01. Release 3 has additional features. This manual is intended for use with Release 2.2. It covers most of the commonly-used features of spreadsheets and several new features in Release 2.2. However, Lotus 1–2–3 has many useful features, and only some of these are covered in this manual. The manual presents enough for you to get started; it is up to you to explore the rest.

LOTUS 1–2–3 RELEASES

Lotus 1–2–3 Release 1A was introduced in 1983. It was upgraded with Releases 2, then 2.01, in subsequent years. In 1989, Lotus Development Corporation released two upgrades of Lotus 1–2–3: Release 2.2 and Release 3.

Release 2.2, covered in this manual, requires an IBM micro or compatible with at least 512K of memory, either two floppy diskette drives or a hard drive and one floppy drive, and a printer.

If you are not familiar with earlier releases of Lotus 1–2–3, this manual will guide you through the basics and show you some of the advanced features. However, if you are familiar with an earlier release, you may want to know how Release 2.2 is different from earlier releases. Most features of Release 2.2 are identical to those of Release 2.01. The upgrades include the following features:

- A *Learn feature* that allows the user to save a range of keystrokes that can later be named and used as a macro.

- *Setting sheets* that display on screen the current settings when you print, graph, or query data. These identify the ranges and options selected, save time, and prevent confusion. There are also setting sheets for global and default settings.

CREATING A SIMPLE SPREADSHEET **67**

- *File linking*, referencing a cell in another file on disk, which is accomplished using a straightforward convention. This feature allows one worksheet to contain formulas that reference values calculated in another worksheet, which resides on disk.

- An *Add-in Manager*, which is built in. Two add-ins are included in the Release 2.2 package: Allways and the Macro Library Manager.

- An *Undo key*, which allows you to undo the effects of your most recent command or entry.

- A */ Graph Group* command, which lets you specify all the graph ranges (X, A, B, C, and so on) with a single command.

- *Video drivers*, which allow more than 25 lines and 80 columns on screen if the appropriate monitor is available. In this manual, however, the screen displays are shown for a 25-line display screen. Users with enhanced display capabilities will have screen displays that differ slightly from those appearing in this manual.

- A *Run key*, which offers an alternative way to invoke macros. The (ALT)-L method works for \L macros, but the Run key can be used to invoke a macro of any name.

Release 3 requires a more powerful computer: at least an 80286 machine with a hard disk and 1 Mbyte memory (3 Mbytes if you use the OS/2 operating system). It is also similar to Release 2.01. It includes the features noted above for Release 2.2, except for linking (which is enhanced over Release 2.2) and Setting sheets (which are omitted). Some of its enhancements relate to size (capacity). Release 3 also includes the following improvements:

- *Three-dimensionality*, achieved by allowing up to 256 worksheets in memory at once. Up to three layers of worksheets can be viewed at a time.

- *Graphics* with more ways to display graphs and the ability to print graphs without leaving the spreadsheet part of Lotus 1–2–3.
- *Multiple-key sorts* that let you sort with as many keys as you need, as compared with two-key sorts (primary and secondary) given in earlier releases.
- Additional *Criteria options,* which allow more flexibility in data querying.
- A *Three-way data table* feature, which extends the two-way data table into a third dimension.
- A *Range Name Note* command, which lets you attach text to any range, to serve as reminder notes or for other purposes.
- Additional *Macro keywords* that apply to databases, graphics, and screen displays.

Users familiar with Release 2.01 will find either Release 2.2 or Release 3 to be similar in many ways. A person who wants to learn Release 3 can benefit from learning Release 2.2 from this manual, since almost every feature presented in the following lessons exists in Release 3.

STARTING LOTUS

To use this manual, you need Lotus 1–2–3 Release 2.2 installed on a hard disk, on a network file server, or on floppy diskettes. You also need a formatted data disk.

Lotus 1–2–3 may be configured in a variety of ways to suit your system. Your software may be installed on a network, or it may be installed on a hard disk system. It can also be on floppy disks to be used on a computer with two floppy disk drives. The manner in which you start the program depends on your particular setup. Ask your instructor for your specific setup.

USING A FLOPPY DRIVE SYSTEM

The computer must be started with a DOS system disk. You cannot use the Allways add-in feature if you are using Lotus installed on floppy diskettes. Your Lotus 1–2–3 Release 2.2 software should be correctly installed on the floppy diskettes.

1. Insert the DOS system disk into drive A and close the door.

2. Switch on the monitor and computer, and enter the date and time when requested.

3. Remove the DOS system disk and place the Lotus 1–2–3 system disk into drive A.

4. Enter the command **LOTUS** and press the (ENTER) key.
   ➤ In a moment, the Lotus Access System screen is displayed, as shown in Screen Display 4–1.

Whenever you attempt to access the Help system, the bottom of the screen will display the message:

```
Cannot find 123.HLP help file
```

To access the Help system, you need to replace the System diskette with the Help diskette and press (F1) again.

When you attempt to use the PrintGraph utility, the screen will go blank and a message will appear:

```
Insert the PrintGraph Disk into your diskette
drive
Press (ENTER) to continue or (ESC) to quit
```

To enter Print Graph, replace the System diskette with the PrintGraph diskette and press (ENTER). A similar message appears when you attempt to use the Translate utility or reenter 1–2–3 after using one of these utilities. Follow the directions and insert the proper diskette into drive A.

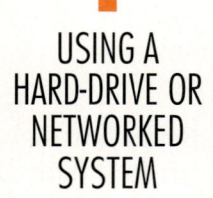

USING A HARD-DRIVE OR NETWORKED SYSTEM

Your Lotus 1–2–3 Release 2.2 software should be correctly installed on the hard drive or on a network.

1. Start up the computer either from the hard disk or through the network.

```
1-2-3   PrintGraph   Translate   Install   Exit
Use 1-2-3


               1-2-3 Access System
               Copyright  1986, 1989
              Lotus Development Corporation
                 All Rights Reserved
                    Release 2.2

The Access system lets you choose 1-2-3, PrintGraph, the Translate utility,
and the Install program, from the menu at the top of this screen.  If
you're using a two-diskette system, the Access system may prompt you to
change disks.  Follow the instructions below to start a program.

o  Use → or ← to move the menu pointer (the highlighted rectangle
   at the top of the screen) to the program you want to use.

o  Press ENTER to start the program.

You can also start a program by typing the first character of its name.

Press HELP (F1) for more information.
```

Screen Display 4–1   Lotus Access System screen.

2. Change the directory to where Lotus 1–2–3 is located.

3. Type **LOTUS** and press (ENTER).

   ➤ In a moment, the Lotus Access System screen appears, as shown in Screen Display 4–1.

USING A PRINTER

You will need a printer to do the lessons in this manual. Furthermore, if you plan to print graphics, you will need a printer that is capable of printing graphics. The manual assumes that the correct printer has been installed and that the hardware setup in PrintGraph has been specified and saved.

STARTING OFF

Start Lotus 1–2–3 on the computer, following the instructions given in the introduction, so that the Access System screen is displayed.

THE 1–2–3 ACCESS SYSTEM

The top line on the screen, with 1–2–3 highlighted, contains the menu. Just as a menu in a restaurant tells you what dishes are available, this menu shows you what commands are now available.

The 1–2–3 Access System menu has the following menu options:

1–2–3	Enter the Lotus Worksheet/Graphics/Database program
PrintGraph	Enter the Lotus Graphics Printing program
Translate	Interchange files between 1–2–3 and other program formats
Install	Start the Lotus Install procedure
Exit	Quit Lotus and return to DOS

To make a selection from the menu, you either use the ← or → key to move the highlight, known as the menu pointer, and then press the (ENTER) key, or press the key of the first letter of the option you want (you may use either uppercase or lowercase letters).

The first option, 1–2–3, is highlighted; it is the default option. A *default* option is the one preselected. That is, if you were simply to press (ENTER), without pressing a specific key, this is the selection you would have made.

The second line in the box displays a short description of the highlighted option in the menu. When you use the arrow keys, also called the pointer movement keys, to highlight another menu option, the second line updates the description each time you move the highlight.

Note: If the rightmost option is highlighted and you press the → key, the menu pointer moves to the leftmost option, and vice versa.

■
PRACTICE TIME

Use the → key to move the menu pointer through all the options. As you move to each option, read the second line.

ENTERING 1-2-3

To enter the Lotus 1–2–3 program:

■ Highlight 1–2–3 and press (ENTER).

➤ After a few moments for the disk access to load the program, the blank worksheet shown in Screen Display 4–2 appears.

The top three lines on the screen make up the *control panel*. The line at the bottom of the screen displays the *status line*. The area between them is the *worksheet area*.

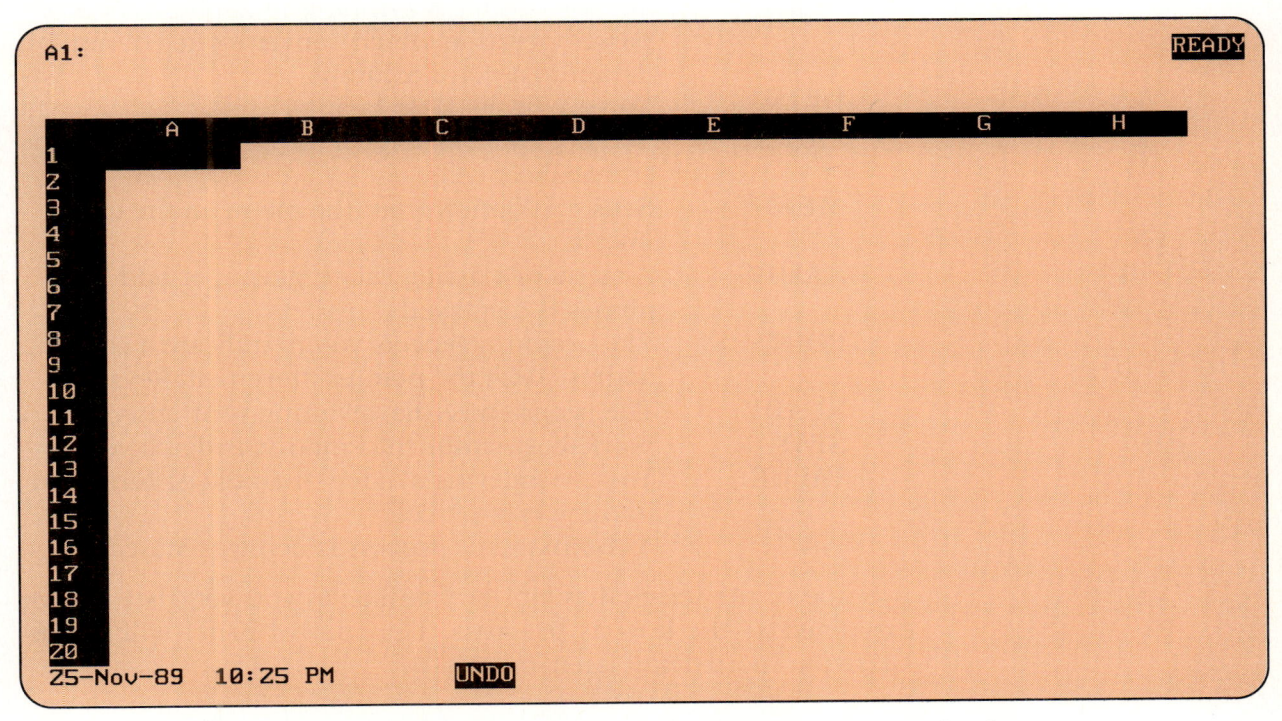

Screen Display 4–2   The initial worksheet display.

CREATING A SIMPLE SPREADSHEET   73

THE CONTROL PANEL

The control panel consists of three lines. The first line displays information about the current cell and the *mode* you are in. The second line displays what you are entering or editing, or menu options available to you. The third line contains further options or an explanation of the menu option highlighted on the entry line.

The first line currently displays the word A1: at the left (this will be explained later) and the mode indicator READY at the right. The *mode indicator* tells you what the program is doing and what kind of entry is expected. The program can be in one of the following modes:

EDIT	Use the keyboard to edit the entry and press (ENTER).
ERROR	An error has occurred; press (ESC) or (ENTER) to clear it.
FILES	A menu of file names is displayed.
FIND	The program is in the data-search mode.
FRMT	You are editing a format line during a data parse operation which converts one column of data into several columns.
HELP	You are in the Help facility.
LABEL	You are entering a label into the current spreadsheet cell.
MENU	Select an option from the menu on the entry line.
NAMES	A menu of existing range, graph, or add-in names is displayed.
POINT	The program expects you to indicate a cell address with the pointer-movement keys.
READY	The program is idle, awaiting your entry.
STAT	Worksheet-status information is displayed.
VALUE	You are entering a value (formula or function) into the current cell.
WAIT	A command or process is being executed.

Some of the terms may not be familiar to you yet; they will be explained as the lessons progress. The control panel will be discussed in more detail later.

THE WORKSHEET AREA

The worksheet area has highlighted borders at the top and to the left of the screen. The top border has letters that identify the columns displayed, while the left border has the numbers that identify the rows displayed. Initially, 8 columns and 20 rows are displayed. Each intersection of a row and a column contains a *cell* in the worksheet. Each cell is identified by specifying the letter and number of its column and row, called its *address,* such as A1 or G8.

THE STATUS LINE

The bottom line on the screen is the *status line*. It displays the time and date, according to your computer's internal memory. It also displays the following status indicators as appropriate:

CALC	Formulas in the worksheet need to be recalculated.
CAPS	The (CAPS LOCK) key is on; all letters are entered in uppercase.
CIRC	A circular reference has been created (not discussed in this manual).
CMD	The program is pausing while a macro is in use.
END	The (END) key has been pressed in the READY mode.
MEM	Memory warning: Available memory is less than 4,000 bytes; you may get ‹Memory Full› message if you add data.
NUM	The (NUM LOCK) key is on; the numeric keypad will input numbers rather than pointer movements.
OVR	The (INS) key has been pressed; the worksheet is in the overwrite mode.
RO	(Networks only) The current file has read-only status (not discussed in this manual).
SCROLL	The (SCROLL LOCK) key has been pressed; pointer-movement keys move the worksheet under the cell pointer, which stays at the current cell.
SST	A macro in single-step mode is waiting for input (not discussed in this manual).

CREATING A SIMPLE SPREADSHEET

    STEP   The single-step mode is on (not discussed in this manual).

    UNDO   Pressing UNDO ([ALT]-[F4]) cancels changes made to the worksheet since it was last in the READY mode.

As you can see, there are quite a few status indicators. Their uses will become clear as the lesson progresses.

MOVING THE CELL POINTER

The inverse-video rectangle (a bright, solid bar) you see at cell A1 (column A, row 1) is the *cell pointer*. You can enter data on the spreadsheet at the cell where the cell pointer is located. This cell is referred to as the *current cell*, and its address is displayed on the first line of the control panel. If you want to enter data elsewhere (in this case, other than A1), you must move the cell pointer to the entry position. You can move the cell pointer by using the pointer-movement keys, also called the arrow keys, located at the right of the main keyboard. The four arrow keys move the cell pointer one cell at a time in the indicated direction. The [HOME] key moves the cell pointer directly to cell A1.

PRACTICE TIME

Move the cell pointer around the worksheet using the keys just described. Press the [→] key at least 10 times, then the [↓] key at least 25 times. As you do so, notice the changes in the first line on the control panel and in the column and row headings.

SIZING THE WORKSHEET

As you pressed the arrow keys, you noticed the column and row headings changed. The cell pointer can move to the right beyond column H and down beyond row 20. Altogether, the worksheet contains 256 columns, labelled A through Z, AA through AZ, BA through BZ, and so on, through IV. The worksheet also contains 8192 rows. Because of the space limitation imposed by your screen size, however, you can see only as many rows and columns as your screen can display at any one time. The screen display, referred to as the *window*, has twenty or more rows; the number of columns displayed depends on the width of the columns.

As you continue pressing the (→) key, new columns appear to the right and the leftmost columns disappear. This is called *scrolling* to the right. That is, you are moving the window to the right. As you continue pressing the (↓) key, new rows appear on the bottom and the top rows disappear; you are scrolling down, or moving the window down. It is as though you were looking at a map with a magnifying glass. You see just one portion of the map at a time, but you can move the magnifying glass around to look at the whole map.

If you want to move the cell pointer a little faster, just hold the arrow key down. If you want to move the cell pointer around even faster, you can use the page-up and page-down ((PGUP) and (PGDN)) keys to move the cell pointer one screen up or down at a time. You can move the cell pointer fast to the left or right, too: Pressing the (TAB) key moves the cell pointer right to the next screen of columns, and pressing (SHIFT)-(TAB) (holding down the (SHIFT) key while you press the (TAB) key) moves the cell pointer one screen to the left. In fact, if you press the (END) key followed by the (→) key, the cell pointer will move to the rightmost column, or column IV. If you press the (END) key followed by the (←) key, it will move to the leftmost, or A, column. You might guess what the (END) key followed by the (↑) or (↓) key will do.

One more key to note is the (SCROLL LOCK) key. When you press the (SCROLL LOCK) key, the status indicator, SCROLL, appears at the bottom of the screen. When you press the (←) and (→) keys, the cell pointer stays at the same location on the screen, but the cells under it scroll. When you press the (SCROLL LOCK) key the second time, the arrow keys will go back to their normal function.

Try out all these key-combinations on your screen.

THE GOTO KEY ((F5))

Sometimes you want to move the cell pointer to a particular cell without these gymnastics; there is a way. Use the GOTO command (the (F5) function key) by following the instructions below.

If you make an error in typing, you can press the Backspace key ((BACKSPACE) key—the key with the left arrow inscribed on it, located above the (ENTER) key) to back up and retype.

CREATING A SIMPLE SPREADSHEET **77**

- Press the (F5) function key.
  ➤ The following message

  `Enter address to go to:`

  appears on the second line of the control panel, followed by the address of the current cell.

  ➤ The mode indicator shows that you are in the POINT mode.

The current cell is the default address. That is, if you were to press (ENTER) without entering an address, the cell pointer would not move. You need to indicate the cell to which you want to move the cell pointer.

- Enter the address of the cell where you want to move the cell pointer. If you want to move the cell pointer to cell L56, then type **L56** and press (ENTER).

  ➤ The cell pointer has moved to the specified cell.
  ➤ 1–2–3 is in the READY mode.

PRACTICE TIME

1. Move the cell pointer to cell C115 using the GOTO command.

2. Move the cell pointer to cell F23 using the GOTO command.

3. Move the cell pointer to other cells.

4. When you are satisfied that you can move the cell pointer to any location you choose, move it to cell A1, using (HOME).

THE COMMAND STRUCTURE

When you work with a spreadsheet, you are either inserting data to be processed or giving a command for 1–2–3 to carry out immediately. When you make entries at the current cell, you are *inserting data*. When you give an instruction for 1–2–3 to carry out, such as

78 USING LOTUS 1-2-3

moving data or printing the spreadsheet on a printer, you are *giving a command*. Most commands are selected through menus, beginning with the / (slash). The / key is just to the right of the . (period) key on the main keyboard.

Note: The / (slash) key and the \ (backslash) key look similar on the keyboard, but they have different meanings in Lotus 1–2–3. Be sure you always select the correct key.

When you press the / (slash) key, the second and third lines in the control panel display menu options and information about the option at the menu pointer. After you select an option, additional menus may appear.

- Press / (no (ENTER)).

    ➤ The second line on the control panel displays the menu options available to you.

Below the menu line, the submenu options or a description of the command at the menu pointer is displayed. The available command menu options are the following:

Worksheet	These commands affect the entire worksheet.
Range	These commands affect part of the worksheet.
Copy	This command lets you copy any part of a worksheet to another area.
Move	This command lets you pick up and relocate any part of the worksheet.
File	These commands let you access disk storage to save, retrieve, or combine worksheets.
Print	These commands let you print any part of your worksheet.
Graph	These commands let you create graphs from data in your worksheet.
Data	These commands let you sort or retrieve data in your worksheet.
System	This command allows you to exit temporarily to DOS.
Add-in	This command allows you to add or remove add-in utilities designed to work with Lotus 1–2–3 .
Quit	This command ends the 1–2–3 session and returns you to the Lotus Access System.

As noted earlier, you can make a selection from the command menu either by typing the first character of the command you want, or by using the ⭠ and ⭢ keys to move the menu pointer to your selection and pressing ENTER.

If you make a mistake and select an option or command that you do not want to pursue, you can exit from that command by pressing the ESC key.

The third line of the control panel displays either the submenu or a description of the command at the menu pointer.

■ PRACTICE TIME

1. Press the ⭢ key once. Notice that the menu pointer moves to the Range command and the third line displays the Range command submenu options.

2. Continue to press either the ⭢ or ⭠ key to move the menu pointer to all the menu items. Do not press ENTER, but notice the submenus for each.

/ ERASING AN ENTRY (/RE)

Let's try a menu command. You will make an incorrect entry in a cell, and then erase that entry using a Range command. First you will make an entry.

- Press the ESC key repeatedly, if needed, until the command menu disappears and the mode indicator says READY.

- Move the cell pointer to cell H1.

- Type MISTAKE and press ENTER.

Range commands are those commands that affect specific cells or a set of adjacent cells. In this case, you want to erase the entry in a specific cell.

- Press **/R** to select the Range commands option.

  ➤ The Range menu options are displayed on the second line of the control panel. The following Range options are displayed:

80 USING LOTUS 1-2-3

Format	Sets display format for a cell or a range of cells.
Label	Modifies the alignment of a label or a range of labels (Left, Right, or Center).
Erase	Erases the contents of a cell or a range of cells.
Name	Assigns a name to a cell or range of cells.
Justify	Reformats a column of label cells.
Prot	(Protect) Disallows changes to a range.
Unprot	(Unprotect) Allows changes to a range.
Input	Restricts worksheet cell-pointer movement to unprotected cells only, within a specified range.
Value	Copies formulas in the source range and converts them to values in the target range.
Trans	(Transpose) Moves the source range to the target range, transposing the rows and columns.
Search	Find or replace a specific string in a given range.

➤ Again, the third line displays either the description of, or submenu for, the highlighted command.

■ Press **E** for Erase.

➤ The message

```
Enter range to erase: H1..H1
```

appears on the control panel (H1 is the current cell in this instance).

A *range* is a group of cells that forms a rectangle. You have to specify the top left and bottom right corner cell of the range. In this case, since there is only one cell in the range, both corners are the same. You will be specifying larger ranges in later lessons.

■ Press (ENTER) to erase only the entry at the cell pointer.

➤ The cell at the cell pointer becomes blank.

To erase an entry at a cell other than the current cell, you type the cell address. (When you are responding to a menu or following

CREATING A SIMPLE SPREADSHEET **81**

through on a command by entering a range, the location of the cell pointer is not affected.)

As you become more familiar with the 1–2–3 menu commands, you will not need to pause to look at the menu options after entering each character of a command. For example, you will be able to erase an entry in the current cell by entering /RE and pressing (ENTER).

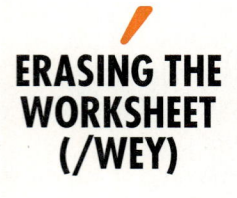

ERASING THE WORKSHEET (/WEY)

You will now clear the entire worksheet using a Worksheet command. Additional worksheet commands are discussed in the next lesson. Note that when you clear an entire worksheet, the 1–2–3 program asks you for confirmation to carry out the command. This is to make sure that you are aware of what you are doing. After all, you are wiping out the whole worksheet: If you have not saved it, it will be gone.

- Now, clear the entire screen (erase the worksheet) by typing **/WE** then **Y**.

LABELS AND VALUES

The use of a spreadsheet requires more than just entering numbers, called *values*, needed for calculations. You need to enter various headings or texts, called *labels*, in order to identify what the numbers in the cells stand for. Thus at each cell in the worksheet, you have the option of entering either a label or a value. A label is any word or words you enter in the cell, while a value is either a numeric value or an expression which, when evaluated, yields the number to be displayed at that cell.

The program distinguishes an entry as a value or a label by the first character entered.

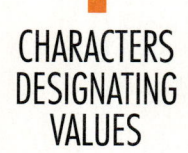

CHARACTERS DESIGNATING VALUES

A value begins with a digit or one of the following special characters: + (plus), – (minus), . (period), @, #, $, or ((left parenthesis).

CHARACTERS DESIGNATING LABELS

A label begins with a letter of the alphabet or any special character other than a / (slash) or the characters indicating values.

You will see examples of both values and labels as the lesson progresses. As soon as the first character of an entry is typed, the mode indicator displays whether a label or a value is being entered. Always check to be sure of your entry.

ENTERING LABELS

Labels are entered by positioning the cell pointer at the appropriate cell, typing the characters, and pressing either (ENTER) or a pointer movement key. If you want a label to begin with a digit or another character indicative of a value, such as + or $, the label needs to be preceded by a *label-prefix character*. The label-prefix characters are also used to position the entry within the cell. The five label-prefix characters are these:

' (apostrophe)	left-justifies the entry in the cell.
" (quotes)	right-justifies the entry in the cell.
^ (carat)	centers the entry in the cell.
\ (backslash)	indicates a repeating label, which is discussed in Lesson 5.
| (vertical bar)	indicates a format line, which is discussed in Lesson 12.

If no label-prefix character is entered, the program uses the global setting, which is left justification.

UPPERCASE

To enter uppercase characters in your label entry, hold the (SHIFT) key down while you press the character, just as you would on a typewriter. The (SHIFT) keys are the keys inscribed with wide up-arrows, located at either end of the main keyboard. If you want to type the whole entry in uppercase, press the (CAPS LOCK) key. The **CAPS** status indicator will appear on the bottom line of the screen. To get out of all uppercase, simply press the (CAPS LOCK) key again. When entering special characters (nonalphabetic shifted characters), you need to hold the (SHIFT) key down even if the (CAPS LOCK) has been pressed.

CREATING A SIMPLE SPREADSHEET

CORRECTING ERRORS

Occasionally, you make a typing error. It is important to know how to correct errors, either during typing or after you have pressed (ENTER) or a pointer movement key.

If you notice a typing error while you are inputting an entry, you can erase characters in the entry by pressing the (BACKSPACE) key. As already noted, the (BACKSPACE) key is the key inscribed with a long left arrow, located above the (ENTER) key, and is not to be confused with the (←) key.

If you notice an error after an entry has been input, you can retype the entire entry by moving the cell pointer to the cell with the error and then entering the correct data.

You can also edit the entry by moving the cell pointer to the cell with the error, then pressing the (F2) function key. You will see the cell contents on the control panel, followed by the cursor. The cursor is the underscore character that indicates where the change that you enter will be made. When you are editing an entry, there are several things you can do. You can move the cursor to the part you want to correct using the arrow keys. (The (HOME) and (END) keys move the cursor to the very beginning or end of the entry.) To delete unwanted characters, use the (BACKSPACE) or (DEL) keys. Finally, type in the corrections, then press (ENTER) to complete the editing.

ENTERING VALUES

Entering values means you want numbers (such as 150, 2, and –37) to appear in cells. You will not necessarily be entering the values that will appear at those positions, however. As you will see later, you can enter a *formula* (a mathematical expression) to calculate the value to be displayed in the corresponding cell.

To enter a numeric value, you position the cell pointer in the appropriate cell, type in the value, and then either press a pointer movement key or the (ENTER) key. If you make a typing error, you can correct it the same way as when entering labels.

PREPARING THE WORKSHEET

The various features of 1–2–3 will be illustrated through several examples. In the first you will help Susan, who started a new business and wants to keep track of her income and expense using a spreadsheet. She wants to find out what her profit is each day.

Start by setting up the worksheet for the first day. In the next several lessons, you will add more entries and expand and modify the worksheet.

Right now, Susan will use the heading "Income" for income, "Expense" for expense, and "Profit" for profit.

- Move the cell pointer to cell A1.

- Type in the word **^Income**. (Do not press (ENTER).) If you mis-type a letter, press the (BACKSPACE) key to back up and make corrections.

  ➤ The second line of the control panel displays ^Income.
  ➤ The mode indicator displays LABEL.

- Press the (↓) key.

  ➤ The word Income is centered in cell A1, and the cell pointer has moved to A2.

- Type **^Expense** and press the (↓) key.

  ➤ The word Expense is centered in A2, and the cell pointer has moved to A3.

Are you getting the hang of it yet? When you press the ^ (caret) key, you are setting the label prefix that specifies that the label is to be centered in the cell. When you press the (↓) key, it is equivalent to pressing (ENTER) followed by the (↓) key. The entry is terminated, and the cell pointer is moved in the direction of the arrow.

- Enter the label Profit in cell A3. Be sure to center it.

Susan earns $600 the first day, and she spends $400 in advertising. Enter these values in the worksheet.

- With the cell pointer on cell B1, type **600** (do not press (ENTER)).

  ➤ Notice that as you type the numbers, the mode indicator reads VALUE.

- Now, press the (↓) key.

CREATING A SIMPLE SPREADSHEET **85**

- Enter the value **400** in cell B2.

ENTERING FORMULAS (MATHEMATICAL EXPRESSIONS)

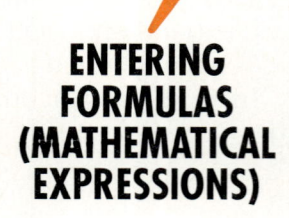

Instead of entering a value in cell B3, you will enter a formula (a mathematical expression) that will cause the computer to calculate the profit. The formula is "income minus expense." That is, the program is to determine the value in B1 minus the value in B2, or B1 minus B2. The result will be displayed as the profit.

When a formula is entered, the formula itself will appear on the first line of the control panel as the content of that cell. In the cell, however, the result of evaluating the formula will appear.

In a formula, the operator + indicates addition, − indicates subtraction, * indicates multiplication, and / indicates division. These operators are evaluated from left to right. Multiplication and division take precedence over addition and subtraction unless the latter operations are enclosed in parentheses. For example: 6+4/2 will result in 8, whereas (6+4)/2 will result in 5.

Let's go on with Susan's business:

- The formula for profit is B1−B2 (in 1−2−3, spaces are not used between values and operators). With the cell pointer in cell B3, type **B1−B2**. (Do not press (ENTER)).

Do you see a problem? Look at the mode indicator: It displays LABEL, not a value as you intended.

Because the first character of this formula is "B," a letter of the alphabet, the 1−2−3 program assumes that you are entering a label. When a formula starts with a cell address, type the special character + first. That is, instead of simply typing in B1, type **+B1**. Thus, the formula to use is +B1−B2.

You have not yet pressed (ENTER); you will now edit the entry.

- Press the (F2) function key.
  - ▶ The mode indicator displays EDIT.
  - ▶ The control panel displays B1−B2 followed by the cursor.

- Press the (HOME) key to send the cursor to the beginning of the line.

- Type **+** so that the entry reads +B1–B2, then press (ENTER).

  ➤ The top line shows the content of cell B3 as the expression +B1–B2.
  ➤ Cell B3 shows the number 200, which is the result of the formula (600 − 400).

- In cell B2, enter any number other than 400, say **250**. Did you notice what happened to the number at B3? If you missed it, type in another number.

  ➤ The number at B3 changes. The program saves the formula for the value in B3. This cell will always display the result of the expression +B1–B2. Thus, the computer value at B3 is recalculated every time you change the values in B1 or B2.

Are you beginning to see the power of an electronic spreadsheet? As you wrote the formula used above, you may have had to check to see which cell contained the number for income and which cell contained the number for expense. If this had been a large spreadsheet, you may have had trouble remembering which cell contained which value. If the cells you wanted had scrolled off the window, you would have had to move the cell pointer to find them; when you found them, you would have had to note their positions, move the cell pointer back to the cell where you wanted to make the entry, and then enter the formula. The program can make this process a little easier.

- Put the cell pointer in B3 and enter **/RE**, followed by (ENTER) to clear the entry at cell B3.

- Press the **+** key. (Do not press (ENTER).)

  ➤ The mode indicator shows that a value is being entered.
  ➤ The second line of the control panel shows + followed by the cursor.

- Use the (↑) key to move the cell pointer to the cell where the value for income appears.

  ➤ Look at the control panel. It now reads +B1.

CREATING A SIMPLE SPREADSHEET

- ➤ The mode indicator shows POINT; that is, you are in the process of entering a cell address.
- ■ Now press the – (minus) key.
  - ➤ The cell pointer jumps back to B3, the cell where you are entering the formula.
- ■ Enter the second part of the formula by pointing to it with the cell pointer. Press the ⓣ key once to place the cell pointer in the cell containing the value for the expense.
  - ➤ The control panel now reads +B1–B2.
- ■ To enter the formula as it is shown on the control panel, press the (ENTER) key.
  - ➤ The cell B3 displays the appropriate value.

You can see that the results of pointing to cells with the cell pointer, known as the POINT mode, are the same as for entering the cell addresses directly from the keyboard.

- ■ Enter the value **400** at B2.

PRACTICE TIME

1. Susan decides that 25 percent of her profit should go toward purchasing new equipment. Enter the label **Equipment** in cell A4, and the formula for evaluating the amount for equipment in cell B4. The formula is .25 multiplied by the value in cell B3.

2. Susan wants to know her net profit after purchasing equipment. Enter in row 5 the label –Net– centered and the formula used to calculate it. The formula for net is profit minus equipment, or B3–B4 (+B3–B4 in notation for 1-2-3), as shown in Screen Display 4–3.

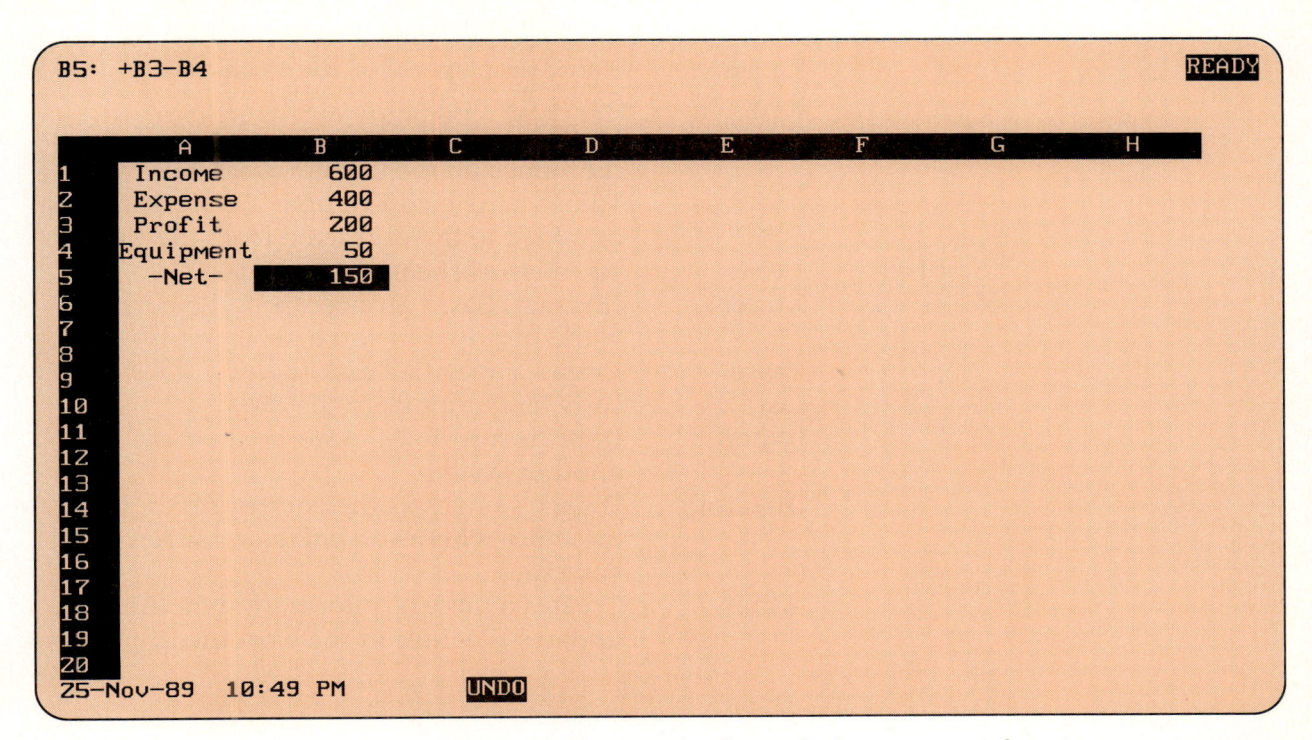

```
B5: +B3-B4                                                    READY

          A         B         C         D         E         F         G         H
 1    Income      600
 2    Expense     400
 3    Profit      200
 4  Equipment      50
 5     -Net-      150
 6
 7
 8
 9
10
11
12
13
14
15
16
17
18
19
20
25-Nov-89  10:49 PM              UNDO
```

Screen Display 4–3 The formula for net is profit minus equipment.

FILE COMMANDS (/F)

The spreadsheet you see in front of you is in the main memory of the computer; therefore, when you turn the computer off, all the information you have input in the current version will be gone. Most of the time, a worksheet is developed in one or more sessions, and then used over and over again in subsequent sessions. Thus, it is important to be able to save the worksheet by some convenient means. You will insert a formatted data disk in drive B to save the contents of the worksheet.

In this and the following lessons, the text assumes that your data disk is in drive B. Your instructor may give you alternative instructions, depending on your computer system.

- Insert the data disk into drive B.
- Press **/F** to select the File option in the Command Menu.

  ➤ The following options are available in the File menu.

CREATING A SIMPLE SPREADSHEET   **89**

Retrieve	Retrieves a specified file from disk.
Save	Saves the current worksheet to disk.
Combine	Combines values from a specified file with the values on the current worksheet. Values can be copied onto the worksheet or added to or subtracted from the values on the worksheet.
Xtract	(Extract) Saves a range from the current worksheet to a file on disk.
Erase	Erases a specified disk file.
List	Lists filenames from the disk.
Import	Imports into 1–2–3 a file created on another system.
Directory	Displays or resets the current disk directory where you will store or retrieve your files.
Admin	Creates a table of information on files, or updates file links in the worksheet.

SPECIFYING A DIRECTORY (/FD)

Next, you want to change the current disk directory, since you want to save your worksheet on the disk in drive B.

- Press **D** to select the Directory option in the menu.

  ➤ The following message appears:

  `Enter current directory: C:\123`

  You want to change this to B:.

- Type **B:** and press (ENTER).

  ➤ The worksheet returns to the READY mode.

SAVING A FILE (/FS)

Now you are ready to save the worksheet.

- Press **/FS** for File Save.

  ➤ The following message appears:

  `Enter name of file to save: B:\*.WK1`

Since you can save more than one worksheet on a disk, each worksheet on a disk must have a unique name. The saved information is called a *disk file*, and the name that identifies the file is called a *filename*.

A valid filename can be from one to eight characters in length and must be letters, numbers, or the underscore character (_). When you enter the filename, the extension .WK1 is added by the 1–2–3 program. For example, if you were to call the file MYFILE, it is stored as MYFILE.WK1. Letters may be entered in upper- or lowercase but are converted to uppercase.

To continue, use the filename LOTUS1.

- Type **LOTUS1** and press (ENTER).

   ➤ The light on the disk drive goes on, and the worksheet is stored on disk.

PRINTING FILES (/PP)

Now let's print the worksheet.

- Make sure you are working with a personal computer that is connected to a printer. Also, make sure that the printer is turned on and ready for use. If you are using continuous fanfold paper, make sure that the perforation is at the print head.

- Send the cell pointer to A1.

- Type **/P** for Print.

   ➤ There are two options in the second-level menu:

   Printer   Prints using the printer.
   File   Stores the print image as a file on disk.

You want to send the worksheet to the printer to be printed.

- Type **P** to select Printer.

   ➤ The print settings are displayed in a box, as shown in Screen Display 4–4.

You can remove the print settings box to view the worksheet by pressing (F6). (F6) is a toggle that allows you to turn setting boxes off and on. The box displays the print settings and their current values.

```
A1: ^Income                                                    MENU
Range Line  Page  Options  Clear  Align  Go  Quit
Specify a range to print
                          ─ Print Settings ─
   Destination:   Printer

   Range:

   Header:
   Footer:

   Margins:
     Left 4       Right 76     Top 2    Bottom 2

   Borders:
     Columns
     Rows

   Setup string:

   Page length:   66

   Output:        As-Displayed (Formatted)

25-Nov-89  10:53 PM
```

Screen Display 4–4   The print menu and print settings box.

For example, the destination has been set to printer, but the range, header, footer, setup string, and borders have not been specified. The margins and page length are already set for your printer.

At the top of the screen, the following menu options let you modify any of the settings:

Range	Specifies a range to print.
Line	Advances paper one line.
Page	Advances paper to top of page.
Options	Sets header, footer, margins, borders, setup, page-length, and others (explained in Lesson 11).
Clear	Resets some or all print settings.
Align	Resets to top of page (after adjusting paper).
Go	Prints the specified range.
Quit	Exits the Print mode.

Before you can print the worksheet, you must specify which rectangular portion, or range, of the worksheet you want printed. You cannot always print the whole worksheet on a single sheet of paper. On 8 1/2 by 11-inch paper, 8 columns of 9 characters width can be printed at 10 characters per inch.

- Select Range.

    ➤ The control panel shows the following message:

    `Enter print range: A1`

The cell initially specified is the cell pointer's position. You want to specify the top left and bottom right corner cells of the rectangle to be printed. In the present example, which is a very small spreadsheet, you can print the whole thing. The range is A1 for the top left corner cell and B5 for the cell in the bottom right corner. You type a . (period) between these addresses to indicate a range.

- Type **A1.B5** and press (ENTER).

    ➤ The menu and print settings are displayed again.
    The range shows A1..B5, indicating you set it.

You are now ready to print the worksheet. First, however, you must align the paper. 1–2–3 keeps track of the number of lines printed, and after the appropriate number are printed (taking top and bottom spacing into account), it leaves several blank lines at the bottom and top margins. Hence you need to tell 1–2–3 that the printer is, indeed, at the top of the paper.

- Select Align.
- Select Go.

    ➤ The worksheet is printed.

- Select Page to advance the paper to the top of next page.
- Select Quit to exit the print mode.

END OF LESSON 4

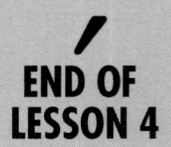

This is the end of the fourth Lotus 1–2–3 lesson.

- Type **/Q** then **Y** to exit 1–2–3 and return to the Lotus Access System.
- Type **E** to exit to DOS.
- Remove your data disk from the drive and carefully store it.
- Turn off the monitor, computer, and printer.

SUMMARY

In this lesson, many of the terms and concepts that are necessary to use spreadsheets effectively are introduced.

- The control panel consists of three lines. The first line displays the cell-pointer location, cell content, and mode indicator. The second line displays input/edit contents or the command menu being accessed. The third line gives the next level of commands for, or explanation of, the highlighted menu option on the second line.
- The mode indicator tells you what the program is doing.
- Status indicators tell you which keys have been pushed.
- The cell pointer highlights the cell where the entry is being made. You can move it around the spreadsheet using the following keys:

Key	Action
→, ←, ↑, ↓	Move cell pointer in the direction of the arrow.
TAB	Moves cell pointer to the next screen of columns to the right,
SHIFT-TAB	Moves the cell pointer one screen to the left.
HOME	Moves the cell pointer to cell A1.
PGUP or PGDN	Moves the cell pointer up or down one screen.

(END)(↓)	Moves the cell pointer to the last row or column in the direction of the arrow.
(F5)	Moves the cell pointer to the location specified.

- Uppercase letters are entered using either the (SHIFT) key or the (CAPS LOCK) key. To enter special characters that appear on the upper half of a key, the (SHIFT) key must be held down even if the (CAPS LOCK) key has been pressed.

- Errors can be corrected by using the (BACKSPACE) key, by re-entering the information for a cell, or by editing the cell content using the (F2) function key. You can also cancel a command by pressing the (ESC) key.

- A cell may contain either a label or a value. A label is used to identify the information; a value is numerical information.

- Values can be arithmetic expressions, such as formulas. A cell address can be entered in a formula by pointing to the cell with the cell pointer.

- A label-prefix character is used to position a label entry in a cell.

- A range is rectangular. It is referred to by specifying the addresses of top left and bottom right corner cells, separated by a period.

- Commands in 1-2-3 are invoked with the / (slash) key.

- The following commands are discussed:

(F2)	Edit—edits the content of the current cell.
(F6)	Window—turns setting boxes off in order to view worksheet.
(F5)	Goto—moves cell pointer to a specified address.
/FD	File Directory—specifies the directory (disk drive) to use.
/FS	File Save—saves the spreadsheet file to disk.
/RE	Range Erase—erases contents of a range of cells.

/WEY	Worksheet Erase Yes—erases the entire worksheet.
/PP	Prints spreadsheet using printer.
A, for Align	Aligns line counter in program.
G, for Go	Prints range.
P, for Page	Advances paper to the beginning of the next page.
Q, for Quit	Exits the print menu.
R, for Range	Selects a range to print.
/QY	Quit Yes—Quits 1–2–3.

REVIEW QUESTIONS

1. How do you send the cell pointer to a particular cell without using the pointer movement, or arrow, keys?
   Go To (F5)

2. What information do you see on the top line of the control panel? *Displays cursor position – where you are*

3. How do you invoke commands in 1–2–3?

4. How does 1–2–3 distinguish a label entry from a value entry? *(information) numerical info.*

5. What are the label-prefix characters and when do you use them? *' left just   " right just. | format line   ^ centers   \ repeating label*

6. How do you enter a value that starts with a cell address?
   +

7. How do you move the cell pointer one screen down at a time? *PGDN*

8. How do you correct a data entry error in a cell?
   F2

9. How do you blank (erase) an entry in a cell?
   /RE

10. Give the commands needed to print a worksheet.
    /PP

EXERCISES

1. a) Design and create a telephone directory, that is, a spreadsheet that holds names and phone numbers. Phone numbers are entered without area codes. Think very carefully whether a phone number is a value or label.

   b) Enter first names and phone numbers of ten friends.

   c) Save the file as EX4_1 (it will be needed in a later exercise).

   d) Print the entire spreadsheet.

2. a) Design and create a spreadsheet that holds the scores of ten students from three exams.

   b) Enter first names of 10 students and scores (1 to 100).

   c) Save the file on disk as EX4_2 (it will be needed in a later lesson).

   d) Print the entire spreadsheet.

LESSON 5
ENHANCING THE SIMPLE SPREADSHEET

OBJECTIVES

Upon completion of the material presented in this lesson, you should be able to perform the following features and processes:

- Use the 1–2–3 Help system
- Retrieve a spreadsheet file from a disk
- Insert a row in a worksheet
- Copy cell contents to other locations
- Enter repeated labels
- Change the width of a column
- Use a simple function
- Use the Undo feature
- Change the display format of the numeric entries
- Save a file using a different filename
- Assign range names
- Print a spreadsheet by sections

STARTING OFF

Start 1–2–3 so that a blank spreadsheet is displayed; also, insert your data disk in drive B. In this lesson, you will retrieve the spreadsheet file you prepared in Lesson 4. You will also learn new commands to extend the basic principles of using electronic spreadsheets that you have already learned.

THE HELP SYSTEM (F1)

If you have difficulty understanding something on the screen, you can use the extensive Help system included in 1–2–3. The Help system is accessed using the F1 function key. Lotus 1–2–3 offers *context-sensitive* help, which means that if you seek help when you are in the Ready mode, you will get the main help index; if you are in the midst of a keystroke sequence when you seek help, you will get help about the particular command, and so forth.

- With 1–2–3 in the Ready mode, press the (F1) function key.

  ▶ The 1–2–3 Help Index is displayed.

To select a topic, use the pointer-movement keys to move the menu pointer and press (ENTER). To quit the Help facility and return to the worksheet, press (ESC).

If you need help on a specific command, move the menu pointer to the command in the index and press (ENTER). The instructions at the bottom of the screen indicate how to navigate the Help facility to find information on the topic you seek.

If you press the (F1) function key when you are in a menu or in the middle of making an entry into a cell, the initial Help screen will relate to what you are doing. An example is given in the section on Retrieving a File.

- Press the (ESC) key.

THE UNDO COMMAND ((ALT)-(F4))

Sometimes you might make a mistake and enter information in the wrong cell of a worksheet: If the cell contained information, that information will have been overwritten. Lotus 1–2–3 has an Undo feature that allows you to undo your last entry. To demonstrate this feature, you will make an entry that overwrites some information and then use the Undo feature to retrieve the overwritten information.

- Move the cell pointer to cell E5, type the value 2.7853 and press (ENTER).

- Now, enter the label **OOPS** at E5 (press (ENTER) to complete the entry).

  ▶ The content of cell E5 has been overwritten. You need to correct the error, but suppose you had forgotten the value that should be in this cell.

- Press ALT-F4, the Undo key.

    ➤ The previous content of cell E5, the value 2.7853, replaces OOPS as the cell contents.

The Undo feature in 1–2–3 is limited to the last entry you have made. If you had made another entry after entering **OOPS**, then ALT-F4 would replace the later entry and you would have no way of undoing the mistake at E5.

The Undo feature is used to recover data overwritten by changes to the worksheet. If you are in a menu and make a wrong entry, you can usually back out to the previous menu by pressing ESC.

RETRIEVING A FILE (/FR)

You will retrieve the file from the disk, but before you can do this, you have to tell the computer where your data disk is.

- Type **/F** for File.

If you need to find out what each menu option does, beyond what is displayed on the third line of the control panel, you can access Help from the menu.

- Press the F1 function key.

    ➤ The Help screen shows a more extensive definition of the menu options displayed.

- Within the Help screen select Directory.

    ➤ Another screen appears, giving a more detailed explanation of the command and an example of its use.

- Press the ESC key to exit Help.

- Type **D** for Directory.

- Type **B:** and press ENTER to indicate that your data disk is in drive B.

Now you are ready to retrieve the file.

- Type **/FR** for File Retrieve.

ENHANCING THE SIMPLE SPREADSHEET **101**

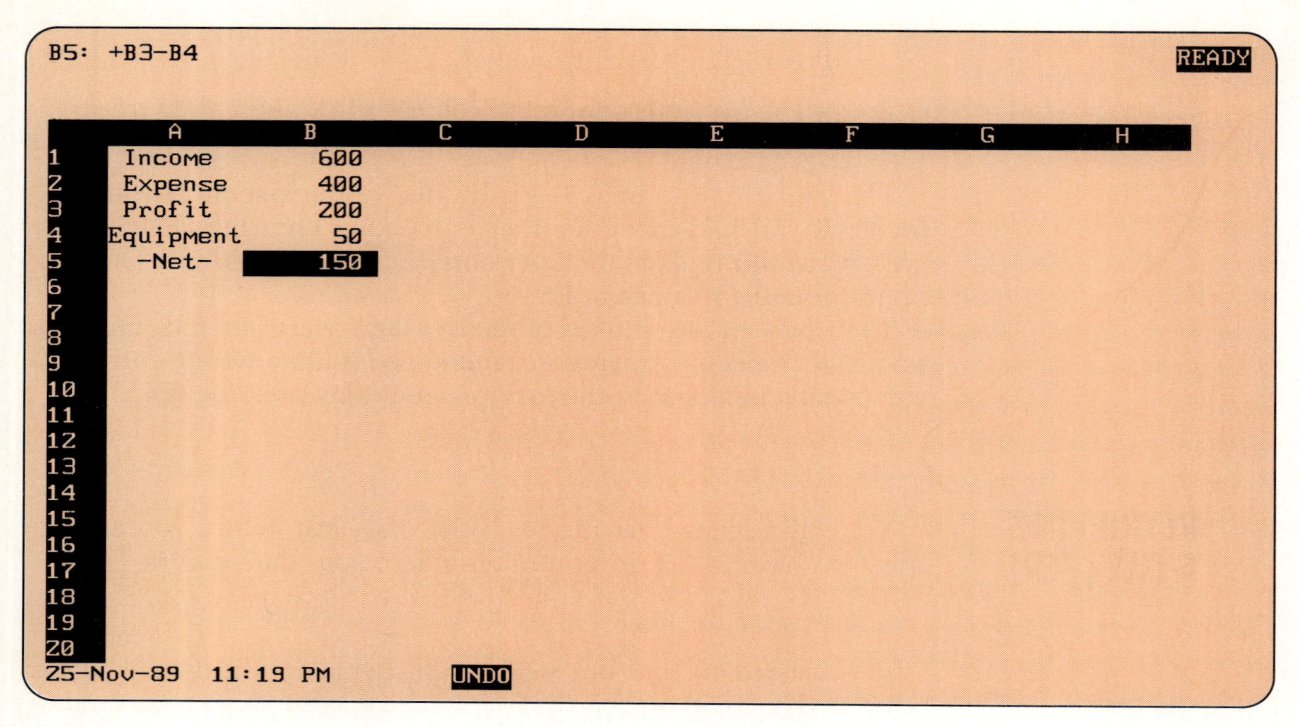

```
B5:  +B3-B4                                                    READY

        A          B        C       D       E       F       G       H
   1   Income      600
   2   Expense     400
   3   Profit      200
   4   Equipment    50
   5    -Net-      150
   6
   7
   8
   9
  10
  11
  12
  13
  14
  15
  16
  17
  18
  19
  20
  25-Nov-89  11:19 PM            UNDO
```

Screen Display 5–1   LOTUS1.WK1 has been retrieved from disk.

➤ The message appears:

   `Name of file to retrieve: B:\*.WK?`

➤ The third line of the control panel displays the names of worksheet files on the disk in drive B. LOTUS1.WK1 should be one of the files displayed.

To specify the file you want retrieved, you can simply type whatever filename you gave at the end of the previous lesson and press the (ENTER) key or move the menu pointer in the usual manner and press (ENTER) when the filename you want is selected.

■ With LOTUS1 selected, press (ENTER).

➤ The selected file is loaded into the worksheet, as shown in Screen Display 5–1.

INSERTING ROWS (/WIR)

Right now your worksheet shows values for one day. You will now extend these entries to show ten days of business activity. You will enter the figures for the second day in column C, for the third day in column D, and so on. To identify the values easily, you give these columns headings.

Column headings should be placed on row 1. Do you see a problem? Row 1 already has some entries. You could erase the whole spreadsheet and start over again, putting Income in row 2, Expense in row 3, and Profit in row 4, and so on. However, there is an easier way: You can insert a row.

- Place the cell pointer on row 1, for example, in cell A1.

- Type **/W** for Worksheet.

  ➤ The following Worksheet submenu options are displayed:

Global	Gives commands that affect the entire worksheet.
Insert	Inserts blank column(s) or row(s).
Delete	Deletes entire column(s) or row(s).
Column	Sets display width of one or more columns.
Erase	Erases entire worksheet in memory.
Titles	Sets horizontal or vertical titles.
Window	Lets you select how the screen is split and whether scrolling is synchronized.
Status	Displays the global format, column-width, and recalculation settings, and memory available.
Page	Inserts a page-break symbol above the current cell in the worksheet.
Learn	Records keystrokes in the worksheet for making macros.

- Select Insert.

ENHANCING THE SIMPLE SPREADSHEET

➤ The Worksheet Insert submenu displays the following:

    Column   Inserts one or more blank columns to left of cell pointer.
    Row   Inserts one or more blank rows above the cell pointer.

■ Select Row since you want to insert a row.

➤ The following message appears:

`Enter row insert range: A1..A1`

Since you want to insert a row only at row 1, you need only press (ENTER).

■ Press (ENTER).

➤ All the information on the spreadsheet moves down one row, and row 1 is now blank.

Now proceed with putting headings on the columns. First you will label row 1.

■ Enter **^Day** at cell A1.

■ Enter **1** (numeric) in cell B1 as a column heading.

Now you will enter 2 in C1, 3 in D1, up to 10 in K1. To do this, you could press the (→) key, make an entry, press the (→) key, make an entry, and so on. But try another way. Each entry is one greater than the previous entry: The entry in C1 is the entry in B1 plus 1; the entry in D1 is the entry in C1 plus 1; and so on. Therefore, you could enter the formula +B1+1 in C1, +C1+1 in D1, and so on.

■ With cell pointer on cell C1, type **+B1+1** and press (ENTER).

➤ The cell C1 shows the value 2.

Consider for a moment. You will have to enter the formula +C1+1 at cell D1, +D1+1 at cell E1, and so on up to +J1+1 at K1. How tedious to enter a similar formula over and over. Yet, in this example, you need to do this only nine times. What if you were setting up the worksheet for a month or a year?

THE COPY COMMAND (/C)

There is an easier way: Use the Copy command. This command can be used to make copies of formulas, labels, numbers, blank entries, and so on, across columns, down rows, and wherever you want.

- With the cell pointer at C1, type **/C** for copy.
  ➤ The following message appears:

```
Enter range to copy FROM: C1..C1
```

The 1–2–3 program wants to know what to copy. You want to copy the formula at C1, that is, the range is one cell: C1. All you have to do is press (ENTER).

- Press (ENTER).
  ➤ Another message appears:

```
Enter range to copy TO: C1
```

You have told the 1–2–3 program to copy the formula in C1; now the program needs to know where to copy to. You are entering headings for 10 days (columns B to K). Since you have already inserted headings for columns B and C, the target range is D1 to K1. You could type in the range D1.K1 (using the period as the delimiter of the range), but this time you will point to the cell with the cell pointer. (This method was discussed in Lesson 4.)

- Move the cell pointer to cell D1, the first cell in which you want to copy the information.
  ➤ The destination range now reads D1.

If you were copying the formula to just one cell, you would press (ENTER) at this point. However, you want to copy the formula to more than one cell: to the range of cells whose upper left-corner cell is D1 and bottom right-corner cell is K1; therefore, you press the period (.) key.

- Type a period (.).
  ➤ The destination range now reads D1..D1.
- Use the arrow keys to highlight cells D1 through K1. As you do this, the screen will scroll to the side. If you

ENHANCING THE SIMPLE SPREADSHEET **105**

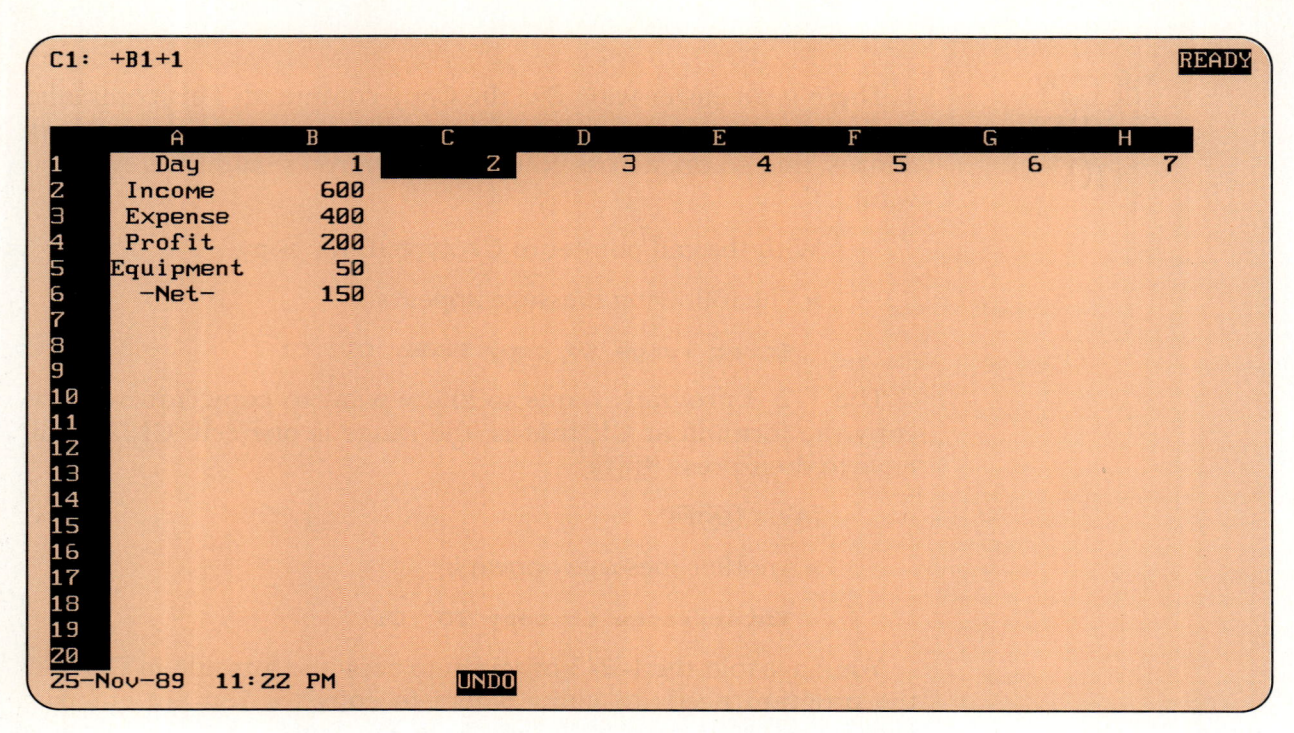

```
C1:  +B1+1                                                           READY

              A         B         C         D         E         F         G         H
     1      Day         1         2         3         4         5         6         7
     2   Income       600
     3   Expense      400
     4    Profit      200
     5  Equipment      50
     6    -Net-       150
     7
     8
     9
    10
    11
    12
    13
    14
    15
    16
    17
    18
    19
    20
    25-Nov-89   11:22 PM            UNDO
```

Screen Display 5–2   The formula at C1 has been copied to D1..K1

move too far to the right with the → key, you can move back with the ← key.

- Press ENTER.

    ► The cell pointer appears at C1 and numbers appear in columns D through K, as shown in Screen Display 5–2.

- Move the cell pointer along row 1, and notice the content of each cell as displayed on the top line of the control panel.

You will notice that 1–2–3 inserted the *relative formula* in each cell; that is, rather than copying the formula +B1+1 in each cell, it copied a formula that specifies "content in the cell to the left plus one." So, at cell F1, it wrote +E1+1. If you really want the *absolute formula* +B1+1 copied into all the cells in the target range, you would have to enter the original formula in C1 with $ (dollar) signs preceding the cell's column label and row number; that is, the formula would be +$B$1+1. This will be discussed in more detail later.

■ **PRACTICE TIME**

Insert a blank line at row 2, as shown in Screen Display 5–3.

REPEATING LABELS (\)

You want the spreadsheet to read attractively, so you will put hyphens across the spreadsheet at row 2, columns A through K, to separate the headings from the values.

- With the cell pointer at A2, type \ (backslash).
  - ➤ The mode indicator shows that you are entering a LABEL.

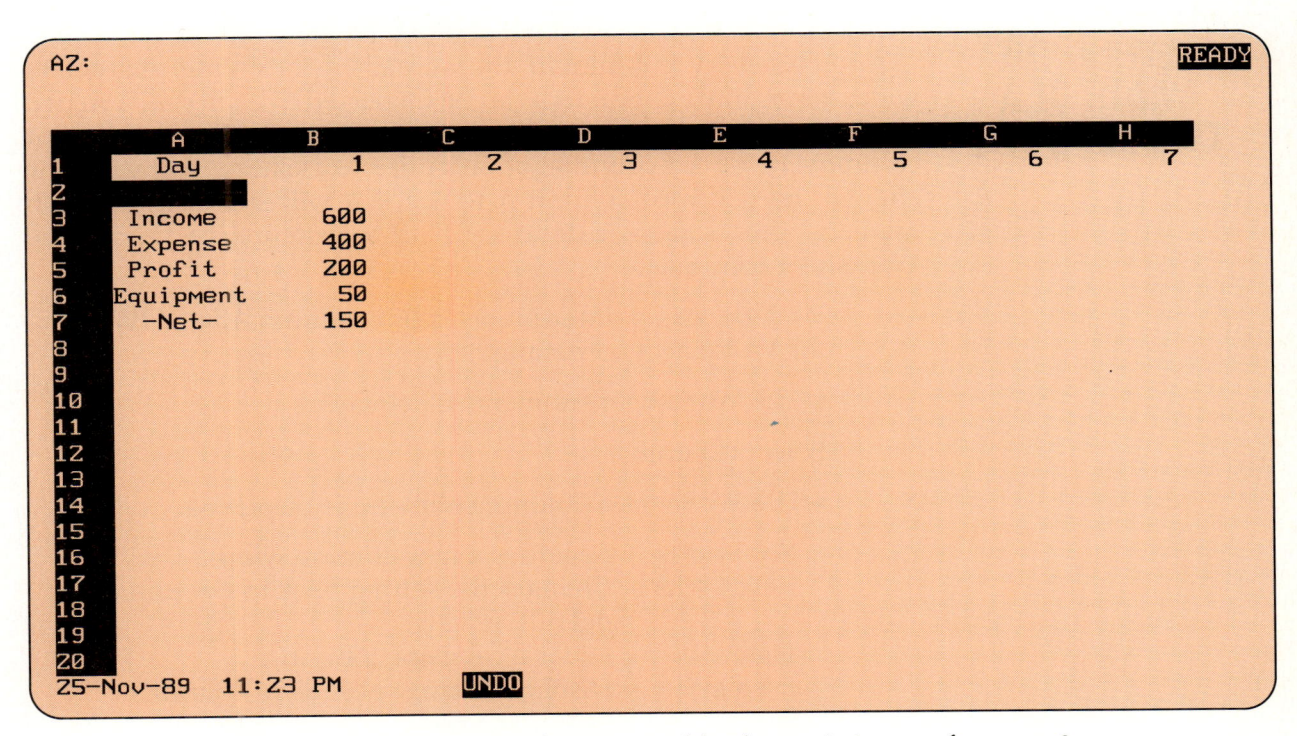

```
A2:                                                              READY
      A        B        C        D        E        F        G        H
 1   Day       1        2        3        4        5        6        7
 2
 3  Income   600
 4  Expense  400
 5  Profit   200
 6 Equipment  50
 7   -Net-   150
 8
 9
10
11
12
13
14
15
16
17
18
19
20
25-Nov-89  11:23 PM          UNDO
```

Screen Display 5–3   A blank row is inserted at row 2.

ENHANCING THE SIMPLE SPREADSHEET   **107**

You are to enter the character you want repeated across the width of the cell.

- Type **-** and press (ENTER).

    ➤ Cell A2 is filled with hyphens. In fact, cell A2 is filled with hyphens regardless of its column width, as you will see in the next section.

You will now copy this entry to the range B2 through K2.

- With cell pointer in cell A2, type **/C** for copy.
- The source range is just A2, so press (ENTER).
- The destination range is cell B2 at the top-left corner and cell K2 at the bottom-right of the range rectangle; therefore, type **B2.K2** and press (ENTER).

    ➤ Row 2 has hyphens from A2 through K2.

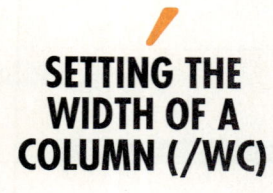

SETTING THE WIDTH OF A COLUMN (/WC)

Initially, every column in the spreadsheet is nine characters wide; that is, nine characters can be displayed in each cell. You can change the width of a particular column, of several adjacent columns, or of the columns of an entire worksheet. You will now change the width of column A to see if it will still be filled with hyphens after you have done so. This is accomplished using the Worksheet command.

- With the cell pointer in any cell in column A, type **/W** for Worksheet command.

    ➤ The Worksheet submenu is displayed.

- Select Column.

    ➤ The Worksheet Column submenu is displayed.

Set-Width	Specifies a new column width.
Reset-Width	Changes the setting back to the initial, or default, setting.
Hide	Hides a range of columns.
Display	Displays a range of hidden columns.

Column-Range	Changes the width of columns across a specified range.

- Select Set-Width.

    ➤ The control panel displays the following message:

    `Enter column width (1..240): 9`

The default, or preset, value is 9. Suppose you want to change the default to 12. You can either press the → key until the column width is increased to 12, or type 12, then press ENTER.

- Type **12** and press ENTER.

    ➤ The width of column A changed to 12. Notice that even though the column width changed from 9 to 12, cell A2 is still filled with hyphens.

Note: If a label is too long to be displayed, the excess characters will be displayed in the consecutive cell(s) to the right, provided that these cells do not contain data; if a value is too large to be displayed in a cell, the cell will fill with asterisks (*). In either case, it is only the display that is affected; the correct data remains in the cell.

PRACTICE TIME

1. Change the width of column A back to 9. This time, use the ← key to decrease the column width, then press ENTER.

2. Enter the following values for days 2 through 5. As you enter these values, note that decimal points are not aligned.

DAY	2	3	4	5
INCOME	300	950	1000	692.5
EXPENSES	275	500	500	600.34

3. Copy the formulas for profit, equipment, and net, as entered in cells B5, B6, and B7, into the range C5 through K5, C6 through K6, and C7 through K7, respectively, as shown in Screen Display 5–4.

ENHANCING THE SIMPLE SPREADSHEET

```
B7:  +B5-B6                                                          READY

         A          B          C          D          E          F          G          H
  1     Day         1          2          3          4          5          6          7
  2    ------------------------------------------------------------------------------
  3    Income      600        300        950       1000        692.5
  4    Expense     400        275        500        500        600.34
  5    Profit      200         25        450        500         92.16      0          0
  6    Equipment    50          6.25     112.5      125         23.04      0          0
  7    -Net-       150         18.75     337.5      375         69.12      0          0
  8
  9
 10
 11
 12
 13
 14
 15
 16
 17
 18
 19
 20
25-Nov-89   11:28 PM            UNDO
```

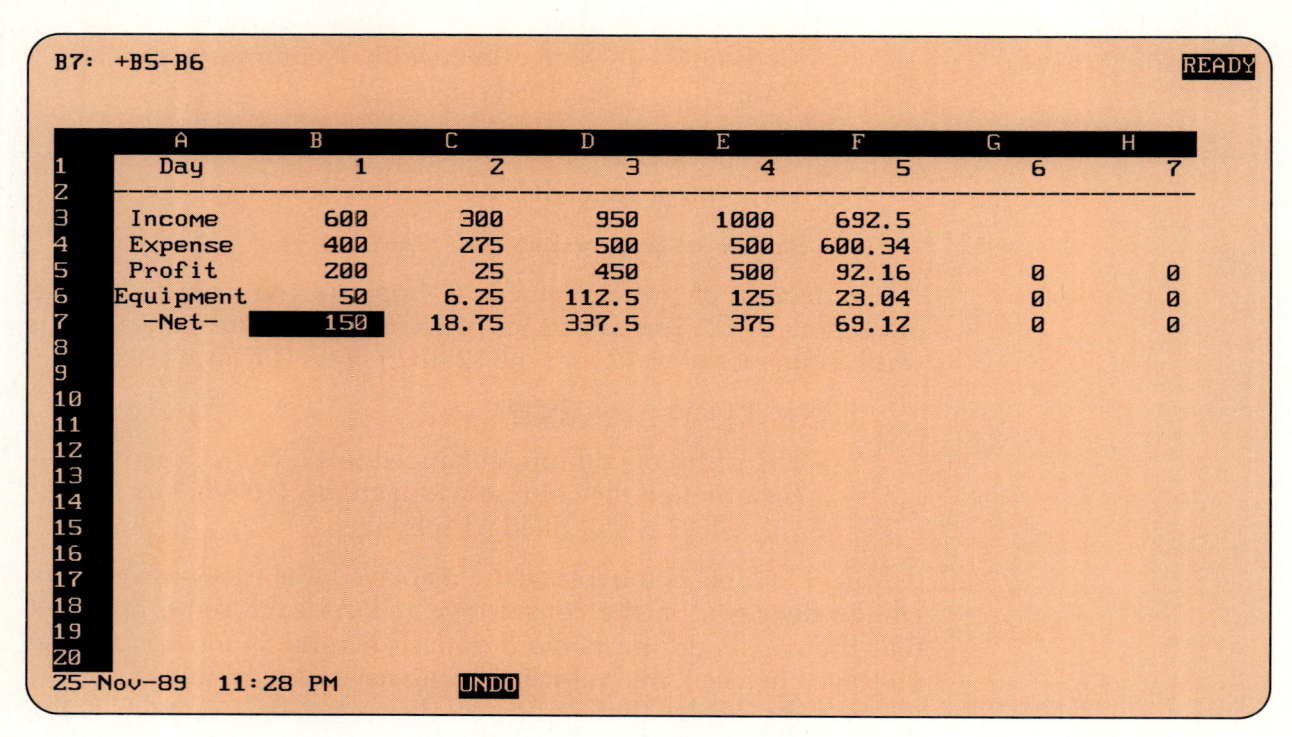

Screen Display 5–4 The worksheet with five days of data.

Susan can now see the profitability of her business at a glance. Columns G through K are blank for the "income" and "expense" rows and show 0 (zero) for the rest. These columns are set up so that as Susan enters values for income and expense on days 6 through 10, profit, equipment, and net will be calculated and displayed automatically.

Note: It is possible to set up an entire spreadsheet without any data in it; it can, nevertheless, contain all the headings and formulas needed, have all columns set to proper width, and have the display format specified. Such a spreadsheet is called a *template*. A template is a prewritten spreadsheet that is ready to accept data: All one has to do to utilize it is retrieve it and enter data into the appropriate cells.

It occurs to Susan at this point that she has a certain amount of cash with which she started the business; call it Cash-on-Hand. She would like to see the change in that value from day to day. She decides that she would like to see this figure on row 3.

PRACTICE TIME

1. Insert a blank row at row 3.

2. Place the row heading "Cash-on-Hand" in cell A3. You will notice that the characters that did not fit in cell A3 appear in cell B3.

3. Adjust the width of column A so that the heading fits.

4. Insert the value 750 in cell B3 as the starting figure, as shown in Screen Display 5–5.

Consider this for a minute. The value for cash-on-hand changes daily depending on the net profit. On the second day the cash-on-hand is cash-on-hand for the first day plus the net profit for the

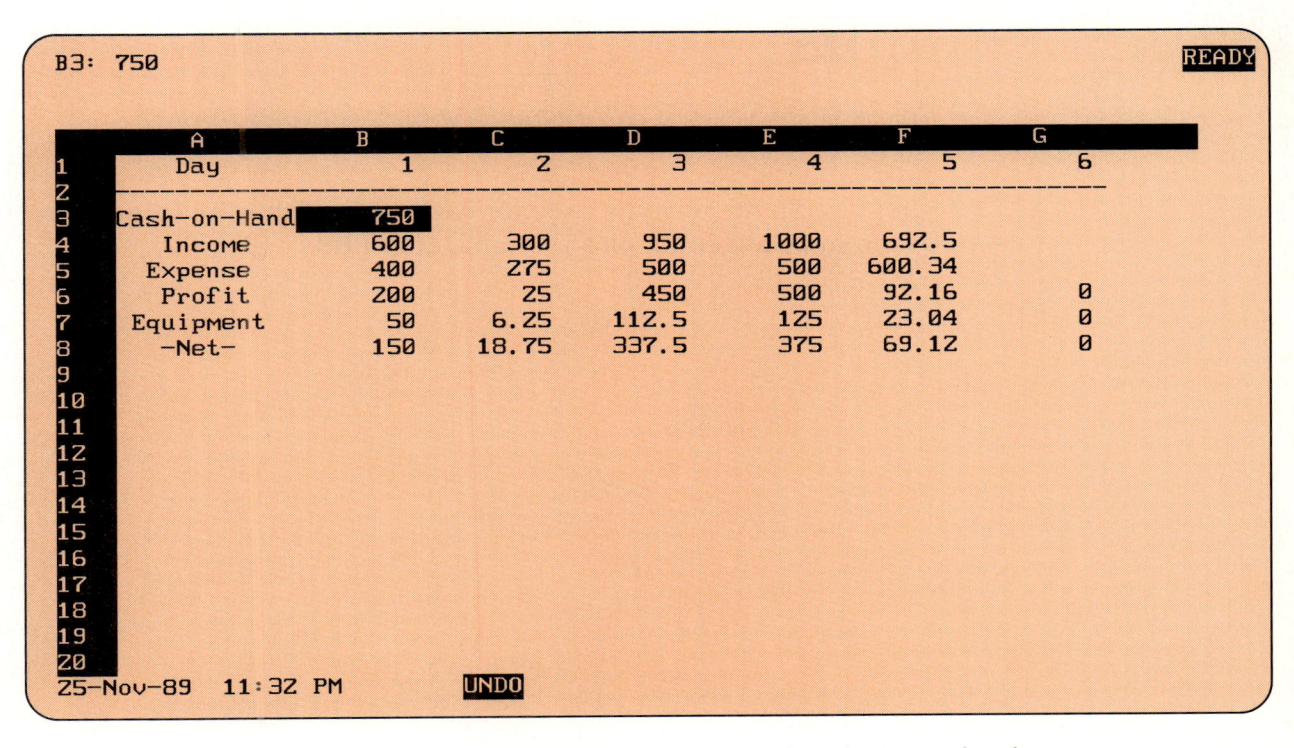

```
B3: 750                                                                  READY

             A           B         C         D         E         F         G
     1      Day          1         2         3         4         5         6
     2     ─────────────────────────────────────────────────────────────────
     3   Cash-on-Hand   750
     4      Income      600       300       950      1000      692.5
     5      Expense     400       275       500       500      600.34
     6      Profit      200        25       450       500       92.16       0
     7    Equipment      50       6.25    112.5       125       23.04       0
     8      -Net-       150      18.75    337.5       375       69.12       0
     9
    10
    11
    12
    13
    14
    15
    16
    17
    18
    19
    20
    25-Nov-89  11:32 PM           UNDO
```

Screen Display 5–5   Cash on hand is initialized.

ENHANCING THE SIMPLE SPREADSHEET

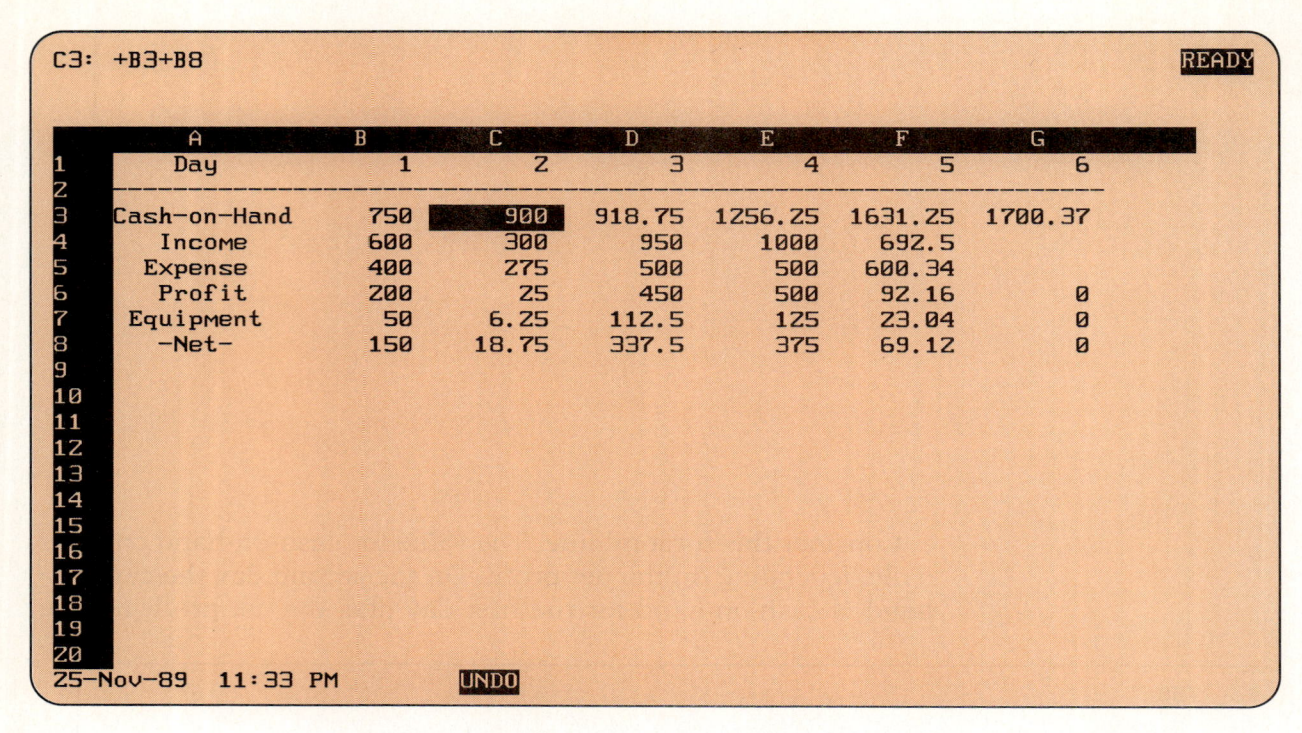

```
C3: +B3+B8                                                              READY

              A           B         C         D         E         F         G
    1        Day          1         2         3         4         5         6
    2       ─────────────────────────────────────────────────────────────────
    3    Cash-on-Hand    750       900      918.75   1256.25   1631.25   1700.37
    4       Income       600       300       950      1000      692.5
    5       Expense      400       275       500       500      600.34
    6       Profit       200        25       450       500       92.16      0
    7      Equipment      50        6.25    112.5      125       23.04      0
    8        -Net-       150       18.75    337.5      375       69.12      0
    9
   10
   ...
   20
   25-Nov-89   11:33 PM              UNDO
```

Screen Display 5–6   Cash on hand formula is copied through worksheet.

first day. So the formula used for cash-on-hand for the second day is the value at cell B3 plus the value at cell B8.

PRACTICE TIME

1. In cell C3, enter the formula for cash-on-hand for the second day.

2. Copy this formula to the range D3 through K3, as shown in Screen Display 5–6.

Cash-on-hand values for days 6 through 10 remain constant since net values are zeros for those days.

THE SUM FUNCTION (@SUM)

For column L, Susan decides that she would like to see totals for income, expense, profit, equipment, and net for the ten-day period. To enter the total income at L4, for instance, you can enter the formula +B4+C4+D4+E4+F4+G4+H4+I4+J4+K4. Suppose you had to find the total income for 60 days? As you might have guessed, there is an easier way to total numbers. You can use the @SUM function.

- With the cell pointer at L4, type **@SUM**, but do not press (ENTER) yet.

You are to indicate what values you want totaled. These values are known as the *arguments* and are entered within parentheses. The arguments you enter can be any of the following:

- A range of cells, such as row 3, column B to E. This is entered as (B3.E3). A period serves as a *delimiter*, or separator, that separates the beginning of the range from the end.
- A list of specific cells separated by commas, such as (B3, C3, D3).
- A combination of range of cells, list of cells, numbers, and formulas, such as (B3.B7,B9,4,7*C9).

In your case, you want to enter a range of cells and you want to total the values in row 4, columns B through K.

- Type **(B4.K4)** and press (ENTER).
  - ➤ The top line on the control panel shows @SUM(B4..K4).
  - ➤ In cell L4, the value 3542.5 appears.

The range could have been specified using the POINT mode. To enter in POINT mode, you type @SUM(then use the pointer movement keys to point to the first cell of the range, type . (period), point to the last cell of the range, type), and press (ENTER). Try this on your own.

All functions start with the @ character. When you enter @, the 1–2–3 program recognizes the entry as a function and knows that the characters between @ and ((left parenthesis) are the name of

ENHANCING THE SIMPLE SPREADSHEET 113

the function. Each function performs a calculation using the value or list of values (its arguments) specified with it, and produces a result. A function can be used as a value entry by itself or as part of a formula, such as .25*@SUM(A1.A6).

There are many functions available in 1–2–3. Some of these are discussed in Lesson 10.

■ PRACTICE TIME

1. Copy the formula at L4 into cells L5 through L8.

    Hint: Copying a formula down a column is done the same way as copying it across a row. The destination range in this case is L5.L8.

2. Insert the column heading Total centered in cell L1.

3. Insert hyphens in cell L2, as shown in Screen Display 5–7.

/ THE GLOBAL DISPLAY FORMAT (/WGF)

At this point, consider the ways by which you can change the display format. The methods for changing the column width have been covered. Now you will learn how to change the way the cell content is displayed, without changing the value in the cell. You can use a Worksheet command to change the entire worksheet (a global change) to, for example, an integer format (whole numbers only). Note that some values in the worksheet have decimals.

- Enter **/W** for Worksheet.

    ➤ The Worksheet menu options are displayed.

- Select Global, meaning that you want the command to affect the entire worksheet.

    ➤ The Worksheet Global submenu is displayed at the top:

Format	Sets format globally.
Label-prefix	Sets label alignment globally.

```
L2:  \-                                                           READY

         E         F         G         H         I         J         K         L
   1     4         5         6         7         8         9         10       Total
   2    ─────────────────────────────────────────────────────────────────────────────
   3  1256.25   1631.25   1700.37   1700.37   1700.37   1700.37   1700.37
   4  1000       692.5                                                        3542.5
   5   500       600.34                                                       2275.34
   6   500        92.16      0         0         0         0         0       1267.16
   7   125        23.04      0         0         0         0         0        316.79
   8   375        69.12      0         0         0         0         0        950.37
   9
  10
  11
  12
  13
  14
  15
  16
  17
  18
  19
  20
25-Nov-89   11:36 PM           UNDO
```

Screen Display 5–7   Column for totals has been created.

Column-width	Sets column width globally.
Recalculation	Sets conditions of recalculation in the worksheet.
Protection	Turns protection on or off.
Default	Defines default disk and printer settings.
Zero	Sets display for cells with value of zero.

The global settings box is displayed in the middle of the screen. These settings are the global default values, which are used unless overridden within a specific cell or range. The menu options can be used to change the settings.

The Format option allows you to specify how values or labels should appear within their cells.

■ Select Format.

➤ The Worksheet Global Format submenu is now displayed.

ENHANCING THE SIMPLE SPREADSHEET   **115**

Fixed	Sets the number of decimal places (0–15).
Sci	(Scientific) Gives exponential notation (x.xxE+xx).
Currency	Shows dollar sign, commas, and decimal point (with specified number of decimal places, 0–15). Negative values are set in parentheses.
,	(Comma) Shows the same as currency, but without dollar sign.
General	Shows no non-significant zeros after the decimal point
+/–	For horizontal bar graph: Shows +'s for positive values, –'s for negative values.
Percent	Shows percent value (value x 100) with percent sign (%).
Date	Formats for displaying date and time.
Text	Displays formula instead of cell contents.
Hidden	Does not display cell contents.

You want to change the entire spreadsheet to integer format (whole numbers only—no decimals).

- Select Fixed.

    ➤ The following message appears:

    `Enter number of decimal places: 2`

The computer prompts you to enter the number of decimal places. If you press (ENTER) without typing any number, it will be set to 2.

- Type **0** (zero) and press (ENTER).

    ➤ Notice that in column F, the decimal portions of the values are not displayed.

Note: The display format affects only the way numbers are displayed on the screen; it does not change the way numbers are stored in the computer's memory.

Since you are dealing with money in this spreadsheet, you probably want your values to show two places to the right of the decimal point (for cents). You can use the Currency format; if you

116 USING LOTUS 1-2-3

do not want to see the dollar signs, you can use the , (comma) format.

PRACTICE TIME

Make a global change to set the format to , (comma) (no dollar sign) with two decimal positions.

THE RANGE FORMAT COMMAND (/RF)

All values on the screen are now displayed with two places to the right of the decimal. Do you see a problem? Even the column headings, showing day numbers, display two places to the right of the decimal, and they are supposed to be integers.

You can change the format of a particular row, column, or entry using the Range (instead of Worksheet) command.

- Type **/R** for Range.

   ➤ The Range submenu is displayed.

- Select Format.

   ➤ The screen displays the Range Format submenu, similar to the one displayed when you changed format through the Worksheet Global command.

- Select Fixed with 0 (zero) decimal places.

In the Range Format command, you specify the range of cells that is to be affected; in this case, the range B1 through K1.

- Type **B1.K1** and press (ENTER).

   ➤ The format of the numerical values in row 1 is changed to integer. The value displayed in cell B1, for example, is 1 instead of 1.00.

- Place the cell pointer in cell B1.

   ➤ The top line in the control panel shows (F0), indicating the value is displayed as Fixed with 0 decimal places.

ENHANCING THE SIMPLE SPREADSHEET   **117**

The format indicator is displayed in the control panel only when it is different from what is done globally, that is, only when the display format was set using the Range option.

ZERO SUPPRESSION

Another thing about the display that is somewhat distracting is the zeros that appear in columns G through K, rows 6 through 9. These cells contain formulas that depend on other cells not containing entries. You can suppress the cell display when the value to be displayed is zero. This is a global option.

- Type **/WG** for Worksheet Global.
- Select Zero.

    ➤ The following options appear:

No	Displays zero values.
Yes	Displays blanks for zero values.
Label	Replaces zeros with a specified label.

- Press **Y** to select Yes.

    ➤ The zeros disappear from the screen.

Zero suppression is a Lotus 1-2-3 feature that is not saved when you save the worksheet on disk.

SAVING A FILE THAT ALREADY EXISTS ON DISK

You need to save your spreadsheet for use during the next lesson. When you are saving the spreadsheet, however, you have to be careful in choosing the filename.

If you enter a filename that already exists on the data disk, a menu appears with the following options:

Cancel	Cancels the command and does not save the file.
Replace	Replaces the file on disk with the current file.
Backup	Renames the existing file into a backup file (with .BAK extension), and saves the current file on disk.

One of these options may be acceptable in some situations. If you use a different filename, however, then both the old and new worksheet files will be stored on disk as .WK1 files.

◼ PRACTICE TIME

Save your spreadsheet using the filename LOTUS2.
Note: The screen displays the name of the file you retrieved earlier in this lesson as the default. To save this file with a different name, simply type the name.

✦ PRINTING THE SPREADSHEET IN SECTIONS

As noted in Lesson 4, a sheet of 8 1/2 by 11-inch paper will hold up to 8 columns of a width of 9 characters at 10 characters per inch. Since this worksheet contains 12 columns (A to L) and column A is wider than 9 characters, the worksheet must be printed in two sections: The first section will contain seven columns (columns A through G), and the second section will contain five columns (columns H through L).

Rather than remembering (or pointing) the top-left and bottom-right corner cells of each section range, you will name these ranges.

- Place the cell pointer in cell A1.
- Type **/RN** for Range Name.

  ➤ The following Range Name submenu is displayed:

Create	Creates a range name.
Delete	Deletes a range name.
Labels	Creates range names from a range of labels.
Reset	Deletes all range names in the worksheet.
Table	Creates a table of range names.

- Select Create.

  ➤ You are prompted to enter the name to use.

A range name can be up to 16 characters in length. Make range names simple and easy to remember. Use the name FIRST for the first section and SECOND for the second section.

ENHANCING THE SIMPLE SPREADSHEET

- Type **FIRST** then press (ENTER).

    ➤ A message prompts you to enter the range of cells that will be named FIRST.

You can assign a name to a single cell or a range of cells. As always, you enter the addresses of the top-left and bottom-right corner cells of the range. Rather than typing these addresses separated by a period, you will point with the arrow keys.

- Press the (→) key until cells A1 through G1 are highlighted.

- Press the (↓) key until the range A1 through G8 is highlighted.

- Press (ENTER).

    ➤ The specified range has been named.

PRACTICE TIME

1. Move the cell pointer to cell H1.

2. Assign the name SECOND to the range H1 through L8.

Note: Assigning range names makes it easy to refer to often used cells and ranges. However, you do have to keep track of these names. You can see all the range names for the current spreadsheet with the Range Name Table command.

Now you are ready to print.

- Type **/PP** to print using the printer.
- Select Range.

At this point, you would ordinarily enter the corner-cell addresses of the range.

- Type **FIRST** and press (ENTER).

    ➤ The Print Printer submenu is displayed again.

- Select Align and then Go.
  ➤ The first section is printed.
- Select Page to advance printer to the top of the next page.
- Select Range again to specify the range of the second section.
- Type **SECOND** and press ENTER.
- Select Go.
  ➤ The second section is printed.
- Select Page and then Quit.

Range names will be discussed in more detail later; in the meantime, use them if you feel comfortable with the concept.

- Save worksheet as LOTUS2 again to preserve the range names. Use the Replace option.

END OF LESSON 5

As you did at the end of Lesson 4:

- Type **/QY** and then select **E** to exit to DOS.
- Remove the disks from the disk drives.
- Turn off the monitor, computer, and printer.

SUMMARY

In this lesson, many of the terms and concepts that are necessary for you to use spreadsheets effectively are introduced.

- Repeating labels are entered by typing \ followed by the character(s) you want repeated across the cell. Even if the column width is changed, the cell is still filled with the specified character(s).
- Functions are introduced with the @SUM function.

- If you save a file to disk a second time using the Replace option, the current spreadsheet contents will write over those of the original file. If you want to keep the original file, the file must be saved under a different name. The Backup option lets you save the existing file with the .BAK extension.

- The Undo function allows you to recover cell contents that were overwritten when the most recent entry was made.

- A cell or a range of cells can be named so that it can be referred by using the name instead of cell addresses.

- If a spreadsheet is too large to be printed on a single sheet of paper, it must be printed in sections.

- The following commands are discussed:

F1	The Help facility.
ALT-F4	The Undo function.
/C	Copy—copies cell contents into another cell or range of cells.
/FR	File Retrieve—reads a spreadsheet file from disk.
/FD	File Directory—specifies the directory (disk drive) to use.
/PP	Print Printer—sends output to printer.
/RF	Range Format—specifies display format for a range of cells.
/RNC	Range Name Create—assigns a name to a cell or a range of cells.
/WCS	Worksheet Column Set-Width—changes the width of a column.
/WGF	Worksheet Global Format—specifies display format of the entire worksheet.
/WGZ	Worksheet Global Zero—suppresses the printing of zeros.
/WIR	Worksheet Insert Row—inserts row(s).

REVIEW QUESTIONS

1. A cell is to contain the formula +B1+C1+C2+C3. What formula can you use instead? *+B1.C3*

2. After you copy the formula 1+B1 in cell C1 to cell D1 using /C command, what formula is stored in cell D1? *+1+C1*

3. After you copy the formula 1+$B$1 in cell C1 to cell D1 using /C command, what formula is stored in cell D1? *1+$B$1*

4. Which command lets you change the width of a column?

5. What do "source range" *(From)* and "destination range" *(To)* mean in a copy command?

6. What does "repeating label" mean? How do you enter it? *\ followed by the character*

7. What is meant by the argument of a function? *the values you want totaled. they are entered within parentheses*

8. What is the difference between setting the display format using the Range command and Worksheet Global command? *R for range of cells   N for entire worksheet*

9. What is the purpose of naming a cell or a range of cells? *So it can be referred to by name instead of cell address*

10. What happens when you save a file the second time using the same filename? *Saves over the original*

EXERCISES

1. Retrieve the spreadsheet EX4_1 prepared in Lesson 4. It occurred to you that your ten best friends have been borrowing considerable amounts of money from you.

   a) Expand the spreadsheet by adding four columns for four weeks (a column for each week). Insert the amount each friend borrowed each week.

   b) Calculate and display the total amount each friend borrowed from you in the four-week period (row totals).

ENHANCING THE SIMPLE SPREADSHEET

c) Calculate and display the total amount you lent each week (column totals).

d) Insert appropriate headings in the worksheet.

e) Select the appropriate display format.

f) Save the spreadsheet as EX5_1.

g) Print the spreadsheet.

2. Retrieve the spreadsheet EX4_2 prepared in Lesson 4.

You as a teacher would like to expand the spreadsheet to calculate your students' total grade points and average.

a) Calculate and display the total grade points of each student after three exams.

b) Calculate and display the average scores of students after three exams. The average is the total divided by the number of exams.

c) Calculate and display the class average for each exam.

d) Insert appropriate headings.

e) Change to an appropriate display format. Averages should show one place to the right of the decimal.

f) Save the spreadsheet as EX5_2.

g) Print the spreadsheet.

LESSON 6
MODIFYING THE DISPLAY FORMAT

OBJECTIVES

Upon completion of the material presented in this lesson, you should be able to understand how to do the following:

- Freeze titles on the screen
- Split the screen into two windows and move the cell pointer to either window
- Move information within the worksheet
- Hide the display of a column
- Delete columns
- Edit cell contents
- Display formulas that were entered in the worksheet
- Get printouts of formulas entered in the worksheet
- Search and optionally replace contents of labels and formulas

STARTING OFF

Start 1-2-3 so that the blank spreadsheet is displayed. Also, insert in drive B the data disk used in the previous lesson.

PRACTICE TIME

1. Change the file directory to drive B.

2. Retrieve the spreadsheet file LOTUS2 from the previous lesson.

FREEZE TITLES COMMAND (/WT)

Scroll your screen so that column L appears. At this point, you cannot see column A, which is the row headings. Without the headings, can you tell which value is which? Since this is a small spreadsheet, you may not have any trouble identifying the values. But if you were working with a large spreadsheet containing many rows of data, you might find it difficult to remember which row contains what data. To eliminate this problem, you can *freeze* the row headings, known as *titles*, on the screen so that they will not scroll off.

- Press (HOME) to move the cell pointer to cell A1.
- Move the cell pointer to cell B1.
- Type **/WT** for Worksheet Title.
  - ➤ The Worksheet Title submenu is displayed:

Both	Freezes all rows and columns to the left and above the cell pointer.
Horizontal	Freezes all rows above the cell pointer.
Vertical	Freezes all columns to the left of the cell pointer.
Clear	Unfreezes all title columns and rows.

You want to freeze the titles that appear in column A, which is the column to the left of the cell pointer.

- Select Vertical.
- Press the → key at least 10 times.
  - ➤ As the screen scrolls to the left (look at the column labels at the top), column A stays on the screen. These titles are "frozen" on the screen.
- Press the ← key repeatedly until the computer beeps.
  - ➤ The cell pointer will not go beyond column B.

If you need to access the "frozen" title cells, use the GOTO ((F5)) command.

- Press the (F5) function key and specify cell A1.

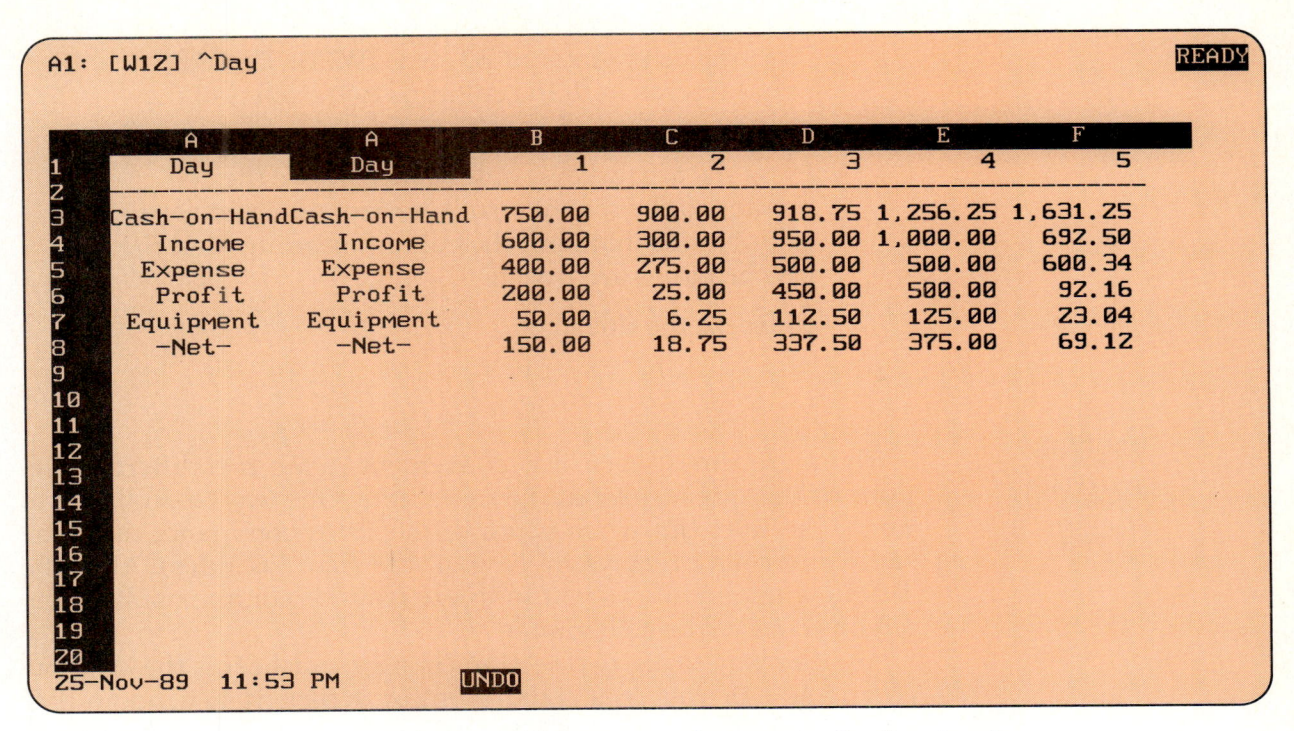

```
A1: [W12] ^Day                                                              READY

              A          A           B        C        D        E        F
     1       Day        Day          1        2        3        4        5
     2      ─────────────────────────────────────────────────────────────────
     3    Cash-on-HandCash-on-Hand  750.00   900.00   918.75 1,256.25 1,631.25
     4       Income     Income      600.00   300.00   950.00 1,000.00   692.50
     5       Expense    Expense     400.00   275.00   500.00   500.00   600.34
     6       Profit     Profit      200.00    25.00   450.00   500.00    92.16
     7      Equipment  Equipment     50.00     6.25   112.50   125.00    23.04
     8       -Net-      -Net-       150.00    18.75   337.50   375.00    69.12
     9
    10
    11
    12
    13
    14
    15
    16
    17
    18
    19
    20
    25-Nov-89  11:53 PM            UNDO
```

Screen Display 6–1   Column A is displayed twice.

➤ A second column A appears on the screen and the cell pointer is on cell A1, as shown in Screen Display 6–1.

If you change the content of cell A1 where the cell pointer is currently located, you will also change the content of the "frozen" cell A1.

- Type **/WTC** to clear title settings. (This command unfreezes the title.)

- Move the cell pointer around and verify that the titles are not frozen.

- With the cell pointer at A3, type **/WTH** for horizontal freeze.

Press the ⬇ key until the screen scrolls up. Notice that rows 1 and 2 stay on the screen.

- Type **/WTC** to unfreeze the title.

MODIFYING THE DISPLAY FORMAT   **129**

- With the cell pointer at B3, type **/WTB.** This command freezes both the columns to the left and the rows above the cell pointer.

- Press the arrow keys, in sequence. Move the cell pointer so the screen scrolls horizontally and vertically. Notice that both the column headings and the row headings are frozen.

- Unfreeze the titles.

WINDOW COMMAND (/WW)

There are times when it is convenient to see two different sections of the spreadsheet at the same time. One way to do this is to freeze the title. But when you give the Titles command, the same set of information stays in view all the time (as titles). Also, the Titles command allows you to freeze rows or columns only to the left or above of the cell pointer.

Another way to see two sections of a spreadsheet is the Window command. As you recall, the monitor screen is a window that allows you to view part of a spreadsheet; the Window command lets you split the monitor screen so you can view two portions of the spreadsheet at the same time. That is, it lets you have two windows on the spreadsheet.

You will now split the screen vertically so that there are two windows side by side.

- Place the cell pointer in the column that will form the left edge of the right-hand window. Place it in column E; say, cell E1.

- Type **/WW** for Worksheet Window.

    ➤ The Worksheet Window submenu is displayed:

Horizontal	Splits the screen horizontally.
Vertical	Splits the screen vertically.
Sync	Synchronizes scrolling in both windows.
Unsync	Scrolls windows independently.
Clear	Returns to full-screen display.

- Select Vertical.

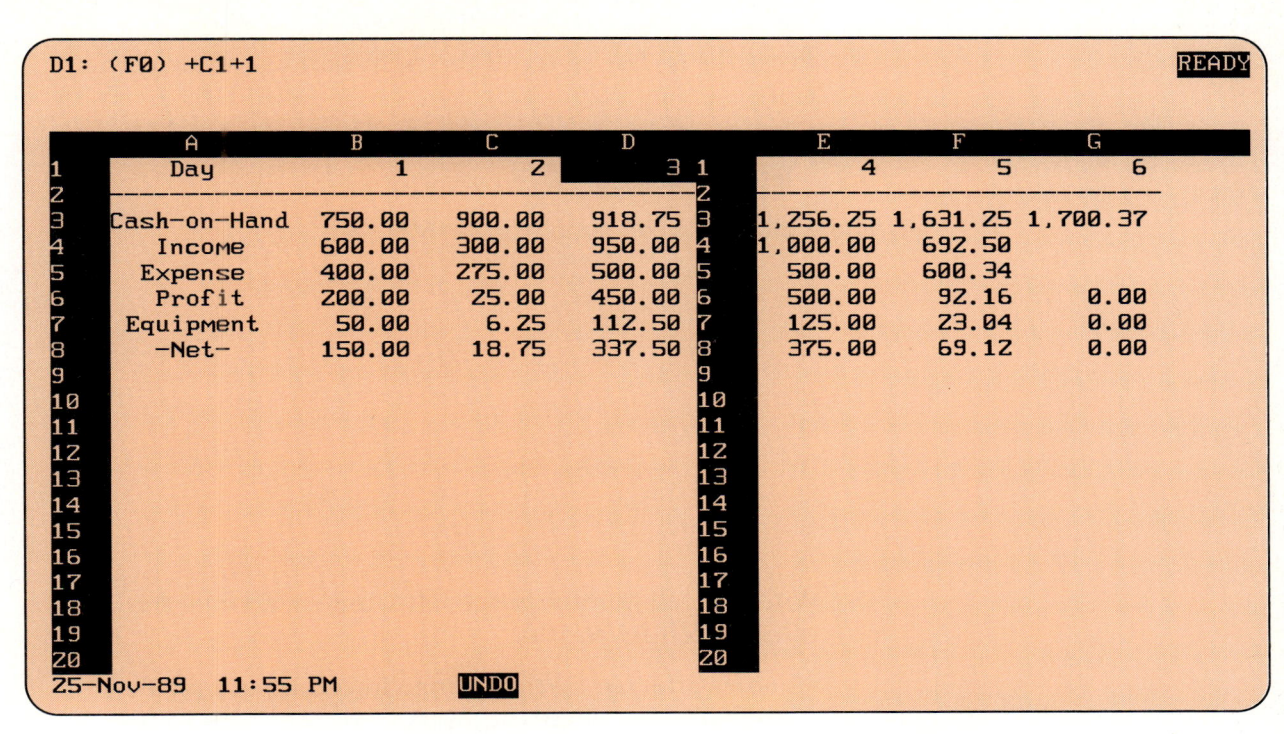

```
D1:  (F0)  +C1+1                                                      READY

        A         B         C         D          E         F         G
1      Day        1         2         3  1       4         5         6
2     ─────────────────────────────────  2    ──────────────────────────────
3   Cash-on-Hand 750.00    900.00    918.75 3  1,256.25  1,631.25  1,700.37
4      Income    600.00    300.00    950.00 4  1,000.00    692.50
5      Expense   400.00    275.00    500.00 5    500.00    600.34
6      Profit   200.00     25.00    450.00 6    500.00     92.16      0.00
7    Equipment   50.00      6.25    112.50 7    125.00     23.04      0.00
8       -Net-   150.00     18.75    337.50 8    375.00     69.12      0.00
9                                            9
10                                          10
11                                          11
12                                          12
13                                          13
14                                          14
15                                          15
16                                          16
17                                          17
18                                          18
19                                          19
20                                          20
25-Nov-89   11:55 PM        UNDO
```

Screen Display 6–2 Screen is split vertically into two windows.

> The cell pointer moves to the right-most column of the window on the left (the same row). The screen is split as shown in Screen Display 6–2.

■ Press the ⊙ arrow key until the left window scrolls.

> As the window on the left scrolls, the window on the right also scrolls.

JUMPING BETWEEN WINDOWS (F6)

You can move the cell pointer to the other window using the F6 function key.

■ Press the F6 function key.

> The cell pointer jumps to the right-hand window.

The F6 function key moves the cell pointer to the other window from whichever window you are currently in.

MODIFYING THE DISPLAY FORMAT   **131**

- Press the ⬇ key to scroll the right-hand window vertically.
  ➤ As the window on the right scrolls, the one on the left also scrolls.

The windows scroll synchronously.

PRACTICE TIME

- Position both windows so that the window on the left displays columns A through D, rows 1 through 20 and the window on the right shows columns J through L, rows 1 through 20.

- With the cell pointer in the left window, change the value in cell B5 to 100.
  ➤ Values affected by the change in cell B5 are recalculated. You can view the effect of the changes in the cells in column L.
- Type **/WWU** so the windows scroll independently.
- Press (PGDN) to scroll the left window down.
  ➤ Only the left window scrolls.
- Type **/WWC** to clear the windows.
- Press (HOME) to move the cell pointer to A1.

PRACTICE TIME

1. Split the screen horizontally so that nine rows appear in the top window.

   Hint: The cell pointer must be placed in the row that will be the top of the lower window. In this case, place the pointer on row 10.

2. Move the cell pointer to the bottom window.

3. Make the windows scroll independently.

4. Press (HOME), then scroll to the right until columns H through L appear in the bottom window.

   You have displayed the entire worksheet in two parts on the screen.

5. Clear the windows.

HIDING A COLUMN (/WCH)

When you printed this spreadsheet at the end of the previous lesson, it was printed in two sections, because the spreadsheet is wider than the 80 characters many printers can print on one line. From Susan's point of view, she does not care to see data for days 6 through 10, because she has not entered that portion. All she wants printed is columns A through F and column L, which displays the totals.

You can hide columns from display, which means that, for all calculation purposes, these columns exist, but they are not displayed on the screen or on the printout.

- With the cell pointer on any column, type **/WC** for Worksheet Column.

- Select Hide to hide one or more columns.

  ➤ The following message is displayed:

  `Select column to hide:`

  followed by the current cell address; that is, if the cell pointer is on cell A1, you see A1.

At this point, you can type **G1.K1** to specify the range. However, let's say that you want to specify the range by pointing to it with the cell pointer. If you want to hide one column, highlight the column and press (ENTER). If you want to hide several columns, highlight one end, then press . (period) to indicate a range, highlight the other end, and then press (ENTER).

- Move the cell pointer to cell G1.

MODIFYING THE DISPLAY FORMAT **133**

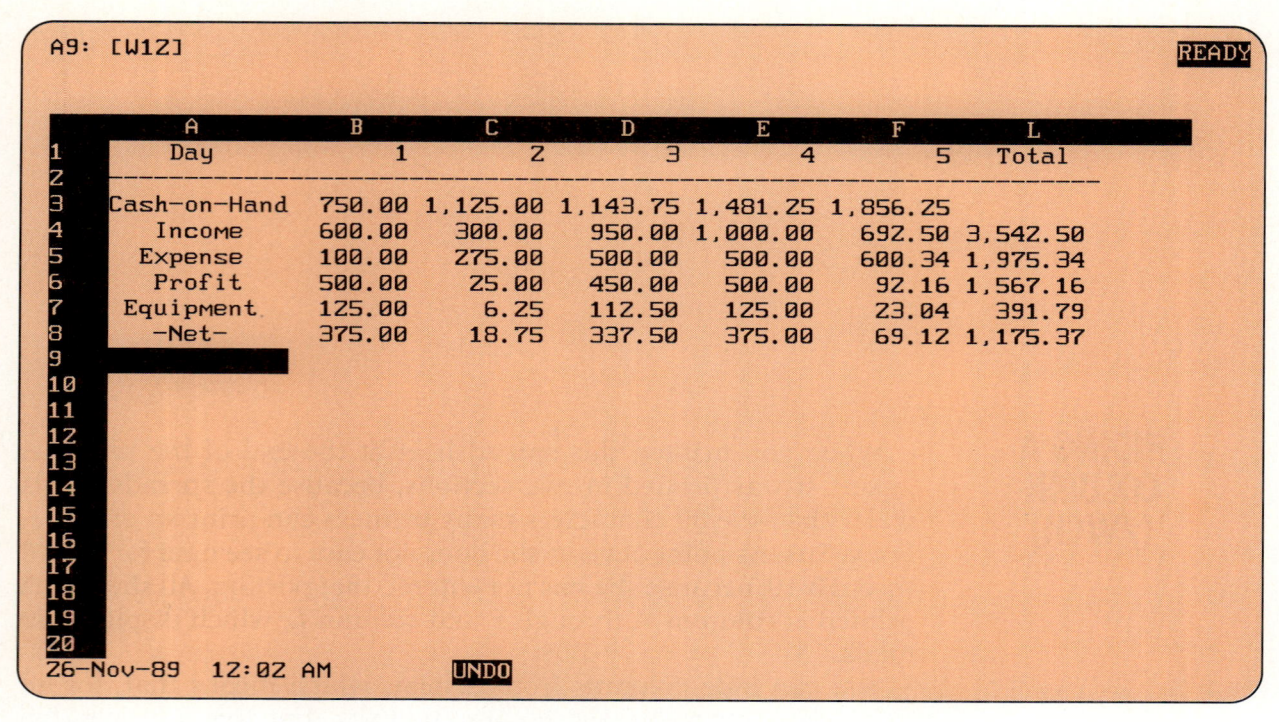

```
A9: [W12]                                                              READY

         A           B         C         D         E         F        L
  1     Day          1         2         3         4         5      Total
  2   ------------------------------------------------------------------
  3  Cash-on-Hand  750.00  1,125.00  1,143.75  1,481.25  1,856.25
  4    Income      600.00    300.00    950.00  1,000.00    692.50  3,542.50
  5    Expense     100.00    275.00    500.00    500.00    600.34  1,975.34
  6    Profit      500.00     25.00    450.00    500.00     92.16  1,567.16
  7   Equipment    125.00      6.25    112.50    125.00     23.04    391.79
  8     -Net-      375.00     18.75    337.50    375.00     69.12  1,175.37
  9
 10
 11
 ...
 20
 26-Nov-89  12:02 AM        UNDO
```

Screen Display 6–3   Columns G through K have been hidden.

- Press . (period).
- Press the → key until cells G1 through K1 are highlighted. Then press (ENTER).
  ➤ Columns G through K disappear, as shown in Screen Display 6–3.

You could print the entire spreadsheet now on one sheet of paper. For now, you will display the columns again.

- Type **/WC**, then select Display.
  ➤ The following message appears:

  `Specify hidden columns to redisplay:`

  followed by the location of the cell pointer. The hidden columns are identified in the border by the asterisks following the column letters.

- Specify the range G1.K1.

134   USING LOTUS 1-2-3

- Press ENTER.
  ➤ All columns appear on the display.

PRACTICE TIME

1. Hide columns G through K from display.

2. Print the entire spreadsheet. The range to print is A1.L8.

3. Reset the column display for columns G through K.

MOVE COMMAND (/M)

Susan decides she would like to see the values for cash-on-hand displayed on the last row on the worksheet, not on the first. You can COPY the entries on row 3 to row 9, then delete row 3. You can also MOVE the entries on row 3 to row 9. The COPY command just copies the values; it leaves the values at the source as is. The MOVE command, on the other hand, actually relocates the values, and hence the source range is left blank; that means, after the MOVE a blank row 3 will be left which you will have to delete.

- With the cell pointer on cell A3, type **/M** for move.

  ➤ The following message appears:

  ```
  Enter range to move FROM: A3..A3
  ```

You need to specify the top left and the bottom right corner cells of the range. Row 3 contains information in columns A through K.

- Specify the range A3.K3.

  ➤ You are prompted with the message:

  ```
  Enter range to move TO: A3
  ```

When you move the data, whatever is currently displayed in the destination range will be overwritten.

You want to move the data to row 9. You specify only cell A9, the upper left corner cell of the range, as the destination. When the source range is larger than the destination range, the extra source-cell contents are placed in the cells below and to the right of the destination range, overwriting the contents of any affected cells.

- Type **A9** and press (ENTER).
    - ➤ Cash-on-hand values appear on row 9, and row 3 is now blank.

You will notice that the formulas in cells C3 through K3 were changed automatically. That is, the formula at C9 (moved from C3), for example, is now +B9+B8, since the content of cell B3 was moved to B9.

DELETING ROWS (/WDR)

You will now delete row 3. The Delete command is very similar to the Insert command.

- Place the cell pointer on row 3, the row you want deleted.
- Type **/WD** for the Worksheet Delete command.
    - ➤ The Worksheet Delete submenu gives you the option of deleting rows or columns.
- Select Row.
    - ➤ The control panel message asks for the range of rows to be deleted.
- Press (ENTER) since you want only row 3 deleted.
    - ➤ The blank row 3 is deleted, and all information on rows 4 through 9 move up one row.

PRACTICE TIME

1. Move contents of row 8 to row 9.

2. Fill row 8 with ='s, as shown in Screen Display 6–4.

3. Save the spreadsheet using the filename LOTUS3.

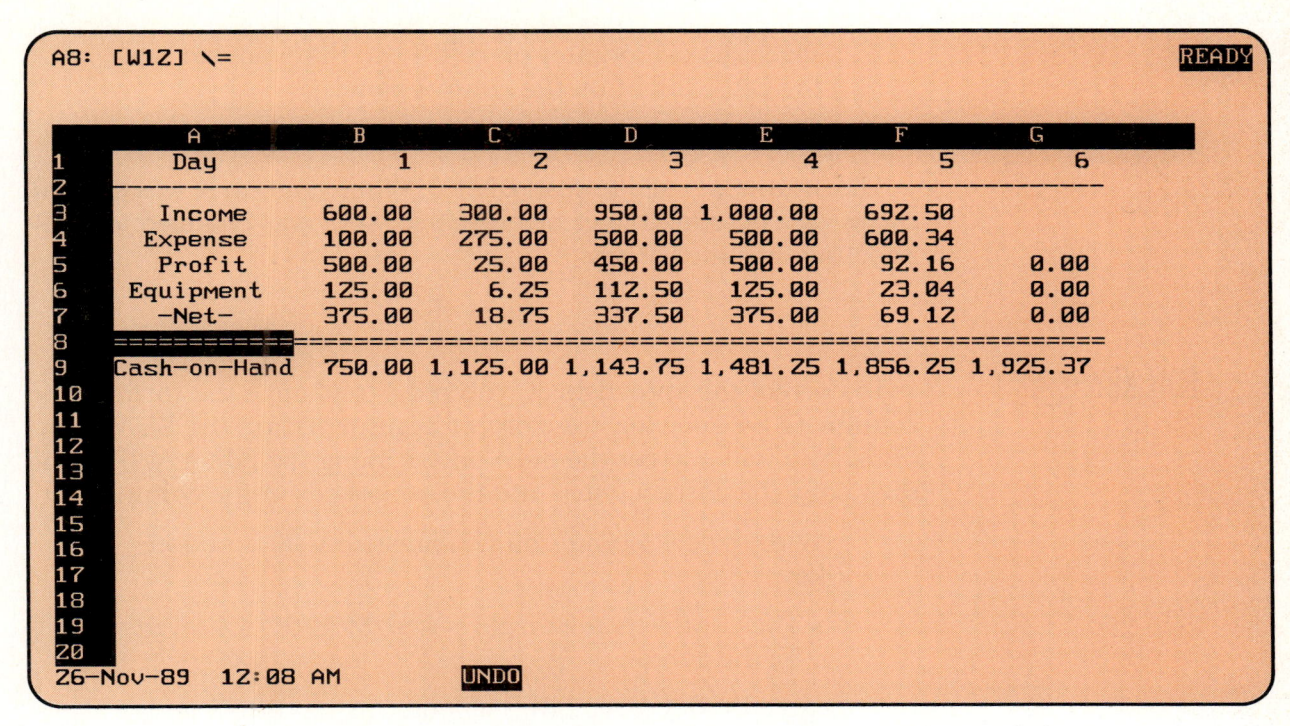

```
A8: [W12] \=                                                          READY

       A         B         C         D         E         F         G
  1   Day        1         2         3         4         5         6
  2  ────────────────────────────────────────────────────────────────
  3   Income   600.00    300.00    950.00  1,000.00    692.50
  4   Expense  100.00    275.00    500.00    500.00    600.34
  5   Profit   500.00     25.00    450.00    500.00     92.16      0.00
  6   Equipment 125.00     6.25    112.50    125.00     23.04      0.00
  7   -Net-    375.00     18.75    337.50    375.00     69.12      0.00
  8  ════════════════════════════════════════════════════════════════
  9   Cash-on-Hand 750.00 1,125.00 1,143.75 1,481.25 1,856.25 1,925.37
 10
 11
 12
 13
 14
 15
 16
 17
 18
 19
 20
 26-Nov-89  12:08 AM          UNDO
```

Screen Display 6–4   *Modified display of the worksheet.*

DELETING COLUMNS (/WDC)

You might have wondered, when hiding display of columns G through K earlier, what would have happened if you had deleted those columns instead. Before starting, note the value 3542.50 that appears as the total income in cell L3.

- Place the cell pointer on column G; say, cell G1.
- Type **/WDC** for Worksheet Delete Columns.
  ▶ The message reads:

    Enter range of columns to delete: G1..G1

- Press the → key until cells G1 through K1 are highlighted, and press (ENTER).
  ▶ "Total" now appears in cell G1.
  ▶ Cells G3 through G7 display ERR.

MODIFYING THE DISPLAY FORMAT **137**

- Place the cell pointer on cell G3 so that you can see the cell content on the control panel.

    ➤ The content reads @SUM(ERR).

The argument used to read B3..K3. When column K was deleted, the range could no longer be evaluated, so it was changed to ERR, affecting the entire entry.

EDIT KEY (F2)

To correct the spreadsheet, you need to change the formulas in column G by entering the correct arguments for the SUM functions. You will correct the entry at G3 using the edit key, F2, and then copy the correct entry into the other cells in the column.

- With the cell pointer on G3, press the F2 function key.

    ➤ The control panel displays @SUM(ERR) followed by the cursor.

You can edit, or correct, the cell entry using the → and ← keys, the BACKSPACE key, and the DEL key.

- Position the cursor and delete ERR.
- Type **B3.F3**, so that the entry reads @SUM(B3.F3), and press ENTER.

    ➤ The total income, cell G3, now reads 3542.50.

PRACTICE TIME

- Copy the formula at G3 into range G4 through G7.

TEXT DISPLAY

The only way you can tell whether a value or a formula was entered in a cell is to move the cell pointer to that cell and look at the cell entry on the top line of the control panel. Therefore, it is very difficult to determine whether values or formulas were entered in all the cells in a worksheet. You can, however, change

```
G3: @SUM(B3..F3)                                                       READY

         A         B         C         D         E         F         G
   1    Day        1         2         3         4         5       Total
   2   ─────────────────────────────────────────────────────────────────────
   3   Income     600       300       950      1000      692.5    @SUM(B3.
   4   Expense    100       275       500       500      600.34   @SUM(B4.
   5   Profit    +B3-B4    +C3-C4    +D3-D4    +E3-E4    +F3-F4   @SUM(B5.
   6   Equipment 0.25*B5   0.25*C5   0.25*D5   0.25*E5   0.25*F5  @SUM(B6.
   7   -Net-     +B5-B6    +C5-C6    +D5-D6    +E5-E6    +F5-F6   @SUM(B7.
   8   ═════════════════════════════════════════════════════════════════════
   9   Cash-on-Hand 750   +B9+B7    +C9+C7    +D9+D7    +E9+E7
  10
  11
  12
  13
  14
  15
  16
  17
  18
  19
```

Screen Display 6–5   Display formatted to show entries, not results.

the display format so that the actual texts of the formulas that were entered are shown rather than the evaluated values.

- Type **/WGF** for Worksheet Global Format.
- Select Text.
  - ➤ The screen display changes appear as in Screen Display 6–5.

One drawback to looking at cell entries this way is that it may not be possible to see the entire text that was entered in a cell without increasing the column widths, and an entry can be very long.

Note: When you change the display format globally, the change does not affect those cells whose formats were set with the Range command.

MODIFYING THE DISPLAY FORMAT   139

PRACTICE TIME

- Make a global worksheet format change to , (comma) with 2 decimal places.

FORMULA PRINTOUT

When you print a worksheet, an image of what is displayed on the screen is printed on the paper. It is also possible to print a spreadsheet with text display format to obtain a paper copy of what was actually entered in each cell. However, there are restrictions, such as the column width as mentioned previously.

A better way to get a printout of the exact entries you made into the worksheet, one cell per line, is called a *formula printout*. You do not need to adjust the column width or the size of the range to be printed when printing worksheet formulas.

- Make sure that you are working with a personal computer connected to a printer, and that the printer is turned on and ready to use.
- Type **/PP** for send print to printer.
- Select Options.

  ➤ The Print Options submenu is displayed at the top:

Header	Prints a given line of text just above the top margin of each page.
Footer	Prints a given line of text just below the bottom margin of each page.
Margins	Sets or clears margins for a printed page.
Borders	Prints a specified range, including column letters and row numbers.
Setup	Specifies the printer setup string.
Pg-Length	Sets the length of the page.
Other	Prints cell formulas, or data without headers, footers, and page breaks.
Quit	Returns to Print menu.

  ➤ The current print settings are displayed in the rest of the screen.

- Select Other.

➤ The Print Options Other submenu is displayed:

As-Displayed	Prints the worksheet as displayed on the screen.
Cell-Formulas	Prints one cell entry per line.
Formatted	Prints with page breaks, headers, footers, and printer setup strings.
Unformatted	Prints without page breaks, headers, footers, and printer setup strings.

You are interested in printing the cell formulas.

- Select Cell-Formulas.

    ➤ In the Print settings box, Output: reads Cell-Formulas (Formatted).

- Select Quit to get back to the Print Printer submenu.
- Select Range to specify the range to print.

The range is the entire spreadsheet, or rows 1 through 9, columns A through G.

- Type **A1.G9** and press (ENTER).
- Select Align.
- Select Go to print.

The indicated range is printed, one cell per line.

```
A1: [W12] ^Day
B1: (F0) 1
C1: (F0) +B1+1
...
A3: [W12] ^Income
B3: 600
C3: 300
D3: 950
E3: 1000
F3: 692.5
```

MODIFYING THE DISPLAY FORMAT

And so forth, to the end:

.
.

```
A9:  [W12]  'Cash-on-Hand
B9:  750
C9:  +B9+B7
D9:  +C9+C7
E9:  +D9+D7
F9:  +E9+E7
```

In the printout, [W12] indicates a column width of 12, (F0) indicates that the format is fixed, with no places to the right of the decimal, and \- indicates a repeating label of hyphens. The label-prefix characters are also displayed.

- Select Page and then Quit to exit the Print menu.

SEARCH AND REPLACE (/RS)

Sometimes you may use a large worksheet in which you need to find cells that contain certain contents. Lotus 1-2-3 has a feature that searches a range for a label or a string contained in a formula (but not a direct numeric entry) and lets you either highlight all the occurrences of it it finds or replace each occurrence with another string. You can use the current worksheet to try out this feature.

- Enter **/RS** for Range Search.

  ➤ You are prompted to enter the range to search.

- Enter the range **B3.F7**.

  ➤ The control panel displays the message,

```
String to search for:
```

You are expected to enter a string: part of the contents of either a label or a formula. Suppose you are interested in finding out which cells contain references to cell E4.

- Enter **E4**.

  ➤ A menu appears with the options Formulas, Labels, and Both.

Lotus 1–2–3 wants to know whether to search for the string you entered in formulas or labels only, or in both. You are interested in searching formulas.

- Select Formulas.
    > Another menu appears, with the options Find and Replace.

If you just want to highlight all the occurrences of the string in the range, you select Find. However, if you want to change the string to something else, you select Replace. Right now, you are just looking.

- Select Find.
    > The cell pointer moves to cell E5. The top line of the control panel displays the contents of the cell, and E4 is highlighted in the formula. The menu options Next and Quit are displayed on the second line of the control panel.

You have the option of either continuing to search for cells containing the search string or returning to the Ready mode.

- Select Next.
    > A message appears on the bottom line of the screen, indicating that no more occurrences of the string were found.
- Press (ENTER) to clear the message and return to the Ready mode.

Replacing one string with another is similar; it is covered in the Practice Time below.

PRACTICE TIME

1. Erase the worksheet.

2. Enter the label **abc** in each of the cells in the range A1..C3.

MODIFYING THE DISPLAY FORMAT **143**

3. Select the Range Search command. The range to search is A1..C3 and the string to search for is **b**. You want to search labels only.

4. Select the Replace option. You want to replace **b** with **r**.

5. When the first occurrence of **b** has been found, that cell is highlighted and you have four menu options. Select All to replace all the occurrences of **b** in the range with **r**. When you have finished, the range A1..C3 contains **arc** in each cell.

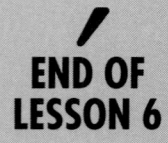

END OF LESSON 6

- Type **/QY**. Type **Y** to abandon the worksheet, then **E** to exit DOS.
- Remove the disks from the disk drive.
- Turn off the monitor, computer, and printer.

SUMMARY

In this lesson, many of the terms and concepts you need to know to change the display format of a spreadsheet are discussed.

- Through the Worksheet Titles command, column and row headings (labels) can remain displayed on the screen as the rest of the worksheet scrolls.
- Two sections of the spreadsheet can be displayed on the screen using the Worksheet Window command. The cell pointer is moved between the windows using the (F6) function key.
- Columns can be hidden from screen display and printing. They still exist and can be used for calculation purposes.
- An entry in a cell can be edited using the (F2) function key.

- The Text display format shows the cell's **actual entry**.
- A formula printout prints the exact entries you made into the worksheet, one cell per line.
- The Range Search command can be used to find a string in a formula or label, and can also replace it with another string.
- The following commands are discussed:

F2	Edit—Makes corrections of the entry in a cell.
F5	GoTo—Moves the cell pointer to a specified cell.
F6	Window—Moves the cell pointer between windows.
/M	Move—Moves specified row(s) or column(s) to another location within the spreadsheet.
/PPOOC	Print Printer Options Other Cell-Formulas—Specifies printing of the cell contents (instead of screen display). You specify the range, then Go.
/RS	Range Search—Searches a range for matches with a specified string, optionally replacing them with another string.
/WCH	Worksheet Column Hide—Hides one or more columns from display.
/WCD	Worksheet Column Display—Redisplays hidden columns.
/WGF	Worksheet Global Format—Changes the display format of the entire worksheet.
/WD	Worksheet Delete—Deletes specified row(s) or column(s).
/WT	Worksheet Titles—Freezes title to the left of and/or above the cell pointer.
/WW	Worksheet Window—Divides the screen into two windows, either side by side or top and bottom. The windows can either scroll synchronously or independently.

REVIEW QUESTIONS

1. What is the purpose of setting titles for the spreadsheet rows? *So the titles will remain on the screen when the worksheet is scrolled*

2. What is the point of splitting the spreadsheet into two windows? *Two sections can be displayed on a screen*

3. What does it mean when both windows scroll synchronously? *They both scroll*

4. What key do you press to move the cell pointer from one window to another? *F6*

5. What is the effect on calculation of hiding the display of a column? Explain. *They exist but they are not displayed on the screen*

6. When you move a cell's contents, what happens to formula entries in other cells that depend on those contents? Explain. *They change*

7. When you move a cell's contents into a cell that already contains data, what happens to the data in the destination cell? *It is overwritten*

8. When you delete a row or column, what happens to formula entries in other cells that depend on the contents in the cells that were deleted? Explain. *They change to ERR*

9. What is the purpose of the edit key (F2)? *To edit an entry in a cell*

10. What is a formula printout? How do you obtain it? *Prints your exact entries.*

EXERCISES

1. Retrieve spreadsheet EX5_1 prepared in Lesson 5.

    a) Hide the column containing telephone numbers.

    b) Get a formula printout of the spreadsheet.

    c) Save the spreadsheet as EX6_1.

2. Retrieve spreadsheet EX5_2 prepared in Lesson 5.
   a) Freeze both the column headings and the students names.
   b) Delete one of the students (delete a row).
   c) Get a formula printout of the spreadsheet.
   d) Save the spreadsheet as EX6_2.

LESSON 7
CREATING PRESENTATION GRAPHICS

OBJECTIVES

Upon completion of the material presented in this lesson, you should be able to:

- Understand the terminology used in 1–2–3 graphics
- Identify various types of graphs
- Create graphs from data in a spreadsheet
- Insert titles and legends in a graph
- Name a graph to associate its settings with the spreadsheet
- Save a graph to a file
- Print a graph

STARTING OFF

Start Lotus 1–2–3 so that a blank worksheet is displayed on the screen. Insert a data disk in drive B and change the file directory to B. To print graphs, you must have access to a printer capable of printing graphics. It is also assumed that the hardware setup of PrintGraph is configured correctly.

GRAPHICS

In this lesson you will learn about the various types of graphs that can be generated from data on a worksheet. Such graphs, also referred to as *presentation graphics,* can be displayed on a monitor or printed. Different types of graphs are useful for different purposes.

- A *pie chart* is used to a show how a certain quantity is divided up. For example, it is used to show how income is generated or how money is distributed, as shown in Screen Display 7–1.

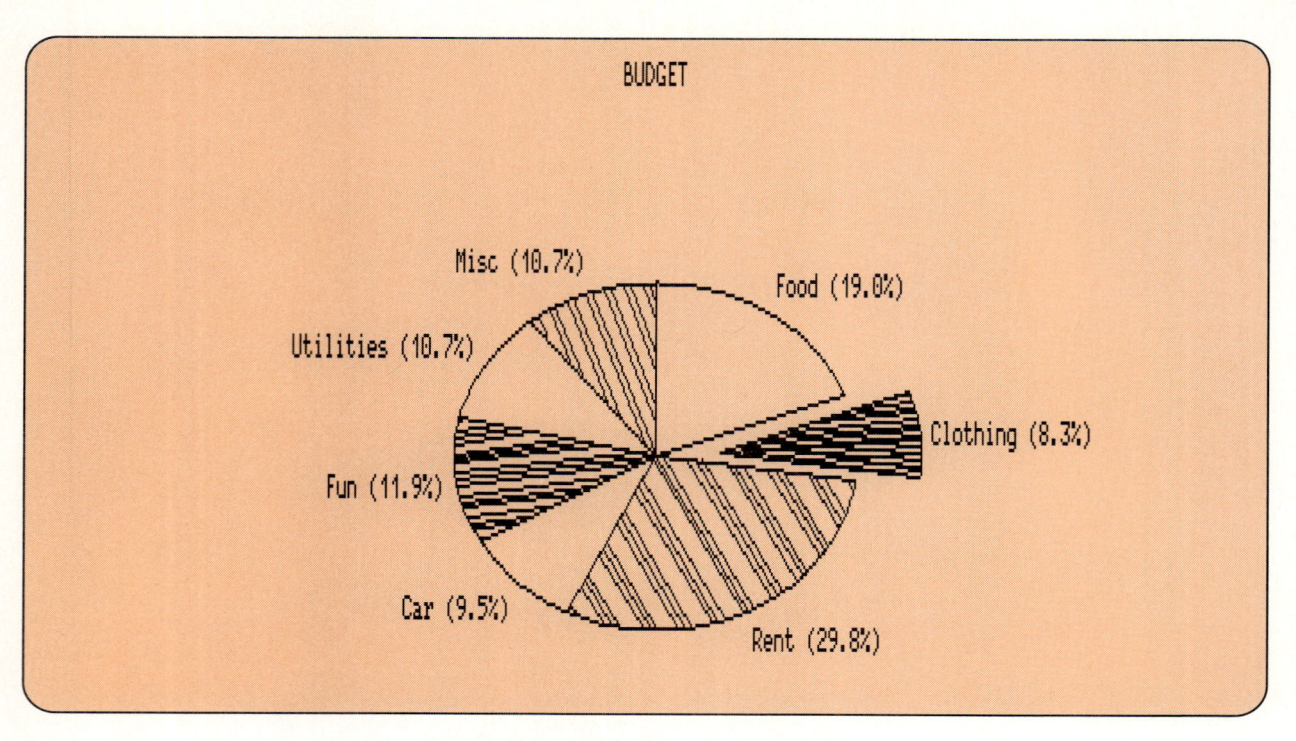

[BUDGET pie chart: Misc (10.7%), Food (19.0%), Clothing (8.3%), Rent (29.8%), Car (9.5%), Fun (11.9%), Utilities (10.7%)]

Screen Display 7–1   Pie chart showing where money goes.

- A *bar chart* is used to show how some quantity varies between different departments, geographical regions, or with time. You may want to compare student enrollment for various departments, as in Screen Display 7–2.

- A *line chart* is used to show trends of one or more quantities. You may want to compare the sales figures for two different brands of a product, as in Screen Display 7–3.

The first step in making a graph is to indicate the type of graph you want. Then you must specify where the data is located. Just as you must specify where the data ranges for copying and printing are, you must indicate the ranges for the various parts of the graph you are making. Finally, if appropriate, you may enter a title, label the horizontal and vertical ranges (*x*- and *y*-axes), and add legends. You can view the graph on the screen at any stage of its creation. When you are satisfied with the graph, you can name it to keep

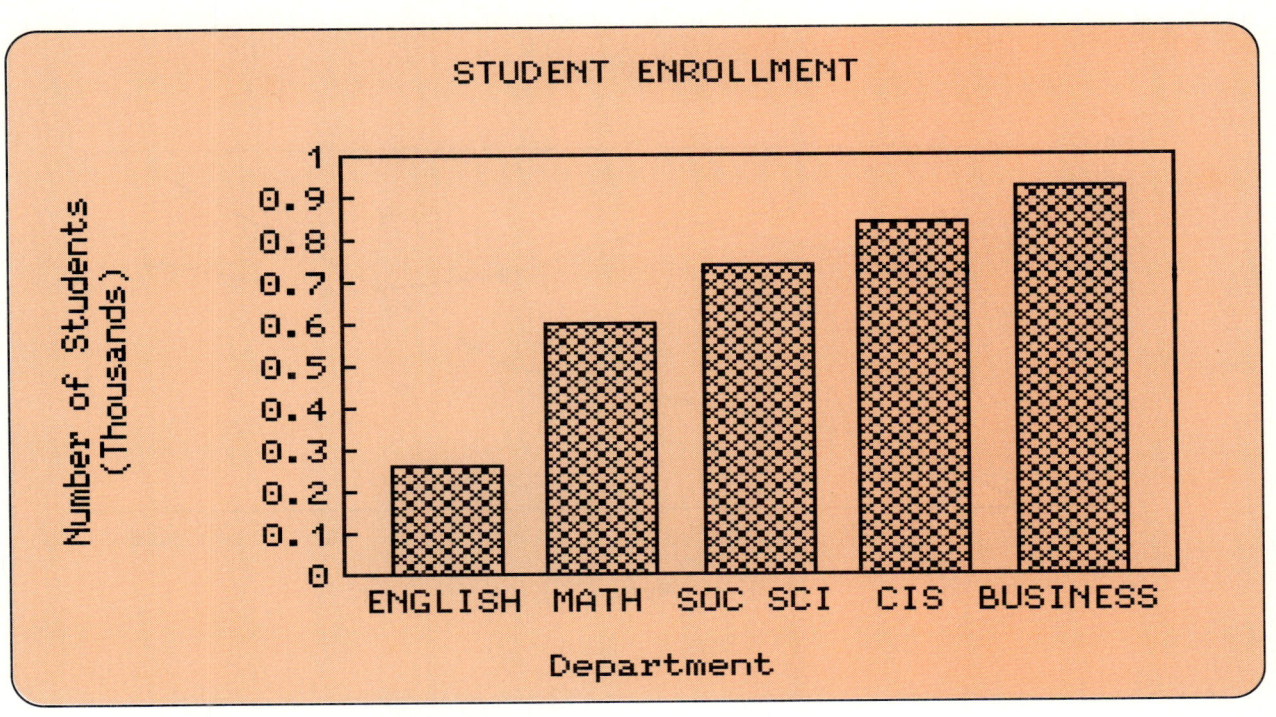

```
                    STUDENT ENROLLMENT
      1
    0.9                                              ▓▓▓
    0.8                                    ▓▓▓       ▓▓▓
    0.7                           ▓▓▓      ▓▓▓       ▓▓▓
    0.6                  ▓▓▓      ▓▓▓      ▓▓▓       ▓▓▓
    0.5                  ▓▓▓      ▓▓▓      ▓▓▓       ▓▓▓
    0.4                  ▓▓▓      ▓▓▓      ▓▓▓       ▓▓▓
    0.3         ▓▓▓      ▓▓▓      ▓▓▓      ▓▓▓       ▓▓▓
    0.2         ▓▓▓      ▓▓▓      ▓▓▓      ▓▓▓       ▓▓▓
    0.1         ▓▓▓      ▓▓▓      ▓▓▓      ▓▓▓       ▓▓▓
      0       ENGLISH   MATH    SOC SCI    CIS     BUSINESS
                              Department
```

Screen Display 7–2   Bar chart showing enrollment for several departments.

track of its settings with your worksheet or you can save it on your data disk, for printing at a later time.

Creating a graph requires some planning. 1–2–3 is extremely flexible, however, and you can change your graph easily. In this lesson, you will look at a few very simple graphs to get an idea of what kinds of graphs can be created and what each type of graph looks like.

PIE CHARTS

A pie chart is a graph consisting of a circle divided into slices, much like a pie. Each section represents one item and shows what fraction it is of the whole. The best way to understand the various settings of a pie chart is to go through the process of setting one up.

Suppose you are evaluating the budget for your business and you want to see a graphic representation of your expense categories.

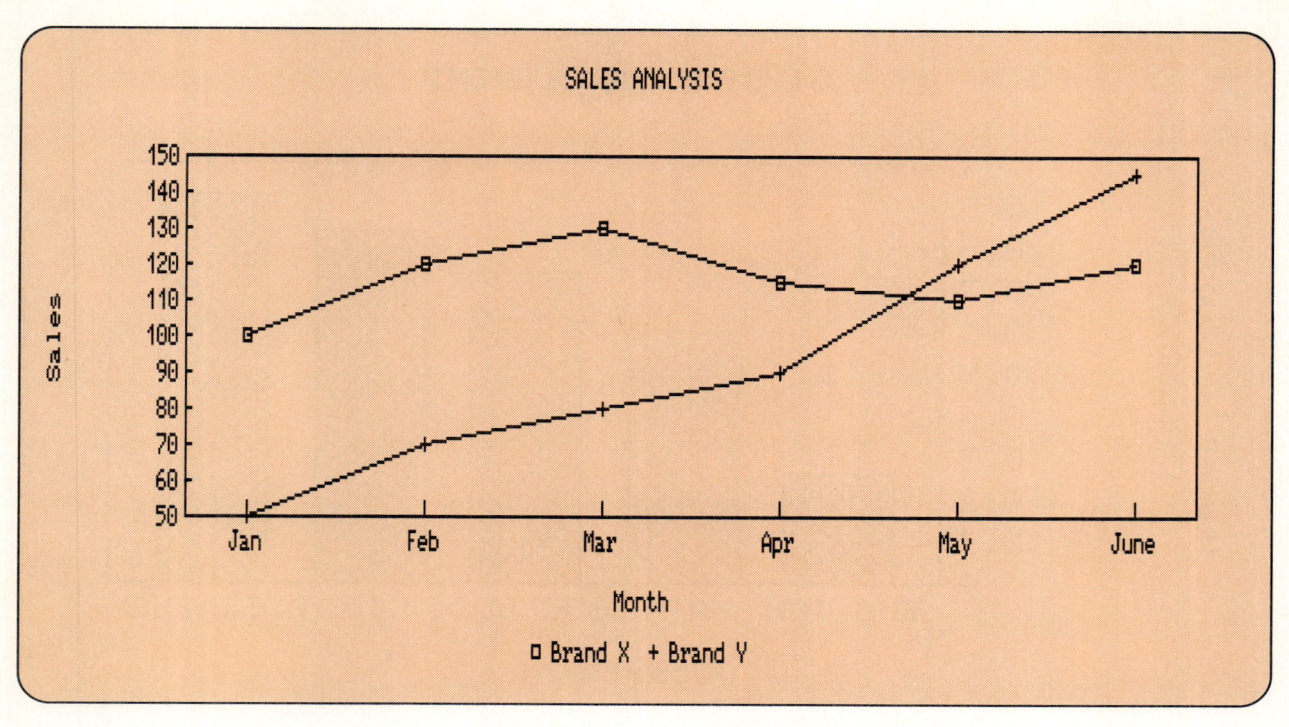

Screen Display 7–3   Line chart showing trends of two quantities.

- Set up a spreadsheet with the following data:

	A	B
1	Salaries	15125
2	Fringes	6595
3	Utilities	875
4	Rent	3450
5	Supplies	650
6	Equipment	1400
7	Travel	3535

After entering the data, do the following:

- Type **/G** for Graph.
    ➤ The Graph submenu and current Graph settings are displayed, as in Screen Display 7–4.

152   USING LOTUS 1-2-3

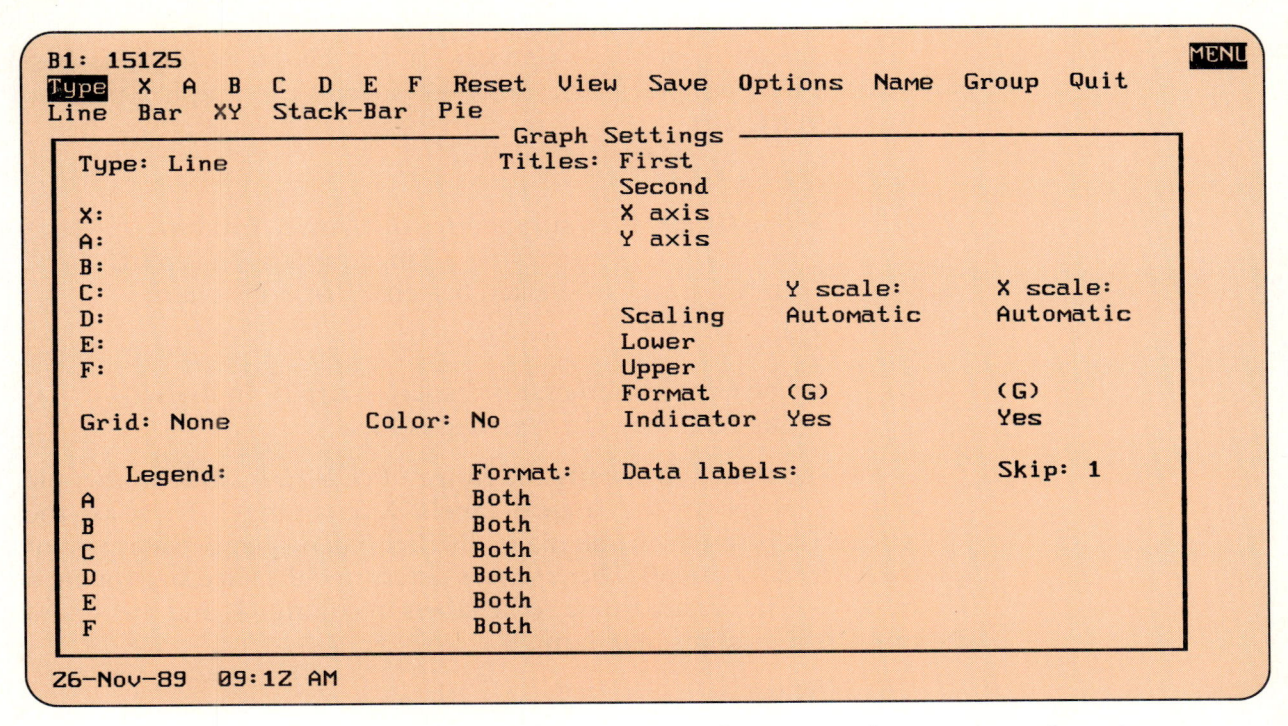

```
B1: 15125                                                           MENU
 Type  X  A  B  C  D  E  F    Reset  View  Save  Options  Name  Group  Quit
 Line  Bar  XY  Stack-Bar  Pie
┌─────────────────────────── Graph Settings ───────────────────────────┐
│  Type: Line                    Titles: First                         │
│                                        Second                        │
│  X:                                    X axis                        │
│  A:                                    Y axis                        │
│  B:                                                                  │
│  C:                                            Y scale:    X scale:  │
│  D:                                    Scaling Automatic   Automatic │
│  E:                                    Lower                         │
│  F:                                    Upper                         │
│                                        Format  (G)        (G)        │
│  Grid: None         Color: No          Indicator Yes       Yes       │
│                                                                      │
│     Legend:            Format:  Data labels:              Skip: 1    │
│  A                     Both                                          │
│  B                     Both                                          │
│  C                     Both                                          │
│  D                     Both                                          │
│  E                     Both                                          │
│  F                     Both                                          │
└──────────────────────────────────────────────────────────────────────┘
26-Nov-89  09:12 AM
```

Screen Display 7–4 Graph menu and current graph settings.

➤ The following Graph submenu is displayed:

Type	Lets you select the type of graph.
X	Sets the X-axis labels or values, or labels for pie chart.
A–F	Sets one to six data ranges for line, bar, XY, and stacked-bar graphs, or sets slice size and shading for a pie chart (ranges A and B).
Reset	Clears all graph settings.
View	Displays the current graph on screen.
Save	Saves the current graph as a file.
Options	Lets you refine the appearance of a graph.
Name	Lets you save the current graph settings with the worksheet.
Group	Sets all the data ranges for the graph.
Quit	Exits the Graph submenu.

The meaning of these options, or the *Graph settings*, is best learned by example. First you must specify the graph type. You want a Pie Chart.

- Select Type.

    ➤ The Graph Type submenu is displayed. You have the options of specifying a Line graph, a Bar chart, an XY graph, a Stacked bar chart, or a Pie chart.

- Select Pie. [handwritten: Stacked Bar]

    ➤ The Graph submenu is displayed again. In the setting box, the type specified is Pie.

Now you need to specify the range of cells to include in this pie chart. First specify the range of labels (X data range). These are the categories into which the pie is divided. Then specify the range of values (A data range). These values determine the slice size for each category. The X data range is the labels in column A, and the A data range is the values in column B.

- Select X.

    ➤ You are prompted to enter the *x* data range.

- Enter the range **A1.A7**. [handwritten: A5]

- Select A.

    ➤ You are prompted to enter the first data range.

- Enter the range **B1.B7**. [handwritten: B5]

You will now view the graph.

- Select View.

    ➤ The pie chart in Screen Display 7–5 is displayed.

The graph looks fine, but a title would improve it.

- Press any key to continue.

    ➤ You are still in the Graph submenu.

- Select Options.

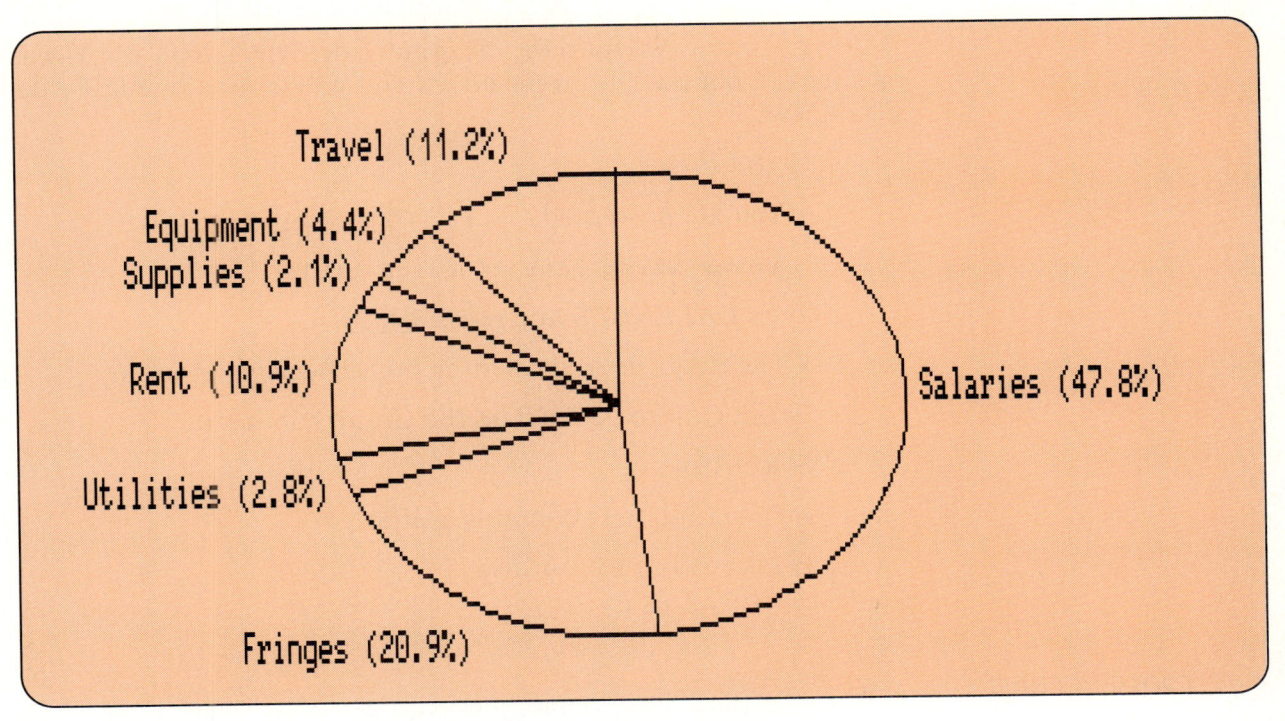

Screen Display 7–5   Pie chart.

➤ The following options are displayed:

Legend	Puts descriptive text in graph.
Format	Selects format for displaying numbers.
Titles	Puts titles in graph.
Grid	Puts grid lines in graph.
Scale	Sets upper and lower limits of graphs.
Color	Sets graph for printing without cross-hatching.
B & W	Adds cross-hatching to graphs.
Data-Labels	Uses worksheet labels as text in graph.
Quit	Exits Options submenu.

■ Select Titles.

➤ The following submenu is displayed:

First	Centers text at top of graph.
Second	Adds a second line to the title.
X-Axis	Places text below the horizontal axis.
Y-Axis	Places text sideways along the vertical axis.

CREATING PRESENTATION GRAPHICS   **155**

You can enter two lines for the graph title. The X-Axis and Y-Axis options are not used for a pie chart. You will enter a one-line title, **EXPENSES**.

- Select First.

    ➤ You are prompted:

    `Enter first line of graph title:`

- Type **EXPENSES** and press (ENTER).

    ➤ The first title in the setting box reflects your entry.

- Select Quit to get back to the Graph submenu.

- Select View.

    ➤ The graph now contains a title.

- Press any key to continue.

CROSSHATCHING A GRAPH

To make the data comparison even easier, you can crosshatch different portions of the pie chart. Lotus 1–2–3 has eight crosshatch patterns.

To generate a crosshatch, you use a B data range, which contains the same number of cells as the A and X ranges. In this data range, you enter a crosshatch code between 0 to 8 for each row in the B data range. (0 or 8 indicates an unshaded pie wedge.)

- Select Quit to exit the graph mode.

- In cells C1 through C7, enter values 1 through 7.

- Type **/GB** to specify the B data range.

- Specify the range **C1.C7**.

- View the graph. It should appear similar to Screen Display 7–6. As you can see, in this case crosshatching each segment made the graph harder to understand.

- Press any key to continue.

EXPENSES

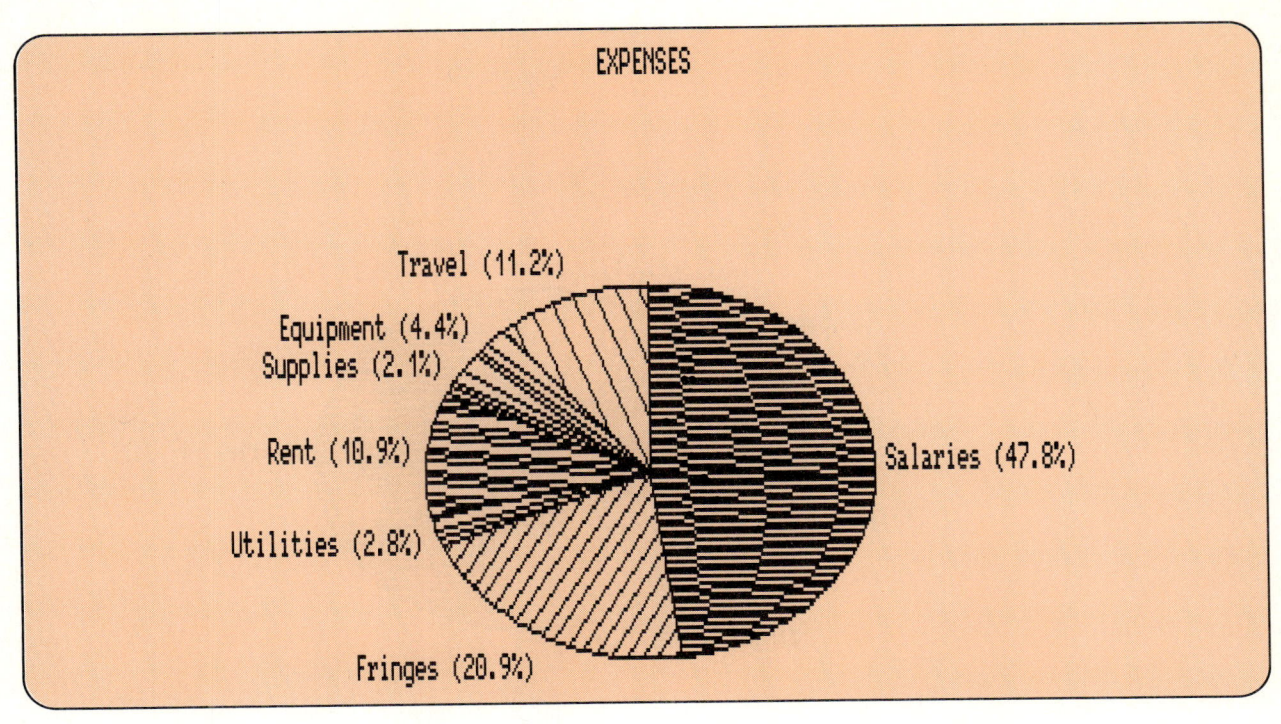

Screen Display 7–6 Pie chart with crosshatching.

EXPLODING A PIE CHART

Sometimes, for emphasis, you want to "explode" a portion of the pie chart; that is, you want to detach one wedge (or more) of the chart from the rest for emphasis. To do this, you simply add 100 to the code entered for crosshatches. For example, to explode the Rent wedge, change the entry at cell C4 from 4 to 104.

- Exit the graph mode, and change the entry at C4 to **104**.

Pressing the F10 function key allows you to look at the current graph (the one defined last) without going through the /Graph commands.

- Press the F10 function key to view the Pie Chart. It should be similar to the one depicted in Screen Display 7–7.
- Press any key to continue.

CREATING PRESENTATION GRAPHICS

EXPENSES

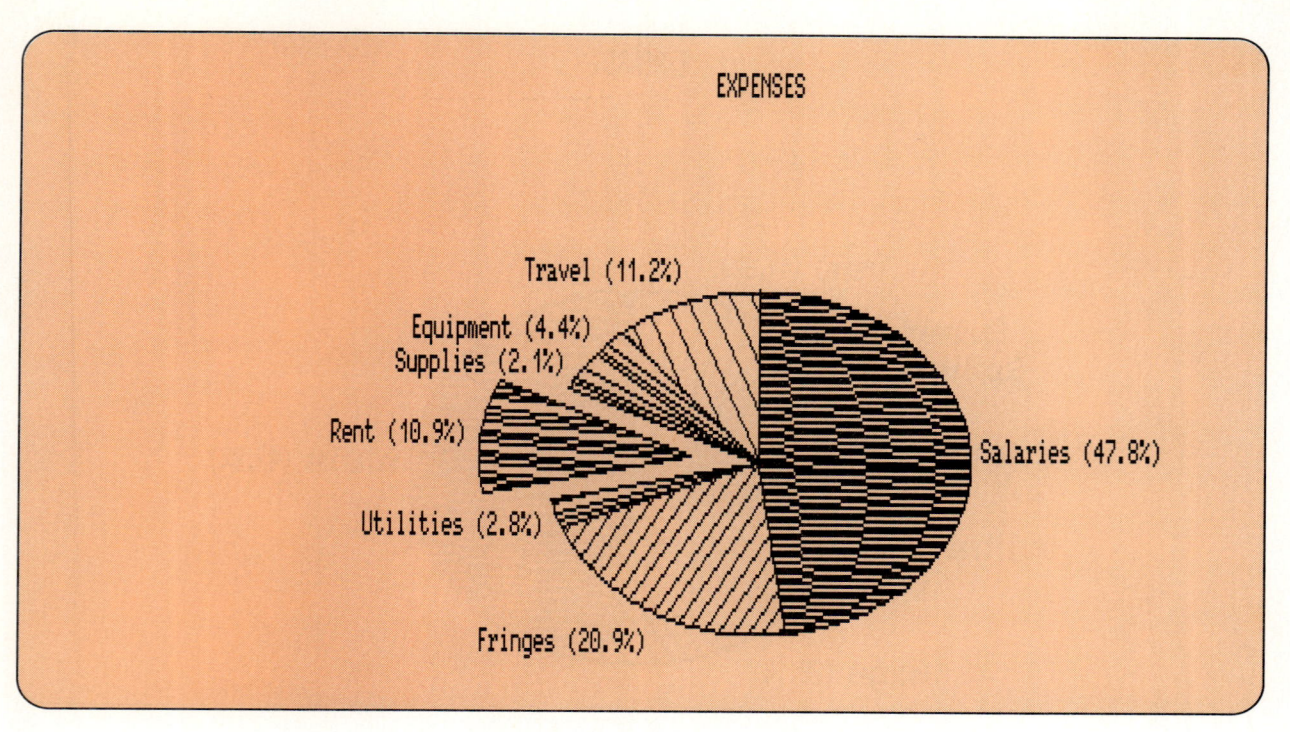

Travel (11.2%)
Equipment (4.4%)
Supplies (2.1%)
Rent (10.9%)
Utilities (2.8%)
Salaries (47.8%)
Fringes (20.9%)

Screen Display 7–7   Pie chart with exploded wedge.

Note: You can eliminate crosshatching or an exploding pie chart by clearing the B data range; that is, you can reset the B data range from the Graph mode. You should also clear those cells that were specified in the B data range using the Range Erase command.

NAMING A GRAPH

Since you may want to work with this graph later, you should name it. Naming a graph does not save the graph in memory; rather, the graph's settings are named and associated with the current spreadsheet. You can recreate the graph later simply by identifying its name. When you save the spreadsheet, the named settings are saved along with it.

- Type **/G** for Graph.
- Select Name.

158   USING LOTUS 1-2-3

➤ The following Graph Name submenu is displayed:

Use	Draws a graph using named settings.
Create	Stores the current graph settings.
Delete	Removes a stored graph name.
Reset	Removes all stored graph names.
Table	Lists all graphs that have been named for the current spreadsheet.

You will create a brand new name.

■ Select Create.

➤ You are prompted as follows:

`Enter graph name:`

A name can be up to 14 characters in length. If you enter an existing name, the old one will be overwritten. Use the name PIE1.

■ Type **PIE1** and press ENTER.

➤ The Graph submenu is displayed again.

The pie chart itself was not saved. <u>Its settings have been named</u> PIE1 and associated with the current spreadsheet. The chart will be saved when the spreadsheet is saved. You can later view the chart even if you have created other graphs in the meantime.

■ Exit the graph mode, and save the spreadsheet as file LOTUS4.

SAVING A GRAPH

The next step is to *save* the graph on disk. This is necessary if you want to print the graph later.

■ Type **/G** to access the Graph menu.

■ Select Save.

➤ The following message appears:

`Enter graph file name: B:`

You are asked to give the graph a name for storage on disk. A filename can be one to eight characters long and can include uppercase and lowercase letters, numbers, and the underscore

CREATING PRESENTATION GRAPHICS   **159**

character (_). Lotus 1-2-3 automatically assigns an extension .PIC to saved graph files.

You will save the graph as PIE1S.

- Type **PIE1S** and press (ENTER).

    ➤ The graph is saved on disk.

Reset the graph settings to get ready for the next graph.

- Select Reset.

    ➤ You have options to reset all the graph settings or just specific ones (such as the X data range or the A data range).

- Select Graph to reset all the settings.

- Select Quit to exit the graph mode.

BAR GRAPH

Another way to represent data graphically is using bar charts, or *histograms*. The heights of the bars in these charts indicate the magnitudes of the various items represented by the bars. Use the data you used for the pie chart once again.

- Type **/GTB** to specify Graph Type Bar.

    ➤ The Graph settings and menu options are displayed.

Now you have to specify the label range (the X data range, or the labels to be displayed horizontally along the bottom axis of the graph) and the values (the A data range).

- Select X.

- The labels you want are contained in column A, so specify the range **A1.A7**.

- Select A.

- The values you want to graph are in column B. Specify the range **B1.B7**.

- Enter a one-line title **BUDGET** (under Options Titles First).

160 USING LOTUS 1-2-3

- Select Quit to return to the Graph submenu.

You might have noticed that although you reset all the settings after you created the pie chart, the only settings that needed to be reset were the B data range and title. Also, you needed to change the graph type to bar.

- Select View.

  ➤ The bar graph is displayed. If you are using a CGA monitor in color mode, the labels on the *x*-axis overlap because of the limited screen resolution.

The height of each bar is determined by the values in column B, and the labels on the *x*-axis (horizontal line) are determined by the labels entered in column A.

If you are using a CGA monitor in color mode, you can shorten the labels to four or five letters each. You can do this without changing any graph settings.

- Exit the Graph menu.

PRACTICE TIME

If your graph display had overlapping labels on the *x*-axis, then shorten the labels as shown below. If your graph was OK, then skip to step 3 below.

1. Change the names of the categories in column A to the following abbreviations:

Salaries	-> Salry
Fringes	-> Frng
Utilities	-> Util
Rent	-> Rent
Supplies	-> Supp
Equipment	-> Equip
Travel	-> Trav

2. Display the graph using the (F10) function key to verify that the shortened names help improve the graph display.

3. Name this graph BAR1.

CREATING PRESENTATION GRAPHICS

4. Quit the Graph mode. (Do not Reset, since you will use these settings in just a while.)

Note that two graphs—PIE1 and BAR1—are now associated with the current spreadsheet. In fact, you can return to graph mode and use the pie chart you have already created.

- Type **/GN** for Graph Name.
- Select Use.
  > You are prompted to enter the name. A submenu displays all the named graphs that are associated with the spreadsheet.
- Highlight PIE1 and press (ENTER).
  > The pie chart is displayed.

  Note: If you are using the B data range in the Pie Chart for crosshatching and exploding the pie chart, you must be careful that the contents in the B data range cells have not changed.

- Press any key to continue.

■
PRACTICE TIME

1. Display the bar graph that was just created.
2. Press any key to continue.
3. Save the graph as **BAR1S**.
4. Quit the Graph menu.

The values in column B are for one month only, and you have decided to put budgets for two more months in columns C and D.

162 USING LOTUS 1-2-3

Furthermore, you would like to see the values for the second and third months on the same bar graph.

- Enter the following values in the spreadsheet.

	C	D	C (handwritten)	D (handwritten)
1	15250	15200	37.13	49.50
2	6610	6600	0	0
3	925	950	4.50	0
4	3450	3450	6.75	0
5	500	825	12.50	5.00
6	1475	1500	3.50	7.00
7	3800	2875		

- Type **/G** for Graph.

You have already specified that you want a bar graph. Also, the X and A data ranges have been specified. Now you need to specify the B data range (values for the second month, column C) and C data range (values for the third month, column D). You can do this with the Group option. In Lotus 1–2–3, the group option in the graph menu lets you specify several ranges at once, either as rows or columns.

- Select Group.

   ▶ The following message appears:

   `Enter group range: A1`

- Enter **A1.D7** [handwritten: O5] to specify the range of data in the worksheet to include in the graph.

   ▶ You are prompted to specify whether the data ranges are organized across rows or down columns.

- Select the menu option Columnwise.

   ▶ Notice that the graph settings for the X, A, B, and C data ranges have been set by the single Group command.

- Select View.

   ▶ The graph in Screen Display 7–8 is displayed.

BUDGET

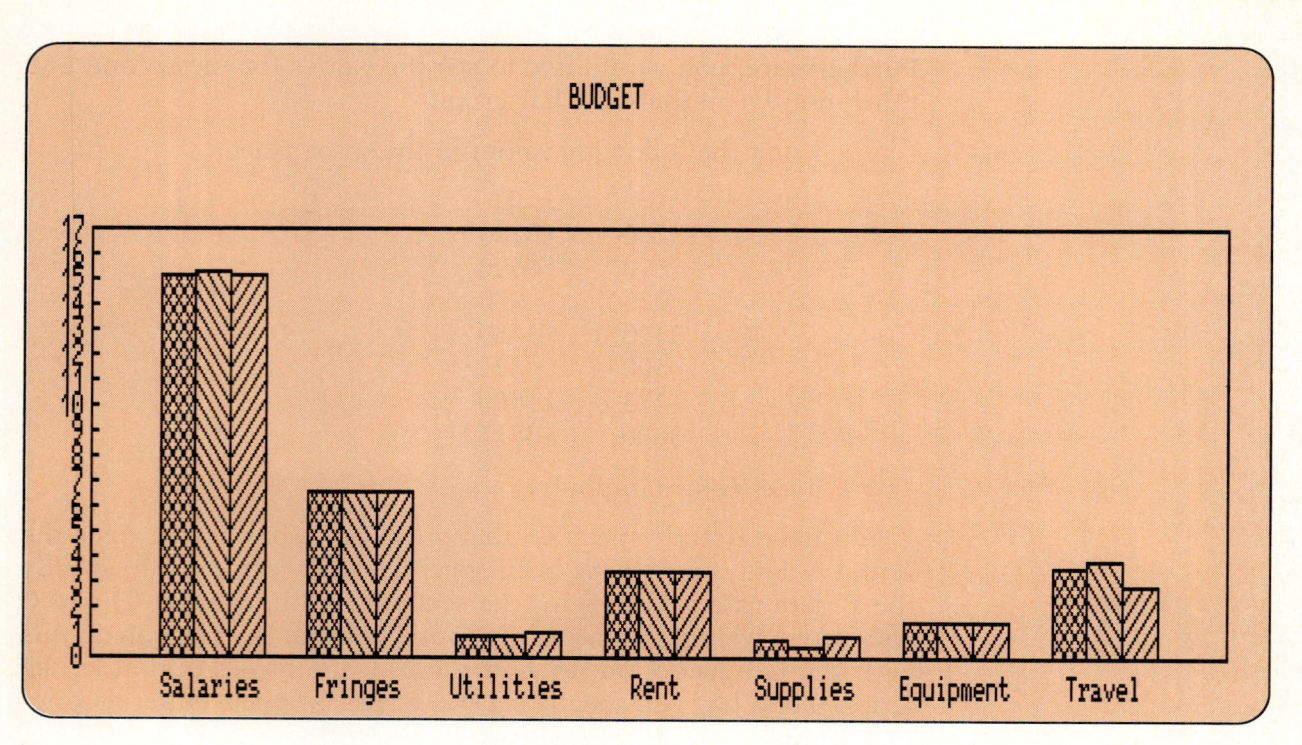

[Bar graph showing Salaries, Fringes, Utilities, Rent, Supplies, Equipment, Travel]

Screen Display 7–8 Bar graph with three data ranges.

The first bar in each category represents the value for the first month (A data range); the second bar, the second month (B data range); and the third bar, the third month (C data range). It would help someone looking at the graph if the graph contained some descriptive information. This can be done by adding a second line to the title, by labeling both the vertical and horizontal axes, and by creating a legend. A *legend* is descriptive text that identifies the patterns on a graph.

- Press any key to continue.

Assume that these figures are for months March, April, and May. You will first add a second line to the title.

- Select Options, Titles, then Second.

  ▶ You are prompted to enter the text for the second line of the title.

- Type **March–May** and press (ENTER).

Now add labels to the horizontal axis (*x*-axis) and vertical axis (*y*-axis).

- Select Title, then X-Axis.
- Type **Expense Categories** [Services] and press (ENTER).
- Select Title, then Y-Axis.
- Type **Amount** and press (ENTER).

You have to add legends for the A, B, and C data ranges.

- Select Legend, then A range.
- Type **March** [Seeding] and press (ENTER).
- Select Legend, then B range.
- Type **April** [Lawn Care] and press (ENTER).
- Select Legend, then C range.
- Type **May** [Cleanup] and press (ENTER).
- Select Quit to exit to the Graph second-level menu.
- Select View. You should see the graph in Screen Display 7–9.
- Press any key to continue.

PRACTICE TIME

1. Name this graph BAR2. [Page 165]
2. Save the graph as BAR2S, then exit the graph mode. [Page 165]
3. Save the spreadsheet as LOTUS5. This spreadsheet has three named graphs associated with it; when you retrieve the spreadsheet later, you will be able to view any of these graphs by giving the name (selecting the Name, then the Use options).

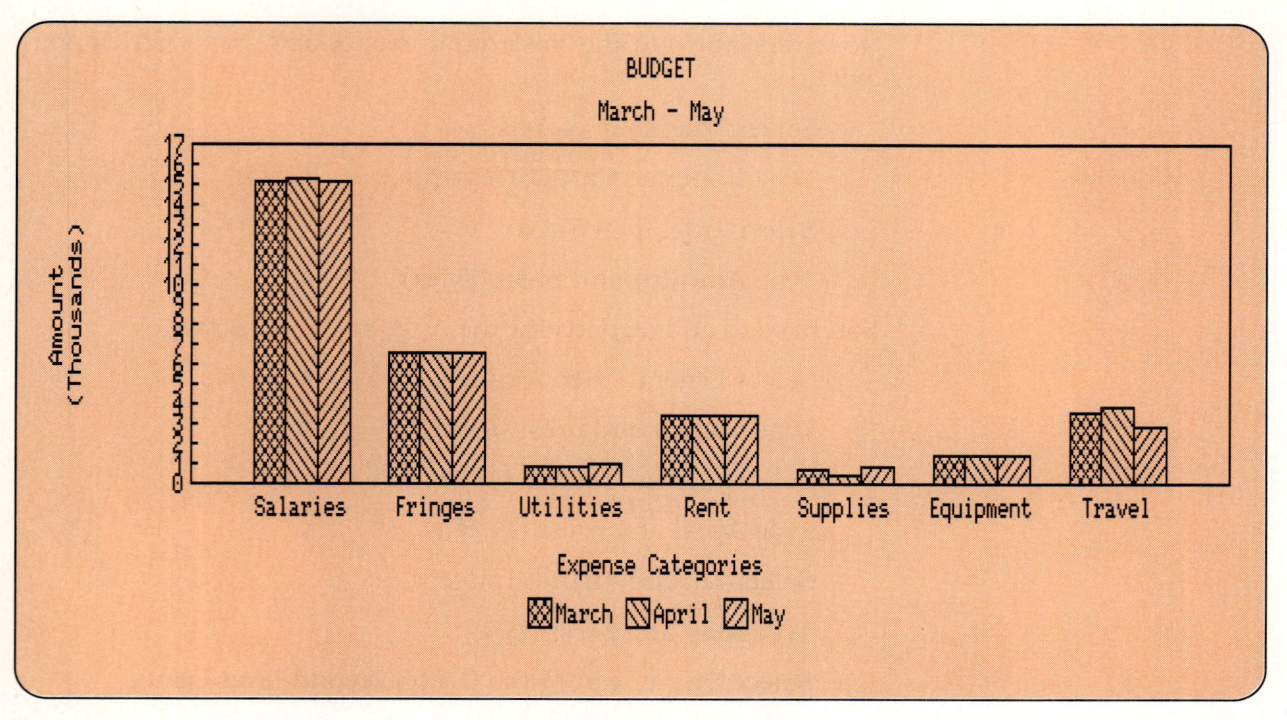

Screen Display 7–9 Bar graph with three data ranges and legends.

STACKED-BAR GRAPHS

Rather than showing bars (one for each month, in our example) side by side, the cumulative values can be seen by stacking the bars. You can switch to a stacked-bar graph by simply changing the graph type.

- Type **/GT**, then select Stack-Bar.
- Select View to look at it.
  - ▶ The graph of Screen Display 7–10 is displayed.
- Exit graph mode.
- Erase the spreadsheet (type **/WEY**).

If you want to stop the lesson at this point, you can: Simply follow the process given at the end of the previous lesson. When you start the next session on the computer, follow the starting-off process at the beginning of this lesson; then continue with the lesson.

166 USING LOTUS 1-2-3

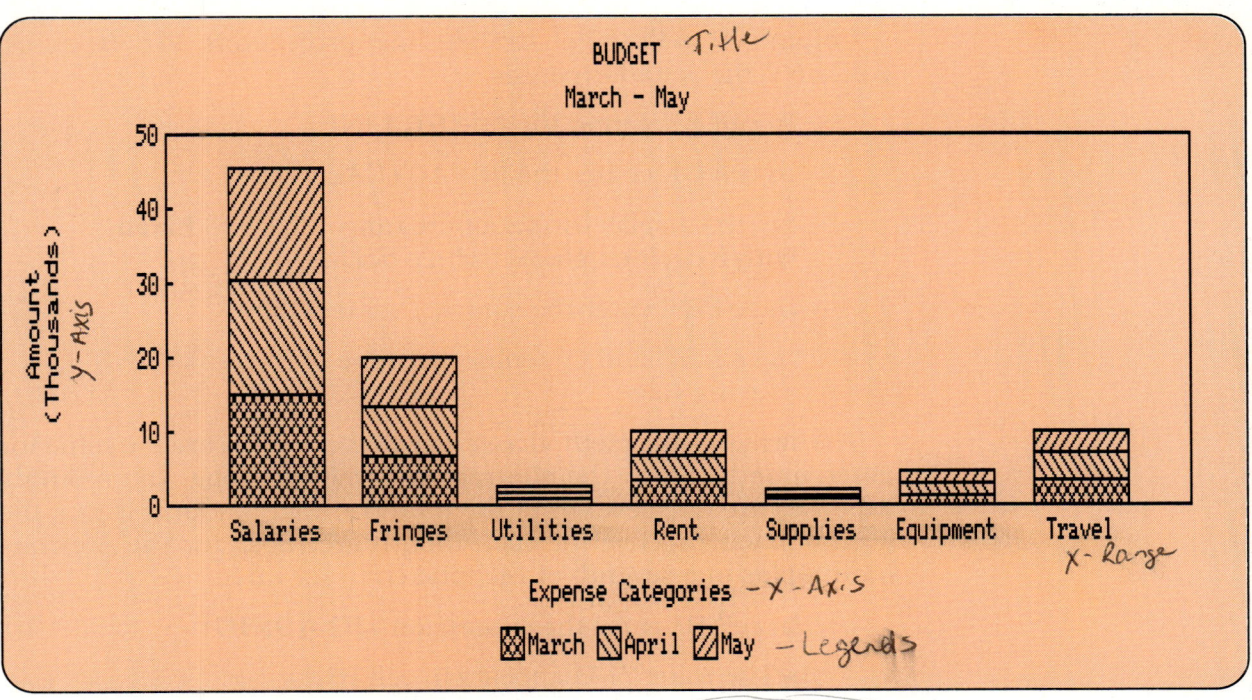

[Annotated figure: a stacked bar graph titled "BUDGET / March – May" with annotations — "Title" pointing to BUDGET, "Y-Axis" next to "Amount (Thousands)", "X-Axis" next to "Expense Categories", "X-Range" next to the category labels, and "Legends" next to the March/April/May key.]

Screen Display 7–10 *Stacked bar graph.*

LINE GRAPH

The heights of the bars in a bar graph represent relative values; the lines in a line graph connect points along the X data range. To learn the latter concept, you will create a spreadsheet to show the projected accumulated expenses (estimated by the straight-line method) and the actual accumulated expenses associated, in Susan's business, with the Madison contract.

The Madison contract began on August 1 and is scheduled to be completed on March 1. Total expenses are not to exceed $50,000. The spreadsheet will show the status of the project by month. In column A of the spreadsheet, you will enter the month names from August through March. Column B will show the projected accumulated expenses, and column C will contain the actual accumulated expenses.

- In column A, rows 1 through 9, enter the following: **MONTH**, **Aug**, **Sep**, **Oct**, **Nov**, **Dec**, **Jan**, **Feb**, and **Mar**.

CREATING PRESENTATION GRAPHICS   **167**

Column B will hold straight-line projections for expenses; column C the actual expenses.

- In cell B1, center the title **ST. LINE**.
- In cell C1, center the title **ACTUAL**.
- Set the display format of the range B2.C9 to **Fixed** with 0 decimal places (whole dollars).
- In cell B9, enter the contract value **50000**.
- In cells B2 and C2, enter the value of **0** (zero), the starting value.

The straight-line method assumes that expenses are the same for every month. Since the contract is 7 months long, the monthly expenses are one-seventh of the total contract amount. Hence the accumulated expense for each month are those for the previous month plus one-seventh of the total contract value.

- In cell B3 enter the expression **+B2+(B$9/7)**.
  ➤ The value 7143 appears in cell B3.

Cell B9 holds the total contract value. As the formula is being copied to other cells in column B, row 9 in the formula must not change. The $ before 9 instructs 1–2–3 not to change the row number as it is copied to other cells. That is, in cell B4, for example, the formula would be +B3+(B$9/7).

- Copy the formula at cell B3 to cells B4.B8.

Now enter the actual expenses for the project. Assume you are in mid-December and have figures for actual accumulated expenses only through the beginning of December.

- Enter the following values into column C in the appropriate rows.

Aug	0
Sep	9235
Oct	18825
Nov	26580
Dec	35320

➤ The worksheet should look like Screen Display 7–11.

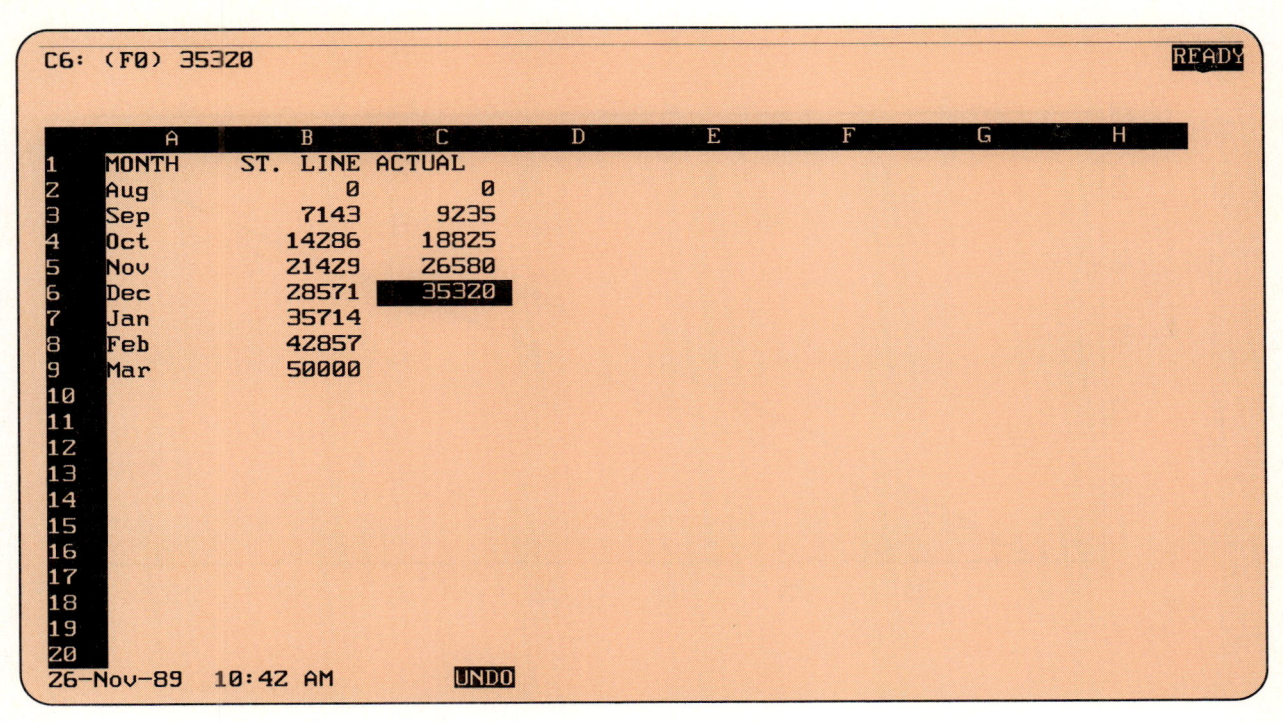

```
C6: (F0) 35320                                                    READY

        A         B         C         D         E         F         G         H
 1   MONTH     ST. LINE  ACTUAL
 2   Aug             0         0
 3   Sep          7143      9235
 4   Oct         14286     18825
 5   Nov         21429     26580
 6   Dec         28571     35320
 7   Jan         35714
 8   Feb         42857
 9   Mar         50000
10
11
12
13
14
15
16
17
18
19
20
26-Nov-89  10:42 AM        UNDO
```

Screen Display 7–11   Worksheet for line graph.

Now you are ready to create a line graph.

- Type **/GTL** for Graph Type Line.
- Select G, for Group.
- Enter the range **A2.C9**, then press (ENTER).
- Select Columnwise.
- Select View.
  ➤ The graph shown in Screen Display 7–12 will appear on your monitor.

Because the last value for actual expenses is for the month of December, it is relatively easy to identify which line is which in this graph. Suppose, however, that you could not tell which line represents projected expenses and which represents actual expenses. You would need a legend to identify the symbols. You will enter two legends, one for each line.

CREATING PRESENTATION GRAPHICS   **169**

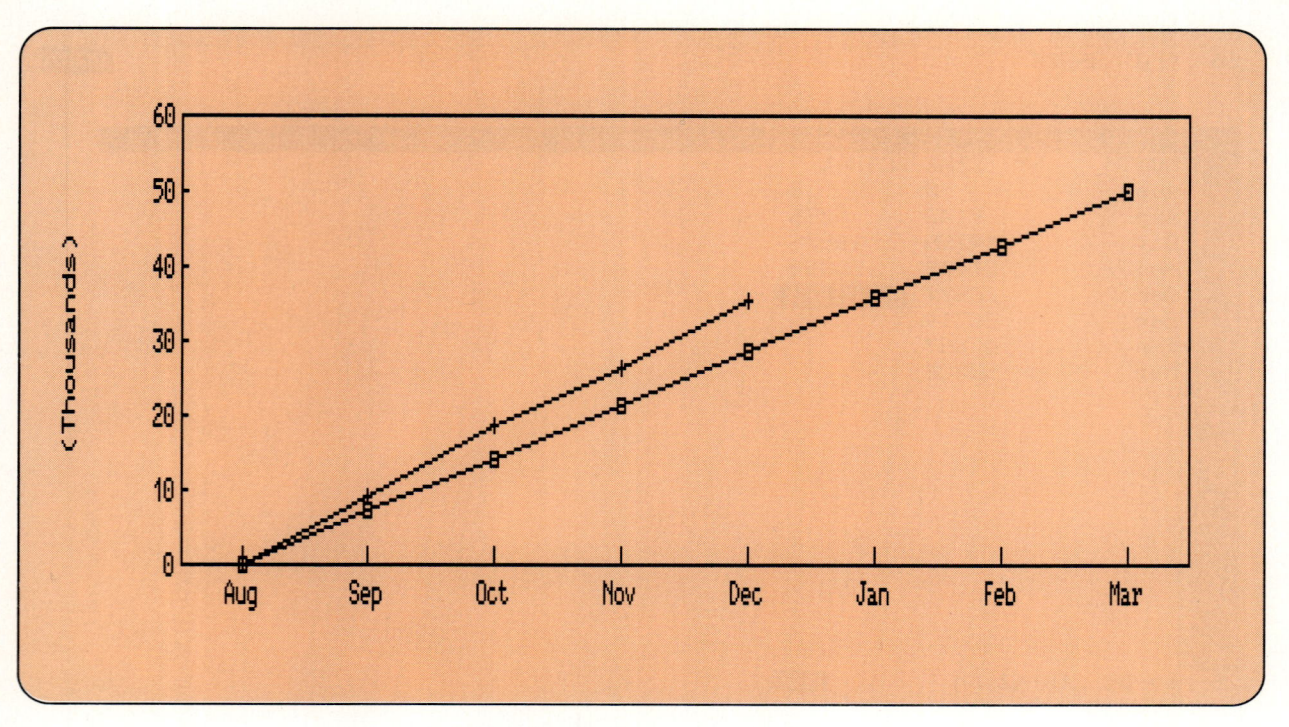

Screen Display 7–12   Line graph.

- Press any key to continue.
- Select Options, then Legend.
  ➤ You are prompted to identify which ranges need legends.

You may either enter the legends separately or, in this case, use the Range option to enter them from a range in the worksheet. The legend for the A data range is in cell B1; the legend for the B data range is in cell C1. To select the two legends with a single command, select Range, then specify the range that contains just the legends you want to use.

- Select Range.
- Enter **B1.C1** to select the range containing the two labels you want to use for legends.

170   USING LOTUS 1-2-3

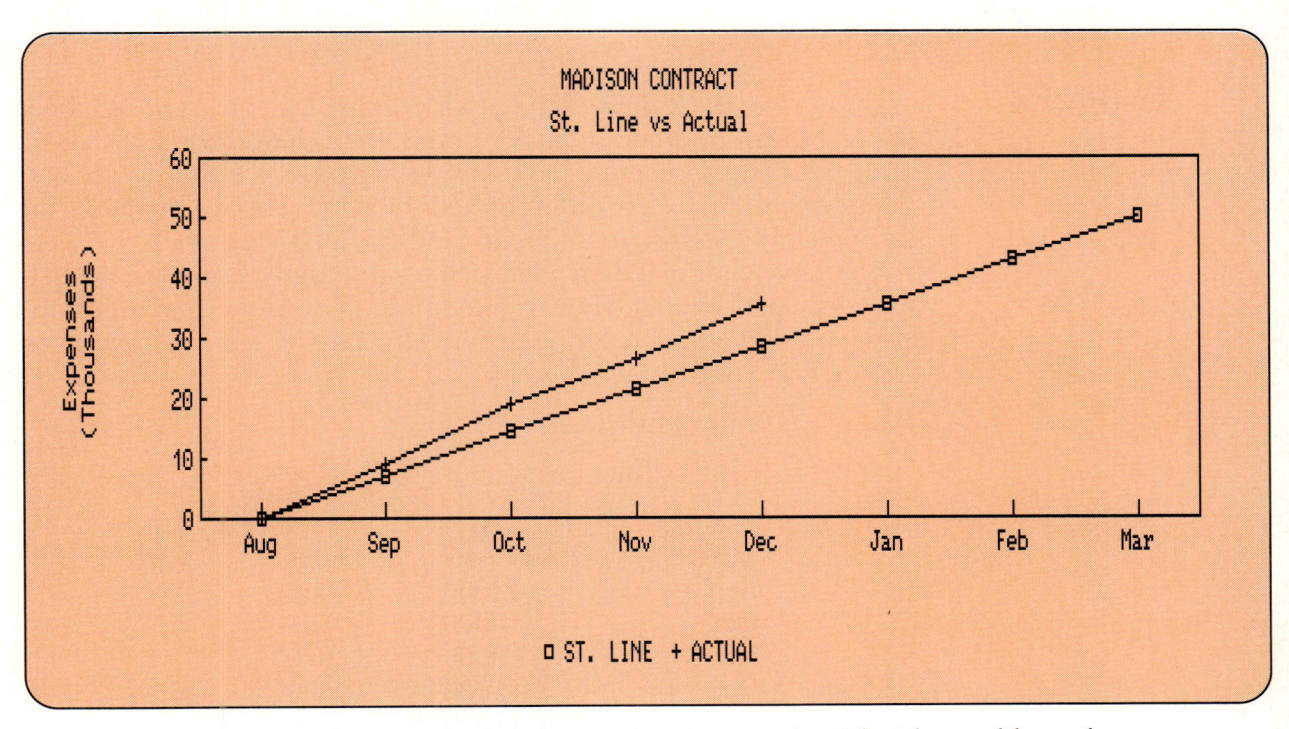

Screen Display 7–13   Line graph with titles and legends.

PRACTICE TIME

1. Enter the title **MADISON CONTRACT** on the first line and **St. Line vs. Actual** on the second line of the graph title.

2. Enter the title **Expenses** along the Y-axis.

3. View the graph shown in Screen Display 7–13.

4. Name the graph LINE1.

5. Save the graph as LINE1S, for printing later.

6. Exit the graph mode and save the spreadsheet as file LOTUS6.

CREATING PRESENTATION GRAPHICS

XY GRAPH

Up to now the *x* data range of all graphs has consisted of labels of one type or another. In an XY graph, the *x* data range consists of numbers. This is useful, for example, if you are trying to see the relationships between different sets of data. The following is an example of how you might create and use an XY graph.

You have conducted an advertising campaign during the past 10 months, spending widely varying amounts of money each month. You would like to determine the effectiveness of your campaign as reflected in your total sales.

- Erase the worksheet.
- Enter the following data.

	A	B	C
1	Month	Ad Costs	Sales
2	Sep	12000	230500
3	Oct	10000	225000
4	Nov	8500	220700
5	Dec	15000	290400
6	Jan	11000	195700
7	Feb	9500	187200
8	Mar	9000	193000
9	Apr	10500	220300
10	May	13000	240500
11	Jun	11500	225100

You will now create an XY Graph of this data.

- Type **/GTX** for Graph Type XY.

The X range is the values to be displayed along the *x*-axis (horizontal), and the A range is the values to be displayed along the *y*-axis (vertical). You want to show the advertising cost along the *x*-axis and sales amounts along the *y*-axis.

- Select Group.
- Enter the range **B2.C11**.
- Specify that the data are **Columnwise**.

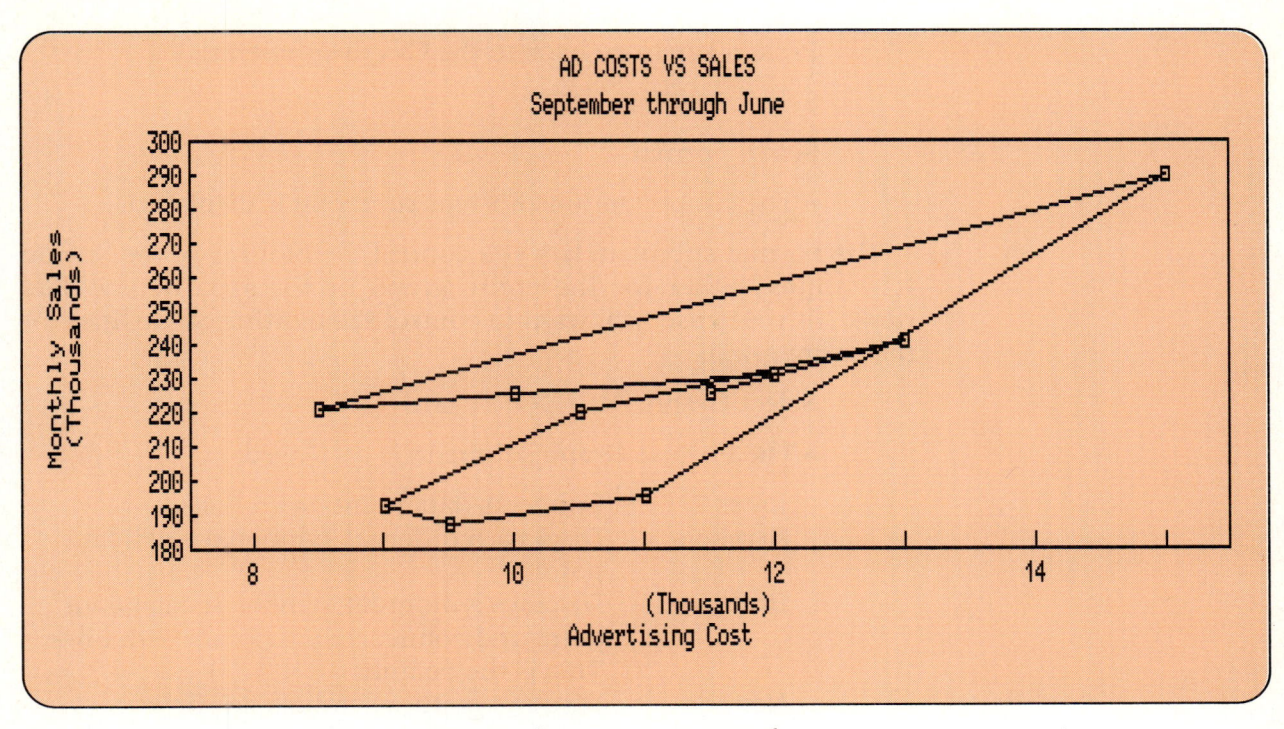

Screen Display 7–14   XY graph.

- Enter the title **AD COSTS VS. SALES** on the first line and **September Through June** on the second line of the graph title.
- Enter the title **Advertising Cost** along the *x*-axis and **Monthly Sales** along the *y*-axis.
- Select Quit to get out of the Option submenu.
- Select View.
    ➤ The graph in Screen Display 7–14 is displayed.

This graph seems rather confusing. The lines connect consecutive rows of data in the spreadsheet, and are not necessary in your analysis. An XY graph is used to make readily apparent the correlation between two sets of data. In this case you want to see if the money you spent on advertising had any effect on your sales. The chronological sequence has no bearing on your analysis; for this reason, you can remove the lines that connect the dots.

CREATING PRESENTATION GRAPHICS   **173**

- Press a key to go back to the Graph submenu.
- Select Options.
- Select Format.
  > The Graph Options Format submenu is displayed.

The Format submenu lets you control the plotting of the line on XY graphs, either for the entire graph or for a particular data range. In your case, you want to control the plotting of the lines for the entire graph.

- Select Graph.
  > The Format Graph submenu is displayed:

Lines	Connects data points with lines.
Symbols	Displays a different symbol at each data point.
Both	Displays a different symbol at each data point and connects data points with lines. This is the default.
Neither	Displays neither symbols nor lines.

- Select Symbols, then Quit to get out of this mode.
- Select Quit again to get out of Options.
- Select View.

With the connecting lines removed, there seems to be a correlation between advertising and sales. It looks like the more money is spent on advertising, the greater are the sales! Note that the ranges of both axes are automatically calculated so that the graph fills the page.

Although this graph contains enough information to tell a reader that it depicts the relationship between sales and advertising figures from September through June, the reader does not know which data point represents which month. You can label each data point with its month, using the information in column A.

- Press any key to continue.
- Select Options, then Data-Labels.

➤ You are prompted to enter the range of data to be labeled.

The data range you want to label is A (there is no other range since you have specified only the X and A data ranges in this XY graph).

■ Select A.

➤ You are prompted to enter the data-label range.

You are to specify the worksheet cells that hold the labels corresponding to the values in the A data range. As you know, column A contains the labels.

■ Enter the range in column A that contains the labels Sep through Jun and press (ENTER).

➤ A menu prompts you to specify the position of a label relative to its corresponding data point.

■ Select Above.

➤ The graph settings box reflects the data labels specified.

■ Select Quit twice.

■ Select View.

➤ The graph shown in Screen Display 7–15 is displayed.

PRACTICE TIME

1. Name this graph XY1.

2. Save the graph as XY1S for printing later.

3. Exit the graph mode and save the spreadsheet as LOTUS7.

MANUAL SCALING

Although Lotus 1–2–3 automatically scales the *x*- and *y*-axes, you have the option of manually scaling the axes.

CREATING PRESENTATION GRAPHICS **175**

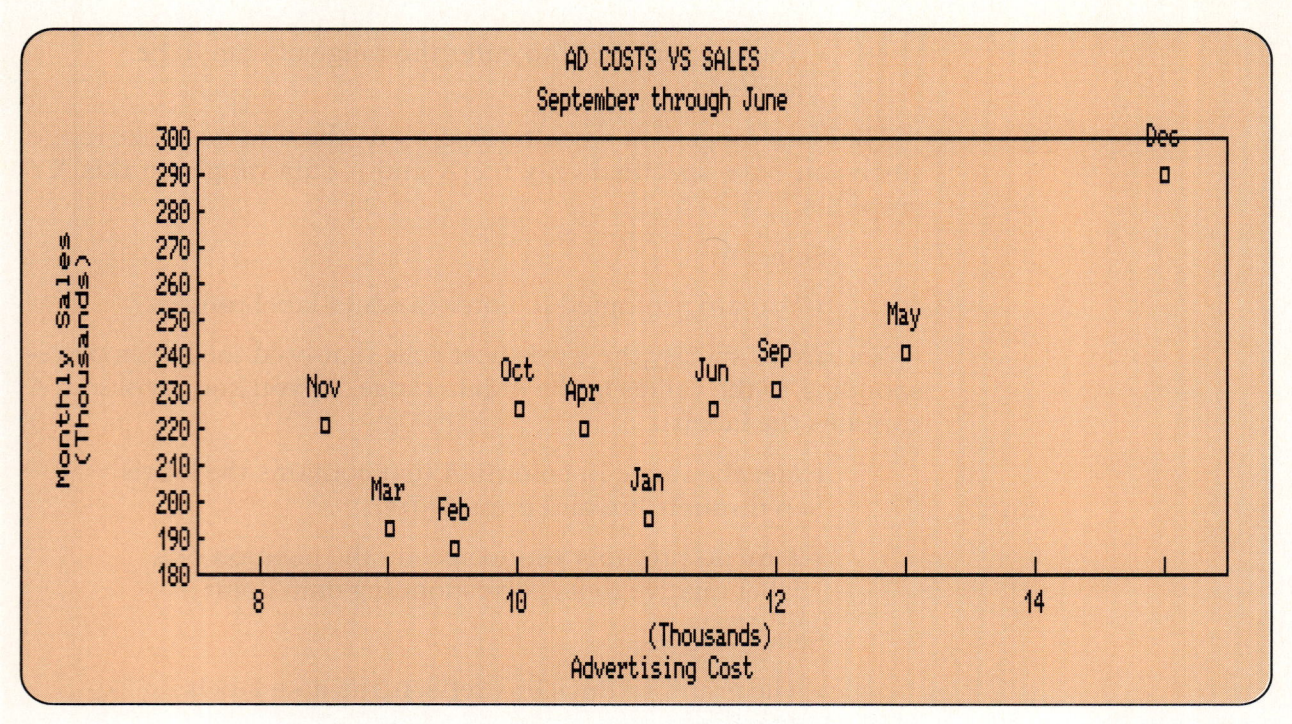

Screen Display 7–15 XY graph with symbols only and data-labels.

- Press the F10 function key.
  - ▶ The XY graph you prepared in the previous section is displayed on the screen.
  - ▶ Note that the scale on the *y*-axis (vertical) goes up to 300000 (indicated as 300 thousand).
- Press any key to continue.

Suppose you just noticed an error in a data entry. The sales for December, 290400, should be 256400.

- Change the entry for December sales to 256400.
- Press F10 again.
  - ▶ The graph is redrawn to reflect the modified data point, though this may be hard to see.
  - ▶ The scale on the *y*-axis now goes up to 260000 (260 thousand).
- Press any key to continue.

When the highest sales value was 290400, the highest value on the *y*-axis was 300000. Now, the highest value on the *y*-axis is 260000. Lotus 1–2–3 adjusts the axis range automatically. However, the Scale option lets you set the values manually or return to automatic scaling.

- Type **/GOS** for Graphics Options Scale.
- The Scale submenu display appears:

Y-Scale	Adjusts the scale of the *y*-axis.
X-Scale	Adjusts the scale of the *x*-axis.
Skip	Specifies a skip factor for the *x*-axis (rather than displaying every value on the *x*-axis, display every *n*th value).

For XY graphs, you can manually set the scales of both the *x*- and *y*-axes. For line, bar, and stacked-bar graphs, you can manually set the scales of the *y*-axis only. Scaling does not apply to pie charts. Also, the skip factor can be specified for the *x*-axis only, and only for line, bar, and stacked-bar graphs.

Here, you will set the *y*-axis range manually.

- Select Y-Scale.

    ▶ The following submenu is displayed:

Automatic	Sets scale automatically (the default option).
Manual	Manually sets the minimum and maximum values along the selected axis.
Lower	Specifies the minimum value to be displayed.
Upper	Specifies the maximum value to be displayed.
Format	Specifies the format of the displayed numbers.
Indicator	Displays or hides the scale indicator.
Quit	Exits the submenu.

- Select Manual.

The *y*-axis displays values ranging from 180000 to 260000. Change them so that they range from 150000 to 300000.

- Select Lower. Type **150000** and press (ENTER).
- Select Upper. Type **300000** and press (ENTER).
  ➤ The graph settings changed with each entry you made.
- Select Quit twice to return to the Graph menu.
- Select View.
  ➤ Notice that the values displayed along the *y*-axis now range from 150000 to 300000.
- Press any key to continue.

GRIDS

Sometimes it is useful to add grids to bar, line, or XY graphs to aid the eye when comparing values.

- Select Options, then Grid.
  ➤ You have a choice of horizontal grids, vertical grids, both horizontal and vertical grids, or no grids.
- Select Horizontal.
- Select Quit, then View.
  ➤ Horizontal grid lines are drawn at each value on the *y*-axis.
- Press any key to continue.
- Exit the graph mode.

PRINTING GRAPHS

Graphs are not printed using the 1–2–3 program, but with the PrintGraph utility. You do not print graphs from worksheet (.WK1) files. Instead, you print graphs which have been saved with the /Graph Save command. When you save a graph, 1–2–3 creates a disk file with the .PIC extension.

All the graphs you will print were previously saved to disk. To print a graph, you must exit the 1–2–3 mode of Lotus and enter the PrintGraph mode.

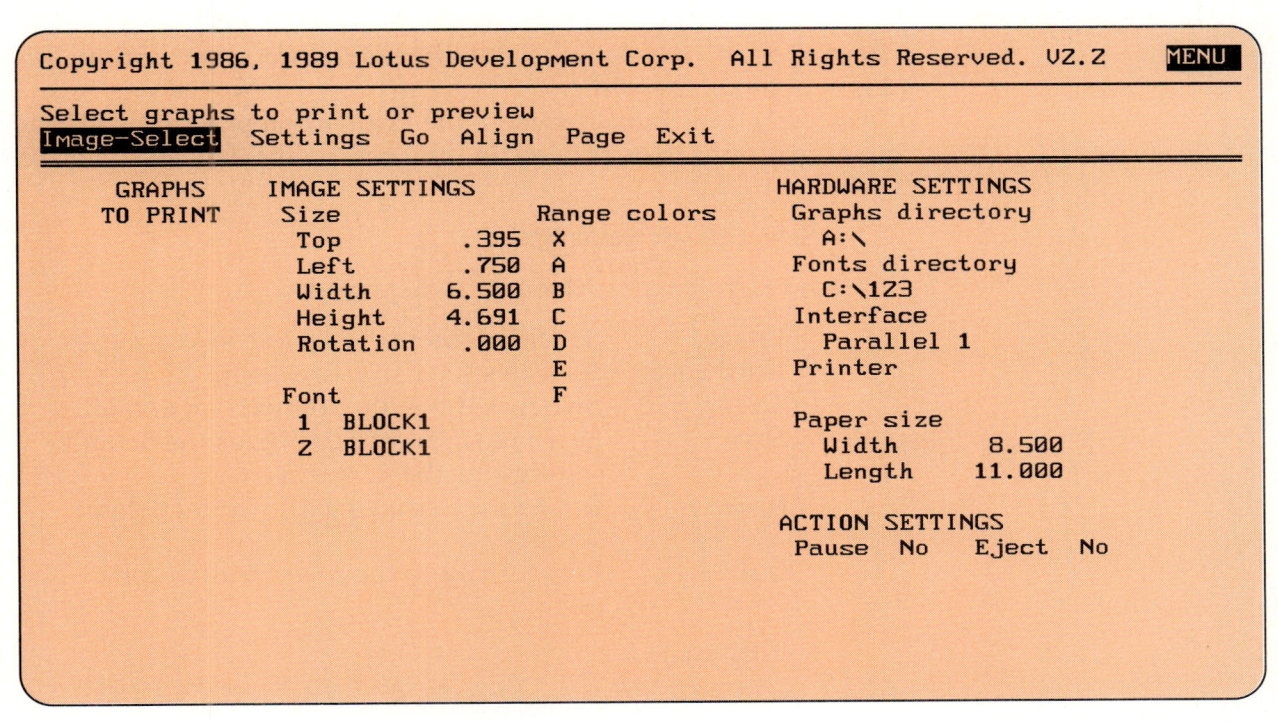

```
Copyright 1986, 1989 Lotus Development Corp.   All Rights Reserved. V2.2   MENU
Select graphs to print or preview
Image-Select  Settings  Go  Align  Page  Exit

      GRAPHS    IMAGE SETTINGS                    HARDWARE SETTINGS
      TO PRINT  Size               Range colors   Graphs directory
                  Top       .395   X                A:\
                  Left      .750   A              Fonts directory
                  Width    6.500   B                C:\123
                  Height   4.691   C              Interface
                  Rotation  .000   D                Parallel 1
                                   E              Printer
                Font               F
                  1  BLOCK1                       Paper size
                  2  BLOCK1                         Width     8.500
                                                    Length   11.000

                                                  ACTION SETTINGS
                                                  Pause  No   Eject  No
```

Screen Display 7–16   PrintGraph main menu and settings screen.

- To exit 1–2–3, type **/QY**, then **Y** to indicate you do not want to save the changes to the current worksheet.

  ➤ The 1–2–3 Access System screen is displayed.

- Select PrintGraph.

  ➤ The PrintGraph menu appears, as shown in Screen Display 7–16. Six options are available from the main menu:

Image-Select	Selects pictures to be printed.
Settings	Defines hardware and graph settings.
Go	Prints the selected graphs.
Align	Sets printer to top of page.
Page	Advances printer to top of next page.
Exit	Exits PrintGraph to the 1–2–3 Access System.

The PrintGraph menu allows great flexibility in setting up exactly how a graph will be printed on the paper. However, you will

CREATING PRESENTATION GRAPHICS   **179**

accept most of the defaults this time. Explore other options on your own at another time.

First, you must indicate where the PrintGraph program will find the saved graphs to be printed, in this case, on the data disk in drive B.

- Select the Settings option.

    ➤ The following submenu is displayed:

Image	Specifies colors, fonts, and size.
Hardware	Specifies the hardware setup.
Action	Switches the Action options on and off.
Save	Saves the current Settings as the default settings for the next session.
Reset	Resets the Settings to the initial default settings.
Quit	Returns you to the main PrintGraph menu.

- Select Hardware.

    ➤ The submenu displays the following options:

Graphs-Directory	Specifies the drive:\path containing graphs.
Fonts-Directory	Specifies the drive:\path containing fonts.
Interface	Specifies the printer interface.
Printer	Specifies the type of graphics printer in use.
Size-Paper	Sets the paper size.
Quit	Returns to previous menu.

- Select Graphs-Directory.

    ➤ The following message appears:

    ```
    Enter directory containing graph (.PIC) files:
    A:\
    ```

- Type **B:** and press (ENTER).

    Note: It is assumed that all other software connections are correct, especially the fonts directory.

```
Copyright 1986, 1989 Lotus Development Corp.  All Rights Reserved. V2.2    POINT
Select graphs to print

    GRAPH FILE  DATE      TIME     SIZE
    ─────────────────────────────────────    Space bar marks or unmarks selection
    BAR2S       11-26-89  10:36    6521      ENTER selects marked graphs
    LINE1S      11-26-89  10:54    1046      ESC exits, ignoring changes
    PIE1S       11-26-89  10:21    3185      HOME moves to beginning of list
    XY1S        11-26-89  11:04    1011      END moves to end of list
                                             ↑ and ↓ move highlight
                                                 List will scroll if highlight
                                                 moved beyond top or bottom
                                             GRAPH (F10) previews marked graph
```

Screen Display 7–17   Image-Select screen.

- Select Quit twice to return to the PrintGraph main menu.

Now you select (specify) the graph file or files to be printed.

- Select Image-Select.

    ➤ A screen display, such as shown in Screen Display 7–17, appears, showing the graph files on disk and several options.

On the left side of the screen is a list of the graph files available on the data disk. On the right side are the commands available in the Select option. You will first select PIE1S.

- Press the ⍗ key, if necessary, to highlight PIE1S, then press the SPACE BAR.

    ➤ A # sign appears in front of PIE1S, indicating that this file has been marked for selection.

As explained on the right side of the screen, the SPACE BAR turns the selection bar on and off. When you press (ENTER), those files marked for selection are selected to be printed.

- Press (ENTER).
  - ➤ The PrintGraph main menu reappears.
  - ➤ The name PIE1S appears under GRAPHS TO PRINT.
- Make sure that the printer is on and ready to print.
- Select Align, then Go to initiate the graphic printout.
  - ➤ The printer begins to print the graph. This is a slow process; you must wait several seconds before the printing begins. It may take a few minutes for the computer to print the graph.

PRACTICE TIME

If time allows, print the other graphs that were saved in this lesson. Each time, select Image-Select, use the SPACE BAR to mark or unmark files for selection, then press (ENTER). You can then select Go.

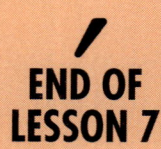

END OF LESSON 7

- When finished, select Exit, then Yes to exit the PrintGraph mode.
- Continue to exit to DOS.
- Remove the disk from the disk drive.
- Turn off the monitor, computer, and printer.

SUMMARY

In this lesson, many of the terms and concepts you need to know in order to use the spreadsheet graphics feature are discussed:

- A pie chart is a graph consisting of a circle divided into slices, much like a pie, and is generally used to show how resources are divided between categories.

- A bar graph uses bar heights to indicate the magnitude of the items represented.

- A line graph connects points in the *x*-range and is used to show trends of one or more quantities.

- An XY graph is a line graph that shows correlation between two sets of values.

- When a graph is named, its settings are identified with a name and the name is associated with the spreadsheet. When the spreadsheet is saved, the settings are associated with the spreadsheet for later viewing.

- A pie graph can be displayed with crosshatching by defining a B data range that contains values from 0 to 8 in each of its cells. Furthermore, the graph can be made into an exploding pie graph (where one or more sections of the pie is detached for emphasis) by adding 100 to the appropriate cell value in the B data range.

- A graph can be saved as a .PIC file on disk for later printing.

- The *x*- and *y*-axis scales can be set automatically or manually.

- Horizontal and vertical grids can be added to graphs.

- Saved graphs can be printed using the PrintGraph utility that comes with Lotus 1–2–3.

- The following commands are discussed:

(F10)	Views current graph.
/GN	Graph Name—Associates graph settings with a name.

CREATING PRESENTATION GRAPHICS

/GOD	Graph Options Data-Labels—Enters labels for each data point on a graph.
/GOG	Graph Options Grid—Displays horizontal and/or vertical grids on a graph.
/GOL	Graph Options Legend—Enters descriptive text to identify types of shading or symbols used in a graph.
/GOS	Graph Options Scale—Sets scale manually or automatically.
/GOT	Graph Options Titles—Specifies titles to be included in the graph.
/GS	Graph Save—Saves the graph on a disk.
/GT	Graph Type—Specifies the type of graph.
/GX, /GA–/GF	Graph ranges X, A–F—Specifies various cells to use in generating a graph.
/GG	Graph Group—Specifies all graph ranges at once.
/GV	Graph View—Displays a graph on the screen.

REVIEW QUESTIONS

1. Name four (out of five) kinds of graphs that can be created using 1-2-3. *Line, Bar, Stack Bar, Pie*

2. For a pie chart, what two ranges must be specified? *X data range, A data range*

3. What is the difference between *naming* a graph and *saving* a graph? Explain. *Naming a graph is mostly for viewing & association w/ worksheet. Saving a graph is mostly for printing*

4. What is a legend? *Enters descriptive text to identify types of shading used in a graph*

5. What are the *x*-axis and *y*-axis? *x-axis places text below the horizontal axis* *y-axis places text sideways along the vertical axis*

6. Explain the difference between a line graph and an XY graph. *XY graph shows correlation between 2 sets of values*

7. How do you manually set the scales on the *y*-axis of an XY graph? */GOS Select Y axis Manual*

8. How do you eliminate the lines that connect symbols in a line graph? GOF S

9. What are data-labels? When would you use them?
To label each data point

10. What does the (F10) function key do?
Views current graph

EXERCISES

1. a) Retrieve the spreadsheet EX6_1 from Lesson 6.
   b) Using the row totals (the amount each friend borrowed from you in the four-week period), create, name, and save a bar graph, a pie chart and a line graph.
   c) Print the graphs.
   d) Save the spreadsheet as EX7_1.

2. a) Retrieve the spreadsheet EX6_2 from Lesson 6.
   b) Using the average for each student, create, name, and save a bar graph and a line graph.
   c) Print the graphs.
   d) Save the spreadsheet as EX7_2.

LESSON 8
USING A SPREADSHEET AS A DATABASE

OBJECTIVES

Upon completion of the material presented in this lesson, you should be able to:

- Understand the database terminology used in Lotus 1–2–3
- Sort data on a spreadsheet
- Query data in the Lotus 1–2–3 database

STARTING OFF

Start Lotus 1–2–3 so that the blank spreadsheet is displayed on the screen. Also, insert the data disk in drive B and change the file directory to B.

DATA MANAGEMENT

The previous four lessons dealt with the fundamentals of setting up and using a Lotus 1–2–3 spreadsheet: entering labels, numbers, and formulas; copying and moving data; setting column widths and formats; inserting rows/columns; and creating and using graphics. In this lesson, the focus is on storing, sorting, and retrieving your data, or *data management*.

A file used as a *database* stores and manages useful historical data that needs to be referred to again and again. Examples of business databases include inventory files and records of customers, suppliers (vendors), and employees. In this lesson you will make and use a database to keep track of inventory.

A database is any collection of *records* about a particular topic. In a customer database, each record contains information about a customer; in an employee database each record holds information about an employee; and in an inventory database each record has information about a product. In a Lotus 1-2-3 database, each row of a spreadsheet is a record.

Each record is composed of a series of related *fields*. A field is the smallest unit of data in a database. A customer record may have

USING A SPREADSHEET AS A DATABASE

fields for that customer's number, name, address, balance, and credit rating. An inventory record may have fields for item number, quantity, and description. In a Lotus 1–2–3 database, each column of a spreadsheet is a field.

A database is only part of the whole spreadsheet. It takes up only as many columns as there are fields and only as many rows as there are records, plus one. The first row in the database holds the *field names,* which are descriptive names of the contents of the corresponding columns. In the remaining rows of the database, you can enter either numeric data (called *values* in previous lessons) or text data (called *labels* in previous lessons). *Numeric data* consists of numbers, expressions, functions, and anything else that can be used in mathematical calculations. *Text data,* also called *string data,* cannot be used in calculations, even if it consists of numeric characters. Note that there should be no extra rows between field names and the database (no hyphens or other means of separating the names from the data).

AN INVENTORY APPLICATION

You manufacture and sell electrical surge/spike suppressors (SSS) and uninterrupted power supplies (UPS), and you want to set up an inventory list, using Lotus 1–2–3.

Each item in your inventory represents a record. Each record has these fields: Part, Type (SSS or UPS), Description (details), (shipping) Weight, Cost (to you), Price (cost to the buyer), Quantity (in stock), and Location (in your warehouse).

The following is the list of inventory items:

PART	TYPE	DESCRIPTION	WEIGHT	COST	PRICE	QUAN-TITY	LOCA-TION
L1003	UPS	200 watt capacity	18.75	195.00	389.00	325	A-8
L1011	UPS	325 watt capacity	36	240.00	479.00	72	C-1
L1029	UPS	450 watt capacity	38.5	315.00	625.00	46	B-1
L1037	UPS	1000 watt capacity	80	625.00	1249.00	12	A-2
L0005	SSS	Modem surge protector	1	30.00	59.90	880	A-6
L1045	UPS	200 watt capacity	15	185.00	369.00	470	C-8
L1052	UPS	325 watt capacity	32	230.00	459.00	112	B-3
L1060	UPS	450 watt capacity	33	300.00	599.00	35	A-3
L1078	UPS	675 watt capacity	68	450.00	899.00	60	B-6
L0013	UPS	1800 watt capacity	14	150.00	299.00	0	A-5
L0047	SSS	2-outlet box	1	25.00	49.95	1480	C-4

L0054 SSS	4-outlet strip	3	29.00	57.95	2257	A-7
L0062 SSS	6-outlet strip	3	33.00	65.95	1326	B-7
L0104 SSS	2-outlet box	5	33.00	64.95	775	C-7
L0112 SSS	6-outlet strip	5	38.00	75.95	1843	A-4
L4502 SSS	Power controller	8.25	50.00	99.85	422	C-5
L4510 SSS	Power controller	9.25	85.00	169.95	633	B-9

■ PRACTICE TIME

Set up the worksheet for the inventory application.

1. Enter field names in row 1. Enter them centered, left-justified, or right-justified, according to your own taste.

2. Determine the appropriate column widths for all fields. Each field should be wide enough to accommodate the longest expression of possible data.

3. In *numeric* fields, enter data in an appropriate data-format type (integer, currency, etc.).

4. In *text* fields, enter data left-justified or centered.

5. Enter the data in the order shown in the list of inventory items, as shown in Screen Display 8–1.

6. Save the spreadsheet with filename LOTUS8.

SORTING

Lotus 1–2–3 allows you to rearrange the records in a file in whatever order you want. You can arrange records in regular or reverse alphabetical order (A to Z or Z to A) or in ascending or descending numerical order, based on any field you select. Such rearranging of records is called *sorting*.

Sort the file, according to Part (first field), in ascending order.

- Type **/D** for the Data command.

   ➤ The following Data submenu is displayed:

Fill	Fills a range with a sequence of values.
Table	Creates a table of values.

USING A SPREADSHEET AS A DATABASE

```
H18: 'B-9                                                          READY

      A      B         C              D      E       F       G       H
 1  PART   TYPE    DESCRIPTION      WEIGHT  COST    PRICE  QUANTITY LOCATION
 2  L1003  UPS   200 watt capacity   18.75 195.00   389.00    325   A-8
 3  L1011  UPS   325 watt capacity   36    240.00   479.00     72   C-1
 4  L1029  UPS   450 watt capacity   38.5  315.00   625.00     46   B-1
 5  L1037  UPS  1000 watt capacity   80    625.00  1249.00     12   A-2
 6  L0005  SSS   modem surge protector 1    30.00    59.90    880   A-6
 7  L1045  UPS   200 watt capacity   15    185.00   369.00    470   C-8
 8  L1052  UPS   325 watt capacity   32    230.00   459.00    112   B-3
 9  L1060  UPS   450 watt capacity   33    300.00   599.00     35   A-3
10  L1078  UPS   675 watt capacity   68    450.00   899.00     60   B-6
11  L0013  UPS  1800 watt capacity   14    150.00   299.00      0   A-5
12  L0047  SSS   2-outlet box         1     25.00    49.95   1480   C-4
13  L0054  SSS   4-outlet strip       3     29.00    57.95   2257   A-7
14  L0062  SSS   6-outlet strip       3     33.00    65.95   1326   B-7
15  L0104  SSS   2-outlet box         5     33.00    64.95    775   C-7
16  L0112  SSS   6-outlet strip       5     38.00    75.95   1843   A-4
17  L4502  SSS   power controller     8.25  50.00    99.85    422   C-5
18  L4510  SSS   power controller     9.25  85.00   169.95    633   B-9
19
20
26-Nov-89  11:32 AM      UNDO                                      CAPS
```

Screen Display 8–1 Database of inventory.

Sort	Sorts records in ascending or descending order.
Query	Finds all records that satisfy given criteria.
Distribution	Calculates frequency distribution of the values in a range.
Matrix	Multiplies and inverts matrices.
Regression	Calculates linear regression.
Parse	Converts a column of long labels into a range of labels or numbers.

- Select Sort.

    ▶ The Data Sort menu options and Sort Settings appear, as in Screen Display 8–2.

The Data Sort menu options are as follows:

Data-Range	Specifies the range to be sorted.
Primary-Key	Specifies the field (column) used to sort the records.

```
H18: 'B-9                                                          MENU
Data-Range  Primary-Key  Secondary-Key  Reset  Go  Quit
Select records to be sorted
                          ┌──────── Sort Settings ────────┐
    Data range:

    Primary key:
      Field (column)
      Sort order

    Secondary key:
      Field (column)
      Sort order

11  L0013 UPS  1800 watt capacity   14  150.00  299.00     0  A-5
12  L0047 SSS  2-outlet box          1   25.00   49.95  1480  C-4
13  L0054 SSS  4-outlet strip        3   29.00   57.95  2257  A-7
14  L0062 SSS  6-outlet strip        3   33.00   65.95  1326  B-7
15  L0104 SSS  2-outlet box          5   33.00   64.95   775  C-7
16  L0112 SSS  6-outlet strip        5   38.00   75.95  1843  A-4
17  L4502 SSS  power controller   8.25   50.00   99.85   422  C-5
18  L4510 SSS  power controller   9.25   85.00  169.95   633  B-9
19
20
26-Nov-89  11:33 AM
```

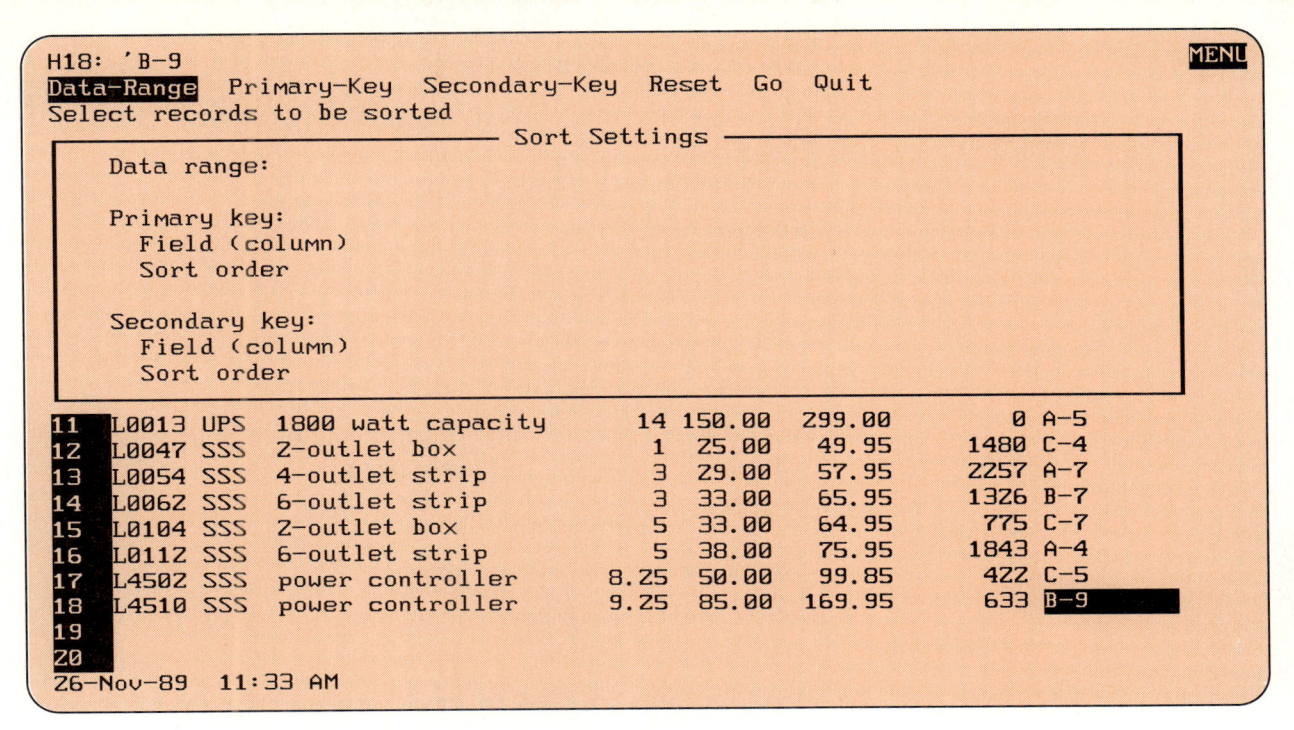

Screen Display 8–2   Sort settings and sort menu.

Secondary-Key	Specifies a second field (column) to sort when there are identical primary-key entries.
Reset	Clears the sort settings.
Go	Performs the sort.
Quit	Exits the sort mode.

Your first step is to specify the data range.

■ Select Data-Range.

➤ A message like the following appears:

Enter data range: H18

Just as for printing, you need to specify the top left-corner and bottom right-corner cells of the range to be sorted. Since you want to sort the entire database (except the headings on row 1), the data range is A2.H18.

USING A SPREADSHEET AS A DATABASE   **191**

- Type **A2.H18** and press (ENTER).

  ➤ The Sort Settings box indicates the data range has been set.
  ➤ The menu is displayed again.

- Select Primary-Key.

  ➤ The control panel displays the following message:

  ```
  Primary sort key: H18
  ```

Your primary key is the Part field, or column A.

- Place the cell pointer anywhere in the part field column (column A), and press (ENTER).

  ➤ The control panel prompts:

  ```
  Sort order (A or D): D
  ```

- Type **A** and press (ENTER), since you want to sort the records in ascending order.

The secondary key is used in case of a tie. For example, employees are often sorted in alphabetical order. The primary key is Last Name; the secondary key, First Name. If two employees have the same last name, then the secondary key is used to break the tie. You do not need a secondary key in this example, because all items have unique part numbers.

- Select Go.

  ➤ The worksheet is sorted, as shown in Screen Display 8–3.

After sorting, each row is intact but has moved up or down according to the entry in the primary-key field.

PRACTICE TIME

1. Sort the spreadsheet in ascending order by Cost.

2. Re-sort the spreadsheet in ascending order by Part.

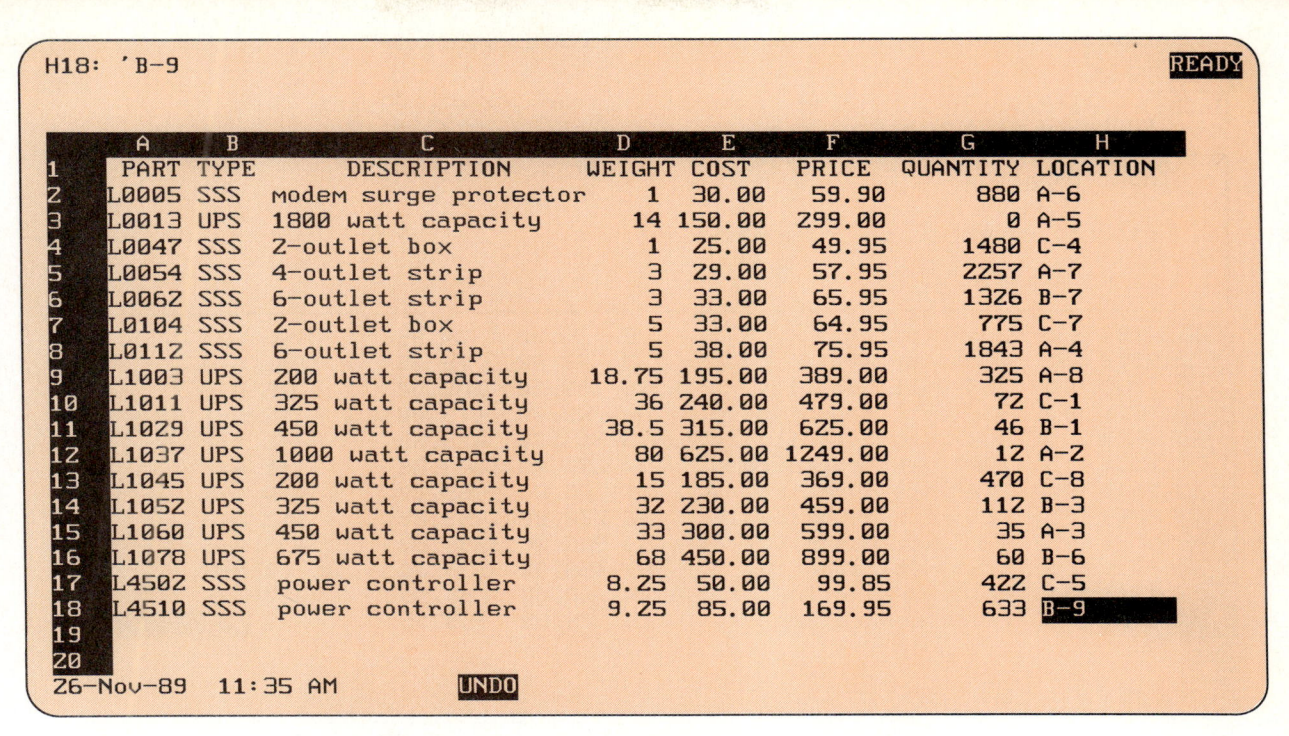

```
H18: 'B-9                                                      READY
     A      B          C             D      E       F        G        H
 1  PART   TYPE    DESCRIPTION     WEIGHT  COST   PRICE    QUANTITY  LOCATION
 2  L0005  SSS   modem surge protector   1   30.00   59.90     880    A-6
 3  L0013  UPS   1800 watt capacity     14  150.00  299.00       0    A-5
 4  L0047  SSS   2-outlet box            1   25.00   49.95    1480    C-4
 5  L0054  SSS   4-outlet strip          3   29.00   57.95    2257    A-7
 6  L0062  SSS   6-outlet strip          3   33.00   65.95    1326    B-7
 7  L0104  SSS   2-outlet box            5   33.00   64.95     775    C-7
 8  L0112  SSS   6-outlet strip          5   38.00   75.95    1843    A-4
 9  L1003  UPS   200 watt capacity   18.75  195.00  389.00     325    A-8
10  L1011  UPS   325 watt capacity      36  240.00  479.00      72    C-1
11  L1029  UPS   450 watt capacity    38.5  315.00  625.00      46    B-1
12  L1037  UPS   1000 watt capacity     80  625.00 1249.00      12    A-2
13  L1045  UPS   200 watt capacity      15  185.00  369.00     470    C-8
14  L1052  UPS   325 watt capacity      32  230.00  459.00     112    B-3
15  L1060  UPS   450 watt capacity      33  300.00  599.00      35    A-3
16  L1078  UPS   675 watt capacity      68  450.00  899.00      60    B-6
17  L4502  SSS   power controller     8.25   50.00   99.85     422    C-5
18  L4510  SSS   power controller     9.25   85.00  169.95     633    B-9
19
20
26-Nov-89  11:35 AM            UNDO
```

Screen Display 8–3   Database sorted by Part.

DATA QUERY

Suppose you had a very large database, containing several hundred items, and you need to look up the data for some item. You could scroll the screen up or down and search sequentially to find the item, but this takes time. Fortunately, you can use the Data Query command instead. The <u>Data Query command lets you select all records that meet any criteria you specify</u>. The selected records can be highlighted, copied to another location on the worksheet, or deleted. The criteria allow flexibility in searching. For example, you can specify criteria to find part number L0104, to find all UPS's that cost you under $500 or to find an item warehoused in location B–6.

- Type **/DQ** for Data Query.

    ▶ The Query Settings box is displayed, as in Screen Display 8–4.

USING A SPREADSHEET AS A DATABASE

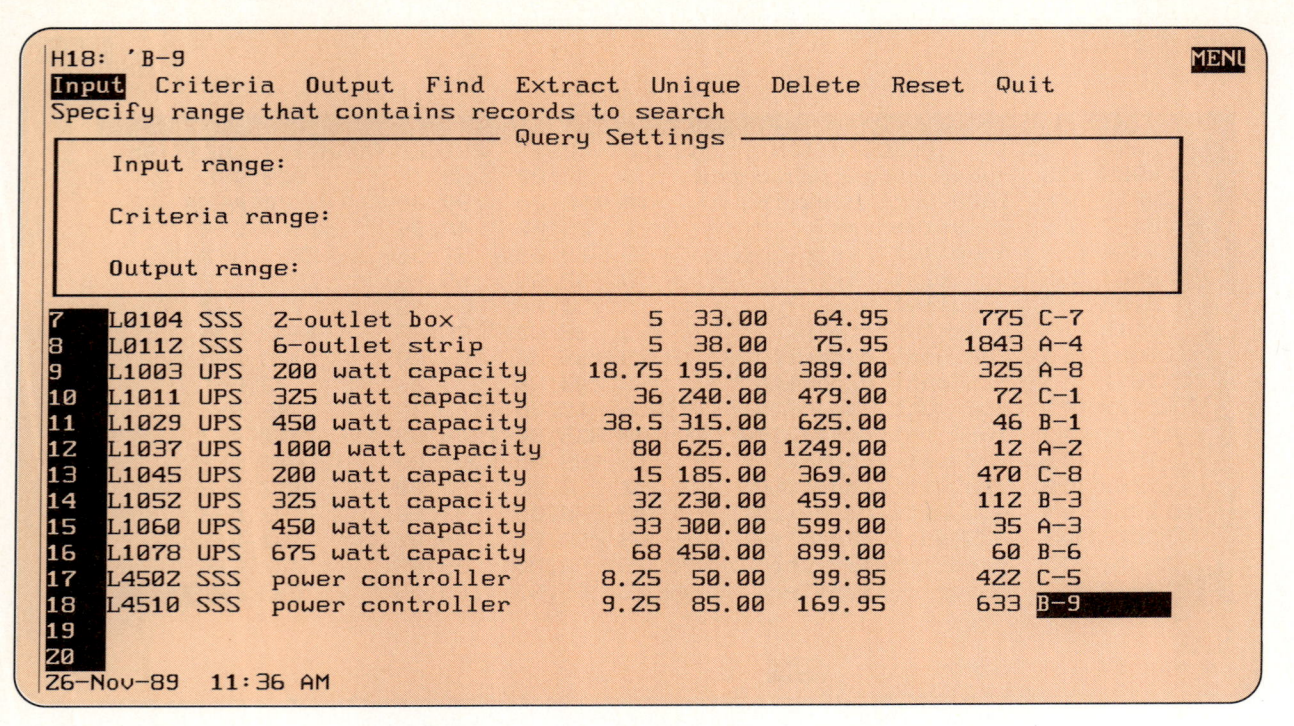

```
H18: 'B-9                                                              MENU
Input  Criteria  Output  Find  Extract  Unique  Delete  Reset  Quit
Specify range that contains records to search
                        ─── Query Settings ───
    Input range:

    Criteria range:

    Output range:

7    L0104  SSS  2-outlet box           5   33.00    64.95   775  C-7
8    L0112  SSS  6-outlet strip         5   38.00    75.95  1843  A-4
9    L1003  UPS  200 watt capacity  18.75  195.00   389.00   325  A-8
10   L1011  UPS  325 watt capacity     36  240.00   479.00    72  C-1
11   L1029  UPS  450 watt capacity   38.5  315.00   625.00    46  B-1
12   L1037  UPS  1000 watt capacity    80  625.00  1249.00    12  A-2
13   L1045  UPS  200 watt capacity     15  185.00   369.00   470  C-8
14   L1052  UPS  325 watt capacity     32  230.00   459.00   112  B-3
15   L1060  UPS  450 watt capacity     33  300.00   599.00    35  A-3
16   L1078  UPS  675 watt capacity     68  450.00   899.00    60  B-6
17   L4502  SSS  power controller    8.25   50.00    99.85   422  C-5
18   L4510  SSS  power controller    9.25   85.00   169.95   633  B-9
19
20
26-Nov-89  11:36 AM
```

Screen Display 8–4 Data query settings and menu options.

▶ The following Data Query submenu is displayed:

Input	Specifies the range that contains records to search.
Criteria	Specifies the range that contains search criteria.
Output	Specifies the range to which extracted data are copied.
Find	Highlights each record that matches criteria.
Extract	Copies all records that match criteria to output range.
Unique	Copies records that match criteria to output range, eliminating duplicates.
Delete	Deletes all records that match criteria.
Reset	Clears the Input, Criteria, and Output ranges.
Quit	Exits Data Query submenu.

To query the database file, you must first specify the input and criteria ranges. The input range includes all the records in the database, and the criteria range consists of the cells where you specify the selection criteria. You will also specify the output range, if needed. The output range consists of the cells into which selected records will be copied. You are then ready to specify Find, Extract, Unique, or Delete options. The output range is needed for the Extract and Unique options only. You will use the Find and Extract options here.

- Select Input.

    ▶ The message prompts you to enter the input range.

The Input range is the entire database, including the field names.

- Type **A1.H18** and press (ENTER).

    ▶ The input range is specified in the Query Settings box.
    ▶ The menu options are displayed again.

At this point, you will exit the Query mode to set up the criteria range. That is, you will enter the selection criteria in cells that will be reserved for that purpose.

- Select Quit.

The criteria range is used to specify the conditions for matching records in the database. The criteria range must not be contained within the input and output ranges and must contain at least two rows: <u>The first row contains the field names to be matched, and the remaining rows contain the values or formulas used for matching</u>. You will use rows 20 and 21 for this purpose.

Right now, although you will select on just the Part field, the easiest way to set up the first row of the criteria range is to enter all field names from the database by copying the field names on the first row of the input range to the first row of the criteria range. It is important that field names be entered on the first row of the criteria range exactly as they are spelled in the first row of the database spreadsheet; the Copy command will thus ensure exact duplication. If you don't enter a comparison value for a field, that comparison will be ignored. That is, if you enter no condition

USING A SPREADSHEET AS A DATABASE **195**

under a field name (on the second row), then all the records with any entry in that field name will be selected. Thus, you may include more fields than needed for selection criteria without affecting the query.

A range of cells can be copied with just one COPY command. Include all the cells to be copied as the source cell-range. For the destination range, you need only specify the first cell of the range. When the destination cell is smaller than the source cell, the extra source cell contents will be copied in the cells to the right and below the destination range.

- Type **/C** for Copy.

- Specify the range **A1.H1** as the source range.

- For destination, just place the cell pointer on cell A20 and press (ENTER).

Now enter the comparison value, which is L0104.

- On row 21, under the heading PART (column A), type **L0104** and press (ENTER).

Now that the criteria range is set up, you can return to the Data Query command and specify the criteria range in range A20.H21.

- Type **/DQC**.

    ► The message prompts you to enter the criteria range.

- Type **A20.H21** and press (ENTER).

    ► The settings box reflects your entry.

Now find the record that meets the stated criteria. When using the Find option, you do not need to specify the output range.

- Select Find.

    ► Row 7, which contains the record for part number L0104, is highlighted, as shown in Screen Display 8–5.

- Press (ENTER) to continue.

    ► The Data Query settings and menu options are displayed again.

```
A7: [W6] 'L0104                                                    FIND
         A    B        C              D      E      F       G    H
    2  L0005 SSS  modem surge protector   1   30.00   59.90    880 A-6
    3  L0013 UPS  1800 watt capacity     14  150.00  299.00      0 A-5
    4  L0047 SSS  2-outlet box            1   25.00   49.95   1480 C-4
    5  L0054 SSS  4-outlet strip          3   29.00   57.95   2257 A-7
    6  L0062 SSS  6-outlet strip          3   33.00   65.95   1326 B-7
    7  L0104 SSS  2-outlet box            5   33.00   64.95    775 C-7
    8  L0112 SSS  6-outlet strip          5   38.00   75.95   1843 A-4
    9  L1003 UPS  200 watt capacity   18.75  195.00  389.00    325 A-8
   10  L1011 UPS  325 watt capacity      36  240.00  479.00     72 C-1
   11  L1029 UPS  450 watt capacity    38.5  315.00  625.00     46 B-1
   12  L1037 UPS  1000 watt capacity     80  625.00 1249.00     12 A-2
   13  L1045 UPS  200 watt capacity      15  185.00  369.00    470 C-8
   14  L1052 UPS  325 watt capacity      32  230.00  459.00    112 B-3
   15  L1060 UPS  450 watt capacity      33  300.00  599.00     35 A-3
   16  L1078 UPS  675 watt capacity      68  450.00  899.00     60 B-6
   17  L4502 SSS  power controller     8.25   50.00   99.85    422 C-5
   18  L4510 SSS  power controller     9.25   85.00  169.95    633 B-9
   19
   20  PART  TYPE    DESCRIPTION      WEIGHT  COST    PRICE   QUANTITY LOCATION
   21  L0104
26-Nov-89   11:40 AM
```

Screen Display 8–5 The record matching criteria is highlighted.

To extract records that meet the selection criteria, you have to specify an output range, since the extracted records will be copied to the output range. The first row of the output range needs to contain only those field names for which data are to be extracted. To enter these field names, you have to exit the Data Query mode.

- Select Quit.

The output range will be rows 25 to 45. The output range can have more rows than the input range. When records are extracted, the program will use as many rows as needed. Moreover, if you specify just the cells containing field names as the output range, all rows below the field names (to the very bottom of the spreadsheet) will be considered part of the output range.

If you want only part number and description displayed, then you enter only the names of the Part and Description fields in row 25. However, you have to be aware of the column width. If you entered these names in columns A and B, respectively, column B might not be wide enough for entries in the Description field. For this reason, when you are extracting only some of the fields, you might locate the output range in columns at a distance from the input range; in this case, outside columns A through H. If you display Part in column K and Description in column L, you will be able to adjust the column widths of K and L accordingly.

Right now, for the sake of simplicity, you will include all field names in the output range. Thus, copy the headings from row 1 and place them in row 25.

- Copy all the field names from the range A1..H1 to the range A25..H25 (same columns).

- Move the cell pointer so that rows 25 through 30 are visible on the screen.

- Type **/DQO** to specify the output range.

- Type **A25.H25** and press (ENTER).

    ➤ The settings reflect your entry.

- Select Extract.

    ➤ The Data Query submenu appears again.

- Select Quit to exit the Data Query mode.

    ➤ The record for item L0104 appears on row 26, as shown in Screen Display 8–6.

- Save the spreadsheet using the filename LOTUS9.

■
PRACTICE TIME

1. Erase the comparison value in cell A21 using **/RE**.

2. Set the selection criterion as Type = SSS (Enter **SSS** in cell B21).

3. Give the Data Query command and select the Find option.

    ➤ Only the first record with Type = SSS is highlighted. To see others, use the ⬆ or ⬇ keys. Other records are highlighted one at a time. If there are no more

198   USING LOTUS 1-2-3

```
A25: [W6] ^PART                                                              READY

       A    B         C            D       E        F        G       H
11   L1029 UPS    450 watt capacity    38.5  315.00   625.00      46 B-1
12   L1037 UPS   1000 watt capacity      80  625.00  1249.00      12 A-2
13   L1045 UPS    200 watt capacity      15  185.00   369.00     470 C-8
14   L1052 UPS    325 watt capacity      32  230.00   459.00     112 B-3
15   L1060 UPS    450 watt capacity      33  300.00   599.00      35 A-3
16   L1078 UPS    675 watt capacity      68  450.00   899.00      60 B-6
17   L4502 SSS    power controller    8.25   50.00    99.85     422 C-5
18   L4510 SSS    power controller    9.25   85.00   169.95     633 B-9
19
20   PART  TYPE       DESCRIPTION    WEIGHT  COST     PRICE  QUANTITY LOCATION
21   L0104
22
23
24
25   PART  TYPE       DESCRIPTION    WEIGHT  COST     PRICE  QUANTITY LOCATION
26   L0104 SSS    2-outlet box            5   33.00    64.95     775 C-7
27
28
29
30
26-Nov-89   11:49 AM          UNDO
```

Screen Display 8–6 The result of extracting a record.

(above or below) satisfying the criteria, the computer beeps.

4. Press (ENTER) to continue.

5. Now extract records of Type **SSS** by selecting the Extract option of the Data Query command. You have to quit the data query mode before you can scroll the screen to look at the output range.

OTHER TEXT-SELECTION CRITERIA

So far all the selection criteria used were exact matches, or condition(s) equal to a specific label. When dealing with text (and not numeric) entries, you can also use "wild card" symbols, like the ones used in DOS:

* All items with any text at and after the position of this symbol are selected.

USING A SPREADSHEET AS A DATABASE **199**

> ? All items with any letter in the position where ? appears are selected.
> ~ Any text that is NOT the same as the text that follows the ~ (a tilde) is selected.

For example, if you want to find all items whose part number starts with the letter L, insert L* in the comparison-value cell. If you want to find all items whose part numbers are L1202, L1212, L1222, ..., L1292 (the first three characters are L12 and the last character is a 2, with any character in the fourth position), you use L12?2 in the comparison value cell.

For practice, extract all items whose Part field contains L00 in the first three positions.

- Make sure that input range, criteria range, and output range are still defined as before.
- Erase all entries on row 21, columns A through H.
- Enter **L00*** (the comparison value for the part number) in cell A21.
- Type **/DQE**, then quit the Data Query mode.

Now examine the output range shown in Screen Display 8–7.

■ PRACTICE TIME

1. Extract all the records whose part number contains L in the first position, 0 in the third position, and 3 in the last position. *Hint:* Use ? in second and fourth positions.

2. Try other text criteria.

■ FORMULA CONDITIONS

To select a record based on fields containing numeric data, you must use *formula conditions* as criteria. On the second line of the criteria range, you enter the formula to be used when testing the first record for selection. Other records are then tested using a *relative* formula condition; that is, the cell address is replaced with the appropriate one as each record is evaluated. You have to precede row and column cell-address numbers with $ if the cell

```
A26: [W6] 'L0005                                                    READY

         A     B          C              D      E       F       G      H
    11  L1029 UPS   450 watt capacity    38.5  315.00   625.00   46 B-1
    12  L1037 UPS  1000 watt capacity    80    625.00  1249.00   12 A-2
    13  L1045 UPS   200 watt capacity    15    185.00   369.00  470 C-8
    14  L1052 UPS   325 watt capacity    32    230.00   459.00  112 B-3
    15  L1060 UPS   450 watt capacity    33    300.00   599.00   35 A-3
    16  L1078 UPS   675 watt capacity    68    450.00   899.00   60 B-6
    17  L4502 SSS   power controller      8.25  50.00    99.85  422 C-5
    18  L4510 SSS   power controller      9.25  85.00   169.95  633 B-9
    19
    20  PART  TYPE      DESCRIPTION      WEIGHT COST    PRICE   QUANTITY LOCATION
    21  L00*
    22
    23
    24
    25  PART  TYPE      DESCRIPTION      WEIGHT COST    PRICE   QUANTITY LOCATION
    26  L0005 SSS   modem surge protector  1    30.00    59.90  880 A-6
    27  L0013 UPS  1800 watt capacity    14    150.00   299.00    0 A-5
    28  L0047 SSS   2-outlet box           1    25.00    49.95 1480 C-4
    29  L0054 SSS   4-outlet strip         3    29.00    57.95 2257 A-7
    30  L0062 SSS   6-outlet strip         3    33.00    65.95 1326 B-7
26-Nov-89  12:41 PM             UNDO
```

Screen Display 8–7 Extracting with a wildcard in the criteria range.

address used in the formula condition is to be an absolute one. This usually happens when the cell being referenced is outside the input range.

When the formula condition is evaluated, the result will be logically "true" or "false." That is, the formula contains a relational operator that, when evaluated, gives the result of "true" or "false." True yields the value 1 and false yields 0. When the result is true (value 1), the record is selected.

Relational operators include:

<	Less than
>	Greater than
=	Equal to
<>	Not equal to
<=	Less than or equal to
>=	Greater than or equal to

USING A SPREADSHEET AS A DATABASE   **201**

Practice by extracting the records of all items that cost you more than $100. You use the formula +E2>100 because E2 is the cell in the first record whose value is to be compared to the value 100.

- Make sure that input range, criteria range, and output range are still defined as before.
- Erase all entries on row 21, columns A through H.
- With the cell pointer on cell E21 (cost comparison value), type **+E2>100** and press (ENTER).
- 0 (zero) appears in cell E21.

The zero means that in the first record, the value in cell E2 is *not* greater than 100 and that this record has therefore not been selected.

Rather than seeing the logical result 0 in cell E21, it would be more meaningful for you to see the selection criteria that you typed in displayed. This can be accomplished by changing the display format to Text.

- Type **/RF**, select Text, then press (ENTER) to format cell E21 only.
  ➤ The text entered is displayed at cell E21.
- Type **/DQE**, then select Quit.
  ➤ The output range contains the records of all items with values greater than 100 in the Cost field, as shown in Screen Display 8–8.

The Data Query command can be quite frustrating to use at first. Make sure to be careful when you specify the input, output, and criteria ranges. Also, try initially to avoid selection criteria that are overly complex.

PRACTICE TIME

1. Extract records of all items with values less than $500.00 in the Price field.

2. Extract all records of Cost > $300. Get a printout of the output range.

```
E21: (T) [W8] +E2>100                                           READY

        A      B           C              D       E       F        G         H
   15  L1060  UPS   450 watt capacity      33    300.00  599.00      35  A-3
   16  L1078  UPS   675 watt capacity      68    450.00  899.00      60  B-6
   17  L4502  SSS   power controller      8.25    50.00   99.85     422  C-5
   18  L4510  SSS   power controller      9.25    85.00  169.95     633  B-9
   19
   20  PART   TYPE      DESCRIPTION      WEIGHT   COST   PRICE   QUANTITY LOCATION
   21                                            +E2>100
   22
   23
   24
   25  PART   TYPE      DESCRIPTION      WEIGHT   COST   PRICE   QUANTITY LOCATION
   26  L0013  UPS   1800 watt capacity     14    150.00  299.00       0  A-5
   27  L1003  UPS    200 watt capacity   18.75   195.00  389.00     325  A-8
   28  L1011  UPS    325 watt capacity     36    240.00  479.00      72  C-1
   29  L1029  UPS    450 watt capacity   38.5    315.00  625.00      46  B-1
   30  L1037  UPS   1000 watt capacity     80    625.00 1249.00      12  A-2
   31  L1045  UPS    200 watt capacity     15    185.00  369.00     470  C-8
   32  L1052  UPS    325 watt capacity     32    230.00  459.00     112  B-3
   33  L1060  UPS    450 watt capacity     33    300.00  599.00      35  A-3
   34  L1078  UPS    675 watt capacity     68    450.00  899.00      60  B-6
   26-Nov-89   12:43 PM               UNDO
```

Screen Display 8–8   Extracting with a relative formula condition.

MULTIPLE SELECTION CRITERIA

Sometimes you need to select records that meet several selection criteria. For example, in an automobile insurance database, you may want to find records of policy holders who are "male" *and* "over 25 years of age." This is called an *AND condition*. In the example inventory database, you may want to select all items that are type SSS *and* cost more than $35. All you need to do is to specify both criteria in the *same row* of the criteria range.

- Clear entries in row 21.

- Specify the criterion for Type = SSS in the appropriate cell in row 21.

- Specify the criterion for Cost > 35 in the appropriate cell in row 21.

- Extract the records and quit the Data Query mode.

```
E21: (T) [W8] +E2>35                                              READY

        A    B          C              D       E       F        G       H
15    L1060 UPS    450 watt capacity   33    300.00  599.00     35 A-3
16    L1078 UPS    675 watt capacity   68    450.00  899.00     60 B-6
17    L4502 SSS    power controller   8.25    50.00   99.85    422 C-5
18    L4510 SSS    power controller   9.25    85.00  169.95    633 B-9
19
20    PART  TYPE      DESCRIPTION     WEIGHT  COST    PRICE   QUANTITY LOCATION
21          SSS                              +E2>35
22
23
24
25    PART  TYPE      DESCRIPTION     WEIGHT  COST    PRICE   QUANTITY LOCATION
26    L0112 SSS    6-outlet strip       5     38.00   75.95   1843 A-4
27    L4502 SSS    power controller   8.25    50.00   99.85    422 C-5
28    L4510 SSS    power controller   9.25    85.00  169.95    633 B-9
29
30
31
32
33
34
26-Nov-89   12:45 PM           UNDO
```

Screen Display 8–9   Extracting with AND condition.

➤ There are records that meet both criteria, as shown in Screen Display 8–9.

There are other occasions when you want to select records that meet one of two (or more) conditions. For example, in a customer database file, you want to select those customers who owe you more than $10,000 *or* who are delinquent on payment by more than two months. This is called an *OR condition*. In the example inventory database, you may want to extract records of those items that are somewhere in location A (A*) *or* have quantity less than 50. Criteria to be used in an OR condition are specified in *different rows* of the criteria range. In this particular case, you need to expand the criteria range to three rows.

- Clear entries in row 21.

- In row 21, enter the criterion for LOCATION = A*.

- In row 22, enter the criterion for QUANTITY < 50.

- Specify the criteria range as A20.H22.

```
A20: [W6] ^PART                                                    READY

        A      B         C            D       E        F        G         H
   20  PART   TYPE    DESCRIPTION   WEIGHT   COST    PRICE   QUANTITY  LOCATION
   21                                                                    A*
   22                                                         +G2<50
   23
   24
   25  PART   TYPE    DESCRIPTION   WEIGHT   COST    PRICE   QUANTITY  LOCATION
   26  L0005  SSS   modem surge protector  1   30.00   59.90     880    A-6
   27  L0013  UPS   1800 watt capacity    14  150.00  299.00       0    A-5
   28  L0054  SSS   4-outlet strip         3   29.00   57.95    2257    A-7
   29  L0112  SSS   6-outlet strip         5   38.00   75.95    1843    A-4
   30  L1003  UPS   200 watt capacity  18.75  195.00  389.00     325    A-8
   31  L1029  UPS   450 watt capacity   38.5  315.00  625.00      46    B-1
   32  L1037  UPS   1000 watt capacity    80  625.00 1249.00      12    A-2
   33  L1060  UPS   450 watt capacity     33  300.00  599.00      35    A-3
   34
   35
   36
   37
   38
   39
   26-Nov-89  12:48 PM           UNDO
```

Screen Display 8–10 *Extracting with OR condition.*

■ Extract the records and quit the Data Query mode.

▶ You will see the records of those items that meet either condition, as shown in Screen Display 8–10.

■ **PRACTICE TIME**

Extract those items that are Type = SSS and Cost < $30 *or* Type = UPS and Cost < $250.

■ **UNIQUE OPTION**

Sometimes the same information appears twice in a database; that is, you may have two identical records in a database. If you use the extract option, both occurrences of the records will be extracted (since they both meet the same conditions). If you use the unique option instead, only one occurrence of the record will be extracted. In order for a selected record to be excluded by the

USING A SPREADSHEET AS A DATABASE **205**

unique option, it must be identical in all fields to another selected record.

DELETE OPTION

This option permanently deletes records from a database file, based on specified selection criteria. Before you use this option to delete records, make sure that your selection criteria are correct. Once you delete records, you cannot retrieve them (unless you have kept a copy of the original file on a disk).

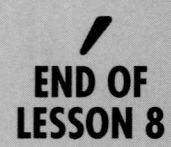

END OF LESSON 8

- Type **/QY**, then **Y** to exit 1–2–3, then press **E** to exit to DOS.
- Remove the disks from the disk drive.
- Turn off the monitor, computer, and printer.

SUMMARY

In this lesson, many of the terms and concepts required to use a spreadsheet file as a database are discussed.

- A database file is a collection of records about a particular topic. Each record, in turn, is composed of a series of fields.

- When a spreadsheet is used as a database, each row is a record and each column is a field. The first row of the database contains field names. Before a query can be made, the input range and criteria range must be specified. The output range is used for the extract and unique options.

- Data in a database may be numeric data (previously called values) or text data (previously called labels).

- Rows in a spreadsheet (or records in a database) may be sorted in whatever order, alphabetical or numerical, specified.
- Records in a database input-range can be selected or queried based on criteria you specify. Selected records can be highlighted, copied to another location, or deleted.
- When querying a database based on text entries, "wild card" symbols can be used.
- When querying a database based on numeric entries, formula conditions are used.
- When querying a database based on selection criteria under the AND condition, the various criteria are specified on the same row. Under the OR condition, the criteria are specified on different rows.
- When the unique option is used, duplicate records are not extracted.
- The data-query delete option is used to delete records based on selection criteria.
- The following commands are discussed:

  /DQ   Data Query—Selects records from a database according to specific selection criteria.

  /DS   Data Sort—Arranges records (rows) of a worksheet in ascending or descending order.

REVIEW QUESTIONS

1. What is the purpose of the secondary-key in a sort?
2. What is a record in a database? a field? Relate them to a spreadsheet.

3. What is the minimum number of data management "pieces" (such as ranges) that have to be specified before a query can be performed on a database?

   Specify Input + Criteria range

4. When do you have to specify the output range for the Data Query? *Same time*

5. When entering field names in the criteria or output range, how important is it to match the names with those given in the input range? *Very*

6. Which records are selected when a field in the criteria range is blank?

7. How are the wild card symbols used in a query? Explain. *When dealing w/ text or non numeric entries*

8. Explain how formula conditions work in a query.

9. What is the difference between an AND condition and an OR condition in a query with multiple selection criteria?

10. What is the difference between the extract and unique options? *When the unique option is used, duplicated ranges are not extracted*

EXERCISES

1. Retrieve the spreadsheet EX5_1 from Lesson 5.

   a) Sort the spreadsheet, based on the Name field.

   b) Query the spreadsheet to extract the names of friends whose telephone numbers have a common exchange (the first three digits are identical). You will need to provide the exchange number in the criteria range.

   c) Get a printout of the entire spreadsheet.

   d) Query the spreadsheet to extract the names of those friends who owe you more than $10 (or another appropriate value) in total.

e) Get a printout of just the criteria and output ranges.

   f) Save the spreadsheet as EX8_1.

2. Retrieve the spreadsheet EX5_2 from Lesson 5.

   a) Sort the spreadsheet by the Name field.

   b) Resort the spreadsheet in ascending order on Total Points.

   c) Query the spreadsheet to extract the names of those students whose average is below 80 (or another appropriate value).

   d) Get a printout of the entire spreadsheet.

   e) Query the spreadsheet to extract the records of students who received more than 90 points on the first exam but whose average is lower than 90.

   f) Get a printout of just the criteria and output ranges.

   g) Save the spreadsheet as EX8_2.

LESSON 9
USING OTHER DATA FEATURES

OBJECTIVES

Upon completion of the material presented in this lesson, you should be able to:

- Enter a sequence of evenly spaced numbers using the Data Fill command
- Set up a data-distribution table
- Name cells using labels in adjacent cells
- Create a table showing the range names and their locations
- Do what-if analysis using data-table commands

STARTING OFF

Start Lotus 1-2-3 so that a blank worksheet is displayed on the screen. Insert a data disk in drive B and change the file directory to B.

DATA DISTRIBUTION

When working with a database containing many rows of data, it is sometimes useful to know the distribution of data. For example, in the inventory example, you might need to know how many items of certain price categories exist within the database. The Data Distribution command displays how values are divided between arbitrarily chosen categories, or *bins*.

- Retrieve the spreadsheet LOTUS9.

You will create a table of the cost distribution of items. Since the cost varies from $25 to $625, you will categorize items by cost in $100 increments. That is, you will find out how many items have a cost of between 0 and $100, how many items have cost of between $100 and $200, how many between $200 and $300, and so on. This

USING OTHER DATA FEATURES **211**

requires the use of two adjacent blank columns. You will use columns J and K.

In column J, the cells will contain the values for the upper limit of a each bin; that is, the first cell will contain the value 100, the second 200, the third 300, and so on, to 700.

When the Data Distribution command is carried out, column K will show the distribution. That is, cell K1 will show the number of items in the cost range less than or equal to 100 (since the value 100 will be stored in cell J1), K2 will show the number of items in the cost range greater than 100 but less than or equal to 200 (since the value 200 will be stored in cell J2), and so on.

■ DATA FILL

When you need to enter a sequence of evenly spaced numbers, as you will do in column J, you do not have to enter each value. Instead, you can fill a range (a column or row) by giving the Data Fill command.

- Place the cell pointer on cell J1.
- Type **/DF** for Data Fill.
    ➤ The control panel displays the following message:

    `Enter fill range: J1`

You are prompted to enter the range of cells to fill with numbers. The fill range specified can be larger than actually needed. 1–2–3 will use only the cells needed to carry out the instruction.

Note: If the fill range specified is too small, all the numbers you require may not be inserted.

- Type **J1.J20** and press (ENTER).
    ➤ A message prompts you for the start value.
- Type **100** and press (ENTER).
    ➤ You are now prompted for the step, or increment, value.
- Type **100** and press (ENTER).
    ➤ You are now prompted for the stop, or ending, value.

DISTRIBUTION TABLE

- Type **700** and press (ENTER).
  - ➤ The appropriate values appear in column J, rows 1 through 7.

Now you can obtain the data distribution.

- Type **/DD** for Data Distribution.
  - ➤ The following message prompts:

    `Enter values range: J1`

You are to enter the range on which the **distribution is based**. In this case, it is COST, or cells E2 through E18.

- Type **E2.E18** and press (ENTER).
  - ➤ The control panel displays the prompt:

    `Enter bin range: J1`

The bin range is the range of values in column J.

- Type **J1.J7** and press (ENTER).
  - ➤ Cells K1 through K8 displays the distribution, as seen in Screen Display 9–1.

As you can see, there are eight items whose cost is below $100, three items that cost between $100 and $200, and so on to one item (shown in cell K7) that costs over $600. K8 displays the number of items whose values exceed the highest value entered in the bin range.

- Save the spreadsheet as LOTUS10.

PRACTICE TIME

Find the weight distribution of the items in your spreadsheet. The bins start at 20 pounds or less and are incremented by 20 pounds to 100 pounds.

USING OTHER DATA FEATURES

```
J1: 100                                                           READY

       D       E       F        G        H        I       J       K
 1  WEIGHT  COST    PRICE    QUANTITY LOCATION                100     8
 2   18.75  195.00  389.00      325   A-8                     200     3
 3      36  240.00  479.00       72   C-1                     300     3
 4    38.5  315.00  625.00       46   B-1                     400     1
 5      80  625.00 1249.00       12   A-2                     500     1
 6       1   30.00   59.90      880   A-6                     600     0
 7      15  185.00  369.00      470   C-8                     700     1
 8      32  230.00  459.00      112   B-3                             0
 9      33  300.00  599.00       35   A-3
10      68  450.00  899.00       60   B-6
11      14  150.00  299.00        0   A-5
12       1   25.00   49.95     1480   C-4
13       3   29.00   57.95     2257   A-7
14       3   33.00   65.95     1326   B-7
15       5   33.00   64.95      775   C-7
16       5   38.00   75.95     1843   A-4
17    8.25   50.00   99.85      422   C-5
18    9.25   85.00  169.95      633   B-9
19
20
26-Nov-89   12:54 PM         UNDO
```

Screen Display 9–1   Data distribution of item cost.

RANGE NAMES

One concept, which is both a time-saver and a tool for effectively designing a spreadsheet, is that of range names. This was covered briefly in Lesson 5. You can assign a range name to a cell or range of cells so that when a cell or range address is required, you can use a meaningful name rather than a cell address consisting of row and column numbers.

To name a range, you need to specify the name itself and the cell or cells included in the named range. Let's review by giving a range name to cell C3.

- Clear the spreadsheet (**/WEY**).

- With the cell pointer in cell C3, type **/RN** for Range Name.

    ▶ The Range Name submenu is displayed:

Create	Lets you create a range name.
Delete	Lets you delete a range name.

214   USING LOTUS 1-2-3

Labels	Lets you name a cell or range of cells using their adjacent labels.
Reset	Lets you delete all range names in the worksheet.
Table	Lets you see a list of range names and their ranges.

- Select Create.

    ➤ The following message prompts:

    `Enter name:`

Range names can be up to fifteen characters long, and may consist of letters (entered in either upper- or lowercase since they will be made uppercase by Lotus 1-2-3), digits, and the underscore character. You should keep your range names simple so they are easily remembered. Use the name TEST for this range.

- Type **TEST** and press (ENTER).

    ➤ The program prompts you to enter the range of cells to call TEST. The default displayed is C3..C3.

- Since you want to name just cell C3, press (ENTER).

Now that cell C3 has been named TEST, you can use the range name TEST the same way you used address C3. For example, if you want the contents of cell C3 to be displayed at cell F7, you would have entered +C3 at cell F7; now, you can enter +TEST instead. (If you type TEST without the + sign, you will enter a label instead of an expression.)

- Insert the value **100** at cell C3.
- Move the cell pointer to F7.
- Type **+TEST** and press (ENTER).

    ➤ Note that the formula you entered, +TEST, is displayed in the control panel.

- Change the value at C3 to **250** and see what happens at F7.

RANGE NAME LABEL COMMAND (/RNL)

If you have a number of cells to name, you can name them all with the Range Name Label option. You will now create a spreadsheet that analyzes a loan to determine monthly payments, given the principal, interest rate, and term of the loan. You will also calculate the total interest that would be paid over the lifetime of the loan. The cells for the five quantities just noted will be created and named.

- Clear the spreadsheet (**/WEY**).
- In cell A1, enter the label **PRINCIPAL**.
- In cells A2, A3, and A4, enter the labels **RATE**, **TERM**, and **PAYMENT**, respectively. The labels may be entered in uppercase, lowercase, or mixed. When they are used to name cells, they will be considered uppercase by the program.

Next, the cells to the right of the four labels will be named, using the labels you just entered. That is, you will name B1 PRINCIPAL, B2 RATE, and so on.

- Type **/RNL** for Range Name Label.

    ➤ The following menu options are displayed:

Right	The label will name the cell to the right.
Down	The label will name the cell below.
Left	The label will name the cell to the left.
Up	The label will name the cell above.

- Select Right.

    ➤ A message prompts for the range where the labels are to be found.

The labels in question are in range A1 through A4, therefore:

- Type **A1.A4** and press (ENTER).

The four cells, B1 through B4, to the right of the cells with the labels, have been named by the respective labels.

216 USING LOTUS 1-2-3

RANGE NAME TABLE COMMAND (/RNT)

If you forget which cell you named what, you can display the required information using the Range Name Table command. This command creates a table showing the range names and their corresponding cell addresses. The table becomes part of the worksheet. If you don't want the table to become a permanent part of the worksheet, you must erase it.

- Place the cell pointer in a cell that will not interfere with the other worksheet entries; say, cell G1.
- Type **/RNT** for Range Name Table.

  ➤ The following message appears:

  ```
  Enter range for table: G1..G1
  ```

- Press (ENTER).

  ➤ The table is created, as seen in Screen Display 9–2.

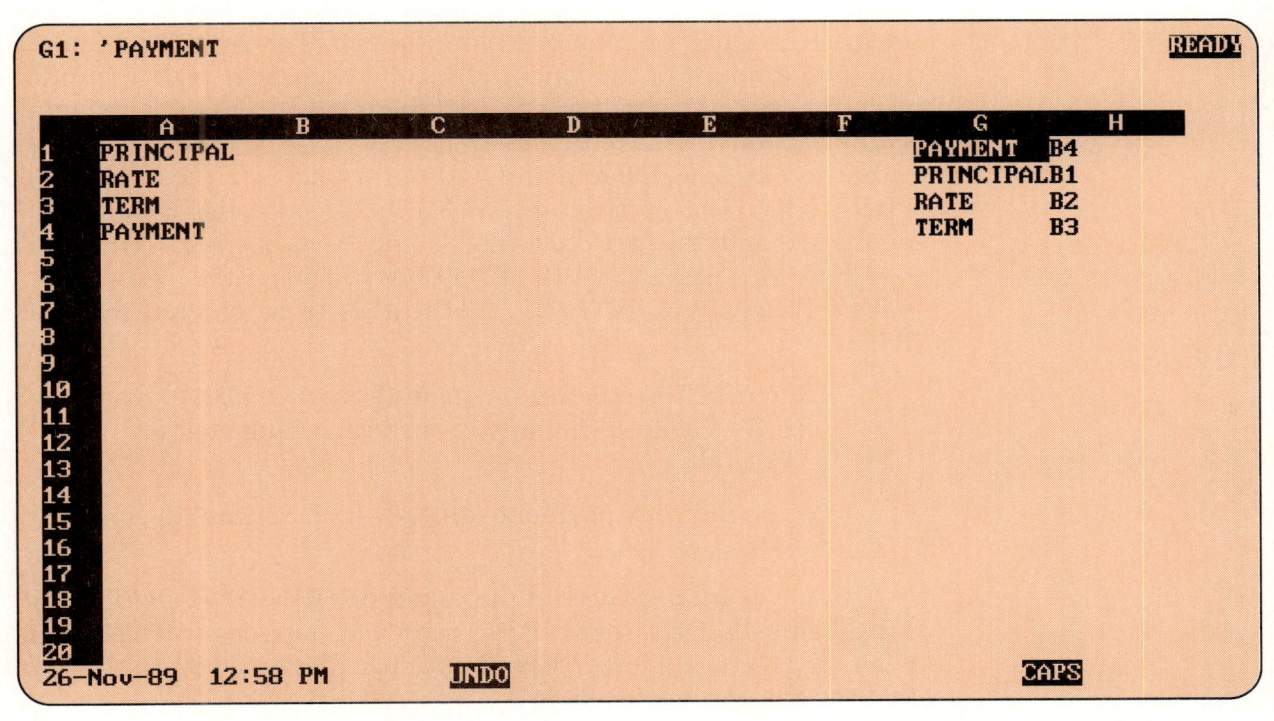

```
G1: 'PAYMENT                                                        READY

         A         B         C         D         E         F         G         H
 1  PRINCIPAL                                                   PAYMENT   B4
 2  RATE                                                        PRINCIPAL B1
 3  TERM                                                        RATE      B2
 4  PAYMENT                                                     TERM      B3
 5
 6
 7
 8
 9
10
11
12
13
14
15
16
17
18
19
20
26-Nov-89  12:58 PM          UNDO                                    CAPS
```

Screen Display 9–2 The Range Name Table command results.

USING OTHER DATA FEATURES **217**

- Erase the table.

You are interested in taking out a loan of $20,000 at an interest rate of 10 percent per year for 10 years, paid in monthly payments. You will enter the principal, annual interest rate, and number of years to term, and then enter the formulas to determine the monthly payment and the total interest paid over the lifetime of the loan.

- Enter the value **20000** in cell B1.
- Enter the value **0.1** (for 10 percent) in cell B2.
- Enter the value **10** (for 10 years) in cell B3.

If you know how to compute the monthly payment, great! However, Lotus 1–2–3 has an @PMT function that will calculate the payment for you. Functions were discussed briefly in Lesson 5 using the @SUM function. The @PMT function uses three arguments (the values within the parentheses). The first argument is the total amount of the loan, the second argument is the periodic rate (rate per payment period), and the third argument is the total number of payments to be made.

In this example, the total amount of the loan is in the cell named PRINCIPAL. The periodic rate is RATE/12, since RATE is the annual rate and the periodic rate is the monthly rate. The total number of payments is 12*TERM. Thus, the expression @PMT(PRINCIPAL,RATE/12,12*TERM) is to be entered into cell B4.

- Enter the formula for payment (as shown above) in cell B4. Make sure that you spell each range name correctly.
  ➤ The monthly payment value, 264.30, appears in cell B4.

You may want to play with the values of PRINCIPAL, RATE, and TERM in cells B1 through B3 to see what happens to PAYMENT when you change them. When done experimenting, return them to their original values.

PRACTICE TIME

1. Enter the label **INTEREST** in cell A5.

2. Name cell B5 using the label in A5.

3. Cell B5 is to display the total interest paid over the lifetime of the loan, or the total of all payments made, minus the amount of the loan. The formula is +PAYMENT*12*TERM-PRINCIPAL.

4. Change the display format of cells B4 and B5 to **fixed** with two places to the right of decimal, as seen in Screen Display 9–3.

When you place the cell pointer in cell B5 and view its contents in the control panel, the formula displayed makes a bit more sense because of the use of range names. Also, the @PMT function

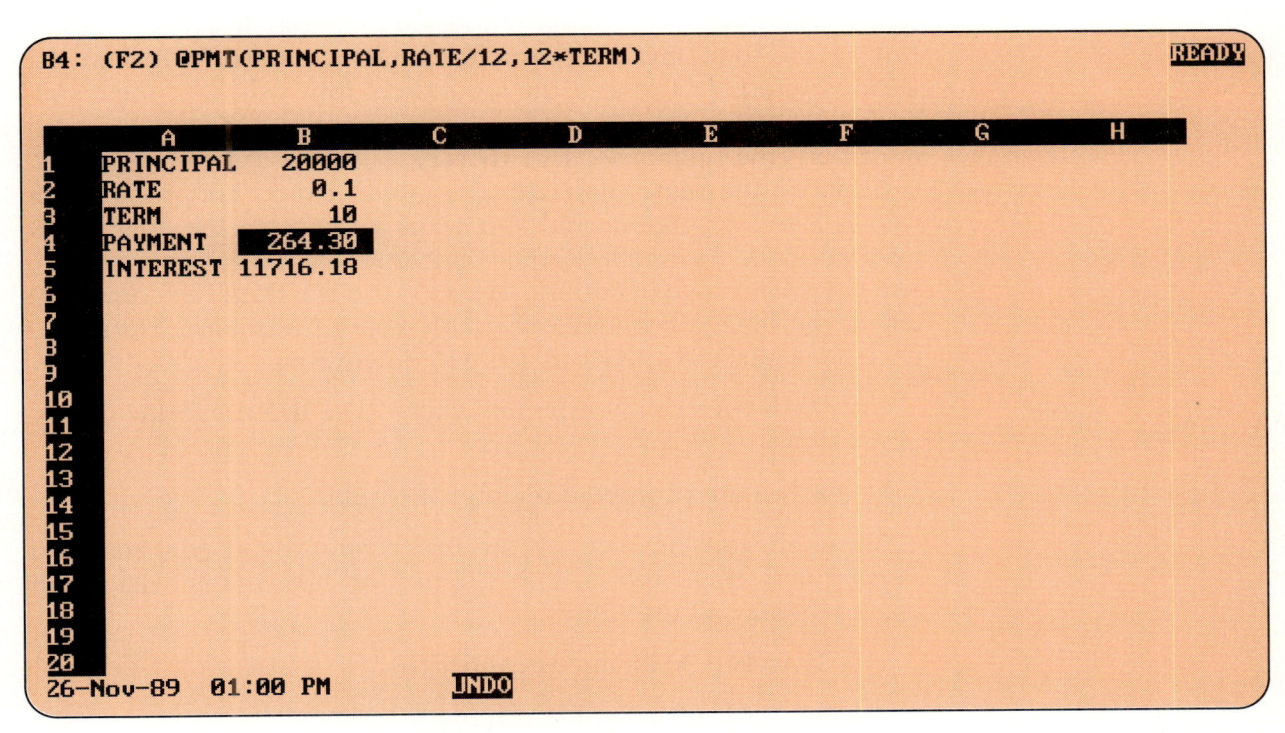

```
B4: (F2) @PMT(PRINCIPAL,RATE/12,12*TERM)                    READY

         A         B         C         D         E         F         G         H
   1  PRINCIPAL   20000
   2  RATE          0.1
   3  TERM           10
   4  PAYMENT     264.30
   5  INTEREST  11716.18
   6
   7
   8
   9
  10
  11
  12
  13
  14
  15
  16
  17
  18
  19
  20
  26-Nov-89  01:00 PM          UNDO
```

Screen Display 9–3 *Loan with total interest paid over its lifetime.*

greatly reduced the difficulty of calculating the payment amount. The two concepts presented here, range names and the @PMT function, can greatly ease your investigation of financing a loan.

DATA TABLE

Isn't it amazing that a ten-year loan at 10 percent will end up costing you 55 percent of the principal in interest? Suppose you want to compare monthly payments for a variety of interest rates. By the time you have entered a number of different rates and written down the results, you've hardly done the work the easy way. Instead, you can create a Data Table that shows various interest rates and corresponding payment amounts.

The Data Table commands are used to do "what if" calculations on the spreadsheet. They handle the entry of various values and keep track of results for you. Your next exercise will be to create a one-way data table with two columns. A one-way data table investigates the effects of changing one quantity, such as the interest rate of the loan. In this example, the first column will hold the various interest rates and the second column will hold the corresponding payment amounts calculated using the formula entered at cell B4 (the cell named PAYMENT).

Suppose the reasonable range you can expect for the interest rate is 8 to 12 percent, and you want to perform the analysis at intervals of 0.25 percent. Rather than enter each value in a column, you can fill a range (a column or row) with the Data Fill command when you have a sequence of evenly spaced numbers. Here, you want the values to appear in cell A10 downward.

- With your cell pointer anywhere, type **/DF** for Data Fill.

    ➤ You are prompted to enter the range.

Although you can specify the exact range, you can enter an exaggerated range and let 1–2–3 figure out how many cells it will take to display all the values.

- Type **A10.A100** and press (ENTER).

    ➤ A message prompts you for the starting value.

- Type **.08** and press (ENTER).

> You are now prompted for the step, or increment, value.

- Type **.0025** and press (ENTER).

> You are now prompted to enter the stop, or ending, value.

When performing a data fill with fractional step values, such as .0025, numeric truncation may cause the data fill to omit the ending value. If you enter .12 as the ending value, the data fill starts at .08 and terminates at .1175. So, if your step values are less than 1, you should add a little bit (less than the step value) to the ending value to make sure it will be included.

- Type **.121** and press (ENTER).

> The interest rates appear in the column A, rows 10 to 26.

- Change the display format of the range A10.A26 to Percent with two places to the right of the decimal, as seen in Screen Display 9–4.

- At cell A9, enter the label **RATE** centered.

ONE-WAY DATA TABLE (/DT1)

The data table you are building will cover columns A and B, rows 9 through 26. Column A, rows 10 through 26, contains various interest rates to consider. Cell B9 will contain the expression to be used to calculate the values in column B, rows 10 through 26. The values displayed in column B will correspond to the values in column A.

The expression you want in cell B9 is the one that was entered in the cell named PAYMENT. You want cells B10 through B26 to show payment amount evaluated using this expression, as values in column A are substituted for RATE. That is, you want cell B10 to show the payment value when the value in cell A10 (8%) is used for RATE; cell B11 to show the payment value when the value in cell A11 (8.25%) is used for RATE; and so on.

- At cell B9, enter **+PAYMENT**.

> Cell B9 displays the same value displayed in cell B4.

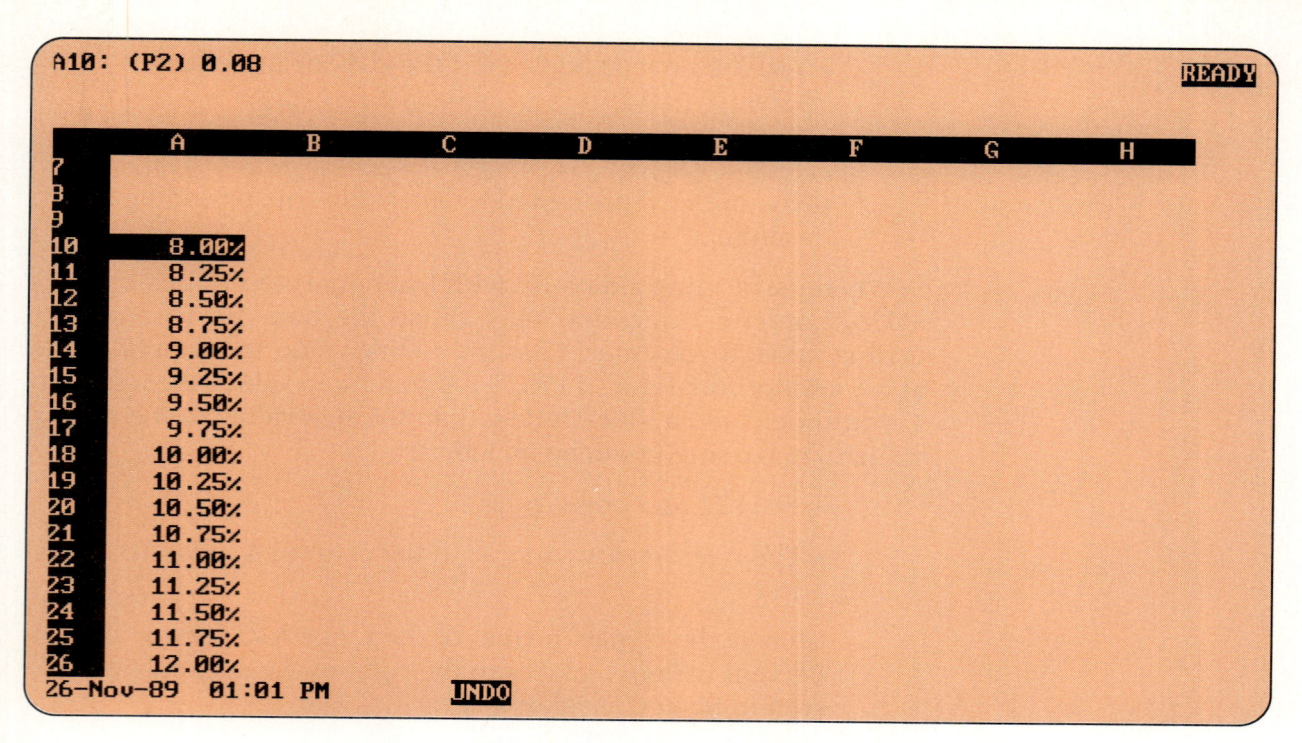

```
A10: (P2) 0.08                                                    READY

         A        B        C        D        E        F        G        H
 7
 8
 9
10     8.00%
11     8.25%
12     8.50%
13     8.75%
14     9.00%
15     9.25%
16     9.50%
17     9.75%
18    10.00%
19    10.25%
20    10.50%
21    10.75%
22    11.00%
23    11.25%
24    11.50%
25    11.75%
26    12.00%
26-Nov-89  01:01 PM          UNDO
```

Screen Display 9–4   Data fill of interest rates.

Now you will create the data table.

- Type **/DT** for Data Table.

    ➤ The following options are displayed.

    1   Creates a data table with one input cell and one or more dependent formulas by inserting trial values from the first column of the table, one at a time, into a single input cell, then recording the resultant values of dependent formulas in the table.

    2   Creates a data table with two input cells and one dependent formula. The left most column and topmost row contain the lists of trial values inserted into the two inputs, and the effects of each possible pair of trial values on a single dependent formula are displayed in the table.

Reset   Clears table ranges and input cells for all data tables.

Since you are trying different values for one input cell only (interest rate), you want 1 (one-way data table).

- Select 1, for one-way data table.

  ➤ A message prompts you to enter the table range.

- Type **A9.B26** and press (ENTER).

  ➤ A message prompts you to enter input cell 1. Input cell 1 is the cell where the values in the table range you just specified will be substituted to produce the results in your data table.

- Type **RATE** and press (ENTER).

  ➤ The results of evaluating PAYMENT, substituting various values (specified in column A) for RATE, are displayed in column B.

You will change the display format so that the screen is easier to read.

- Change the display format of column B, rows 10 through 26, to **currency** (two decimal places).

Cell B9 serves a dual purpose as both the expression to be used in calculation and the heading for the column. Rather than have the value for payment (the same value displayed at cell B4) displayed, it makes more sense to show the expression, +PAYMENT. You can do this by changing the display format to text. Text format shows the entry for the cell, rather than the calculated value.

- With the cell pointer in cell B9, type **/RFT** and press (ENTER).

  ➤ +PAYMENT appears in cell B9, as seen in Screen Display 9–5.

PRACTICE TIME

1. Expand the table so that in column C, rows 10 through 26, total interest paid (INTEREST) for various interest

USING OTHER DATA FEATURES **223**

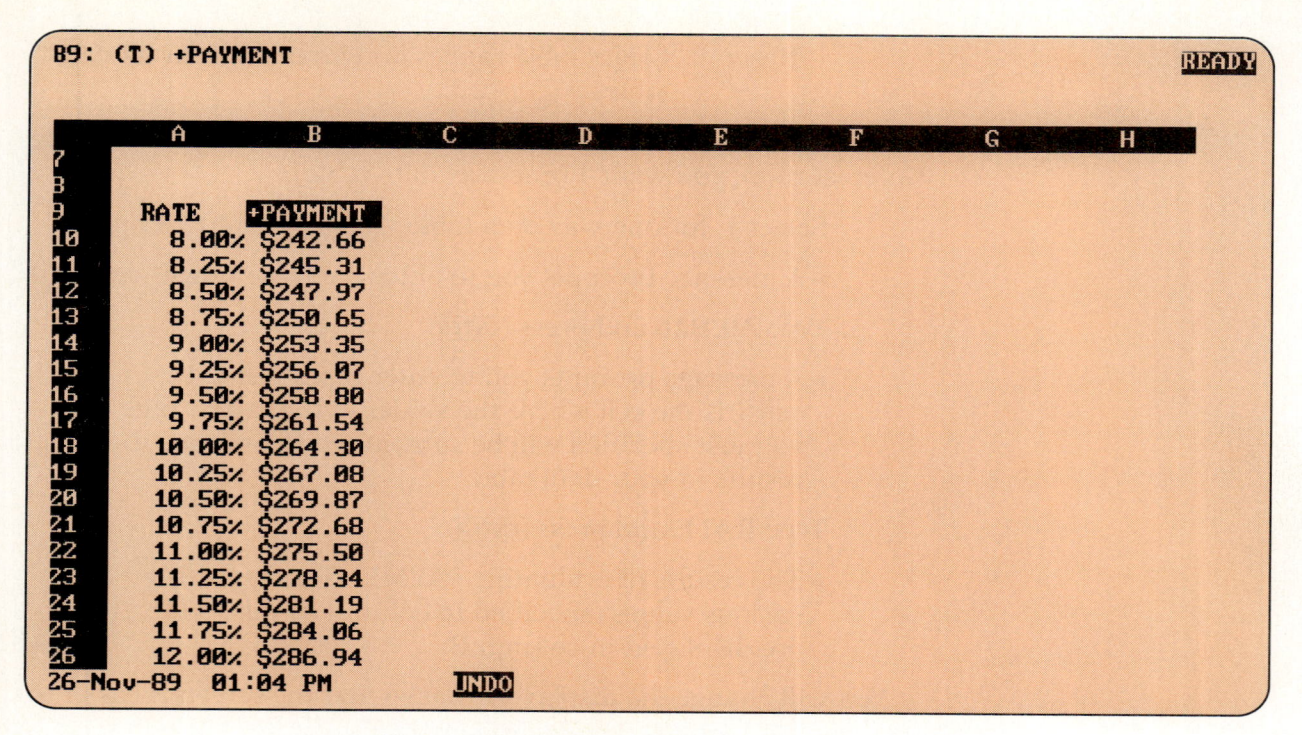

```
B9: (T) +PAYMENT                                                    READY
          A      B        C        D        E        F        G        H
     7
     8
     9    RATE  +PAYMENT
    10    8.00% $242.66
    11    8.25% $245.31
    12    8.50% $247.97
    13    8.75% $250.65
    14    9.00% $253.35
    15    9.25% $256.07
    16    9.50% $258.80
    17    9.75% $261.54
    18   10.00% $264.30
    19   10.25% $267.08
    20   10.50% $269.87
    21   10.75% $272.68
    22   11.00% $275.50
    23   11.25% $278.34
    24   11.50% $281.19
    25   11.75% $284.06
    26   12.00% $286.94
26-Nov-89  01:04 PM         UNDO
```

Screen Display 9–5   Results of a one-way data table.

rates is displayed. You have to enter the expression used for calculation in cell C9. The table range is A9 through C26.

Note: You will have to change the width of column C to accommodate the values.

2. Change the display formats for cell C9 and the range C10 through C26, as seen in Screen Display 9–6.

3. Save the spreadsheet as LOTUS11.

TWO-WAY DATA TABLE (/DT2)

It is pretty clear that if you have a range of interest rates, you will pay the lowest payment and least total interest with the lowest rate. But, suppose you have two variables to consider: rate and term.

224   USING LOTUS 1-2-3

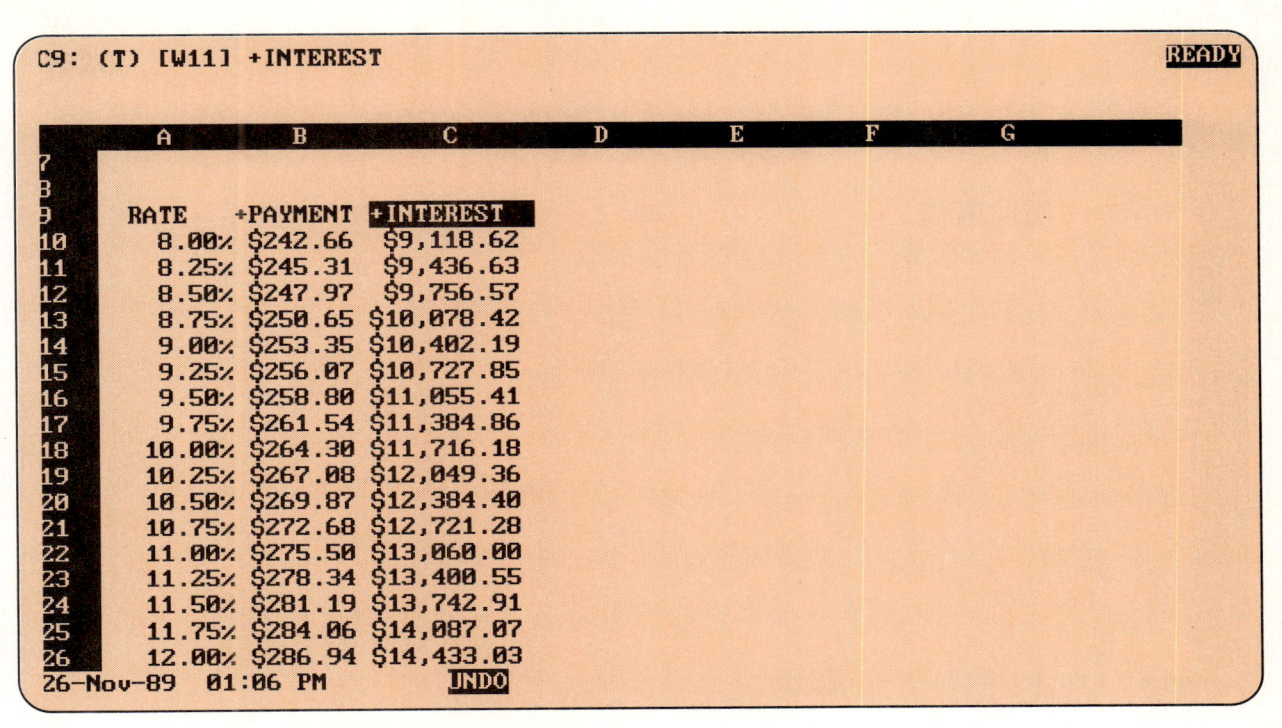

```
C9: (T) [W11] +INTEREST                                    READY

        A       B         C        D      E      F      G
 7
 8
 9    RATE    +PAYMENT  +INTEREST
10    8.00%   $242.66   $9,118.62
11    8.25%   $245.31   $9,436.63
12    8.50%   $247.97   $9,756.57
13    8.75%   $250.65   $10,078.42
14    9.00%   $253.35   $10,402.19
15    9.25%   $256.07   $10,727.85
16    9.50%   $258.80   $11,055.41
17    9.75%   $261.54   $11,384.86
18   10.00%   $264.30   $11,716.18
19   10.25%   $267.08   $12,049.36
20   10.50%   $269.87   $12,384.40
21   10.75%   $272.68   $12,721.28
22   11.00%   $275.50   $13,060.00
23   11.25%   $278.34   $13,400.55
24   11.50%   $281.19   $13,742.91
25   11.75%   $284.06   $14,087.07
26   12.00%   $286.94   $14,433.03
26-Nov-89  01:06 PM             UNDO
```

Screen Display 9–6   A one-way data table with two dependent formulas.

That is, many institutions will offer you lower rates if you take shorter terms, so you need to know whether the higher monthly payments over a shorter period are worth the difference in total interest paid. In other words, there are two values you need to try in your calculations. This is done with a two-way data table.

- Erase the range B9.C26 (**/RE**). Do not erase column A because you will use these values again.

- Reset the display formats for range B9.C9 (**/RFR**). This clears whatever display format (currency and text format, in this case) that you set earlier.

- Reset the Data Table settings by typing **/DTR**. Again, the previous data table settings are cleared.

- Reset the width of column C using the **/WCR** command.

```
B9: 10                                                              READY

         A         B         C         D         E         F       G
  7
  8
  9     +PAYMENT       10        15        20        25        30
 10        8.00%
 11        8.25%
 12        8.50%
 13        8.75%
 14        9.00%
 15        9.25%
 16        9.50%
 17        9.75%
 18       10.00%
 19       10.25%
 20       10.50%
 21       10.75%
 22       11.00%
 23       11.25%
 24       11.50%
 25       11.75%
 26       12.00%
26-Nov-89  01:09 PM           UNDO
```

Screen Display 9–7   The two-way data table is set for calculating payments.

In the two-way data table, the leftmost column contains the first variable, and the top row contains the second variable. The expression to be used in calculation goes in the upper-left-corner cell of the table range: cell A9 in this case. The expression to be calculated is the payment amount.

- Enter +PAYMENT in cell A9. Change the display format of cell A9 to TEXT.

- Use the Data Fill (**/DF**) to insert the values from 10 to 30 in increments of 5, into the cells B9 through F9, as seen in Screen Display 9–7.

Now you will generate the two-way data table. This substitutes amounts that appear in column A for RATE (cell B2) and values that appear in row 9 for TERM (cell B3) and then computes the corresponding PAYMENT (cell B4). The calculated amount will be displayed in the table in the corresponding row and column.

- Type **/DT2** for Two-Way Data Table.

  ➤ You are prompted to enter the table range.

- Type **A9.F26** and press (ENTER).

  ➤ You are prompted to specify where to substitute the values in the leftmost column of the data table.

- Type **RATE** and press (ENTER).

  ➤ You are prompted to specify where to substitute the values in the top row of the data table.

- Type **TERM** and press (ENTER).

  ➤ The word WAIT appears at the status indicator while payment amounts are being calculated.
  ➤ The table is filled with the appropriate payment amounts.

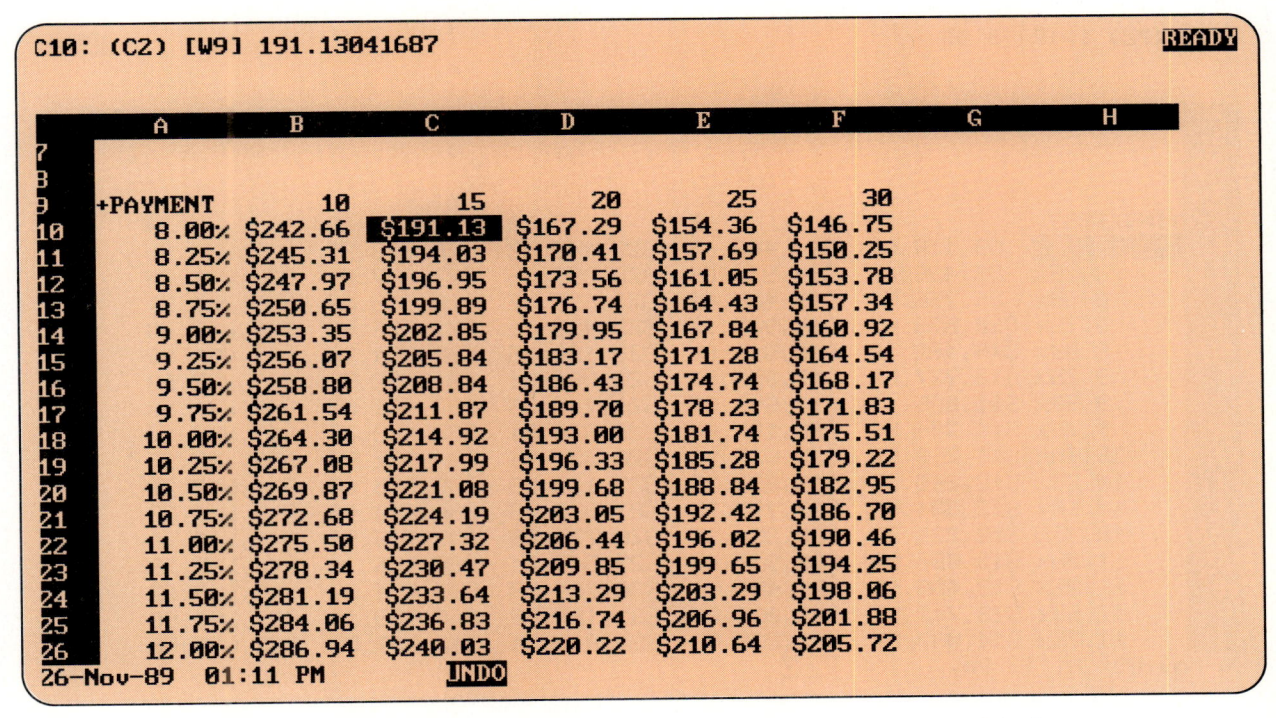

```
C10: (C2) [W9] 191.13041687                                    READY

            A         B         C         D         E         F          G        H
  7
  8
  9    +PAYMENT      10        15        20        25        30
 10      8.00%   $242.66   $191.13   $167.29   $154.36   $146.75
 11      8.25%   $245.31   $194.03   $170.41   $157.69   $150.25
 12      8.50%   $247.97   $196.95   $173.56   $161.05   $153.78
 13      8.75%   $250.65   $199.89   $176.74   $164.43   $157.34
 14      9.00%   $253.35   $202.85   $179.95   $167.84   $160.92
 15      9.25%   $256.07   $205.84   $183.17   $171.28   $164.54
 16      9.50%   $258.80   $208.84   $186.43   $174.74   $168.17
 17      9.75%   $261.54   $211.87   $189.70   $178.23   $171.83
 18     10.00%   $264.30   $214.92   $193.00   $181.74   $175.51
 19     10.25%   $267.08   $217.99   $196.33   $185.28   $179.22
 20     10.50%   $269.87   $221.08   $199.68   $188.84   $182.95
 21     10.75%   $272.68   $224.19   $203.05   $192.42   $186.70
 22     11.00%   $275.50   $227.32   $206.44   $196.02   $190.46
 23     11.25%   $278.34   $230.47   $209.85   $199.65   $194.25
 24     11.50%   $281.19   $233.64   $213.29   $203.29   $198.06
 25     11.75%   $284.06   $236.83   $216.74   $206.96   $201.88
 26     12.00%   $286.94   $240.03   $220.22   $210.64   $205.72
26-Nov-89  01:11 PM                  UNDO
```

Screen Display 9–8   Result of two-way data table for payments.

- Set the display format for range B10.F26 to currency with two decimal places, as seen in Screen Display 9–8.

PRACTICE TIME

1. Get a printout of the PAYMENT table.

2. Save the spreadsheet as LOTUS12.

3. Create a two-way data table for INTEREST. You might start it at cell A30. Make the appropriate display format and column width changes (set width globally to 12) as seen in Screen Display 9–9.

4. Get a printout of the INTEREST table.

5. Save the spreadsheet as LOTUS13.

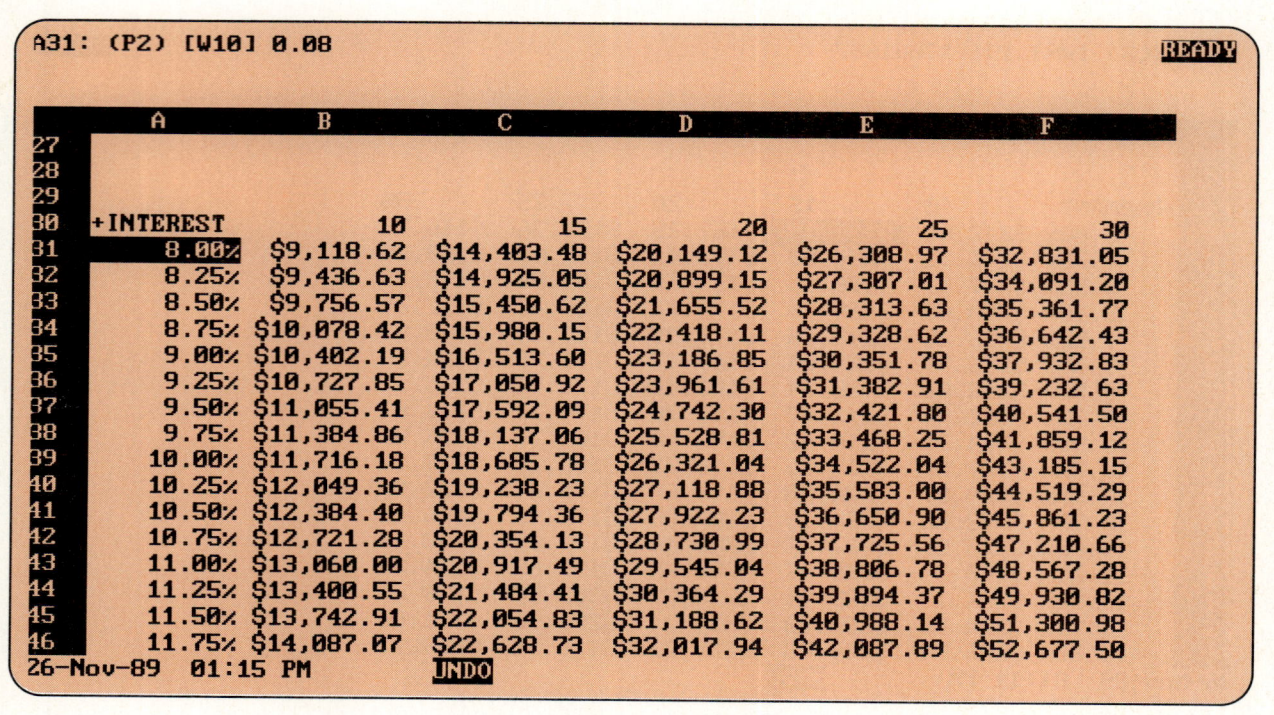

```
A31: (P2) [W10] 0.08                                              READY

           A          B           C           D           E           F
27
28
29
30   +INTEREST        10          15          20          25          30
31      8.00%   $9,118.62  $14,403.48  $20,149.12  $26,308.97  $32,831.05
32      8.25%   $9,436.63  $14,925.05  $20,899.15  $27,307.01  $34,091.20
33      8.50%   $9,756.57  $15,450.62  $21,655.52  $28,313.63  $35,361.77
34      8.75%  $10,078.42  $15,980.15  $22,418.11  $29,328.62  $36,642.43
35      9.00%  $10,402.19  $16,513.60  $23,186.85  $30,351.78  $37,932.83
36      9.25%  $10,727.85  $17,050.92  $23,961.61  $31,382.91  $39,232.63
37      9.50%  $11,055.41  $17,592.09  $24,742.30  $32,421.80  $40,541.50
38      9.75%  $11,384.86  $18,137.06  $25,528.81  $33,468.25  $41,859.12
39     10.00%  $11,716.18  $18,685.78  $26,321.04  $34,522.04  $43,185.15
40     10.25%  $12,049.36  $19,238.23  $27,118.88  $35,583.00  $44,519.29
41     10.50%  $12,384.40  $19,794.36  $27,922.23  $36,650.90  $45,861.23
42     10.75%  $12,721.28  $20,354.13  $28,730.99  $37,725.56  $47,210.66
43     11.00%  $13,060.00  $20,917.49  $29,545.04  $38,806.78  $48,567.28
44     11.25%  $13,400.55  $21,484.41  $30,364.29  $39,894.37  $49,930.82
45     11.50%  $13,742.91  $22,054.83  $31,188.62  $40,988.14  $51,300.98
46     11.75%  $14,087.07  $22,628.73  $32,017.94  $42,087.89  $52,677.50
26-Nov-89  01:15 PM          UNDO
```

Screen Display 9–9 *Result of two-way data table for interest.*

END OF LESSON 9

- Type **/QY** and then press **E** to exit to DOS.
- Remove the disk from the disk drive.
- Turn off the monitor, computer, and printer.

SUMMARY

In this lesson, many of the terms and concepts needed to use the spreadsheet data-command features are discussed:

- The data-fill command is used to fill a range of cells with evenly spaced numbers.
- The data-distribution table shows how values in a range are distributed between arbitrarily chosen categories, or bins.
- The range-name-label command is used to name a range of cells using labels already entered in an adjacent row or column.
- The range-name-table command creates a table in the worksheet showing range names and their locations.
- The @PMT function is used to calculate payment amounts given principal, rate, and term length of a loan.
- A data table lets you do "what-if" analysis by creating a table that shows evaluated results when either one (one-way) or two (two-way) values in an expression are replaced by values taken from the table.
- The following commands are discussed:

/DF	Data Fill—Enters a series of numbers into a range when the increment or decrement is fixed.
/DD	Data Distribution—Tabulates the frequency distribution of a specified range of values.

/DT1	One-Way Data Table—Creates a data table that shows the various results when one value of an expression is replaced by other values.
/DT2	Two-Way Data Table—Creates a data table that shows the various results when two values of an expression are replaced by other values.
/RNL	Range Name Label—Names a range of cells using labels found in adjacent cells.
/RNT	Range Name Table—Creates a table showing named ranges and their locations.

REVIEW QUESTIONS

1. What is the purpose of the Data Fill command?

2. Explain what is meant by data distribution and how it is done.

3. What is the difference between Range Name Create and Range Name Label?

4. Is Range Name Table a permanent part of a spreadsheet? Explain.

5. Explain the purpose of a Data Table.

6. What are the differences between one-way and two-way data tables?

7. Explain the values entered in the first column of the one-way Data Table?

8. What is entered in the first row of the second column of a one-way Data Table?

9. Explain the values in the first column of the two-way Data Table?

    In the first row of the two-way Data Table?

10. In a two-way Data Table, where do you enter the expression to be evaluated?

EXERCISES

1. Retrieve the spreadsheet EX8_1 from Lesson 8.

   a) Find the distribution of the amounts of money owed to you. Use whatever bin values that are appropriate.

   b) Insert appropriate headings.

   c) Print the distribution table.

   d) Save the spreadsheet as EX9_1.

2. Retrieve the spreadsheet EX8_2 from Lesson 8.

   a) Find the distribution student averages. Find out how many students have an average of 60 or below, 61 to 70, and so on.

   b) Insert appropriate headings.

   c) Print the distribution table.

   d) Save the spreadsheet as EX9_2.

3. Set up the following One-Way Data Table.

   a) Enter Labels MILES, MPH, and TIME in column A.

   b) Use labels in column A to name cells in column B.

   c) Given a distance, MILES, of 50 miles you must travel to get to a certain destination and a speed of 35 mph at which you drive, MPH, calculate how long it will take you to get to your destination, TIME (TIME is +MILES/MPH).

   (The TIME is given as a fraction of an hour. If you are ambitious, you can convert time to minutes.)

   d) Obviously, the faster you drive, the sooner you will get there. So, create a data table containing various MPHs

USING OTHER DATA FEATURES **231**

that show the corresponding TIME. MPH can be in the range of 35 mph to 65 mph, at 5 mph increments.

e) Put appropriate headings on the data table. Also, change to the appropriate display format. Then print the spreadsheet.

f) Save the spreadsheet as EX9_3.

4. a) Set up a Two-Way Data Table by expanding on exercise 3 to show various distances (say, 25 to 200 miles in 25-mile increments); the two values being substituted are MILES and MPH. You are to calculate how much time it takes to travel a given distance, MILES, at a set speed, MPH.

b) Put appropriate headings and changes to the display format. Then print the spreadsheet.

c) Save the spreadsheet as EX9_4.

LESSON 10
USING BUILT-IN FUNCTIONS

OBJECTIVES

Upon completion of the material presented in this lesson, you should be able to:

- Understand Lotus 1–2–3 built-in functions
- Recognize various types of functions that are available
- Use some of the more common functions

STARTING OFF

Start Lotus 1–2–3 so that the blank spreadsheet is displayed on the screen. Also, insert the data disk in drive B and change the file directory to B.

FUNCTIONS

In Lessons 5 and 9, you were exposed to two built-in functions, @SUM and @PMT. A built-in function is a pre-written formula, which, like any other formula or expression, produces a numerical or logical result. In addition, some functions let you manipulate alphanumeric data or return information regarding the current cell or the file currently in use. Lotus 1–2–3 has over 90 built-in functions that are divided into eight categories: mathematical (including trigonometric), statistical, logical, financial, date/time, database, string, and special. In addition, third-party software developers who create add-in programs can develop add-in @ functions that perform specific tasks. Some of the more commonly used functions are presented here. Since this is not a lesson in mathematics or finance, the discussions do not always explain how these functions are used. Also, there are a very limited number of **PRACTICE TIMES** in this lesson. The intent of the lesson is to expose you to the availability and operation of the functions. Users who need other functions not covered here can find descriptions of their use in the on-screen help displays (the (F1) function key).

All functions begin with the @ character. The function name may be entered in upper- or lowercase letters. Most functions require that you enter arguments within parentheses, although there are some that do not require any arguments. For example, in the @SUM function, you need to enter the quantities (or cell locations of the quantities) you want added together, and in the @PMT function, you need to enter the principal amount, monthly interest rate, and number of months of the loan. The arguments may be a number, a formula (including other built-in functions), a cell, a range of cells, a list of cells, a named range, or a combination of these.

A function is said to *return* a value or a result. That is, when the function **@PMT(PRINCIPAL, RATE/12, 12*TERM)** is entered in a cell, the function is evaluated and the payment value is substituted, or returned, in place of the function. Although the control panel shows the function you entered, the cell displays the result of evaluating the function.

In this lesson, when arguments are required for the function, they are indicated in lowercase, and the following syntax rules are used:

- If a single numeric argument is required, it is denoted as 'x.' If more numeric arguments are required, they may be denoted as x1, x2, and so on, as in @MOD(x1,x2).

- If the argument needs to be an integer or a cell(s) or range name containing integers, it is denoted as 'n,' as in @ROUND(x,n).

- If a list of numeric arguments can be used, it is denoted 'list,' as in @MIN(list).

- If a list of characters (alphanumeric entry) is required, it is denoted 'string,' as in @LENGTH(string).

- Some variables in financial, date/time, and other functions are given names indicative of the values they represent.

If the syntax above sounds confusing, the examples presented in each section should be helpful in clarification. To begin with, you will place some values in certain cells.

- In cell D1, enter **–7.253**.
- In cell D2, enter **6.62**.

MATHEMATICAL FUNCTIONS

Mathematical functions are used to handle algebraic expressions, equations, trigonometric functions, and formulas.

@ABS(x) returns the absolute value of x. That is, the value of x without a sign (positive or negative) is returned.

- In cell A1, enter **@ABS(D1)**.
  - The value 7.253 appears in the current cell.
  - The expression **@ABS(D1)** appears on the control panel.

@INT(x) returns the integer part, or the whole-number part, of x. It does not round off x to the nearest integer; it simply truncates everything to the right of the decimal.

- In cell A2, enter **@INT(D2)**.
  - 6, which is the integer part of 6.62, is displayed in the cell.
  - The control panel shows **@INT(D2)**.

@MOD($x1,x2$) returns the modulus or remainder when $x1$ is divided by $x2$.

- In cell A3, enter **@MOD(22,6)**.
  - Cell A3 displays 4, which is the remainder when 22 is divided by 6.

@ROUND(x,n) rounds the value of the x to n places to the right of the decimal point. The second argument must be an integer.

- In cell A4, enter **@ROUND(D2,0)**.
  - The cell A4 displays 7. Can you tell the difference between @ROUND and @INT?

@SQRT(x) returns the square root of x. The square root is the value which, when multiplied by itself, yields the argument (x). The argument cannot be less than zero.

- In cell A5, enter **@SQRT(81)**.
  - ➤ The cell displays 9.

@PI returns the value (π), the ratio of the circumference of a circle to its diameter. This function does not require an argument.

- In cell A6, enter **@PI**.
  - ➤ Cell A6 contains 3.141592.

@RAND is another function without an argument. It returns a random number between 0 and 1 (greater than 0, but less than 1). In fact, each time the worksheet recalculates, it recomputes the random number.

- In cell A7, enter **@RAND**.
  - ➤ Some number between 0 and 1 is displayed in cell A7.
- Press the (F9) function key, for CALC (recalculates the worksheet).
  - ➤ Some other number between 0 and 1 is displayed.
- Press the (F9) function key several times more.
  - ➤ Each time you press (F9), a different number between 0 and 1 is displayed.

In functions that use arguments, you may use as arguments a cell address, a named range, or a formula. Also, functions can be nested; that means, other functions may be used as arguments or as a part of arguments. For example, if you want to simulate rolls of dice by randomly generating integer numbers in range 1 to 6, you can use the function @INT(6*@RAND)+1. That is, when you multiply a number between 0 and 1 (result from @RAND) by 6, you get some number greater than 0 but less than 6. So, @INT of that gives 0, 1, 2, 3, 4, or 5. Add 1 and you have numbers between 1 and 6.

Lotus 1–2–3 has the standard trigonometric functions @COS(x), @SIN(x), @TAN(x), @ACOS(x), @ASIN(x), and @ATAN(x). The angle is always given, or returned, in radians. These functions are not discussed here.

PRACTICE TIME

Suppose your service club holds a lottery at its monthly meetings and you are asked to have the computer generate six (integer) random numbers, each ranging from 0 to 99. You decide to generate seven random numbers (the last one in case of a duplicate).

1. In cells B10 through B16, enter the labels **ONE**, **TWO**, ..., **SIX**, **ALTERNATE**.

2. Enter the appropriate formula in cell C10 and copy it into cells C11 through C16.

3. Press the (F9) (calc) key several times to verify that the function you entered returns integers from 0 to 99 each time.

STATISTICAL FUNCTIONS

Statistical computations may make use of several functions. Statistical terminologies are not explained here. For demonstration purposes, fill 20 cells with random numbers as follows.

- Clear the worksheet using **/WEY**.
- In cell A1, enter **@RAND**.
- Copy the content of A1 into the range A2 through A20.
  - ➤ Cells A1 through A20 are filled with random numbers between 0 and 1.
- Name the range A1 to A20 ARRAY by using **/RNC**.
- Place the cell pointer at cell B1.

@AVG(*list*) returns the average of a given list. As described earlier, the list may consist of values, expressions, cell locations, cell ranges, or range names.

- In cell B1, enter **@AVG(ARRAY)**.
  - ➤ Cell B1 displays the average of values in the cell range A1 through A20.

USING BUILT-IN FUNCTIONS

@COUNT(*list*) returns the number of cells in a given list, counting only cells with values, except that the minimum value returned is 1, regardless of whether or not any values are present.

- In cell B2, enter **@COUNT(ARRAY)**.
    - ➤ Cell B2 displays 20, which is the number of cells in the named range ARRAY.

@SUM(*list*) returns the sum of the values in the list. This was introduced in lesson 5.

@MAX(*list*) returns the maximum value in the list.

- In cell B3, enter **@MAX(ARRAY)**.
    - ➤ Cell B3 displays the greatest value in the list (which, in this case, changes each time the spreadsheet is recalculated).

@MIN(*list*) returns the minimum value in the list.

- In cell B4, enter **@MIN(ARRAY)**.
    - ➤ Cell B4 displays the lowest value in the list.

@STD(*list*) returns the population or unadjusted standard deviation, ignoring blank cells in the list. A standard deviation shows the average value by which values deviate from the mean.

- In cell B5, enter **@STD(ARRAY)**.
    - ➤ Cell B5 displays the population standard deviation.

@VAR(*list*) returns the population variance of the list. The variance is the square of the standard deviation.

- In cell B6, enter **@VAR(ARRAY)**.
    - ➤ Cell B6 displays the population variance.

PRACTICE TIME

1. Retrieve the spreadsheet LOTUS3 from Lesson 6 containing Susan's spreadsheet, as seen in Screen Display 10–1.

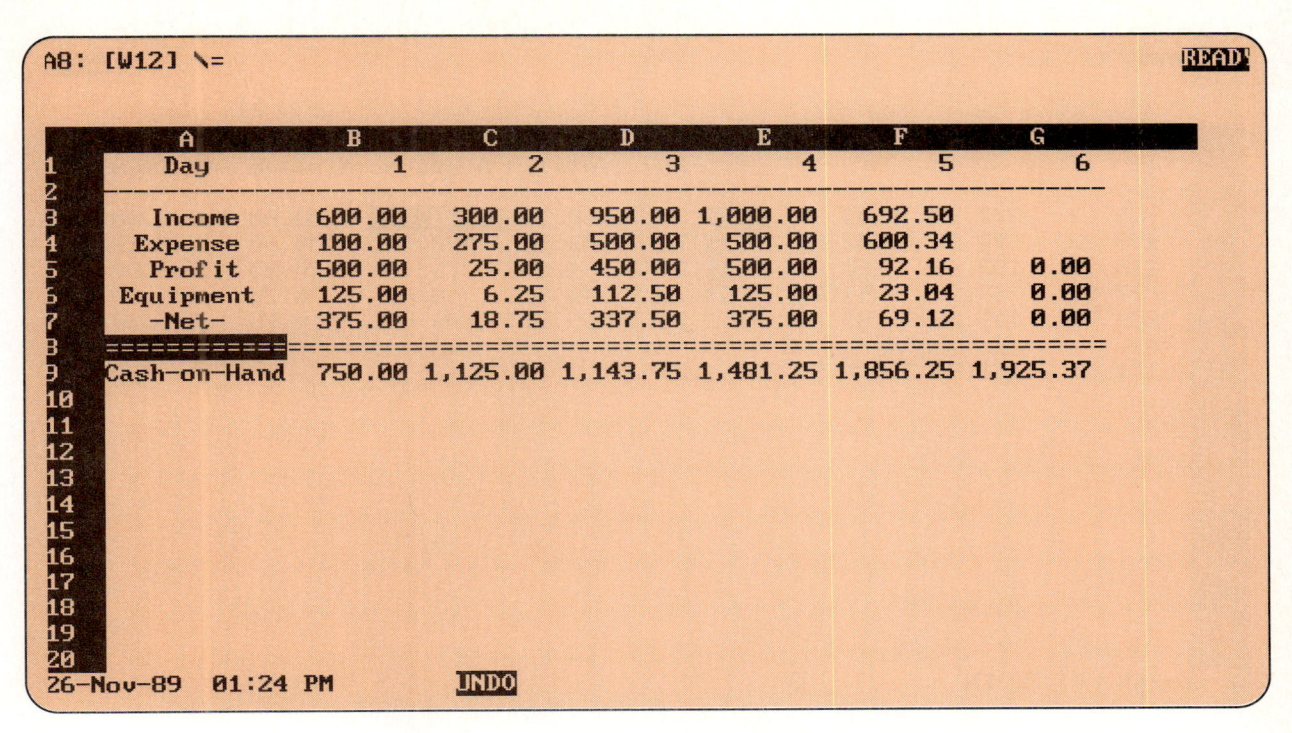

```
A8: [W12] \=                                                                    READY

       A         B        C        D        E         F        G
  1   Day        1        2        3        4         5        6
  2   ─────────────────────────────────────────────────────────────
  3   Income    600.00   300.00   950.00 1,000.00    692.50
  4   Expense   100.00   275.00   500.00   500.00    600.34
  5   Profit    500.00    25.00   450.00   500.00     92.16     0.00
  6   Equipment 125.00     6.25   112.50   125.00     23.04     0.00
  7   -Net-     375.00    18.75   337.50   375.00     69.12     0.00
  8   ==============================================================
  9  Cash-on-Hand 750.00 1,125.00 1,143.75 1,481.25 1,856.25 1,925.37
 10
 ...
 20
26-Nov-89  01:24 PM           UNDO
```

Screen Display 10–1   Worksheet of income and expenses.

2. Enter the following values for Income and Expense in columns G through K.

	G	H	I	J	K
Income	589.35	769.63	872.33	949.28	935.35
Expense	328.28	459.32	678.88	742.25	719.74

3. In column M, display the average income, expense, profit, equipment, and net, using the @AVG function.

4. In column N, display the minimum value for income, expense, profit, equipment, and net, using the @MIN function.

5. In column O, display the maximum value for income, expense, profit, equipment, and net, using the @MAX function, as seen in Screen Display 10–2.

6. Save the spreadsheet as LOTUS14.

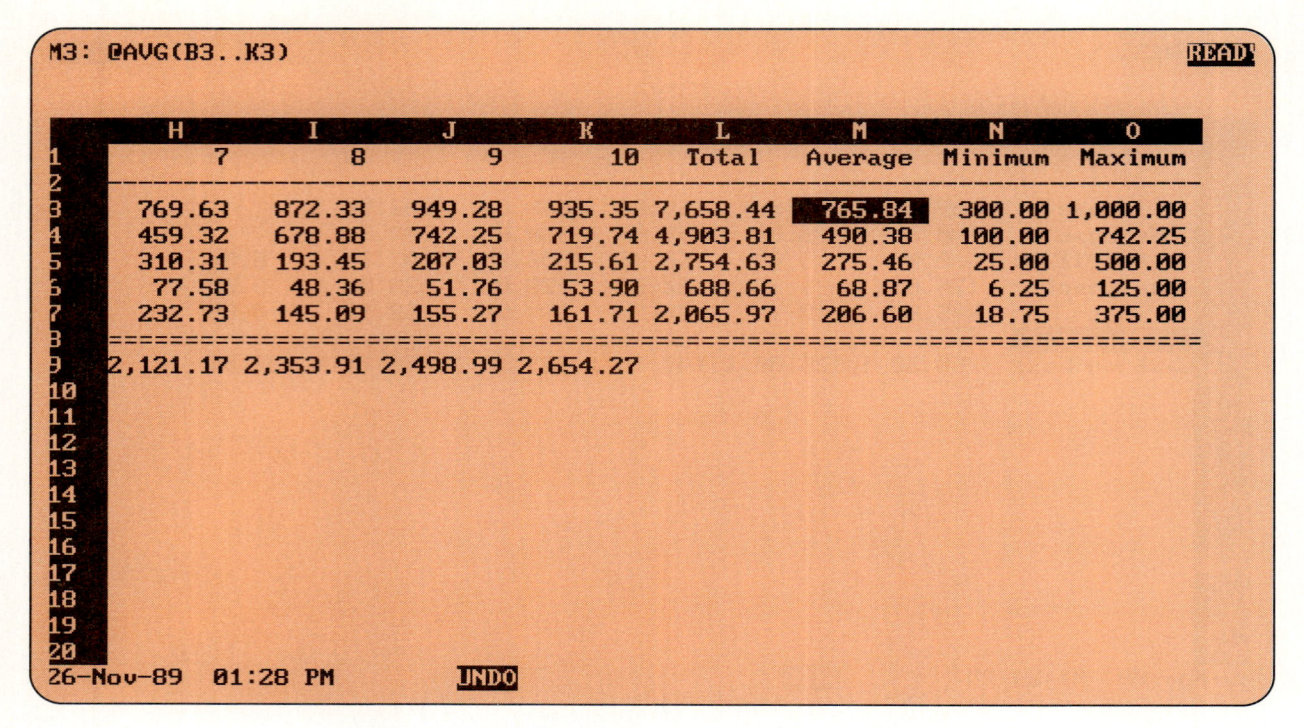

```
M3: @AVG(B3..K3)                                                    READY

        H         I         J         K        L        M        N        O
1       7         8         9        10      Total   Average  Minimum  Maximum
2     ─────────────────────────────────────────────────────────────────────────
3     769.63    872.33    949.28    935.35  7,658.44  765.84   300.00  1,000.00
4     459.32    678.88    742.25    719.74  4,903.81  490.38   100.00    742.25
5     310.31    193.45    207.03    215.61  2,754.63  275.46    25.00    500.00
6      77.58     48.36     51.76     53.90    688.66   68.87     6.25    125.00
7     232.73    145.09    155.27    161.71  2,065.97  206.60    18.75    375.00
8     ==========================================================================
9   2,121.17  2,353.91  2,498.99  2,654.27

26-Nov-89   01:28 PM         UNDO
```

Screen Display 10–2 *Computation of average, minimum, and maximum.*

LOGICAL FUNCTIONS

Logical functions lend flexibility to the spreadsheet by giving it a decision-making capability. They give you the ability to display an answer, choose a course of action, or make a selection based on values or conditions entered on the worksheet. You saw how the logical decision process works in Lesson 8 while doing database queries based on formula conditions.

A result of a condition is either 'true' or 'false.' A condition tested is usually a comparison of two values. That is, you are testing whether one value on the worksheet is:

=	equal to another value;
>	greater than another value;
<	less than another value;
<>	not equal to another value;
<=	less than or equal to another value; or
>=	greater than or equal to another value.

These are the six relational operators that may be used in a condition. A condition must be entered without spaces between the operators and the values being tested. If you enter a condition with such spaces, Lotus 1-2-3 will not accept the entry and you will have to edit the spaces out.

A condition may be compound; that is, you can test for a multiple condition such as for a number greater than zero, but less than 1. In order to do this, the logical operators #AND#, #OR#, and #NOT# are used. Use of these three logical operators is shown below, with spaces given before and after the operators for the sake of clarity only.

> Condition-1 #AND# condition-2 returns 'true' if both condition-1 and condition-2 are 'true.'

> Condition-1 #OR# condition-2 returns 'true' if at least one of the conditions is 'true.'

> #NOT# condition returns 'true' only if condition is 'false.'

Lotus 1-2-3 allows only numerical values to be returned by logical functions: a 'true' result is represented by the value 1, and 'false' is represented by the value 0. Additionally, in the logical evaluation of a value, any nonzero value is equivalent to 'true,' and zero is equivalent to 'false.' These points will become clear in the following examples.

The following steps introduce the use of logical functions.

- Clear the spreadsheet using **/WEY**.

- In cell A1, enter **5=5**.

    ➤ The value 1 appears in cell A1, indicating that the condition, 5=5, is 'true.'

- In cell A2, enter **4=2**.

    ➤ The value 0 appears at cell A2, indicating that the condition, 4=2, is 'false.'

Let's try some compound conditions.

- In cell A3, enter **3<4#AND#4<2**.

    ➤ Since the second condition (4<2) is 'false,' the entire condition is 'false.' Hence, the value 0 is displayed in A3.

- Edit the entry in A3 and change #AND# to #OR#.
    - ➤ Since the first condition (3<4) is 'true' (notice the 1 in cell A1), the entire condition is 'true.' Hence, the value 1 is displayed in A3.

Next, let's enter a compound condition using cell addresses containing conditions.

- In cell A4, enter **A1#OR#A2**.
    - ➤ Since the condition in A1 is 'true' (notice the 1 in cell A1), the entire expression is 'true.'

Recall that, as mentioned, any non-zero number is 'true.'

- In cell A5, enter **7#AND#5**.
    - ➤ Cell A5 displays 1. Since 7 and 5 are both nonzero, they are considered 'true,' and since both conditions are 'true,' the entire expression is 'true.'

Conditions and relational operations are important concepts involved in @IF functions, which are described next.

@IF(*condition,x1,x2*) evaluates a given condition. If the condition is 'true' (not zero), *x1* is returned; if it is 'false,' *x2* is returned. The condition may be a number, an expression containing relational operators or logical operators (or both), or a cell location. The last two arguments, *x1* and *x2*, may be either numeric or strings (enclosed in quotes).

- Enter the value **14** in cell C1 and **7** at C2.
- In cell C3, enter **@IF(C2=0,0,C1/C2)**.
    - ➤ The value 2 appears in cell C3.

This expression evaluates the condition C2=0. Since C2 is 7 and not 0, the expression is 'false.' Hence, the last argument C1/C2 is returned.

- Change the entry at C2 to **0**.
    - ➤ Since the condition is now 'true,' the second argument is returned. Hence, C3 displays 0.

@TRUE and @FALSE can be used to indicate explicitly that you are setting some cells 'true' or 'false.' These functions are often associated with the @IF function to indicate explicitly that you are setting something 'true' or 'false' to see the effect of this condition on the rest of the spreadsheet. They may also be useful in the last two arguments of an @IF function.

- In cell C4, enter **@IF(C2=0,@TRUE,@FALSE)**.

    ➤ Since the condition is 'true,' @TRUE, or 1, is returned in cell C4.

@ISERR(x) returns 'true' if x has the value ERR (error value). Otherwise, 'false' results. An error value occurs when a negative square root is taken, division by zero is attempted, or a function has an expression too large or too small for evaluation. In such cases, the word ERR is placed in the cell of concern. The argument, x, in this case is a cell address, and if the condition in the cell is in error, then @ISERR returns 'true.'

- In cell D1, enter **7**.

- In cell D2, enter **0** (zero).

- In cell D3, enter **+D1/D2**.

    ➤ ERR is displayed in cell D3. Since this is 7 divided by zero, division by zero results in an error.

- In cell D4, enter **@IF(@ISERR(D3),D1,D3)**.

    ➤ Since cell D3 contains an error, the condition is 'true,' and hence the value at D1 is displayed.

- Change the value in cell D2 to **3**.

    ➤ Now that cell D3 does not contain ERR, the condition in the expression in cell D4 is 'false' and hence the value at D3 is displayed.

PRACTICE TIME

1. Retrieve the spreadsheet LOTUS14.

2. Change the value at C4 to 375. Now, the value for expense exceeds that of income; hence the profit is $-75.00 (loss of $75.00). It really does not make sense to purchase any equipment when there is a loss. Change

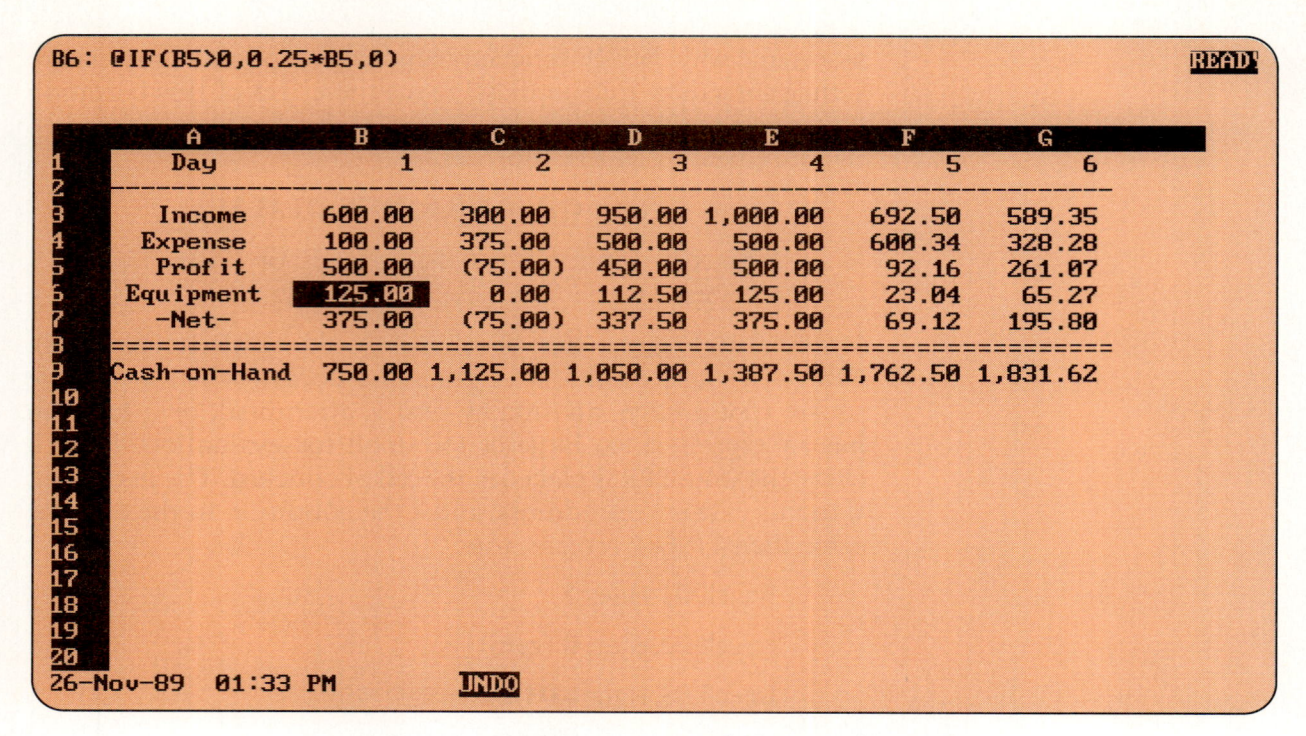

```
B6: @IF(B5>0,0.25*B5,0)                                                    READY

        A           B         C         D         E         F         G
  1    Day          1         2         3         4         5         6
  2   ------------------------------------------------------------------------
  3   Income      600.00    300.00    950.00  1,000.00    692.50    589.35
  4   Expense     100.00    375.00    500.00    500.00    600.34    328.28
  5    Profit     500.00    (75.00)   450.00    500.00     92.16    261.07
  6   Equipment   125.00      0.00    112.50    125.00     23.04     65.27
  7    -Net-      375.00    (75.00)   337.50    375.00     69.12    195.80
  8   ========================================================================
  9   Cash-on-Hand 750.00 1,125.00  1,050.00  1,387.50  1,762.50  1,831.62

 26-Nov-89  01:33 PM         UNDO
```

Screen Display 10–3   Worksheet with @IF functions.

the entry for equipment at B6 so that if the entry for Profit is zero or less, the equipment is zero (none purchased); otherwise it is to display .25 times Profit.

3. Copy the formula at B6 to range C6 through K6, so that your screen resembles that seen in Screen Display 10–3.

4. Save the spreadsheet as LOTUS15.

5. Clear the spreadsheet.

FINANCIAL FUNCTIONS

Lotus 1–2–3 has several useful financial functions. Only three are described here. As with other functions, a detailed explanation of how these functions are used will not be presented here.

@PMT(*prin,i,term*) is a function that calculates the payments on a loan, given the principal (*prin*), the rate of interest for each period (*i*), and the number of periods (*term*). This function was described in Lesson 9.

@FV(*pmt,i,term*) is a function that returns the future value of payments made to you, given the amount of payment each period (*pmt*), the interest rate per period (*i*), and the number of periods (*term*). This could be used to see how much your contributions to a college fund grow. Suppose you are interested in making monthly payments of $100 to a fund at 6% annual interest (0.5% per term) for 50 months.

- In cell E1, enter **@FV(100,0.06/12,50)**.

  ➤ You will have 5664.516.

PRACTICE TIME

Change the display format of cell E1 so that it is $ (Currency) with two places to the right of the decimal. Adjust the column widths accordingly.

@NPV(*i,range*) calculates the net present value of payments (the entries in the range given in the argument), based on an interest rate (*i*) per period between payments. This gives you the equivalent value that such payments would be worth to you right now if you could invest that money at interest rate *i*.

Suppose you could invest money at 8 per cent per year, but your brother-in-law has asked for a business start-up loan of $25,000. He promises to pay you back $5000 at the end of the first year, $11,000 at the end of the second year, and $18,000 at the end of the third year. The following is how you can figure out which investment yields the greater return (aside from family politics).

- Enter the values 5000, 11000, and 18000 in cells E2 through E4.
- In cell E5, enter **@NPV(.08,E2.E4)**.

  ➤ Cell E5 displays the value 28349.336.

The answer is the amount of money, invested at 8 percent per year, that would yield the payments your brother-in-law has

USING BUILT-IN FUNCTIONS **247**

promised. That is, in order to make the amount of money your brother-in-law has promised, you would have to invest $28,349.34 at 8 percent for three years.

DATE/TIME FUNCTIONS

There are fifteen functions for manipulating dates and time. The date values used for manipulations are in whole numbers in the range 0 (January 1, 1900) to 36525 (December 31, 1999). The time used is a 24–hour clock.

@DATE(*year,month,day*) returns the date value for the date entered. The three arguments required are year (1900 as 0), month, and date. For example, September 1, 1990 is entered as @DATE(90,9,1). The date value is useful in determining how many days have elapsed since a given date, such as when determining people who are 30 days delinquent in their payments.

- Clear the spreadsheet.
- In cell A1, enter the present date using @DATE function.

    ➤ A number somewhere between 32000 and 34000 is displayed.

Since this number does not make much sense to someone looking at the screen, you need to change the display.

- Type **/RF**, then select Date.

    ➤ The following options are displayed:

1	(DD–MMM–YY)	21–Nov–90
2	(DD–MMM)	21–Nov
3	(MMM–YY)	Nov–90
4	(Long Intn'l)	11/21/90
5	(Short Intn'l)	11/21
Time		Time formats

- Select **1** (DD–MMM–YY).

    ➤ You are prompted to enter the range to format.

- Press (ENTER) to specify the current cell.
- Increase the column width so the date is displayed.

- In cell A2, enter **+A1+30**. This allows you to determine the date 30 days from the present. Again, change the display format.

@DAY(*date*) returns the day of the month. The date in the argument must be given in date value.

- In cell A3, enter **@DAY(@DATE(90,7,4)+100)**.
  - The cell displays 12, indicating that 100 days after the 4th of July in 1990 is the 12th of a certain month.

@MONTH(*date*) returns the month number (1–12) of a date, entered as a date value. You will try the same example as above.

- In cell A4, enter **@MONTH(@DATE(90,7,4)+100)**.
  - The cell displays 10.

Now you know that Columbus Day (October 12) follows the Fourth of July by exactly 100 days!

@YEAR(*date*) returns a number representing the year. However, to find the year, add 1900 to the number returned. Thus, 101 becomes 2001 and –33 becomes 1867.

You can find out the year in which you will be exactly 20,000 days old. If you were born on March 31, 1968, enter **@YEAR(@DATE(68,3,31)+20000)+1900**. (This person turns 20,000 days old in the year 2023.)

- In cell A5, enter the expression appropriate for your birthday.

@TODAY returns today's number, based on the computer's clock. If you did not set the time and date at the beginning of the session (when you booted the system), you could end up with today being given as January 1, 1980.

- In cell A6, enter **@TODAY**.
  - A number between 32000 and 34000 is displayed. Remember, the date value is displayed. You have to change the display format to see something more familiar.

USING BUILT-IN FUNCTIONS **249**

If you look at the control panel, @INT(@NOW) is displayed instead of @TODAY, which you entered. The @NOW function is explained next.

@NOW returns a whole number followed by a decimal fraction. The integer portion is the date value, as you just saw, and the fraction represents the present time (as a fraction of the day). Using the appropriate display format, you can see the time. @NOW will not work properly, however, unless (a) you previously set the time when you turned the computer on or (b) the computer's time was set from a battery-driven clock/calendar.

- In cell A7, enter **@NOW** and set the format to display the time. Time can be displayed as a 24–hour clock or as AM/PM time.

The time is not updated automatically. It is updated only when the spreadsheet is recalculated.

You can use the @HOUR, @MINUTE, and @SECOND functions in a similar manner to date functions. Try these on your own.

DATABASE FUNCTIONS

All seven statistical functions are supplied for use in a database as well. They perform the same operations as the statistical functions, but they have three arguments instead of one, to make them more suitable for calculations with databases. The three arguments are the input range, the offset (from the first column of the input range), and the criteria range. Only those records meeting the given criteria are selected from the input range for evaluation.

You will retrieve file LOTUS9 to see how database statistical functions can be used.

- Retrieve file **LOTUS9** containing the input, criteria, and output ranges for a database query.
- Range erase A21..H21 to clear the criteria range.

Suppose you want to find the total quantity of parts warehoused in section A. You can use the @DSUM function.

- In cell H21, enter **A*** to represent all the locations beginning with A.

250   USING LOTUS 1-2-3

Note that the Quantity column, column G, is the sixth column from the left edge of the database. To find this, count with column A as zero, B as 1, and so on.

- In cell A23, enter **@DSUM(A1.H18,6,A20.H21)**.

➤ The value 5352 is returned in A23.

STRING FUNCTIONS

String functions work on the alphanumeric entries in the spreadsheet. These allow you to manipulate a series of characters, or *strings*. A string that you enter in an argument may be a cell address or a series of characters enclosed in quotes (example: "hello").

- Clear the spreadsheet.
- In cell A1, enter the name **Keiko Pitter**.

@LEFT(*string,n*) lets you extract *n* number of characters from the left side of the string.

- In cell A2, enter **@LEFT(A1,5)**.

➤ Cell A2 displays `Keiko`, or the first five characters of the string in cell A1.

@RIGHT(*string,n*) lets you extract *n* number of characters from the right side of the string.

- In cell A3, enter **@RIGHT(A1,6)**.

➤ Cell A3 displays `Pitter`, or the right six characters of the string in cell A1.

@LENGTH(*string*) returns the number of characters in a string.

- In cell A4, enter **@LENGTH(A1)**.

➤ Cell A4 displays `12`.

@FIND(*string1, string2, n*) returns the starting location of string1 within string2. The first position is 0 (instead of 1).

Note: When working with strings, position always starts with 0. In the string ABCDEF, the character A is at position 0, B at position 1, and so on.

USING BUILT-IN FUNCTIONS   **251**

You will find the position of the blank character (" ") in the entry at cell A1. You want to start the search at the first position.

- In cell A5, enter **@FIND(" ",A1,0)**.
  - ➤ Cell A5 displays `5`.

You might note that the location of a blank character is also the number of characters that exist in the string before the blank character. By combining the functions given above, you can do some fancy manipulations.

- In cell A6, enter **Charles Darwin**.
- In cell A7, enter **@LEFT(A6,@FIND(" ",A6,0))**.
  - ➤ This returns `Charles`.

The expression in cell A7 says to return some characters from the left part of the entry in cell A6. To return the first word, use the @FIND function to find its length. The next example shows how to get the remainder of the contents in cell A6.

- In cell A8, enter **@RIGHT(A6,@LENGTH(A6)–@FIND(" ",A6,0)–1)**.
  - ➤ This returns `Darwin`.
- Now enter your name in cell A6.

@MID(*string,position,n*) returns *n* number of characters in the string, starting at the position specified. Remember, the first character of the string is at position 0.

- In cell A9, enter **@MID(A1,3,2)**.
  - ➤ Cell A9 displays `ko`.

@LOWER(*string*) converts a string to all lowercase.

- In cell C1, enter **@LOWER(A1)**.
  - ➤ Cell C1 displays `keiko pitter`.

@UPPER(*string*) converts a string to all uppercase.

- In cell C2, enter **@UPPER(A1)**.
  - ➤ Cell C2 displays `KEIKO PITTER`.

@REPLACE(*string1,position,n,string2*) replaces *n* number of characters in string1, starting at the specified position, with string2.

- In cell C3, enter **@REPLACE(A1,0,5,"Jackie")**.
  - ➤ Cell C3 displays `Jackie Pitter`.

@STRING(*x,y*) converts numeric value *x* to a string (alphanumeric—it cannot be used in calculation), displaying *y* digits to the right of the decimal.

- In cell E1, enter **@STRING(123.45,0)**.
  - ➤ Cell E1 displays `123` left justified (which means label).

@VALUE(*string*) works the reverse of the @STRING function; that is, given a number entered as a string (alphanumeric), @VALUE converts it to a numeric value.

- In cell E2, enter **'45.6** (number 45.6 entered as a label).
- In cell E3, enter **@VALUE(E2)**.
  - ➤ Cell E3 displays numeric `45.6` (right justified).

SPECIAL FUNCTIONS

These functions return various informational items. Try them on your own.

@CELL(*attribute,location*) returns information regarding a cell at the specified location in the worksheet. You request any one of the items of information by specifying the appropriate attribute. The attribute must be enclosed in quotes.

address	Cell's address
col	Cell's column position
contents	Cell's contents (an empty cell returns 0)
filename	The name of the current file, including path
format	Cell's format
prefix	Cell's label prefix character (for label entry)
protect	Cell's protection status
row	Cell's row number

USING BUILT-IN FUNCTIONS **253**

type   Cell's type of data (b=blank,l=label,v=value or formula)
width   Cell's column width

For example, to display the content of cell A1, enter **@CELL("contents",A1)**.

@CELLPOINTER(*attribute*) works just like the @CELL function except that it returns information about the cell where the cell pointer is currently located.

@COLS(*range*) returns the number of columns in a range.

@ROWS(*range*) returns the number of rows in a range.

The special functions also include four Lookup functions—@HLOOKUP, @VLOOKUP, @CHOOSE, and @INDEX. These functions make table lookup easier.

@HLOOKUP AND VLOOKUP are useful ways to use a table of values. Examples of cases where lookup functions can be used include the U.S. Tax Rate Schedules and determining a grade in a class. You will try the latter example.

You are a teacher, and you have the semester total points for students in a class. You assigned a possible 843 points, and you use 90% as the cutoff for A, 80% for cutoff for B, 70% for C, 60% for D. Given the number of points each student earned, you want the spreadsheet to assign a grade using the criteria just mentioned.

The @VLOOKUP(*x,range,offset*) function requires three arguments. The first argument is the value to look up. The second is a range (or name of a range) that holds test values in the first column and numbers to be returned in one of the remaining columns. The third argument, the offset, is the number of columns from the test column to the column containing the values to be returned. The program looks for the row with a test value closest to, but not less than, the first argument (*x*). This row is used, and the offset determines which column contains the value to be returned.

This will become clearer as you proceed with the exercise. Rather than entering students' test grades, you will just enter their total points.

■ Clear the spreadsheet using **/WEY**.

- Enter student names in column A and total points in column B along with the appropriate headings, as follows:

	A	B	C
1	NAME	TOTAL	GRADE
2	JOHN	725	
3	LARRY	690	
4	MARY	668	
5	SUE	769	
6	LINDA	580	
7	HELEN	622	
8	GINGER	500	
9	---
10	POSSIBLE	843	

This area of the worksheet contains your data. You want to see what letter grade each student is to receive.

- Name cell B10 as TOTAL. This saves time later on.

- Starting at cell B12, enter the following table. The score goes in column B and grade goes in column C.

	B	C
12	SCORE	GRADE
13	0	F
14	.6*TOTAL	D
15	.7*TOTAL	C
16	.8*TOTAL	B
17	.9*TOTAL	A
18	+TOTAL	

➤ Your spreadsheet should appear as shown in Screen Display 10–4.

- Name the range from B13 to C18 **TABLE**.

TABLE contains the lookup table. It is called a vertical table because the numbers appear in columns. A horizontal table would have the numbers appearing in rows.

At C2 through C8, you will enter the expression that will cause the numbers in column B to be compared with TABLE, and the appropriate grade in column C returned for each student.

USING BUILT-IN FUNCTIONS **255**

```
B18:  +TOTAL                                                    READY

           A           B           C       D       E       F       G       H
      1  NAME        TOTAL       GRADE
      2  JOHN          725
      3  LARRY         690
      4  MARY          668
      5  SYE           769
      6  LINDA         580
      7  HELEN         622
      8  GINGER        500
      9  ------------------------------
     10  POSSIBLE      843
     11
     12               SCORE       GRADE
     13                   0       F
     14               505.8       D
     15               590.1       C
     16               674.4       B
     17               758.7       A
     18                 843
     19
     20
     26-Nov-89  01:54 PM         UNDO                                    CAPS
```

Screen Display 10–4 Worksheet for determining student grades.

■ In cell C2, enter **@VLOOKUP(B2,TABLE,1)**.

➤ The grade of B appears in cell C2.

In this particular case, 725 (the value at cell B2) was compared along the first column of TABLE (column B, starting at B13). 725 is greater than 674.4 but less than 758.7, therefore row 16 was selected. Then, the program returned the value located one (the value found in the third argument) column away from the test values in column B. That is the entry in column C, which is B.

While you should be familiar with copying expressions along a row, which you want to do to get the grades for the remaining students, you should realize that Lotus 1–2–3 treats the copying of range names (such as TABLE, in this instance) as relative copies. Thus, since TABLE refers to the range B13..C18, when you copy this expression to C3, it sets the second argument to B14..C19. Obviously, you do not want to do this, so you need to force the reference to TABLE to be absolute. To do this, the range name needs to have a $ preceding it.

- Edit the entry at cell C2 to read
  @VLOOKUP(B2,$TABLE,1).

- Copy the entry in cell C2 down the column to get the grades of the remaining students, as seen in Screen Display 10–5.

- Save the spreadsheet as LOTUS16.

@HLOOKUP works like @VLOOKUP, except that the table values are in one row, in adjacent columns. The third argument is the offset, that is, the number of rows offset (down) from the test row to the row containing the values to be returned.

@CHOOSE(x,y0,y1,y2,...,yn) returns one value from the series *y0* to *yn* that corresponds to the value of *x*. That is, if *x* = 3, *y3* is returned; if *x* = 0, *y0* is returned.

- Clear the worksheet.

```
C2: @VLOOKUP(B2,$TABLE,1)                                          READY

         A          B         C        D        E        F        G        H
  1   NAME       TOTAL     GRADE
  2   JOHN         725     B
  3   LARRY        690     B
  4   MARY         668     C
  5   SYE          769     A
  6   LINDA        580     D
  7   HELEN        622     C
  8   GINGER       500     F
  9   ─────────────────────────────
 10   POSSIBLE     843
 11
 12              SCORE     GRADE
 13                  0     F
 14              505.8     D
 15              590.1     C
 16              674.4     B
 17              758.7     A
 18                843
 19
 20
 26-Nov-89  01:56 PM                UNDO
```

Screen Display 10–5 Worksheet with student grades.

Let's say that there are three levels of pay that a clerk might earn.

- In cell B10, enter $5.50.
- In cell B11, enter $6.00.
- In cell B12, enter $6.50.

You are creating a spreadsheet for a payroll.

- In cell A1, enter the label **CLERK NAME**. Set the column width to 12.
- In cell B1, enter the label **SALARY**.
- In cell A2, enter **Bill Bowers**.
- In cell A3, enter **Jane Randall**.

Bill Bowers earns level 2 pay, and Jane Randall earns level 3 pay. Remember that the first cell in the range $y0$ to yn is chosen if $x = 0$.

- In cell B2, enter **@CHOOSE(1,B10,B11,B12)**.

PRACTICE TIME

Jane Randall earns level 3 pay. Make the proper entry in cell B3.

@INDEX(*range,col#,row#*) returns the value at column *col#* and row *row#* of the specified range. Col# and row# are locations relative to the beginning of the range. Also, the first position for either number is zero (0).

- Clear the worksheet.
- Create a table at columns B through E, rows 10 through 12 by entering the following:

	B	C	D	E
10	Jane	Mary	Janet	Chris
11	Nancy	Paula	Barbara	Karen
12	Susan	Vicky	Joan	Ava

- Name the table (the range B10.E12) **GIRLS**.

- In cell A1, enter **@INDEX(GIRLS,2,1)**.
  - ➤ In cell A1, the name `Barbara` is displayed.

Note that Barbara is in the second column from the left-most column of the range, and the first row down from the top row of the range.

PRACTICE TIME

In cell A2, enter the expression to retrieve the name Vicky.

END OF LESSON 10

- Type **/QY**, then **Y** to exit 1–2–3, then press **E** to exit to DOS.
- Remove the disks from the disk drive.
- Turn off the monitor, computer, and printer.

SUMMARY

In this lesson, many of the terms and concepts that are necessary to use built-in functions are discussed:

- A built-in function is a pre-written formula, which, like any other formula or expression, produces (returns) a numerical or logical result. In addition, some functions let you manipulate alphanumeric data or return information regarding the worksheet.

- Most functions require that you enter arguments (that is, inputs to the function). Arguments are enclosed in parentheses and can be a string, a number, formula, a cell, a range of cells, a list of cells, a named range, or a combination of all of these.

- Mathematical functions are used to handle algebraic expressions, equations, and formulas. The following mathematical functions were covered: @ABS, @INT, @MOD, @ROUND, @SQRT, @PI, @RAND. The mathematical functions also include the trigonometric functions: @COS, @SIN, @TAN, @ACOS, @ASIN, @ATAN.

- Statistical functions covered were: @AVG, @COUNT, @SUM, @MAX, @MIN, @STD, and @VAR.

- Logical functions make it easier to make decisions using a spreadsheet. The functions covered were: @IF, @TRUE, @FALSE, and @ISERR.

- Financial functions covered were: @PMT, @FV, and @NPV.

- Date/time functions manipulate date and time using date values in the range from 0 (January 1, 1900) to 36525 (December 31, 1999). Times are given as a fraction of a day. Date/time functions covered were: @DATE, @DAY, @MONTH, @YEAR, @TODAY, and @NOW.

- All the statistical functions were supplied in forms applicable for use with a database. The @DSUM function was covered.

- String functions let you manipulate alphanumeric entries. Such functions covered were: @LEFT, @RIGHT, @LENGTH, @FIND, @MID, @LOWER, @UPPER, @REPLACE, @STRING, and @VALUE.

- Special functions return various kinds of worksheet information. Such functions covered were: @CELL, @CELLPOINTER, @COLS, and @ROWS. Special functions also help with retrieving information from tables. @HLOOKUP, @VLOOKUP, @CHOOSE, and @INDEX were covered in this lesson.

REVIEW QUESTIONS

1. Name eight categories of functions and give an example of each.

2. What are arguments in a function? Give types of arguments and examples of each.

3. What is the difference in the result between @INT and @ROUND?

4. Give the purpose of each of the following functions:
   @AVG
   @COUNT
   @MAX
   @MIN

5. When does an #AND# operator return the logical result of 1?
   The #OR# operator?

6. Explain the arguments used in the @IF function.

7. Explain how date values are displayed in date/time functions.

8. If cell A1 contains the string COMPUTER, what is returned from
   @RIGHT(A1,4)?
   @LEFT(A1,3)?
   @LENGTH(A1)?
   @FIND("TE",A1,0)
   @MID(A1,2,3)

9. What does the @CELL function do?

10. Explain how @VLOOKUP and @HLOOKUP work.

EXERCISES

1. a) Retrieve the spreadsheet EX6_1 from Lesson 6.

   b) In rows just below the current spreadsheet, enter the average and total amounts that your friends borrowed each week.

   c) You decided that if a friend borrows money from you every week during the period given, you will charge a $1.00 service charge. In column H, enter a function that returns a service charge of $1.00 if a friend has borrowed money from you each week for three weeks.

   d) In column I, enter the total amount owed to you (sum of columns H and I).

   e) Save the spreadsheet as EX10_1.

   f) Print the spreadsheet, both displays and formulas.

2. a) Retrieve spreadsheet EX6_2.

   b) Create a lookup table to determine student grades. The average of 90 and above is an A (value 4), 80 to 89 is a B (value 3), 70 to 79 is a C (value 2), and 60 to 69 is a D (value 1); below 60 is an F (value 0).

   c) Save the spreadsheet as EX10_2.

   d) Print the spreadsheet, both displays and formulas.

LESSON 11
PRINTING REPORTS

OBJECTIVES

Upon completion of the material presented in this lesson, you should be able to:

- Understand the default print settings
- Use various print setting options to produce reports formatted to your specification

STARTING OFF

Start Lotus 1–2–3 so that a blank spreadsheet is displayed on the screen. Also, insert the data disk in drive B and change the file directory to B.

Although you printed spreadsheets in most of the previous lessons, for the most part you used the default settings. Lotus 1–2–3 also offers several options to make the spreadsheet into a report that is useful and meaningful. This lesson introduces many of the printing options available in Lotus 1–2–3. Additionally, Lesson 15 covers an add-in program, Allways, which can be used to produce high-quality printouts of reports.

PRINTER DEFAULT SETTINGS

When Lotus 1–2–3 is installed, the user identifies the type of printer in use. Most printers can print 10 characters per inch (called 10 pitch) and use 8-1/2-by-11-inch continuous paper. The printer-setting defaults are 80 print columns, or characters, and 66 lines per page. The left, right, top, and bottom margins are set accordingly. You can change these settings manually, however.

Lotus assumes that when you begin a session, the printer head is located at the first line on the page. If the perforation is not at the printer head, you should adjust it manually. Lotus 1–2–3 keeps track of the number of lines it has printed on the current page, and when the appropriate number have been printed (taking the top and bottom spacings into account), it leaves several blank lines for the top and bottom margins.

If you print a worksheet that is wider than 80 characters, minus the left- and right-margin allowances, the worksheet will print on more than one page. The portion that extends beyond the right margin will be printed on the next page.

If you want to stop, or abort, the printing process for any reason, hold the (CTRL) key down and press the (SCROLL LOCK) key. Depending on the type of printer you are using, the printer may not stop right away. While printing, the computer is not available for other use, and you cannot work on the spreadsheet until the entire file has been sent to the printer. Since the program can send the file to the printer faster than the printer can print the file, some printers have buffer memories that store the file to be printed, thus freeing the computer sooner for use. If the printer has a buffer, the printer will not stop until the buffer is emptied. (CTRL)-(SCROLL LOCK) stops the computer's role in the printing process on the computer; it does not affect the printer's role.

If you want to pause while printing, then hold the (CTRL) key down and press the (NUM LOCK) key. You can then press any key to resume printing. For printers with buffers, printing will not stop immediately after you press these keys.

PRINTER SETTINGS

You can look at the current printer settings. Initially, the screen shows the default settings.

■ Type **/PP**.

➤ You see Screen Display 11–1.

Beneath the control panel the Print Settings box is displayed. Most of the settings should be self-explanatory; the Borders settings will be discussed later in this lesson.

As you change settings, this part of the screen reflects the current settings status. You can change settings through either the Worksheet Global Default Printer command or the Print Printer Option command. In this lesson, you will use the Print Printer Option command sequence.

■ Select Quit to exit the Print command.

```
A1:                                                              MENU
Range  Line  Page  Options  Clear  Align  Go  Quit
Specify a range to print
                           ─── Print Settings ───
  Destination:  Printer

  Range:

  Header:
  Footer:

  Margins:
    Left 4        Right 76    Top 2     Bottom 2

  Borders:
    Columns
    Rows

  Setup string:

  Page length:  66

  Output:       As-Displayed (Formatted)

26-Nov-89  02:01 PM
```

Screen Display 11–1   Default printer settings in print menu.

PRINT COMMAND OPTIONS

You will now retrieve a file and try some Print options. You need a big spreadsheet.

- Retrieve the spreadsheet LOTUS10 from Lesson 9.
- Make sure that the printer is on and the paper is aligned at the perforation. Type **/PP**.

At this point, you specify the range of cells to be printed. The Range setting is blank. You cannot print a spreadsheet until the range has been specified.

- Select Range.

  ➤ The message appears:

      Enter print range:

- Enter **A1..K18**.

PRINTING REPORTS   **267**

Print this spreadsheet even though it is wider than 80 characters.

- Select Align.
- Select Go.

  ➤ As mentioned earlier, the spreadsheet is printed on two pages. Columns A through H appear on the first page; columns I through K on the second page.

If you start printing the next spreadsheet at this point, the printing begins right where the other spreadsheet ended. To advance to the top of the form, you must select Page.

- Select Page.

  ➤ The paper advances to the top of the next page.

The Line option is a "line feed." Every time you select Line, the paper advances one line, and the program adds a line to the number of lines printed. Hence, the program keeps track of where the top of the form is.

If you advance the paper using the controls on the printer (the Line Feed or Form Feed buttons or knobs on the side), however, the line count, as kept by the program and hence the top of the form, is no longer correct. If you are not sure, you need to align the spreadsheet, that is, to reset the top of the form. To do this, make sure that the print head is positioned at the first line on the page and select the Align option.

- Select Quit to exit Print mode.

To test some other features, you need to make the spreadsheet even larger.

- To make the spreadsheet even larger, copy range **A2.H18** to cell A19, and then copy range **A2.H35** to cell A36.

  ➤ You now have a spreadsheet that goes from row 1 through 69 and from column A through H.

- Erase data in columns I through K.

MARGIN SETTINGS

At 6 lines per inch, an 8 1/2-by-11-inch sheet of paper is 66 lines long. (If you are using larger or smaller paper, you can specify the number of lines per page through the Printer Option Page-Length command.) The default for top and bottom margins is 2 lines. In other words, the program will print 62 lines, skip 4 lines, then print the rest of the spreadsheet.

- Align, then print the spreadsheet range A1.H69.
  - ➤ The spreadsheet is printed on two sheets with a space at the perforation to allow for bottom and top margins.
- Select Page.

To change the margin settings, you use the Printer Option command.

- Select Options from the menu.
  - ➤ The Print Options submenu is displayed:

Header	Enters text that will be printed at the top of each page.
Footer	Enters text that will be printed at the bottom of each page.
Margins	Sets page margins (top, bottom, left, right, and none).
Border	Sets border columns and rows to be printed as top and left borders on each page.
Setup	Enters the printer setup string that will be sent to your printer.
Pg-Length	Sets the number of lines on a page. The default is 66.
Other	Determines how the worksheet data will be printed.
Quit	Exits the Print Option mode.

- Select Margins.
  - ➤ You are prompted to specify which margin you want to reset.

- Select Top.

    ➤ You are prompted to enter a number of lines for the top margin. The default setting is 2.

You can set the top margin to any number between 0 and 255. The top margin should be about one inch, or 6 lines.

- Type **6** and press (ENTER).

PRACTICE TIME

1. Set the bottom margin to 6.

2. Quit the Printer Option mode.

3. Align, then again print the spreadsheet (range A1.H69). Notice how the top and bottom margins changed.

4. Select Page.

5. Select Quit to exit the Print mode.

You can also change the left and right margin settings. The left margin setting determines how far the printed spreadsheet is offset from the left edge of the paper. You might change the right margin setting when you are using wider paper, such as computer paper that can accommodate 132 characters (at 10 pitch, or 10 characters to an inch), or when you are using a pitch other then 10, such as 12 pitch or 17 pitch.

SETUP STRING

If you are working with a dot matrix printer, you can change the printer pitch by sending a series of ASCII codes to the printer. You can also change the printer font in a similar manner, if other fonts are available on your printer. The pitch and font are changed using the Setup option. Consult your printer manual to find the particular character string needed for your printer. The codes for commonly found printers are given in the Command Summary.

If the ASCII code for condensed printing (17 pitch) is \015 for your printer, you do the following to change the setting.

- If the spreadsheet you plan to print is wider than 80 characters, change the right margin setting to an appropriate number (for example, 132).
- Type **/PPOS** for Print Printer Option Setup.
  ➤ You are prompted to enter the code.
- Type **\015** and press (ENTER).
- Select Quit to exit the Printer Option mode.
- Align and Print the spreadsheet.
  ➤ The spreadsheet is printed in condensed format.
- Select Page.
- Select Quit.

HEADER AND FOOTER

You can insert text to be printed at the top (as a header) or bottom (as a footer) of each page. This text can be up to 240 characters long, but any text that extends beyond the margins will be cut off.

- Type **/PPOH** for Print Printer Option Header.
  ➤ You are prompted to enter the text to appear as a header.
- Enter **This is a header line**.
- Select Quit to exit the Printer Option mode.
- Align, then print.
  ➤ The header is printed on each page.
- Select Page.

PRACTICE TIME

Print the spreadsheet with the footer "This is a footer."

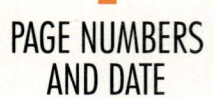

PAGE NUMBERS AND DATE

You can include a page number or date as part of the header or footer. To include the page number, insert the symbol # where you want the page number to appear. To include the current date, insert the symbol @. You can also right-justify, center, or left-justify headers and footers or parts of them. Left justification is the default. Any portion of a footer or header preceded by a single vertical bar (|) will be centered. Any portion after a second vertical bar will be right-justified.

- Change the header to read
  This is a header | TITLE | Page #.
- Change the footer to read **This is a footer||@**.
- Align, then print the spreadsheet.
- Select Page.
  - ➤ The header appears as
    ```
    This is a header      TITLE        Page 1
    ```
  - ➤ The footer appears as
    ```
    This is a footer                  11-Nov-90
    ```

BORDER

When you print a large spreadsheet in sections, the row and column headings are omitted from all pages but the first.

- Type **/PPC** to clear all previous printer settings.
  - ➤ You are given the options to clear all settings or just the range specified, the border specified, or the format specified.
- Select All.
- Select Option.

- Select Border.
  ➤ You are prompted to specify whether you want row headings (the column range) to appear on the left side of the page or column headings (the row range) to appear at the top of the page.
- Select Rows.
  ➤ You are prompted to enter the range.

You want the column headings currently in row 1 to appear at the top of every page.

- Enter **A1.H1**.
- Select Quit to exit the Printer Option mode.

When specifying the range, do not include the rows or columns that have been specified for border. Otherwise, they will be repeated.

- Select Range and enter A2.G69.
- Align, then print.
  ➤ The column heading is printed on all pages.
- Select Page.
- Select Quit.

PRACTICE TIME

1. Retrieve the spreadsheet LOTUS14 from Lesson 10.

2. Print the spreadsheet so that column A appears as a vertical border on every page.

OTHER

You used an option from the Print Other submenu once before, when you printed cell formulas. The remaining menu selections in the Other menu are explained very briefly here; it is left to you to explore them on your own. Make sure to try each of these features.

PRINTING REPORTS **273**

As-Displayed	Prints the worksheet as it is displayed on the screen.
Cell-Formulas	Prints formulas, not values.
Formatted	Prints the worksheet with page breaks, headers, and footers and uses the printer Setup string.
Unformatted	Prints the worksheet, ignoring all settings.

Press (ESC), and then select Quit twice to return to the worksheet.

/ END OF LESSON 11

- Type **/QY**, then press **E** to exit to DOS.
- Remove the disks from the disk drive.
- Turn off the monitor, computer, and printer.

/ SUMMARY

In this lesson, many of the options within /PP necessary to customize reports are discussed:

- Printing can be aborted by entering (CTRL)-(SCROLL LOCK), or paused by entering (CTRL)-(NUM LOCK).

- Before printing a report, make sure that the perforation on continuous paper is at the print head (of the printer), and select the Align option. After that, advance the paper using the Page and Line options in the program.

- The Setup option is used to enter the ASCII code needed to change the pitch and font used by the printer.

- The symbols # and @ are used to include the page number and the date in the header or footer. Also the symbol | is used to specify which portion of the text (in the header/footer) is to be centered or right-justified.

- The Border option is used to specify which rows/columns are to be printed at the top/left of all pages of the report.
- The Other submenu contains other printing options.

REVIEW QUESTIONS

1. If you press (CTRL)-(SCROLL LOCK), will the printing of the report stop immediately? Explain.

2. What are the default settings for range, margins, and paper size?

3. What does it mean to "align the paper"? Why do you need to align it?

4. How do you change the margin settings?

5. How do you change the printer pitch?

6. How do you include the page number and the current date in the header/footer?

7. Can you center or left-justify text in a header or footer? Explain.

8. What does the Border option do?

9. What does the As-Displayed option do?

10. What does the Page-Length option do?

EXERCISES

1. a) Retrieve the spreadsheet EX10_1.
   b) Reveal all columns ("unhide" hidden ones).

    c) Print the spreadsheet so that
 —friends' names appear at the left side of each page.
 —the header "Friends who owe me money" appears left-justified and the page number appears right-justified.

    d) Save as EX11_1.

2. a) Retrieve the spreadsheet EX10_2.

    b) Print the spreadsheet with the header "ENGLISH 101" centered and the current date right-justified.

    c) Save as EX11_2.

LESSON 12
MULTIPLE FILES

OBJECTIVES

Upon completion of the material presented in this lesson, you should be able to:

- Know the various types of files, such as ASCII, DIF, and DBF
- Combine two or more worksheets into one
- Extract a portion of a spreadsheet and save it on disk
- Link information between worksheet files on disk and the worksheet currently in memory
- Know how to import ASCII files
- Parse input into columns of data
- Translate file formats in order to transfer data between Lotus 1–2–3 and other applications programs

STARTING OFF

Start Lotus 1–2–3 so that the blank spreadsheet is displayed on the screen. Also, insert the data disk in drive B and change the file directory to B.

Up to now, when you saved your work, you always saved an entire worksheet. Similarly, when you retrieved a worksheet from the disk, you loaded an entire worksheet. There was no discussion of the format in which the worksheet was saved. Furthermore, when you retrieved a worksheet, any worksheet that was in the computer's memory was replaced by the one you retrieved from the disk, and there was no way to distribute information between worksheets.

There are times when you may not want to save an entire worksheet, or you may want to convert a worksheet to a format compatible with application packages other than Lotus 1–2–3. You may also want to use a data file created using another application package or to work with just a portion of another worksheet.

Furthermore, you may want to combine two or more worksheets into one, or you may want to use information that exists in a worksheet on disk. This lesson discusses the various options you have in saving and retrieving worksheet files, in translating files for transfer between application packages, in combining worksheets, and in linking information between worksheets.

Generally speaking, files created by other applications programs cannot be retrieved directly by Lotus 1–2–3. These other files need to be *translated*, or converted to the .WK1 format before they can be used in 1–2–3. Conversely, worksheets generated in Lotus 1–2–3 may not be directly compatible with other applications programs. These, too, may need to be translated to another format for use in another application.

Fortunately, most application programs are designed to input or output one or more widely-used file formats (such as ASCII and DIF), and Lotus is no exception. The Translate utility, which can be reached through the Lotus Access System menu, performs many common file translations. Hence, it is possible to translate a file between most other application programs and Lotus 1–2–3.

Note: The .WK1 extension identifies the format of Lotus 1–2–3, Release 2.2 files. Lotus 1–2–3 Release 1A stores worksheets as .WKS files, which are in a slightly different format than Lotus 1–2–3 Release 2.2 files. Similarly, formats of other applications programs are often identified by their extensions.

When you translate files, some features of the application program (for example, repeating labels in Lotus 1–2–3) will not be converted.

In Lotus 1–2–3 Release 2.2, the following rules apply:

- A regular file saved in Lotus 1–2–3 Release 2.2 creates files with a .WK1 extension. To use files with the .WK1 extension, you need to *retrieve* or *combine* them.

- ASCII (American Standard Code for Information Interchange) files with the extension .PRN are created by *printing a spreadsheet report to a file* using the /Print File command. To use ASCII files, you need to *import* them. A file in ASCII format includes headers, footers, values as they appear on the report, page breaks, and leading blanks for the left margin. ASCII files can be used by word-processing applications.

These files are sometimes called text files or **DOS** files by other applications programs.

- Any other types of files that need to be transferred between Lotus 1–2–3 and other applications need to be *translated,* using the Lotus Translate Utility. The Translate Utility can translate into Release 2.2 format files from earlier releases of Lotus 1–2–3, dBase database files, DIF (Data Interchange Format) files, Multiplan SYLK files, Symphony files, and VisiCalc files; it can also translate Release 2.2 files into Release 1A or 3, dBase, DIF, or Symphony format. The Translate Utility is covered later in this lesson.

Several common database management programs, including dBase II, III, and IV, use .DBF files for storing databases. However, dBase III and IV have commands that directly import Lotus worksheet files into databases, so you will probably not need to use the Lotus Translate Utility for such transfers.

COMBINING FILES

Imagine that you want to retrieve two completely different worksheets so that they are both present in the computer's memory at the same time. You can save each of them separately and then use the /File Combine Copy command to put them on separate portions of a single worksheet. The File Combine command retrieves all or part of a second worksheet without erasing the current worksheet on the computer. The second worksheet is inserted beginning at the cell-pointer position.

- Retrieve the worksheet LOTUS2 created in Lesson 5.

Next, you want to retrieve a second worksheet and place it in the existing worksheet, without erasing the first one.

- Move the cell pointer to A11, which is a couple of rows below the first spreadsheet.

Type **/F**, and then select Combine.

➤ The following options are displayed

Copy	Combines the values from the second spreadsheet with the worksheet currently in memory, or current worksheet; if there are already values in the cells used to hold the second worksheet's data, the values from the second spreadsheet replace the current contents.
Add	Adds the values from the second spreadsheet to the current contents of corresponding cells.
Subtract	Subtracts the values from the second spreadsheet from the current contents of the corresponding cells.

The Copy option preserves labels and formulas, as well as numbers, and effectively places the second spreadsheet so that the cell A1 of the second spreadsheet is located at the current cell-pointer position.

Note: The values and formulas from the second worksheet will overwrite the labels and values in the current worksheet when using the Copy option.

■ Select Copy.

➤ The following options are displayed:

Entire-File	Copies the second worksheet in its entirety at the current cell-pointer position; column width and range names in the current worksheet are unaffected. Also, range names from the second worksheet are not read into the current worksheet
Named/Specific-Range	Copies a range, either by name or by address. If you use a name, the named range must already exist in the second worksheet

You will select the entire file, or worksheet. Had you wanted to copy just a portion of the second worksheet, you would need to

```
A11: [W12] 'PRINCIPAL                                                    READY

            A          B         C         D         E         F         G
   1       Day         1         2         3         4         5         6
   2       ----------------------------------------------------------------
   3    Cash-on-Hand  750.00    900.00    918.75  1,256.25  1,631.25  1,700.37
   4       Income     600.00    300.00    950.00  1,000.00    692.50
   5       Expense    400.00    275.00    500.00    500.00    600.34
   6       Profit     200.00     25.00    450.00    500.00     92.16      0.00
   7      Equipment    50.00      6.25    112.50    125.00     23.04      0.00
   8        -Net-     150.00     18.75    337.50    375.00     69.12      0.00
   9
  10
  11    PRINCIPAL   *********
  12    RATE            0.10
  13    TERM           10.00
  14    PAYMENT       264.30
  15    INTEREST    11716.18
  16
  17
  18
  19    +B14           10.00     15.00     20.00     25.00     30.00
  20            8.00% $242.66   $191.13   $167.29   $154.36   $146.75
30-Nov-89   08:46 PM          UNDO
```

Screen Display 12–1 Result of combining a second worksheet with the current worksheet.

enter either the range addresses to copy into the current worksheet or the range name to be copied into the current worksheet.

- Select Entire-File.
  ➤ You are prompted to enter a filename.
- Select LOTUS12.
  ➤ Both spreadsheets are now displayed on the current worksheet, as seen in Screen Display 12–1.

The asterisks in cell B11 indicate that the column width is too narrow to display the contents. Do not worry about this right now.

MODULAR SPREADSHEETS

A powerful feature of Lotus 1–2–3 is its ability to "cut and paste" spreadsheets, avoiding the need to reenter data or formulas. Earlier, you used the @VLOOKUP function with a table in order to calculate grades. Since an instructor typically has several classes, it might be convenient to transfer ("lift") the TABLE and its associated cells from the original spreadsheet into another one. Lifting can be done with /File Xtract, and placing can be done with /File Combine, as shown in the previous section.

- Erase the worksheet.
- Retrieve the worksheet LOTUS16 from Lesson 10. It contains the table for the @VLOOKUP function.
- Type **/FX** for file extract.
  ➤ The following options are displayed:

Formulas	Extracts both the cell formulas and values from the current worksheet and saves to a file.
Values	Extracts only the values (not formulas) in displayed (not hidden) cell to a worksheet file.

- Select Formulas.
  ➤ You are now prompted to give a file name.
- Enter the name **GRADES.**
  ➤ You are prompted to enter the range to be extracted.

For the purpose of assigning grades, you need the cell named TOTAL and range named TABLE. (TOTAL is used to calculate values on the first column of TABLE.) Since TOTAL is cell B10 and TABLE is B12.C18, the range to extract is B10.C18.

- Type **B10.C18** and press (ENTER).
  ➤ The extracted cells are saved to GRADES.WK1.
- Clear the spreadsheet (**/WEY**).

284 USING LOTUS 1-2-3

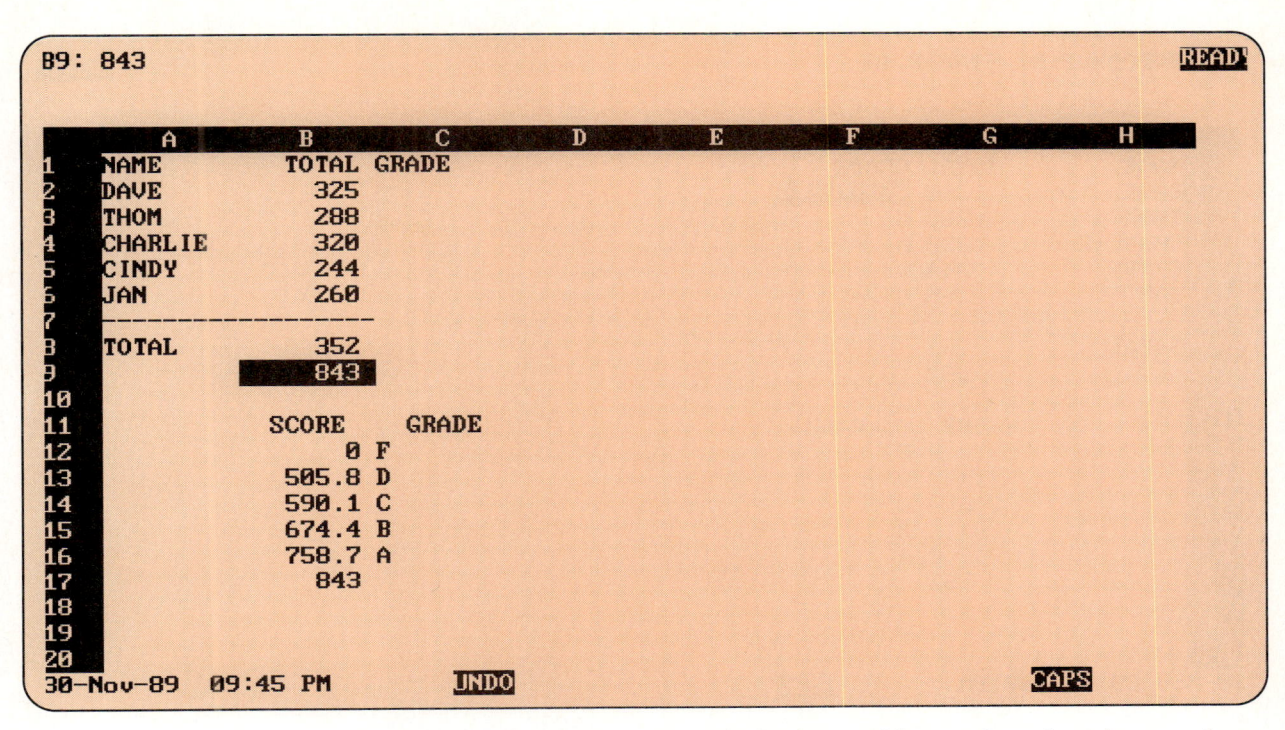

```
B9: 843                                                            READY

       A         B        C        D        E        F        G        H
 1   NAME      TOTAL   GRADE
 2   DAVE        325
 3   THOM        288
 4   CHARLIE     320
 5   CINDY       244
 6   JAN         260
 7   -----------------
 8   TOTAL       352
 9               843
10
11             SCORE   GRADE
12                 0   F
13             505.8   D
14             590.1   C
15             674.4   B
16             758.7   A
17               843
18
19
20
30-Nov-89  09:45 PM              UNDO                              CAPS
```

Screen Display 12–2   Grade-lookup table combined with new class.

- You have a new class. Enter the following information for your new set of students.

	A	B	C
1	NAME	TOTAL	GRADE
2	DAVE	325	
3	THOM	288	
4	CHARLIE	320	
5	CINDY	244	
6	JAN	260	
7	-----------------------
8	TOTAL	352	

- Move the cell pointer to B9.

- Combine the GRADES.WK1 file using **/FCCE** (File Combine Copy Entire-file).

  ➤ Your worksheet looks as shown in Screen Display 12–2.

MULTIPLE FILES   **285**

```
C2: @VLOOKUP(B2,$TABLE,1)                                              READY

         A            B         C         D         E         F         G         H
 1   NAME         TOTAL     GRADE
 2   DAVE           325     A
 3   THOM           288     B
 4   CHARLIE        320     A
 5   CINDY          244     D
 6   JAN            260     C
 7                ---------
 8   TOTAL          352
 9                  352
10
11                SCORE     GRADE
12                    0     F
13                211.2     D
14                246.4     C
15                281.6     B
16                316.8     A
17                  352
18
19
20
30-Nov-89  09:47 PM              UNDO
```

Screen Display 12–3 Grades of new class computed using lookup table.

Do you see a problem? The total appears twice. Cell B8 shows the possible total for this class, and cell B9 (the cell named TOTAL) shows the possible total from the previous worksheet. You need to replace the value in B9 with the one in cell B8.

- At cell B9, enter **+B8**.

  ➤ Cell B9 shows the same value as cell B8.
  ➤ Values in the first column (B column) of the table are readjusted accordingly.

PRACTICE TIME

1. Rename the table. That is, use /RNC to give cells B12.C17 the name TABLE.

2. At cell C2, enter the @VLOOKUP formula and copy it down the column to yield grades as seen in Screen Display 12–3.

ADDING VALUES FROM SEVERAL SPREADSHEETS

Suppose you keep a monthly budget spreadsheet. Each month you enter the values in a different spreadsheet. At the end of the year you want to add all the monthly figures.

To do this most efficiently, you must use exactly the same spreadsheet layout every month. You create a blank spreadsheet form, called a *template*. A template contains all the labels and formulas but no input data. Each month you begin by retrieving the template but save the completed worksheet under the name of the month. When designing the template, then, you must think about all the data categories you will need for the entire year. Again, you see the need for planning.

- Clear the worksheet.
- Create a template using the following information.

	A	B
1	INCOME:	
2	JOB	
3	GIFT	
4	OTHER	
5	--	
6	TOTAL	@SUM(B2.B4)
7		
8	EXPENSES:	
9	FOOD	
10	CLOTHES	
11	RENT	
12	AUTO	
13	SCHOOL	
14	OTHER	
15	--	
16	TOTAL	@SUM(B9.B14)
17		
18	OTHER:	
19	SAVINGS	+B6-B16

- Save the worksheet as file **TEMPLATE**.
- Make sure that the blank template is on the screen.

- Enter some values in column B (cells B2.B4 and B9.B14).

- Save the spreadsheet as **JAN**.

- Retrieve the file TEMPLATE.

- Enter values in column B and save the spreadsheet as **FEB**.

- Do the same for **MAR** and **APR**.

Next, you will create a summary of the four months.

- Retrieve the worksheet JAN.

- With the cell pointer on cell A1, type **/FC** for File Combine.

- Select Add.

  ➤ You are prompted to specify either the entire file or a specified range.

Again, if you want to read a range of the second spreadsheet into the first spreadsheet, enter either the addresses of the range or the range name, which you would have created before saving the second spreadsheet.

- Select Entire-File.

  ➤ You are prompted to enter the filename.

- Select FEB.

  ➤ The values from FEB file are added to those in JAN.

PRACTICE TIME

1. Add the data from the MAR and APR worksheets.

2. Save the worksheet as QTR–1.

It just occurred to you that the first quarter ends in March, not April. You can start all over again, accumulating values for January through March, or you can subtract the values for April from the QTR–1 worksheet.

- Make sure that the QTR–1 worksheet is displayed.
- With the cell pointer on cell A1, type **/FC** and then select Subtract.
- Select Entire-File.
- Enter **APR** as the filename.
  - ➤ The values in the APR worksheet are subtracted from the values in QTR–1, thus giving the total for January through March.
- Save it again as **QTR–1**.
- Erase the worksheet.

LINKING DATA BETWEEN FILES

There are times when you need information from one worksheet for use in another, but the file-extract and file-combine features of Lotus may not be the most efficient ways to do this. Lotus 1–2–3 Release 2.2 has a data-linking feature that allows the currently-displayed worksheet to use data contained in specific cells of other worksheets on disk.

Suppose you own a business that sells fruits and vegetables to retailers. Every day, the prices of the various fruits and vegetables change. Your purchasing agents keep you updated by transferring data to worksheet files on a daily basis. Your salesmen need to know the correct prices in order to make bids for customers.

Barry (a purchasing agent) keeps you updated on prices of several fruits. In his worksheet, BARRY.WK1, he has cells labeled APPLE, BANANA, ORANGE, and GRAPEFRUIT. In these cells, he has the price per pound that he paid to purchase these items.

■ **PRACTICE TIME**

1. Enter the following data into the current worksheet:

	A	B
1	APPLE	0.24
2	BANANA	0.18
3	ORANGE	0.36
4	GRAPEFRUIT	0.30

2. Use the Range Name Labels feature to label the corresponding cells in column B with the labels in column A.

3. Save the worksheet as BARRY.

4. Erase the worksheet.

Another purchasing agent, Howard, keeps you updated on the vegetables he has purchased. In his worksheet, HOWARD.WK1, he has cells named CORN, SQUASH, BEANS, CABBAGE, and CELERY. These cells contain the prices per pound that he paid to purchase those items.

■ **PRACTICE TIME**

1. Enter the following data into the current worksheet:

	A	B
1	CORN	0.28
2	SQUASH	0.22
3	BEANS	0.26
4	CABBAGE	0.37
5	CELERY	0.18

2. Use the Range Name Labels feature to label the corresponding cells in column B with the labels in columnA.

3. Save the worksheet as HOWARD.

4. Erase the worksheet.

With the two above worksheets, your sales agent, Marilyn, can create a worksheet for making bids to clients. In this exercise, you will only go through the steps it takes for Marilyn to obtain the latest costs for produce.

PRACTICE TIME

Enter information in your current worksheet as shown below. The produce names are in column A, and the column headings are in row 1.

	A	B
1	PRODUCE	PRICE
2	APPLE	
3	BANANA	
4	BEANS	
5	CABBAGE	
6	CELERY	
7	CORN	
8	GRAPEFRUIT	
9	ORANGE	
10	SQUASH	

You need information from BARRY.WK1 and HOWARD.WK1 in order to create your bids. You could import these files into your worksheet, but since the information in these files changes daily, you want to *link* the current data in the files on disk with the current worksheet in memory. For example, in cell B4, you need the price you paid for apples. To reference a cell in a worksheet file on disk, you use a *linking formula,* which has the format:

+<<*filename*>>*cellname*

where *filename* is the worksheet filename (including drive and path, if the drive and path are not the default values), and *cellname* is either the address or the name of the cell you are referencing.

Note: When you use a linking formula, it is the only entry you can make in a cell; you cannot use a linking formula as part of an expression or function. However, expressions and functions in other cells can reference a cell containing a linking formula.

MULTIPLE FILES **291**

- With the cell pointer at B2, enter
  +<<BARRY>>APPLE and press (ENTER).
  - ➤ The value 0.24 appears in the cell. You may have noticed your disk drive briefly whirr—the current worksheet looked up the value in BARRY.WK1 at cell named APPLE.

PRACTICE TIME

1. Enter the linking formulas for the other fruits and vegetables in the worksheet.

2. Save the worksheet as MARILYN.

The produce market is never stable. Suppose that, due to rumors of a cold spell, the prices of some fruits have skyrocketed.

PRACTICE TIME

1. Retrieve BARRY and change the values of APPLE, BANANA, ORANGE, and GRAPEFRUIT to 0.42, 0.19, 0.51, and 0.43, respectively, in those cells.

2. Save the file as BARRY, replacing the earlier version.

3. Erase the worksheet.

- Retrieve **MARILYN**.
  - ➤ The file has the changes that Barry recently entered.

When you retrieve a worksheet linked to other worksheets, the values in the links are updated.

- Erase the worksheet.

EXPORTING ASCII FILES

ASCII files are created on disk through the Print File command. They contain the ASCII images of what would have appeared on a printed report. Thus, the file contains all margins, headings, footings, and lines between pages. Formulas are not saved. As noted earlier, other applications may call these text files or **DOS** files.

- Retrieve the spreadsheet JAN.

Note that cell B6 contains the formula @SUM(B2..B4).

- Type **/P** for Print.

Ordinarily, when printing a report, you would select Printer at this point. To save the report as a text file, you select File.

- Select File.
  - ➤ You are prompted to enter a filename.
- Enter **JAN**.
  - ➤ The print options appear.
- Select Range, then specify the range **A1.B19**.
- Align, then Go, just as though you would to print the report.
- Quit the menu.
  - ➤ The report is saved on disk as file JAN.PRN.
- Clear the worksheet.

IMPORTING ASCII FILES

You will now import the ASCII file you just created.

- With cell pointer on A1, type **/FI** for File Import.

You are to enter the type of file to be imported. PRN files are text files that can be imported as "Text" or as "Numbers." You will try both ways to see the difference.

- Select Text.

```
A1:                                                         READY

      A         B         C         D       E      F      G      H
 1
 2
 3
 4
 5
 6    INCOME:
 7       JOB          1200
 8       GIFT            0
 9       OTHER          25
10    ------------------
11       TOTAL        1225
12
13    EXPENSES:
14       FOOD          325
15       CLOTHES       100
16       RENT          350
17       AUTO          275
18       SCHOOL        125
19       OTHER          25
20    ------------------
30-Nov-89  09:59 PM              UNDO
```

Screen Display 12–4   The JAN.PRN file after importing text.

- Select the filename **JAN.PRN**.

   ➤ A screen similar to Screen Display 12–4, but containing the values you entered appears.

Notice that there are five rows at the top for the top margin and two spaces at the left for the left margin.

- Move the cell pointer to A7 and look at the status line for cell content.

   ➤ The content of the cell is the whole line on a report

   `'   JOB   1500`

- Move the cell pointer to B7.

   ➤ Cell B7 is empty.

When you import a file as text, the entire file is imported into a single column in the worksheet. You will see how to separate the data into columns later in this lesson.

294   USING LOTUS 1-2-3

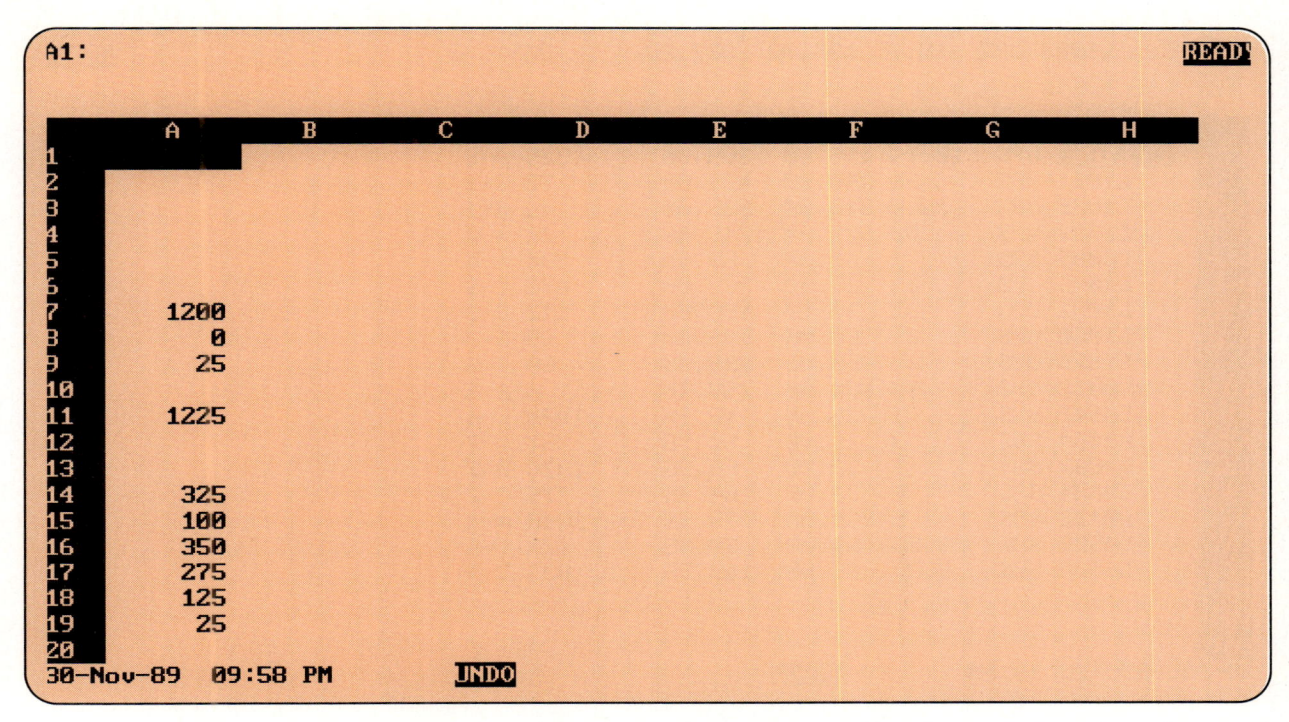

```
A1:                                                              READY

        A       B       C       D       E       F       G       H
 1
 2
 3
 4
 5
 6
 7    1200
 8       0
 9      25
10
11    1225
12
13
14     325
15     100
16     350
17     275
18     125
19      25
20
30-Nov-89  09:58 PM            UNDO
```

Screen Display 12–5   The JAN.PRN file after numbers have been imported.

- Clear the worksheet.
- Import the file JAN.PRN with the Numbers option, as shown in Screen Display 12–5.

The Numbers option retrieves values but ignores any labels unless they are *delimited,* or contained within quotes. The numbers are in the same order as in the JAN spreadsheet, except for the additional rows at the top, and the text and hyphens are missing.

- Move the cell pointer to A11 and look at the control panel for the content.
  ➤ The content is the value as displayed, not the formula.

MULTIPLE FILES   295

```
A1: '          L1003 UPS   18.75 195.00  389.00      325 A-8                    READY
             A      B       C      D       E       F       G       H
    1    L1003  UPS    18.75  195.00  389.00    325 A-8
    2    L1011  UPS       36  240.00  479.00     72 C-1
    3    L1029  UPS     38.5  315.00  625.00     46 B-1
    4    L1037  UPS       80  625.00 1249.00     12 A-2
    5    L0005  SSS        1   30.00   59.90    880 A-6
    6    L1045  UPS       15  185.00  369.00    470 C-8
    7    L1052  UPS       32  230.00  459.00    112 B-3
    8    L1060  UPS       33  300.00  599.00     35 A-3
    9    L1078  UPS       68  450.00  899.00     60 B-6
    10   L0013  UPS       14  150.00  299.00      0 A-5
    11   L0047  SSS        1   25.00   49.95   1480 C-4
    12   L0054  SSS        3   29.00   57.95   2257 A-7
    13   L0062  SSS        3   33.00   65.95   1326 B-7
    14   L0104  SSS        5   33.00   64.95    775 C-7
    15   L0112  SSS        5   38.00   75.95   1843 A-4
    16   L4502  SSS     8.25   50.00   99.85    422 C-5
    17   L4510  SSS     9.25   85.00  169.95    633 B-9
    18
    19
    20
10-Dec-89   10:33 PM            UNDO
```

Screen Display 12–6 *LOTUS8.PRN file as long labels in column A.*

PRACTICE TIME

1. Erase the worksheet.

2. Retrieve file LOTUS8 from Lesson 8.

3. Hide column C, the description field of the database.

4. Create an ASCII file, named LOTUS8.PRN, of the worksheet excluding the column titles in row 1.

5. Erase the worksheet.

6. Import LOTUS8.PRN as Text.

7. Delete the blank rows above the data, so that the worksheet appears as shown in Screen Display 12–6.

DATA PARSING

The File Import Text command enters an ASCII file into the worksheet as "long labels"; that is, each row of text is placed into a single column of the worksheet. In order to convert the long labels to useful worksheet data, the long labels must be separated into columns. The process is called *data parsing.*

Lotus 1–2–3 has a data-parse command that allows you to separate these long labels into columns. The parsing of a long label requires three things: an *input column,* an *output range,* and one or more *format lines.* The input column is the column containing the long labels. The output range is where the separated data will be placed in the worksheet. The format line is a special label entry that identifies how the information is to be divided into worksheet columns. These terms may seem confusing at first, but an example of data parsing will show how it is done. In the following example an imported file of long labels is parsed to illustrate the steps involved in separating the data into worksheet columns.

- Locate the cell pointer at A1.
- Enter **/DP** for Data Parse.

  ➤ A Parse Settings box appears below the control panel.

The easiest way to parse data is to let Lotus 1–2–3 create format lines for you and then to edit them if necessary.

Note: This lesson presents only a brief discussion of the creation of a format-line. For more detail, including advanced use and editing, students should refer to the Lotus reference manual.

- Specify Format-Line and then Create.
- Quit the Data Parse menu in order to view the worksheet.

  ➤ A new row was inserted at the cell pointer and contains the label:

  |****L>>>>*L>>**V>>>>*V>>>>>**V>>>>>*****V>>*L>>

Look at the cell entry as shown on the top line of the control panel. The vertical bar (|) at the beginning of the label is a label-prefix character that indicates it is a format line. Lotus 1–2–3 scanned the long label at the cell pointer and created the format line to

MULTIPLE FILES **297**

indicate the type of data and the number of characters in each field. Letters and characters in the format line indicate how the data was evaluated during the parsing operation:

L	Label.
V	Value.
D	Date.
T	Time.
S	Skip (skip this column of data in the parsing).
>	A subsequent character in a data field (see below).
*	A blank character was parsed; a character in this position will be placed in an adjoining field.

Only one letter is entered in the format line for each field. Subsequent data positions in the field are represented by > characters. Thus, where L1003 was found in the label, Lotus 1–2–3 entered the format-line characters L>>>>, indicating that the field is a label, five characters wide. Where the value 389.00 was found, the format line contains V>>>>>. Where blanks exist in the long label, Lotus 1–2–3 inserts asterisks (*) into the format line. When the input column is parsed, anything that appears at positions containing asterisks is included in adjacent data fields.

The format line lets you to parse the column of labels. The next step is to define the column to be parsed, including its format line.

- Make sure the cell pointer is at cell A1.

- Enter **/DPI** to select Input-Column.

  ➤ You are asked to enter the input column, including the format line and all the data in the column.

- Enter the column range **A1.A18**.

The third part of the data parse which needs to be specified is the output range. You can indicate a single cell, the upper left-corner cell in the output range. You will specify the range to be cell J1.

- Select Output-Range.

  ➤ You are asked to enter the output range.

- Enter **J1**.

```
J1: 'L1003                                                                    READY

         J        K          L        M        N        O      P        Q
 1   L1003      UPS       18.75     195      389      325 A-8
 2   L1011      UPS          36     240      479       72 C-1
 3   L1029      UPS        38.5     315      625       46 B-1
 4   L1037      UPS          80     625     1249       12 A-2
 5   L0005      SSS           1      30     59.9      880 A-6
 6   L1045      UPS          15     185      369      470 C-8
 7   L1052      UPS          32     230      459      112 B-3
 8   L1060      UPS          33     300      599       35 A-3
 9   L1078      UPS          68     450      899       60 B-6
10   L0013      UPS          14     150      299        0 A-5
11   L0047      SSS           1      25    49.95     1480 C-4
12   L0054      SSS           3      29    57.95     2257 A-7
13   L0062      SSS           3      33    65.95     1326 B-7
14   L0104      SSS           5      33    64.95      775 C-7
15   L0112      SSS           5      38    75.95     1843 A-4
16   L4502      SSS        8.25      50    99.85      422 C-5
17   L4510      SSS        9.25      85   169.95      633 B-9
18
19
20
10-Dec-89   10:36 PM         UNDO
```

Screen Display 12–7 ASCII file parsed into columns J through P.

Once the three parts of the data parse have been specified, you can execute the parse by selecting the Go option in the menu.

- Select Go.
  ➤ After parsing the line, Lotus returns you to the Ready mode.
- Position the cell pointer at J1 to view the effect of parsing, as shown in Screen Display 12–7.

Columns J through P contain the data that has been parsed from the long labels in column A. The data-parse command separated the long label into columns of data.

- When finished, erase the worksheet.

MULTIPLE FILES **299**

```
            Lotus  1-2-3  Release 2.2 Translate Utility
   Copr. 1985, 1989  Lotus Development Corporation  All Rights Reserved

What do you want to translate FROM?

        1-2-3  1A
        1-2-3  2, 2.01 or 2.2
        dBase II
        dBase III
        DIF
        Multiplan (SYLK)
        Symphony  1.0
        Symphony  1.1, 1.2 or 2.0
        VisiCalc


           Highlight your selection and press ENTER
            Press ESC to end the Translate utility
            Press HELP (F1) for more information
```

Screen Display 12–8   Initial screen of Translate Utility.

THE LOTUS TRANSLATE UTILITY

When transferring data from another application, you will usually have to convert the data file to one that is compatible with Lotus 1–2–3 Release 2.2. Similarly, if you need to exchange Lotus 1–2–3 worksheet data with another program, you will need to convert the .WK1 file to a file that the other application can use. The Lotus Translate Utility is a menu-driven program that allows you to convert files. The Translate Utility is accessed from the Lotus Access Menu.

- Enter **/QY** to exit 1–2–3 to the Lotus Access Menu.
- Select the Translate option.
   ➤ The Translate utility screen appears, as shown in Screen Display 12–8.

To become familiar with the Lotus Translate Utility, you will convert a .WK1 file to a .DIF file. Each time you convert, or translate, a file, you create a new file with the appropriate exten-

```
        Lotus  1-2-3  Release 2.2 Translate Utility
  Copr. 1985, 1989  Lotus Development Corporation  All Rights Reserved
─────────────────────────────────────────────────────────────────────
Translate FROM: 1-2-3 2.2         What do you want to translate TO?

                                       1-2-3    1A
                                       1-2-3    3
                                       dBase II
                                       dBase III
                                       DIF
                                       Symphony  1.0
                                       Symphony  1.1, 1.2 or 2.0




              Highlight your selection and press ENTER
          Press ESC to return to the source product menu
              Press HELP (F1) for more information
```

Screen Display 12–9   *Select type of file to translate to.*

sion. If you want, you can also change the name or directory of the converted file. For an exercise, you will translate the LOTUS16.WK1 file you created in Lesson 10 to a DIF file.

- Use the ⬇ key to move the menu pointer highlight to the second option, 1-2-3 2, 2.01 or 2.2.

- Press (ENTER) to select that option as the type of file to translate from.

   ➤ The screen now displays the options of types of files that you can translate to, as shown in Screen Display 12–9.

- Similarly, select DIF.

   ➤ A screen concerning information on the type of file translation that you have specified appears, as shown in Screen Display 12–10.

- Press (ESC) to continue.

MULTIPLE FILES   **301**

```
            Lotus  1-2-3  Release 2.2  Translate Utility
     Copr. 1985, 1989  Lotus Development Corporation  All Rights Reserved
   ─────────────────────────────────────────────────────────────────────

    TRANSLATING FROM 1-2-3 TO DIF FORMAT


    Translate will only accept worksheet files created with the
    File Save command.  If you wish to translate a file created
    with the /File Xtract command, you must first save the file
    with /File Save.




                          ═══ Press ESC to continue ═══
```

Screen Display 12–10   Translate Utility note about translation rule.

The screen shown in Screen Display 12–11 lists the .WK1 files in the same directory as the 1–2–3 program. The bottom of the screen has information that may be useful. You want to change the path of the source file to B:\ .

- Press ESC to edit the source file specification.
    - ➤ The source filename is highlighted.
- Change the source file specification to **B:*.WK1** and press ENTER.
    - ➤ The program displays the .WK1 files on the disk in drive B.
- Select LOTUS16.WK1.
    - ➤ The screen indicates that you are to edit the target file specification.

```
        Lotus  1-2-3  Release 2.2 Translate Utility
   Copr. 1985, 1989  Lotus Development Corporation  All Rights Reserved

Translate FROM: 1-2-3 2.2              Translate TO: DIF

Source file: C:\123\*.WK1

 AWSAMPLE WK1    7/19/89     1:23a       2470
        AWSAMPLE WK1




        Highlight the file you want to translate and press ENTER
             Press ESC to edit the source file specification
                  Press HELP (F1) for more information
```

Screen Display 12–11   Menu of .WK1 files in directory of 1–2–3.

The default target-file specification (drive, path, and filename) is identical to that of the source file you specified, except that it has a .DIF extension.

- Press (ENTER) to accept the default specification.
    - ➤ The program asks if you want to proceed with the translation.
- Select Yes.
    - ➤ The screen indicates the progress of the translation.
    - ➤ When the translation is complete, you are given the option of translating another file using the same source and target types or returning to the source specification menu.
- Press (ESC) to return to the initial Translate menu.
    - ➤ The Translate Utility converted B:\LOTUS16.WK1 to B:\LOTUS16.DIF.

MULTIPLE FILES **303**

The Lotus Translate Utility is used to convert files from one format to another. If you are exchanging data between Lotus and another application, check to see if the other application accepts .WK1 files directly. If so, you do not need to convert the files.

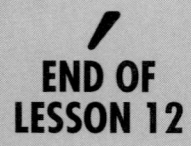

END OF LESSON 12

- Press (ESC), then **Y** to return to the Access menu.
- Type **E** to exit to DOS.
- Remove the disks from the disk drive.
- Turn off the monitor, computer, and printer.

SUMMARY

In this lesson, many of the terms and concepts needed to use functions in Lotus 1-2-3 are discussed:

- Lotus 1-2-3 can save an entire worksheet (/File Save), or a specified range (/File Xtract), as a .WK1 file for later use.
- Worksheets can be combined (/File Combine) with a worksheet in memory in three ways: either by overwriting the existing file in memory (Copy) or by adding or subtracting (Add, Subtract) the values to or from the current worksheet.
- Data can be linked between files on disk and the current worksheet in memory.
- Lotus 1-2-3 can create ASCII files on disk with the .PRN extension (/Print File).
- ASCII files with the .PRN extension can be imported (/File Import) either as labels (Text) or as delimited labels and values (Numbers).
- Data can be parsed from long labels into columns of cells (/Data Parse).

- The Lotus Translate Utility is used to translate files to or from the Lotus 1–2–3 Release 2.2 format (.WK1 extension), for transferring data to and from other applications.
- The following commands are discussed:

    /DP   Data Parse—Converts a long label in a single column, from the /File Import Text command, into separate columns of data.

    /FC   File Combine—Copies, adds, or subtracts content of a second file into the current worksheet.

    /FI   File Import—Reads contents of ASCII disk files into a worksheet.

    /FX   File Extract—Extracts and saves a portion of a spreadsheet onto a disk file.

    /PF   Print File—Prints reports to a disk file, with the .PRN extension, rather than to the printer.

REVIEW QUESTIONS

1. How do you save a specific range of a worksheet only into a .WK1 disk file?

2. How do you move a named range from a .WK1 file into a worksheet, without erasing the existing worksheet in memory?

3. When you combine files, where is the second file placed? Does it have any effect on the contents of the current worksheet?

4. How do the File Combine Add and Subtract commands work?

5. How do you create an ASCII file from a Lotus 1–2–3 worksheet?

6. What does it mean to parse a long label in Lotus 1–2–3?

7. How do you link data in worksheets on disk with the current worksheet?

8. How do you convert a DIF file into a .WK1 file for Lotus 1–2–3?

9. What is the difference between importing a PRN file as "Text" or as "Numbers?"

10. What applications does the Lotus Translate Utility convert files to or from?

EXERCISES

1. You realize that your good friends borrow money from you every month. So you decide to create a spreadsheet for each month and a semester (four-month) summary.

    a) Create a one month template, TEMP10_1, from the worksheet saved in EX6_1.

    b) Using the template, create worksheets for SEPT, OCT, NOV, and DEC. Make up data as needed.

    c) Print all the worksheets.

    d) Combine the monthly worksheets into a worksheet that shows the total amounts loaned.

    e) Save the semester worksheet as EX12_1.

    f) Print the semester worksheet.

2. a) Retrieve the worksheet EX6_2.

    b) Create an ASCII file, EX12_2.PRN, containing the data in the worksheet.

    c) Combine the entire file EX9_2 into the current worksheet.

    d) Print the worksheet.

e) Save the worksheet at EX12_2.WK1.
f) Erase the worksheet.
g) Import file EX12_2.PRN as text.
h) Print the worksheet as cell formulas.

LESSON 13
INTRODUCING MACROS

OBJECTIVES

Upon completion of the material presented in this lesson, you should be able to:

- Explain what a macro is
- Follow the steps to create and invoke macros
- Explain how to enter macros into a spreadsheet
- Create and edit a simple noninteractive macro
- Create a simple interactive macro
- Create a macro using the learn feature
- Use two ways to invoke, or execute, macros
- Create a multiple-line macro

STARTING OFF

Start Lotus 1–2–3 so that a blank worksheet is displayed on the screen. Insert a data disk in drive B and change the file directory to read B.

MACROS

Think back to the previous lessons. How often did you have to give the same series of keystrokes to execute a command? Because Lotus 1–2–3 is menu driven, you often have to enter several keystrokes to accomplish even a very simple task. Of course, the more keystrokes you must enter, the greater the chance of making mistakes. Wouldn't it be nice if you could use one command to invoke a whole series of frequently-used keystrokes? Well, you can.

This lesson introduces the concept of macros in Lotus 1–2–3. As a prefix, "macro" means large or big. In various computing languages, however, a *macro* is a block of code that can be "patched" (inserted or used) into a program at various places, each time with a single command. In Lotus 1-2-3, a macro is a series of worksheet commands or data entries stored in one or more cells and activated, or invoked, with a keystroke command. In this sense, you can think of a macro as a set or series of stored keystrokes. It takes only a few keystrokes to invoke a macro once it is set up. Macros are defined for each worksheet and are stored and retrieved along with the worksheet.

CREATING AND USING MACROS

There are two ways to create macros in Lotus 1-2-3. Either you type the macro commands into the worksheet cells, or you may use the Learn feature to automatically record keystrokes in a range. First, you will enter macros into cells, then you will use the Learn feature.

To create and use a macro:

1. Enter the macro (a series of data and commands) as a label into a worksheet cell or column of cells.

2. Name the first cell of the macro. You can use any valid range name, or you can name the macro \[L], where [L] is any letter. In a range name, lowercase letters are automatically converted to uppercase. You can also name the macro \0, as will be explained later.

3. As often as required after steps 1 and 2, invoke, or execute, the macro with the (ALT)-(F3) (Run) command or, if the macro is named \[L] ([L] is any letter), with the (ALT)-L keystroke combination.

To demonstrate that a macro in Lotus 1-2-3 is a series of stored keystrokes, you will enter something in a cell and make that cell a macro.

- Type your name in cell A1. Press (ENTER) to complete the entry.

Now, you will name the cell with the Range Name command. Macros can be named like any other range name in Lotus 1-2-3, but a macro named with a backslash (\) followed by one (and only one) alphabetic character can be executed directly rather than by accessing a menu and selecting its name.

- Type **/RNC** for Range Name Create.
- Type **MYNAME** and press (ENTER).
- Press (ENTER) again to indicate that you are naming the current cell.
  ➤ Cell A1 is named.

You now have a macro named MYNAME associated with the worksheet. When you execute it, it causes the keystrokes (the keys you typed to enter your name, in this case) in cell A1 to be placed at the current location. You will execute it, or invoke it, to put those keystrokes into cell C3.

- Move the cell pointer to cell C3.
- Press (ALT)-(F3) to run a macro.
  ➤ The range name MYNAME appears on the control panel.
- Select **MYNAME**.
  ➤ The keystrokes for your name appear on the top line of the control panel, but the worksheet has not completed the label entry.
- Press the (ENTER) key to complete the entry.

The keystrokes that make up your name were saved as the macro MYNAME, but the keystroke for pressing the (ENTER) key was not included in the macro. The ~ (tilde) represents pressing (ENTER) in a macro in Lotus 1-2-3.

Once you have entered and named a macro, you can edit it or change its contents.

- Move the cell pointer to A1 (the cell with the macro) and press the (F2) function key to edit the contents of the cell.
- Add the ~ (tilde) at the end of your name and press (ENTER).

INTRODUCING MACROS **311**

- At cell C5, invoke the macro **MYNAME**.

    ➤ Your name is entered into cell C5.

The ~ (tilde) is an important part of macros. When a macro doesn't work the way you think it should, check to see if you forgot to enter a tilde somewhere.

- Save the worksheet as LOTUS17.
- Erase the worksheet.

Macros can be used for almost any sequence of keystrokes you need to make. Suppose you have entered a date in the worksheet with the @DATE function and you need to format the cell. Not only must you change the cell format to date, but the default cell width is too narrow to display the date, therefore you must increase the width of the column to 10. You can enter a macro that does both of these tasks with a single keystroke. Macro keystrokes must be entered as labels in the worksheet, hence you begin the entry with an apostrophe. The command to set the current cell to date (formatted DD–MMM–YY) is /rfd1~, where the ~ (tilde) indicates that you accept the default range. The command to set the column width to 10 is /wcs10~, where the ~ (tilde) indicates the termination of the entry of the column width. Thus, the macro is to be entered as: '/rfd1~/wcs10~. You will enter the macro in cell B4.

- Locate the cell pointer at cell B4.
- Enter the macro **'/rfd1~/wcs10~**.

You have entered the macro. Now you need to name cell B4. Last time, you named the macro MYNAME and you invoked it through the (ALT)-(F3) key. This time, you will name the macro \F, so you can invoke it with the (ALT)-**F** keystroke combination. Note that the macro name begins with a backslash character.

- With the cell pointer in B4, type **/RNC** for Range Name Create.
- Type **\f** and press (ENTER) to specify the range name.
- Press (ENTER) again to indicate that you are naming just the current cell.

    ➤ Cell B4 is named, and hence the macro is named.

Now that the macro has been created and named, you can use it by directly invoking it. But first, you need a date to format.

- Move the cell pointer to cell A1 and enter **@TODAY**.

    ➤ Cell A1 contains a number.

Note: When you are creating macros, sometimes they do not run correctly the first time you try them out. If a macro's instructions are not meaningful to 1–2–3, the program stops the macro execution and places 1–2–3 in the ERROR mode. When this happens, press (ESC), then press (ENTER) to return to the READY mode and edit your macro.

- Press (ALT)-**F**; that is, hold down the (ALT) key and press **F** (in upper- or lowercase) to invoke the \F macro.

    ➤ Today's date appears in cell A1.

Once the macro has been entered and named, it can be used as often as necessary.

- At cell E1 enter **@DATE(90,1,1)+24**. This specifies the date 24 days after New Year's Day, 1990.

    ➤ The number 32898 appears in the cell.

- Press (ALT)-**F** to format the cell.

    ➤ The date 25–Jan–90 appears.

Suppose you want the macro to display the date as 01/25/90. That format is date format 4 (Long Intn'l).

- Move the cell pointer to B4 (the cell with the macro), and press the (F2) function key to edit the contents.

- Use the (←) key to place the cursor on the number 1 after /rfd.

- Press the (DEL) key to erase the 1, then type **4**.

- Press (ENTER) to terminate editing the macro.

- Place the cell pointer at E1 and invoke the macro.

    ➤ The date appears as 01/25/90.

What if, in this macro, you wanted to be able to specify which date format to use? As it is right now, the date format is always set

INTRODUCING MACROS **313**

to Long Intn'l (or, previously, it was always set to DD–MMM–YY). To make the macro interactive, all you have to do is to replace the number 4 with {?} so that macro reads /rfd{?}~~/wcs10~. The bracketed question mark {?} means that the macro waits while the user makes an entry, and continues when the user presses the (ENTER) key. Everything the user types is entered except the (ENTER) keystroke.

- Edit the macro in cell B4 so that it reads **/rfd{?}~~/wcs10~**. Note the second tilde after the {?}.

- Place the cell pointer at E1 and invoke the macro.

  ➤ The screen displays the Range Format Date submenu.

- Select menu option 1 by pressing (ENTER).

  ➤ The date at E1 is displayed in the selected format.

Note: When you use interactive macros for selecting menu options, you should remember that the {?} is concluded when the user presses (ENTER). The additional tilde in the macro then lets the macro select the entry you highlighted.

This macro is part of the spreadsheet. As long as the cell containing a label macro is present in the spreadsheet, the macro exists and can be used.

Let's save this worksheet so that you can retrieve the macro later.

- Save the worksheet as LOTUS18.

- Clear the worksheet using **/WEY**.

PRACTICE TIME

1. Retrieve the spreadsheet LOTUS1 from Lesson 4.

2. In cell F10, create a label macro \p to print the whole spreadsheet. The command keystrokes are /pprA1.B5~agpq. Remember to begin the macro with an apostrophe to indicate that it is a label, as shown in Screen Display 13–1.

3. Invoke macro \p.

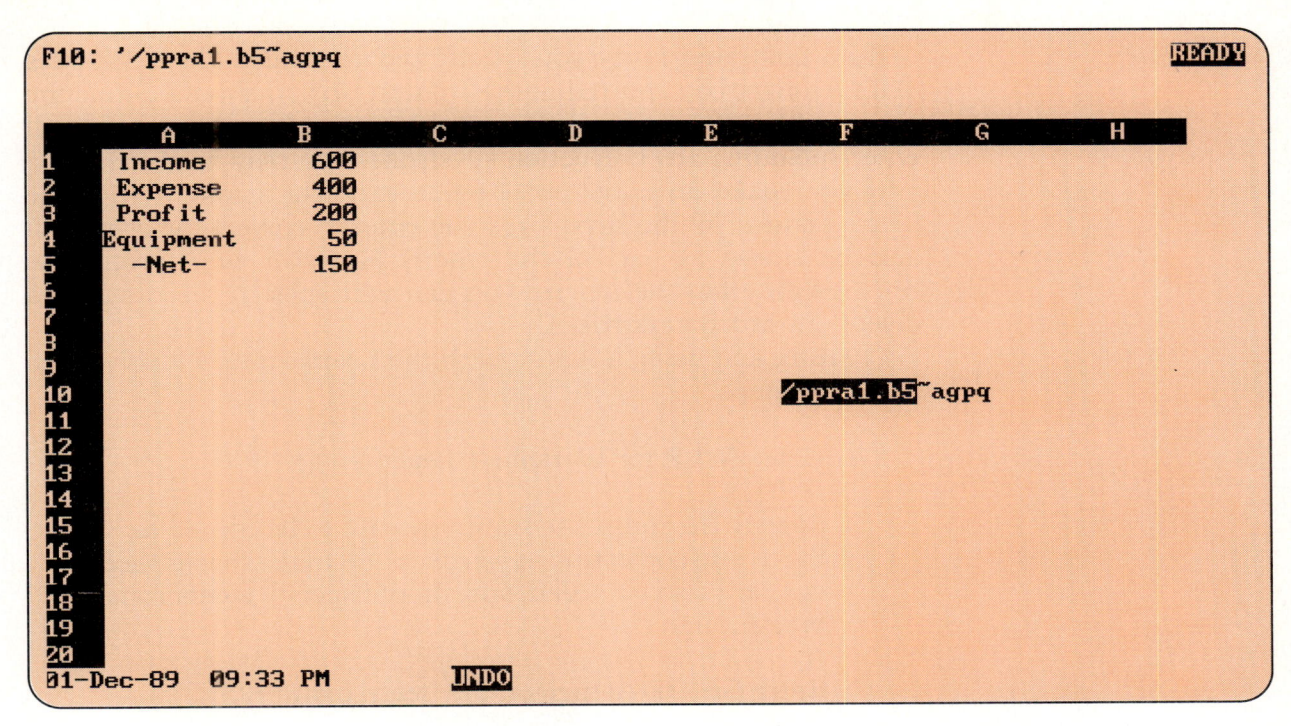

```
F10: '/ppra1.b5~agpq                                            READY

         A         B         C         D         E         F         G         H
  1   Income      600
  2   Expense     400
  3   Profit      200
  4   Equipment    50
  5    -Net-      150
  6
  7
  8
  9
 10                                                /ppra1.b5~agpq
 11
 12
 13
 14
 15
 16
 17
 18
 19
 20
 01-Dec-89  09:33 PM        UNDO
```

Screen Display 13–1   A macro to print the worksheet.

4. Edit macro \p so that the user enters the range to print. Think very carefully about all the keystrokes you must enter to accomplish this task.

5. Test the macro to be sure it works properly.

6. Save the worksheet as LOTUS19.

THE LOTUS LEARN FEATURE

The Learn feature of Lotus 1–2–3 Release 2.2 allows you to capture a series of keystrokes as you enter them, for later use as a macro. The macro commands are assigned to a columnar range of your choice: Each keystroke you make is entered into the columnar range, and each entry is entered into the range using the appropriate notation for macros. When you have entered the command keystrokes, you name the first cell in the column. Then you can execute the column of commands as a macro.

INTRODUCING MACROS   **315**

If the columnar range you specify becomes filled, the keystrokes will no longer be captured in the column, so you should define the range with sufficient length to hold all the keystrokes you will enter, including any correction keystrokes you may need to make.

If you make an entry error while entering a macro with the Learn feature, all the keystrokes you enter to correct the error will also be stored as part of the macro. However, when you have finished entering the macro, you can edit cells in the range and delete unwanted keystrokes.

Creating and using a macro with the Learn feature involves the following steps:

1. Enter **/WLR** for Worksheet Learn Range.

2. Specify the range the keystrokes are to be copied to. Since any correction keystrokes you make (backspace, etc.) are also recorded, you should specify a generously broad range.

3. Enter (ALT)-(F5) to turn on the Learn feature.

4. Enter the keystrokes you want saved as a macro.

5. Enter (ALT)-(F5) again to turn the Learn feature off.

6. Name the first cell in the macro.

7. As often as required after steps 1 through 6, invoke the macro with either the (ALT)-[**L**] keystroke (if the first cell is named \[L], where [L] is any letter), or the (ALT)-(F3) command (Run), which allows you to run any macro.

You will use the Learn feature to capture the keystrokes for a macro that enters the current date and time in two adjacent cells. You will go through the commands once to capture the keystroke sequence (and see the results), and you will use those commands to create the macro.

- Clear the worksheet.

- Type **/WLR** for Worksheet Learn Range.
  - ➤ The following message is displayed:

    `Enter learn range: A1`
- Specify the range **A10.A30**.

Note: The range is specified much longer than you will need.

- Press `ALT`-`F5` to turn on the Learn feature.
  - ➤ The word LEARN appears on the status line, indicating that what you type is entered into the specified range.

From this point on, whatever you enter will be saved as part of the specified range. When you no longer want to save the keystrokes, you will press `ALT`-`F5` again. You will make all the keystrokes necessary to enter (and format) the date in the current cell and the time in the cell directly beneath the current cell.

- With the cursor on cell A1, type **@TODAY** then press `ENTER`.
  - ➤ A number is displayed in cell A1.
- Type **/rfd1** and press `ENTER` to format the current cell to date format.
  - ➤ The cell is filled with asterisks, indicating that the column is not wide enough to display the date.
  - ➤ At A10, @TODAY~ appears.

The Learn feature is approximately one command behind in displaying commands in the learn range. Don't worry, it eventually catches up.

- Type **/wcs10** and press `ENTER` to change the column width to 10.
  - ➤ The current date appears in cell A1.
  - ➤ In cell A11, **/rfd1~** appears.
- Press the `↓` key to move the cell pointer to A2.
  - ➤ In cell A12, /wcs10~ appears.

INTRODUCING MACROS **317**

- Type **@NOW** and press (ENTER) to get the current date and time.

  ➤ A number appears in cell A2.

  ➤ In cell A13, {D} appears.

The D in braces stands for the (↓) keystroke. Most of the function keys and pointer movement keys can be entered in macros as a keystroke instruction similar to {D}. The following table shows most of these keystrokes.

Key	Macro Keystroke Instruction
(↑)	{UP} or {U}
(↓)	{DOWN} or {D}
(←)	{LEFT} or {L}
(→)	{RIGHT} or {R}
(HOME)	{HOME}
(END)	{END}
(PGUP)	{PGUP}
(PGDN)	{PGDN}
(INS)	{INSERT} or {INS}
(DEL)	{DELETE} or {DEL}
(ESC)	{ESCAPE} or {ESC}
(BACKSPACE)	{BACKSPACE} or {BS}
(TAB) or (CTRL)-(→)	{BIGRIGHT}
(SHIFT)-(TAB) or (CTRL)-(←)	{BIGLEFT}
(F2) (Edit)	{EDIT}
(F3) (Name)	{NAME}
(F4) (Abs)	{ABS}
(F5) (Goto)	{GOTO}
(F6) (Window)	{WINDOW}
(F7) (Query)	{QUERY}
(F8) (Table)	{TABLE}
(F9) (Calc)	{CALC}
(F10) (Graph)	{GRAPH}

These keystroke commands are inserted by the Learn feature when you make the keystrokes, but you can also use the bracketed commands when you enter macros from the keyboard.

- Type **/rfdt3** and press (ENTER) to change the format to one that displays time.

    ➤ The current time (according to your computer's internal clock) is displayed in cell A2.
    ➤ In cell A14, @NOW~ appears.

If you stop now, each time the worksheet recalculates, the new time (and maybe date) will be displayed. You want these two cells to freeze their current values. That can be done with the Range Values command. You will move the cell pointer back to cell A1 before executing the Range Values command.

- Press (↑) to move the cursor to cell A1.

    ➤ In cell A15, /rfdt3~ appears.

- Type **/rv** for Range Values and press (↓) once to highlight cells A1 and A2, and then press (ENTER).

    ➤ A message appears requesting the range to copy the values to.

You will copy the values to their same cells. You will use pointer movement keys to keep the movements relative.

- Type **.** (period) and press (↓) to highlight cells A1 and A2, and then press (ENTER).

    ➤ On the top line of the control panel, the content of cell A1 is no longer @INT(@NOW) (the equivalent of @TODAY), but rather a number.
    ➤ In cell A16, {U} appears.

- Since you are now through entering keystrokes, press (ALT)-(F5).

    ➤ CALC appears on the bottom line.

- Press (ENTER).

    ➤ In cell A17, /rv{D}~.{D}~ appears.

- Name cell A10 **DATESTAMP**.

You have created a macro called DATESTAMP, assigned to cell A10. Now you will execute it.

INTRODUCING MACROS **319**

- Move the cell pointer to cell C3.
- Enter ALT-F3.
  ➤ The following prompt appears:
  `Select the macro to run:`

On the third line of the control panel, the range names appear.

- Select **DATESTAMP**.
  ➤ You can watch the macro execute. At the end of the execution, you are left with the date and time entered into cells C3 and C4.

You have created (that is, defined) a Learn range of A10 to A30. Now that your macro has been entered and checked, you should cancel the Learn range to prevent inadvertent entry of other keystrokes into this range.

- Type **/wlc** to cancel the learn range specification.

PRACTICE TIME

1. Use the Learn feature to create a macro (beginning in cell A20) that inserts the months of the year (JAN, FEB, MAR, ... , DEC) across a row, starting at the cursor position, and then sends the cursor to cell A1 (HOME).

2. Name the macro MONTHS.

3. Move the cell cursor to A20. Notice that the series of commands takes up several rows, one entry per row. If you mis-typed something and corrected it, those keystrokes were also recorded.

4. With the cursor in a column other than column A, invoke the macro.

5. Save the worksheet as LOTUS20.

6. Clear the worksheet.

MULTIPLE-LINE MACROS

With the Learn feature you have created two macros that consisted of several rows, or lines. One advantage of writing macros on several lines is that they can be broken up into small pieces, for easier understanding and editing. Once the contents of the *named* cell (the starting cell)—for example, C18—have been executed, Lotus 1-2-3 looks at the cell in the next row down, C19. If C19 is not blank, the macro continues execution. The macro continues until it is stopped or encounters an empty cell.

When you create a macro, it is usually a good idea to use three consecutive columns. Macro commands and keystrokes are entered in the middle column. You should limit the portion of the macro in any given cell to a small piece. You enter the name of the macro (as a label) in the cell to the left of the *named* cell (the starting cell). The third column is used for comments that describe the functions of the cells adjacent to them.

The widths of these columns should be adjusted to accommodate the longest entries. For that reason, it is a good idea to store macros in columns that will not interfere with the rest of the worksheet. You might store them in columns A, B, and C, and then start the worksheet in column D. Or you might use columns to the right of the worksheet entries. In either case, for presentation purposes, you might want to hide the columns that contain macros. Also, in Lesson 15, the Macro Library Manager, an Add-in, will be introduced. The Macro Library Manager is a way to use macros without having them occupy worksheet cells.

You will retrieve the worksheet LOTUS18 prepared earlier in this lesson and change macro \F into a multiple-line macro, defined in columns A, B, and C, as discussed above.

- Retrieve the spreadsheet LOTUS18.

  ➤ The macro displayed in cell B4 is
  `/rfd{?}~~/wcs10~`.

- Edit the label macro in cell B4 so that cell B4 holds the keystrokes to set the date format, and cell B5 contains the keystrokes to change the column width.

- Enter the label \f in cell A4. (Make sure to precede the label with a label prefix character.)

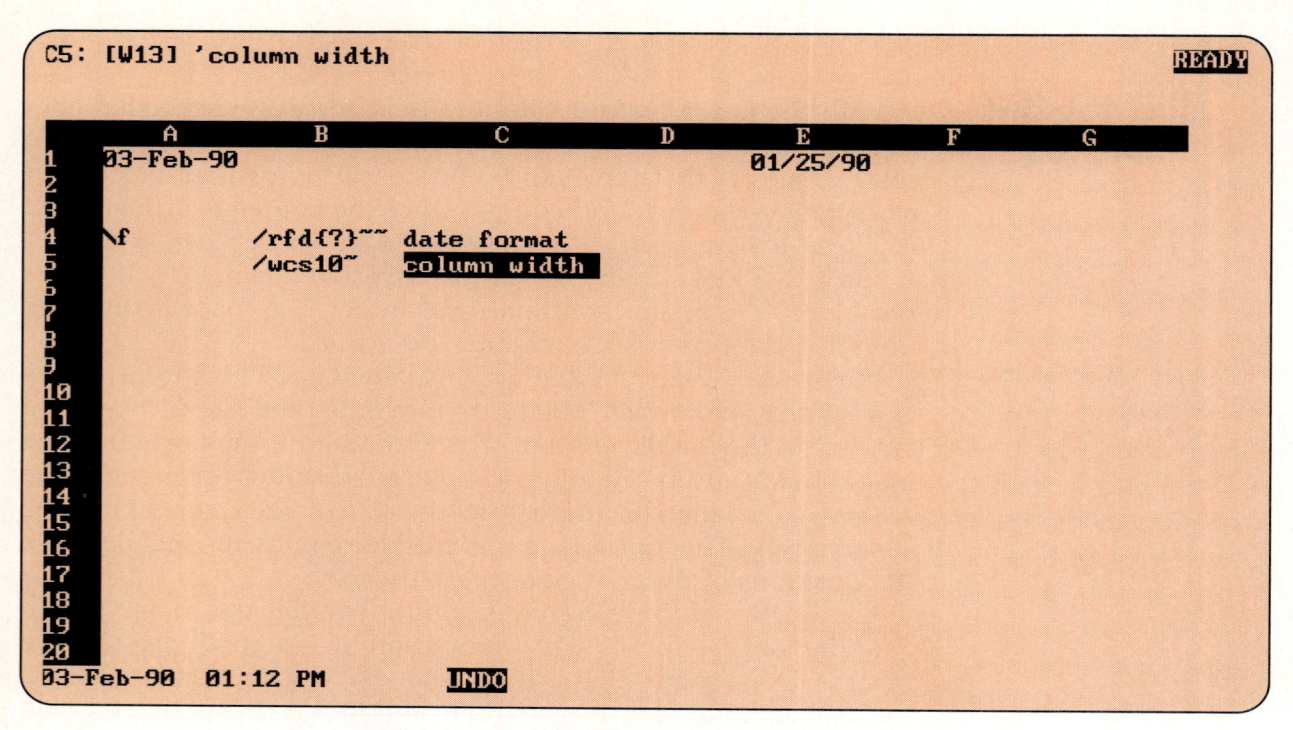

```
C5: [W13] 'column width                                              READY

         A          B           C           D         E         F         G
   1  03-Feb-90                                    01/25/90
   2
   3
   4  \f         /rfd{?}~~   date format
   5             /wcs10~     column width
   6
   7
   8
   9
  10
  11
  12
  13
  14
  15
  16
  17
  18
  19
  20
  03-Feb-90   01:12 PM          UNDO
```

Screen Display 13–2   A multiple-line macro in three columns.

- In cells C4 and C5, describe the functions of the keystrokes in cells B4 and B5 respectively.
- Adjust columns to appropriate widths, as shown in Screen Display 13–2.

This macro will stop executing when the empty cell is encountered at cell B6. You can put in a specific command {QUIT} to stop the macro's execution. However, the effect of leaving cell B6 empty is the same as having the entry {QUIT}.

{QUIT} is an example of a macro command. There are many macro commands available that let you *program* macro instructions. Macro commands are discussed in the next lesson.

■ PRACTICE TIME

1. Enter the date in cell F10 using either @NOW or @TODAY.

2. Use macro \F, which you just divided between two cells, and verify that it works correctly.

3. Save the worksheet as LOTUS21.

/ LEARN FEATURE vs. DIRECT ENTRY OF MACROS

Now that you have tried two ways to enter macros, you probably noticed some advantages and disadvantages for each type.

When you directly enter a macro into the worksheet, you must be certain that all the command keystrokes are correct. You also need to enter special keystroke symbols for (ENTER), arrow keys, and function keys. The procedure can be difficult, error-prone, and tedious, especially if the macro is a long one. By contrast, the procedure for recording a macro with the Learn feature is easier and self-checking.

The Learn feature in Lotus 1–2–3 is a convenient way to record many macros that can benefit your productivity. Virtually any sequence of keystrokes that is often repeated can be recorded and named and then invoked repeatedly.

Macros that are directly entered into the worksheet can use macro commands not available with the Learn feature. Some of these capabilities will be presented in Lesson 14. The capabilities include menus (like the slash commands), more ways to make macros interactive with the user, and different flows of control for the macro (branching, loops, and subroutines).

Macros are contained as part of a worksheet, and hence there is the possibility that someone may accidentally erase cells or delete rows or columns that contain macro commands. You can hide macros in order not to clutter displays and printouts, but the possibility of deleting a row or column containing macro commands still exists. In Lesson 15, a better solution than incorporating macros in the worksheet is presented through a discussion of the Macro Library Manager.

END OF LESSON 13

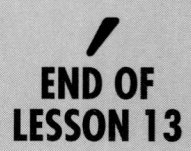

- Type **/QY** and then **E** to exit to DOS.
- Remove the disks from the disk drives.
- Turn off the monitor, computer, and printer.

SUMMARY

In this lesson, the concept of the macro is introduced.

- A macro is a series of worksheet commands or data entries that is stored in a cell or some other memory location and is easily executed with a few keystrokes.
- A macro stores keystrokes as a label in one or more cells in a column. The first cell is named.
- There are two ways to enter macros in Lotus 1-2-3 Release 2.2. Macros may be directly entered into the worksheet as labels, or they may be recorded as you enter the actual keystrokes, using the Learn feature.
- The Learn feature captures keystrokes as the actual entries are made.
- If a macro is named \[L], where [L] is one of the characters A through Z or zero, then it can be directly executed with the (ALT)-[L] keystroke combination.
- In a macro, the ~ (tilde) represents pressing the (ENTER) key; pressing other keys are represented by words within braces. For example, pressing the (→) key is represented by {RIGHT} or {R}.
- User input is accepted during the macro's execution by including {?} in the macro.
- Macro instructions can include keystrokes to enter a label or a value in a cell. In either case, the exact keystrokes needed must be entered in a cell as a label.

- The following commands are discussed:

/WLR	Worksheet Learn Range—defines the range to record a macro.
/WLC	Worksheet Learn Cancel—cancels the learn range setting.
ALT-F3	Runs a macro.
ALT-F5	Toggles learn feature on and off.
ALT-[L]	([L] is any letter) Invokes the \[L] macro.

REVIEW QUESTIONS

1. What is a macro?

2. What are the two ways to enter macros in Lotus 1–2–3 Release 2.2?

3. Explain the steps in creating a macro by direct entry.

4. Explain the steps in creating a macro using the Learn feature.

5. How do you invoke a macro named \Z?

   A macro named WILCO?

6. How do you edit a macro?

7. What happens to the macro name if you move it in the worksheet?

8. What are the advantages of using the Learn feature to enter macros?

9. How does the execution of a multiple-line label macro get stopped?

10. What are the advantages of directly entering macros into the worksheet?

EXERCISES

1. a) Create and test a macro that edits the contents of the current cell and centers an existing label.

   b) Create and test a macro that enters your name as a label in the current cell and then moves the cell cursor down one cell.

   c) Save the worksheet as EX13_1.

   d) Print the macro ranges in the worksheet.

2. a) Create and test the following macro:

   Set the current directory to B:.

   Retrieve (File Combine Copy) a file specified by the user.

   Print to printer a range specified by the user.

   b) Save the worksheet as EX13_2.

   c) Print the macro range in the worksheet.

LESSON 14
ADVANCED MACRO COMMANDS

OBJECTIVES

Upon completion of the material presented in this lesson, you should

- Know what advanced macro commands are
- Know the different types of advanced macro commands
- Be able to use advanced macro commands
- Be able to create a menu using advanced macro commands
- Be able to create and use autoexecute macros

STARTING OFF

Start Lotus 1–2–3 so that a blank spreadsheet is displayed on the screen. Also, insert the data disk in drive B and change the file directory to B.

In the last lesson, Lotus 1–2–3 macros were introduced. You should remember that macros are ways to enhance your productivity in Lotus 1–2–3. They let you do jobs more easily and faster than you could otherwise. Also, because they can store commonly-used keystroke sequences, they eliminate problems with mis-typed commands.

Several macros were introduced in the last lesson. You were also given a brief introduction to the advanced macro commands {?} and {QUIT}. In this lesson, you will learn more advanced macro commands and develop a menu of commands for another person to use.

ADVANCED MACRO COMMANDS

There are some commands used only in macros. These commands are enclosed in curly braces {} and are known as *macro commands*.

Note: /X commands may also be used in macros. However, /X commands, introduced in Lotus 1-2-3 Release 1A, all have equivalent advanced macro commands, which are easier to remember and use. /X commands will not be discussed here.

The format for an advanced macro command is either

- {KEYWORD}

or

- {KEYWORD *argument1,argument2,...*} ,

where keyword is a command such as BRANCH, IF, GETLABEL, and so on. If there are any arguments, they follow a space after the keyword and are separated by commas (no separating spaces). Arguments are one or more of the following:

- an address or a named location (a range)
- a numeric value (a number or an expression)
- a logical formula (for testing a condition)
- a string (a series of characters, enclosed in double quotes)
- a link to another file (not discussed here)

Advanced macro commands can be grouped into five types:

Data-manipulation	Changes the content or format of data in a cell or range.
Flow-of-control	Controls the order in which macro commands are carried out.
Interactive	Allows the macro to accept input from the user during execution.
Screen	Affects the appearance of the screen, including menus.
File-manipulation	Performs operations on disk files (save, print, and so on).

Screen and file manipulation commands will not be discussed here. Some of the commands of the first three types will be discussed in the following sections.

DATA-MANIPULATION COMMANDS

As mentioned above, data-manipulation commands change the content, the format, or both of the data in a cell or range of cells.

{LET location, entry}

This command stores an entry, either a number or a label, at a specific address or location. For example, to store the label TOTAL in cell D5, you enter

- {LET d5,"TOTAL"}

and to enter the value 45 in cell E7, you enter

- {LET E7,45}.

{BLANK location}

This command erases the contents of a cell or range of cells. For example, to erase the contents of range A1.A7, you enter {BLANK a1.a7}. If the range A1.A7 is named RANGE1, then you can enter instead

- {BLANK RANGE1}.

FLOW-OF-CONTROL COMMANDS

As mentioned above, flow-of-control commands control the order in which macro commands are carried out.

{BRANCH location}

In this command, location specifies the cell name or address that contains the next command the macro is to execute. It should not be confused with the {GOTO} command, which stands for pressing the (F5) function key. The {GOTO} command moves the cell pointer to the address specified. The {BRANCH} command tells where to find the next macro instruction.

ADVANCED MACRO COMMANDS

- Retrieve the file LOTUS20.

  ➤ The worksheet has two macros: one that sets the date and time, and one that enters month names in a row.

- Erase the content of range A1.N9 using **/RE**.
- Reset the display format of the same range using **/RFR**.
- Move the DATESTAMP macro to cells B1 and below.
- Move the MONTHS macro to cells B12 and below.
- Enter the macro names in the appropriate rows in column A.
- Enter descriptions of the macros in column C, as shown in Screen Display 14–1.

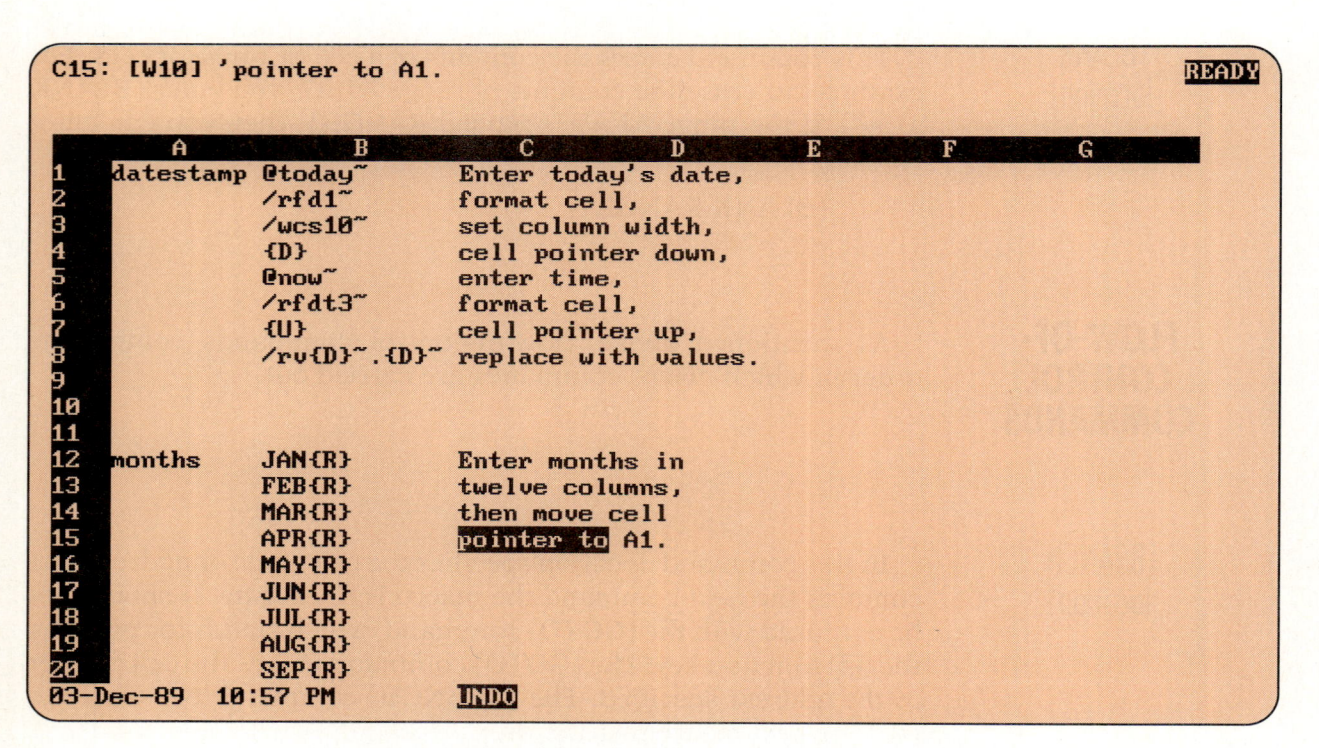

```
C15: [W10] 'pointer to A1.                                          READY

           A          B            C           D        E       F       G
 1    datestamp   @today~      Enter today's date,
 2                /rfd1~       format cell,
 3                /wcs10~      set column width,
 4                {D}          cell pointer down,
 5                @now~        enter time,
 6                /rfdt3~      format cell,
 7                {U}          cell pointer up,
 8                /rv{D}~.{D}~ replace with values.
 9
10
11
12    months      JAN{R}       Enter months in
13                FEB{R}       twelve columns,
14                MAR{R}       then move cell
15                APR{R}       pointer to A1.
16                MAY{R}
17                JUN{R}
18                JUL{R}
19                AUG{R}
20                SEP{R}
03-Dec-89   10:57 PM           UNDO
```

Screen Display 14–1 *Two macros from LOTUS20 with comments.*

You want to enter a third macro, which places the year in a cell, enters the month names across columns beginning two rows down, and then moves the cell pointer to cell A1. The macro at cell B12 (macro MONTHS) already does most of this. Rather than writing all these instructions, you can simply enter the current year, move the cell pointer down two rows, and then transfer the execution sequence to MONTHS.

You should start the worksheet somewhere below and to the right of the existing macros, perhaps at E100. Since you might forget the address, it is a good idea to name the cell START; thus you will be able to get to the macros by pressing Home, and to the worksheet by pressing (F5) (Goto), followed by START.

- Name cell E100 as START (use **/RNC**).

- Move the cell pointer to Start by pressing (F5) then entering **START**.

- Move the cell pointer back to A1 by pressing the (HOME) key.

You decide to start the new macro at cell B28 and to name it HEADING.

- In cell A28, enter **HEADING**.

- Use the Range Name Labels command to give the name HEADING to cell B28.

- In cells B28 to B31, enter the following macro commands:

    {LET START,@YEAR(@NOW)+1900}

    {GOTO}START~

    {DOWN 2}

    {BRANCH MONTHS}

- Press (ALT)-(F3), then select the macro name **HEADING** to invoke the macro.

    ➤ You can watch the macro executing to determine whether it is doing everything correctly.

- Move the cell pointer to START (use the (F5) function key), and check the result.

The macro named HEADING, which begins at B28, consists of four macro commands. Let's go over the commands, line by line.

Cell B28   The command {LET START,@YEAR(@NOW)+1900} enters into the cell named START (cell E100), the year (@YEAR) at the moment (@NOW), according to the computer's internal clock. The @YEAR function returns 90 for 1990; 1900 needs to be added to the value to get the correct year.

Cell B29   {GOTO}START~ moves the cell pointer to START.

Cell B30   The command {DOWN 2} moves the cell pointer down two rows, to E102.

Cell B31   The macro command {BRANCH MONTHS} indicates that the next macro command will be the first command in the macro named MONTHS.

Often, there is more than one way to give commands for macros. For example, in cell B29, you could have entered the location as E100~, and in cell B30, you could have entered {D 2} or {DOWN}{DOWN} instead of {DOWN 2}.

{IF condition}

The format of the {IF} command is *{IF condition}command*. It is very important that you not insert a space between the {IF} statement and the command that follows. The condition is evaluated as either true or false. If true, the command specified is executed. If the condition is not true, the command is skipped and the instruction in the cell below is executed. An example of an {IF} command is {IF a210<b1}{BRANCH c18}. The value in cell A210 is compared with the value in cell B1. If the value in A210 is less than the value in B1, the condition is true and hence the command {BRANCH c18} is executed; that is, the command to be executed will be found in cell C18. If the value in A210 is greater than or equal to the one in B1, the condition is false and hence the instruction in the cell

one row below this command is executed. Note that uppercase and lowercase letters may be used interchangeably for commands and range names.

Note: The following conventions are generally followed when writing macros:

1. Use all lowercase letters for slash (/) command responses and macro names.

2. Use all uppercase letters for range names, functions, macro keywords, and macro keystroke representations.

{QUIT}

You can program the macro to stop by inserting the command {QUIT}. For example, {IF COUNTER>LIMIT}{QUIT} will stop the macro execution when the value in the cell named COUNTER is greater than the value in the cell named LIMIT. This command was discussed briefly in the previous Lesson.

{RETURN}

This command returns control to the calling macro from a macro *subroutine*. A subroutine is a series of macro instructions whose starting cell is named and also terminated with a {RETURN} command. A macro can call a subroutine by specifying the subroutine name (the name of its starting cell) within braces. For example, if the subroutine is named sub1, it can be called using {sub1}. When the subroutine {RETURN} command is executed, the instruction in the calling macro one row below the subroutine call is the next command executed.

Earlier, it was explained that the {BRANCH} command transfers the execution of the macro to the cell specified. After a {BRANCH}, however, instructions on consecutive rows below are executed until either a blank row or a {QUIT} command is encountered to terminate the macro instructions. The instruction does not return to the original macro.

You will see the difference between branching and calling a subroutine in the next example.

- In the row below the last command in MONTHS (near B24), enter **{RETURN}**.
- In cell B31, edit {BRANCH MONTHS} to read {MONTHS}.
- In cell B32, enter **{BEEP}**.

{BEEP} is a macro command that causes the computer to beep when invoked.

- Run macro HEADING again.
  ➤ Since it now calls MONTHS as a subroutine, {RETURN} gives control to the next command in HEADING (the {BEEP} command).

Do you hear the difference between {BRANCH} and a subroutine call?

- Save the worksheet as LOTUS22.

PRACTICE TIME

1. Erase the range E100..P103.

2. Change the first two rows of the HEADING macro to read:

   {GOTO}START~

   {DATESTAMP}

3. Execute the macro and check the results at E100 and E101.

4. Save the worksheet as LOTUS22, replacing the previous file.

INTERACTIVE COMMANDS

As mentioned above, interactive commands allow a macro to accept input from the user at certain points during execution.

{?}

This command suspends macro execution until the user presses (ENTER). It is used to let the user move the cell pointer or enter data, thus making the macro interactive. It is useful when you want to let the user make interactive replies, such as the range to print (since the program displays the prompt), and to select menu options, as you saw in the example in Lesson 13.

{GETNUMBER prompt,location}

This command displays a prompt to indicate what the user is to enter (a value), and then places the numeric input into the location indicated. The prompt must be enclosed in double quotes ("). The prompt is displayed on the control panel when the command is executed. When the user types a number and presses (ENTER), the value is placed in the location indicated by the address in the command.

If you want to place the value in the current cell (the cell where the cell pointer is located), you must first find out the address of the current cell, using the @CELLPOINTER function. @CELLPOINTER("address") returns the address of the current cell. Thus, the macro instruction to place the value into the current cell is {GETNUMBER "Enter value: ",@CELLPOINTER("address")}~. The tilde at the end of the instruction terminates the entry.

{GETLABEL prompt,location}

The label-input command is used, like the numeric input command, when a label (such as a name or telephone number) is to be entered into the worksheet instead. It displays the prompt and then waits for the user to input a label. When the user presses (ENTER), the entry is stored as a label in the cell indicated.

ADVANCED MACRO COMMANDS **337**

{MENUBRANCH location} and {MENUCALL location}

The MENUBRANCH command is used to branch to a macro that displays menu options, whereas MENUCALL makes a subroutine call to the menu macro. Use of these commands and of menu macros is described later in this lesson.

{WAIT time-number}

The {WAIT} command suspends execution of the macro until the time-number is satisfied. The time-number is not the number of seconds to wait but the time of day. If the time-number is invalid or if the time-number has already passed, no suspension of execution occurs. One way to cause a macro to wait, for example, five seconds is to give the following WAIT command:

- {WAIT @NOW+@TIME(0,0,5)}

Macro execution continues after the wait.

MACRO EXAMPLE

As an exercise in writing macros, you will write a macro that can be used to produce a number of copies of printer output. Since Lotus 1–2–3 prints one copy of output at a time, you need to issue the print command again for every additional copy that you require. Also, you need to remember to end each printing with a Page command to make the next printout start at the top of the paper.

For this macro, not only will there be a macro name, \r, but the macro will loop to another cell, named LOOP, and keep two numbers in locations named COPIES and COUNTER. This may sound a bit confusing, but as the macro is explained, these names should become understandable to you.

- Clear the spreadsheet using **/WEY**.
- Enter the spreadsheet as shown below. Note that the initial apostrophes will not be displayed: they are there to make the entries labels.

	A	B	C
1	'\r	'/ppr{?}~q	Multiple copy print
2		{GETNUMBER "How many copies? ",COPIES}~	
3		'/reCOUNTER~	
4	LOOP	'/ppagpq	
5		{LET COUNTER,COUNTER+1}	
6		{IF COUNTER}{BRANCH LOOP}	
7		{QUIT}	
8			
9	COPIES		
10	COUNTER		

Let's go over the macro line by line, starting at cell B1.

Cell B1   This command sets the range to print. The Lotus menu command /ppr gets the user to the range entry in the print command. {?} lets the user set the print range, and the tilde terminates entry of the range. (The user's pressing of (ENTER) terminates the {?} but not the actual entry of the range.) The macro then quits the print command.

Cell B2   The numeric input command {GETNUMBER} prompts for the number of copies and places the user response in the cell named COPIES.

Cell B3   The Range Erase command (/re) erases the contents of the cell named COUNTER.

Cell B4   A single copy of the output is printed. The last p in the command sends a form feed to position the paper at the top of the page. This cell is named LOOP.

Cell B5   The {LET} command increments the value in COUNTER by 1. It places in cell COUNTER the current value in COUNTER plus 1.

Cell B6   The {IF} command checks to see if the value at COUNTER is less than the value at COPIES. (Remember: COPIES contains the number of copies the user requested.) If that value is less, the {BRANCH} command is executed to return to the instruction in the cell named LOOP (B4). Otherwise, the command on the next line is executed.

Cell B7   This command terminates the macro execution.

The description in cell C1 identifies the purpose of the macro. When you have entered the macro, check it carefully for data entry mistakes. Especially check the tildes in cells B1, B2, and B3. Before you can use the macro, you have to name the macro and a few other cells used by the macro.

- Name cells B1 through B10, using the entries in cells A1 through A10.
    - ➤ Since there are only four entries in cells A1 through A10 (A1, A4, A9, and A10), only cells B1, B4, B9, and B10 are named.

Now you can execute the macro by entering (ALT)-**R**. You will test the macro by printing the macro instructions on the worksheet.

- Enter (ALT)-**R**.
- When prompted, enter the range **A1.C10** and press (ENTER).
- Enter **3** in response to the prompt on number of copies.
    - ➤ Note the values in cells B9 and B10 during the three printings of the output.
- Save the worksheet as **LOTUS23**.

MENUBRANCH EXAMPLE

The menubranch macro is used when you create a menu or menu block, like the Lotus 1–2–3 command menu, for your custom applications. This can be especially useful in several situations. For example, if you have several types of reports that you need to print from a worksheet, rather than wade through the Print command submenus for each report or try to remember the macros for each, you can display your options on the command line as a menu, complete with a short description of the highlighted option on the line below. These menu options are selected the same way as the Lotus 1–2–3 menu options; that is, you can either highlight a selection and press (ENTER) or press the key for the first letter of an option. Planning on your part is important, since you should avoid having two menu options beginning with the same first letter. Also, to avoid confusion by the user, you should make the option names single words, hyphenated if necessary.

Because of its sophistication, the menu block is more complex than the commands covered thus far. The menu block requires a block of two to eight columns by at least three rows. The menu block is invoked by either the {MENUBRANCH} or {MENUCALL} command in a macro; it cannot be invoked as a macro by itself.

In the menu block, each column represents one menu option. Hence, you can have up to eight options. Also, the cell in the first row, to the right of the last option, must be blank. For each menu option, the first row contains the short title, up to 9 characters long, that is displayed as the selection name on the command line. The second row contains longer descriptions (or perhaps a list of the commands available in the submenu). These descriptions can each be up to 80 characters long. The third and following rows contain the commands, or the macros, that are executed when the selection is made.

Note: When working with menu blocks, (ESC) does not return the user to the previous menu but terminates the menu.

Suppose you are entering data in a worksheet on real-estate offerings. You need to enter the property type over and over again. Because this worksheet is being used as a database, the exact wording (spelling and upper- and lowercase) of your entry is very important.

You have divided the property types into seven categories: Vacant Land, Business, Warehouse, Single-Family Home, Duplex, Apartment, and Other. When the user selects Other, the user will enter the category type. You want to create a menu that allows the user to select one of these seven categories. As each option is highlighted, you want the second line to show more information about the category. When an option is selected, the appropriate property type is entered in the current cell.

You will set up the menu block starting at cell M1. That is, the first menu option will be entered in column M, the second in column N, the third in column O, and so on, to the seventh option in column S.

- Clear the spreadsheet.
- In cell M1, enter **Vacant**
- In cell M2, enter **Vacant lot or acreage**
- In cell M3, enter **VACANT~**

When the menu is displayed, the word "Vacant" will appear on the command line. When this option is highlighted, the description "Vacant lot or acreage" will appear on the line below. When this option is selected, the macro in cell M3 will be invoked and the label VACANT entered in the current cell.

- Enter the rest of the menu block.

	N		O
1	**Business**	1	**Warehouse**
2	**Business establishment**	2	**Warehousing and shipping**
3	**BUSINESS~**	3	**WAREHOUSE~**

	P		Q
1	**Single**	1	**Duplex**
2	**Single-family home**	2	**Duplex or quadruplex units**
3	**RESIDENCE~**	3	**DUPLEX~**

	R		S
1	**Apartment**	1	**Other**
2	**Apartment or condominium**	2	**Other property type**
3	**APARTMENT~**		

S
3 **{GETLABEL "Enter property type: ", @CELLPOINTER("address")}~**

▶ Your screen may look as shown in Screen Display 14–2.

Entries on the second row may overlap since they are longer than 9 characters, but there is no need for you to widen any columns, unless you want to. Also, note that all the entries in row 3 end with tildes.

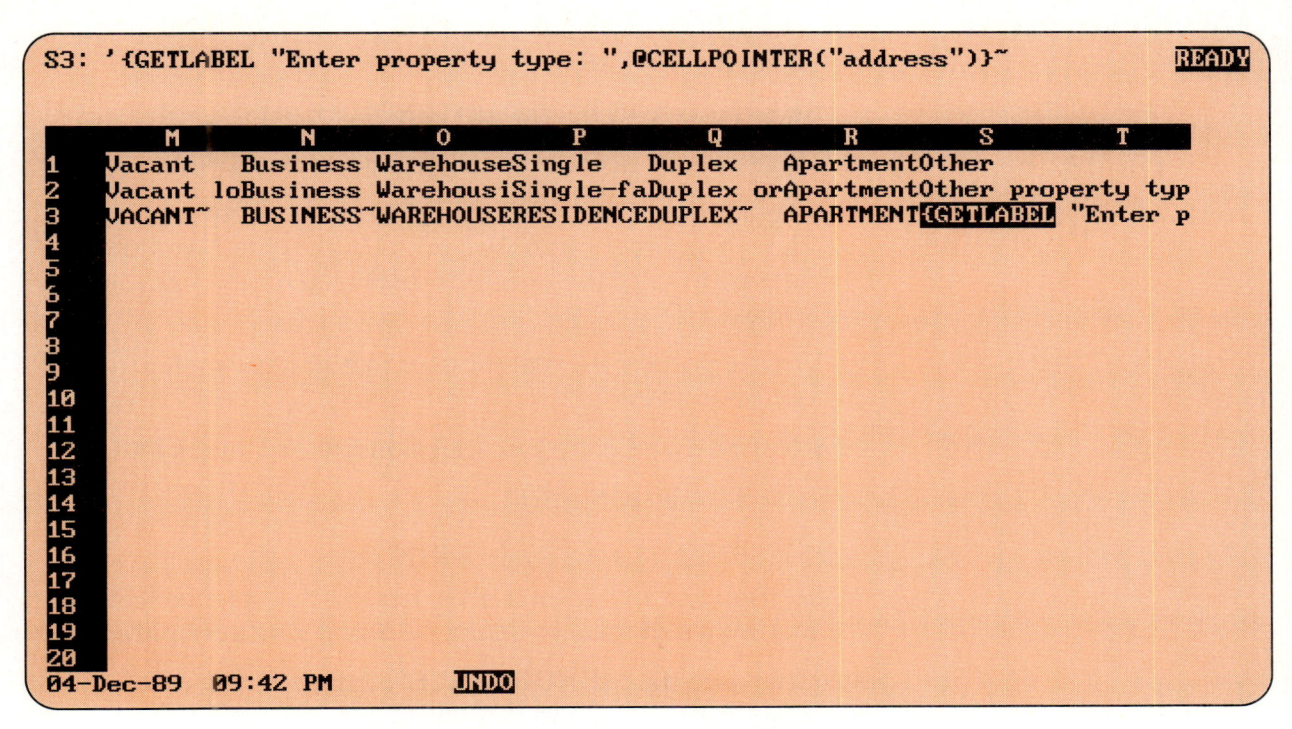

```
S3: '{GETLABEL "Enter property type: ",@CELLPOINTER("address")}~              READY
            M         N        O         P         Q         R         S         T
    1   Vacant    Business WarehouseSingle    Duplex    ApartmentOther
    2   Vacant  loBusiness WarehousiSingle-faDuplex orApartmentOther property typ
    3   VACANT~    BUSINESS~WAREHOUSERESIDENCEDUPLEX~   APARTMENT{GETLABEL "Enter p
    4
    5
    ...
   20
   04-Dec-89  09:42 PM          UNDO
```

Screen Display 14–2   Menu block.

- Move the cell pointer to cell M1, and use **/RNC** to name the cell **PROP**, for property menu.

You will now enter the macro to call the menu you just created.

- In cell M10, enter **'\m**.
- Use the label in M10 to name cell N10.
- In cell N10, enter the command **{MENUBRANCH PROP}**

This is the menu command which says that the menu block starts at the cell named PROP.

- In cell O10, enter the macro description.

    `Property type entry macro`

    ▶ Row 10 looks as follows:

	M	N	O
10	\m	{MENUBRANCH PROP}	Property type entry macro

ADVANCED MACRO COMMANDS **343**

Now the macro is ready.

- Save the spreadsheet as **LOTUS24**.
- Move the cell pointer to cell A1 and press (ALT)-**M**.
  - ➤ Your customized menu appears on the command line. The first option, Vacant, is highlighted, and the description of the option is displayed on the line below.
- Use the pointer movement keys to highlight each option in turn.
  - ➤ Notice the changing descriptions on the line below.
- Type **S** to select Single.
  - ➤ The label RESIDENCE appears in cell A1.
- Position the cell pointer elsewhere in the spreadsheet and invoke the macro again, selecting another option.

Since this uses the MENUBRANCH command, the execution of the macro does not return to the calling macro (\m).

PRACTICE TIME

1. Without erasing the menu block for property type, create a second menu block starting at cell M6. This menu is to help with data entry of city names. Your menu options are:

Menu Option	Description	City name to enter in current cell
Reno	City of Reno	Reno
Sparks	City of Sparks	Sparks
Incline	Incline Village	Incline Village
Carson	Carson City	Carson City
Verdi	Verdi	Verdi
Other	Enter City Name	[see below]

In cell R8, enter the advanced macro command:

{GETLABEL "Enter city or area: ", @CELLPOINTER("address")}~

2. To use the menu block, name cell M6 CITY.

3. In M12, enter the label **'\c**. Use this label to name cell N12.

4. In N12, enter **{MENUBRANCH CITY}**.

5. At O12, enter a description for the macro.

6. Test your \C macro.

7. Save the worksheet as file LOTUS25.

MENUCALL EXAMPLE

Suppose your intent is to set up a worksheet for real estate that contains the property type in the first column, the address in the second column, the city in the third column, and the price in the fourth column. You want to set up a macro that will help with data entry, and use the menu macros you have already created for property type and city—thus, macros will be called from within a macro.

The following series of events are to occur when this data-entry macro is invoked:

1. Data entry starts in cell A1 and continues on subsequent rows.

2. The menu for property type appears.

3. When a selection is made, the appropriate property type appears in the current cell.

4. The prompt for address then appears.

5. The user's response is stored in the cell to the right of the cell containing the property type.

ADVANCED MACRO COMMANDS **345**

6. The menu for city then appears.

7. When a selection is made, the appropriate city name appears in the cell to the right of the cell containing the address.

8. The prompt for price is then displayed.

9. The number the user types appears in proper currency format in the cell to the right of the cell containing the city.

10. The cell-pointer is moved to column A on the next row down.

You will now enter the data-entry macro in cell M14.

- In cell M14, enter the macro name **\d**.
- Label cell N14 using the entry in cell M14.

Starting at cell N14, you will enter the multiple-line keyboard macro for data entry. The first step is to send the cell pointer to cell A1. This step is not repeated.

- In cell N14, enter **{HOME}**.

The next step is to display the menu for property type and make a selection—that is, call the property macro. When the macro for property type is executed, however, you want to return to the next instruction in the data-entry macro; therefore, you use the {MENUCALL} command.

- In cell N15, enter **{MENUCALL PROP}**.

After the property type is entered, the cell pointer is to move to the right.

- In cell N16, enter **{RIGHT}**.

To enter the address, you will use the label-entry command and store the label in the current cell.

- Enter **{GETLABEL "Enter address: ", @CELLPOINTER("address")}~** at cell N17.
(Remember to end the entry with the tilde.)

346 USING LOTUS 1-2-3

You now need to move the cell pointer one cell to the right.

- In cell N18, enter **{RIGHT}**.

You now call the menu macro for city.

- In cell N19, enter **{MENUCALL CITY}**.

After the city has been entered, the cell pointer is to move to the right.

- In cell N20, enter **{RIGHT}**.

The price is entered the same way as the address, except that it is numeric; hence, the numeric-input command is used.

- Enter **{GETNUMBER "Enter price: ", @CELLPOINTER("address")}~** in cell N21.
  (Remember the tilde at the end.)

The entry for price is to be formatted to currency with two places to the right of the decimal.

- In cell N22, enter **'/rfc2~~**.

Move the cell pointer to the next entry location, which is one row down to the extreme left (column A). You accomplish this by moving the cell pointer down and then pressing the (END) key and the (←) key.

- In cell N23, enter **{DOWN}{END}{LEFT}**.

Now you need to loop back to the cell containing commands to display the menu for property type (cell N15). You will name that cell AGAIN.

- In cell N24, enter **{BRANCH AGAIN}**.

Name the cell N15 AGAIN before you forget.

- In cell M15, enter **AGAIN**.
- Name cell N15 using the entry in M15.
  ➤ Your screen looks as shown in Screen Display 14–3.

The data-entry macro has been entered and named. It is important that you check that all the entries are correct, because it is sometimes very difficult to debug errors in keyboard macros.

ADVANCED MACRO COMMANDS **347**

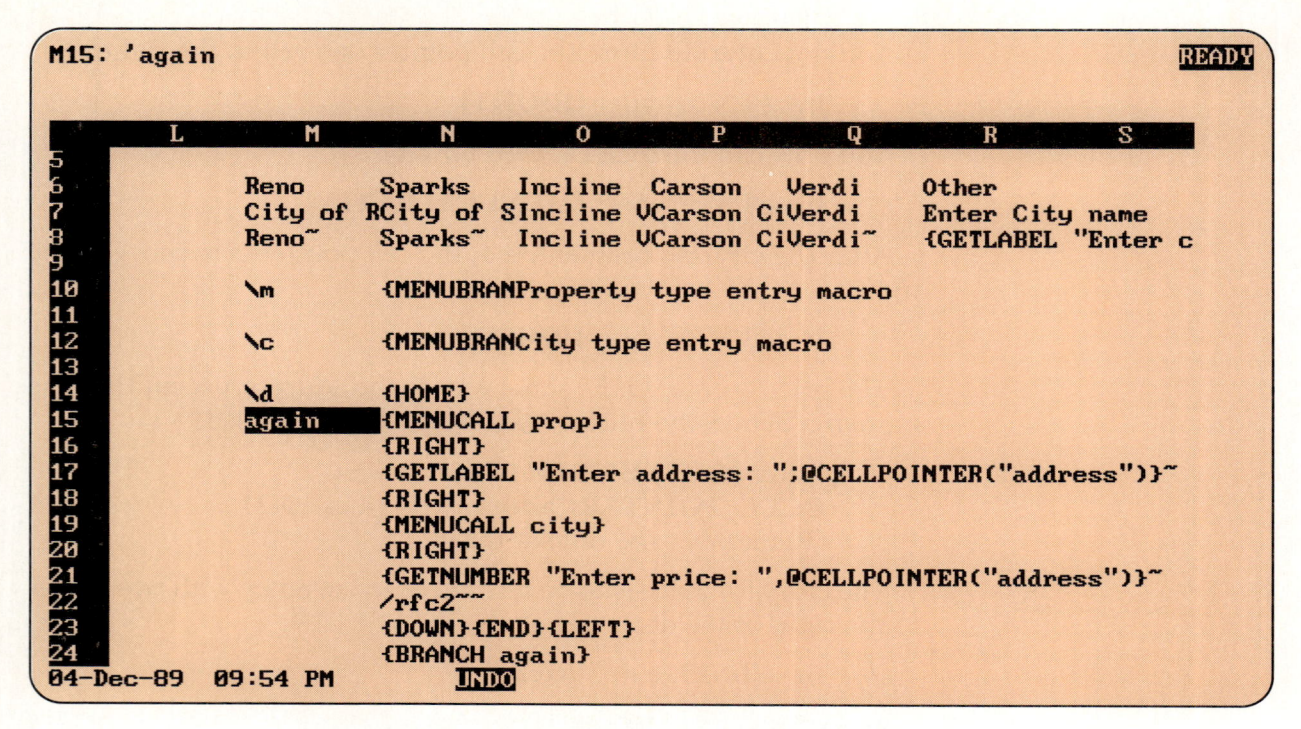

```
M15: 'again                                                          READY

         L        M         N        O        P        Q        R        S
 5
 6                Reno      Sparks   Incline  Carson   Verdi    Other
 7                City of   RCity of SIncline VCarson  CiVerdi  Enter City name
 8                Reno~     Sparks~  Incline  VCarson  CiVerdi~ {GETLABEL "Enter c
 9
10                \m        {MENUBRANProperty type entry macro
11
12                \c        {MENUBRANCity type entry macro
13
14                \d        {HOME}
15                again     {MENUCALL prop}
16                          {RIGHT}
17                          {GETLABEL "Enter address: ";@CELLPOINTER("address")}~
18                          {RIGHT}
19                          {MENUCALL city}
20                          {RIGHT}
21                          {GETNUMBER "Enter price: ",@CELLPOINTER("address")}~
22                          /rfc2~~
23                          {DOWN}{END}{LEFT}
24                          {BRANCH again}
04-Dec-89  09:54 PM         UNDO
```

Screen Display 14–3 Data entry macro calling two menus.

- Erase all the entries that you have made in columns A through D.
- Invoke the data entry macro by entering (ALT)-**D**.
   ➤ The menu for property type is displayed.
- Select Single.
   ➤ The word RESIDENCE appears in cell A1.
   ➤ You are prompted to enter the address.

Because you performed a MENUCALL instead of a MENU-BRANCH, the sequence of instructions returned you to the calling macro.

- Enter **1240 Searchlight Ct.**
   ➤ The menu to select the city is displayed.
- Select Reno.
   ➤ You are prompted to enter the price.

- Enter **89000**.
  - ➤ The number is formatted to currency. Since you have not adjusted the column width yet, the entry may not be displayed properly.
  - ➤ The cell pointer moves to column A, next row down.
- Use the following data for entry.

Residential	123 S. Center	Reno	$89,500
Warehouse	225 Glendale	Sparks	$225,000
Duplex	2473 Eagle Valley	Carson City	$185,000
Apartment	101 Francis Way	Verdi	$550,900
Business	22500 Highway 395	Washoe Valley	$322,000
Vacant	75 Donna Lane	Incline Village	$70,000

Do you see another problem? There is no way to terminate the macro. For now, you can abort the macro by pressing CTRL-BREAK.

- Press CTRL-BREAK, and then press ENTER to terminate the macro execution.
- Adjust the column widths.
- Save the spreadsheet as **LOTUS26**.

You will insert commands to terminate the macro instruction. This will also be a menu.

- Edit cell N24 to read **{MENUBRANCH ANS}**.

PRACTICE TIME

1. Create the following menu macro, starting at cell M28, and name cell M28 ANS.

28	AGAIN?	QUIT
29	Enter another property	Quit data entry
30	{BRANCH AGAIN}	{QUIT}

2. Erase the contents of columns A through D and test the macro \d.

3. Save the spreadsheet again as LOTUS26.

AUTOEXECUTE MACROS

There is a special type of macro that is invoked when the worksheet containing it is retrieved. This type of worksheet can be used by people who are not computer-oriented. For example, you might have a non-computer-oriented data-entry clerk who has been taught how to retrieve the worksheet: When the worksheet is retrieved, the customized menu automatically appears to tells the clerk what he or she is to do for this particular spreadsheet.

The \0 (zero) macro is the autoexecute macro. You will now create an autoexecute macro that branches to the ALT-D macro you just created.

- Erase the entries in columns A through D.
- Change the entry in cell M14 to \0 (backslash zero).
- Label cell N14 using the entry in cell M14.
- Place cell pointer at cell A1.
- Save the worksheet as file **LOTUS27**.
- Clear the worksheet.

Now let's try the autoexecute macro.

- Retrieve file **LOTUS27**.
  ➤ The menu for property type is displayed.

When the worksheet was retrieved, it automatically executed the \0 macro.

- Enter an item and quit the macro.

PRACTICE TIME

1. Clear the worksheet.

2. Create an autoexecute macro that enters the label "DATE" in cell A1, the date in B1, the label "TIME" in A2, and the time in B2, with B1 and B2 properly formatted to display those quantities. *Hint:* Use the Learn feature to enter the macro.

3. Save the worksheet as LOTUS28.

4. Clear the worksheet.

5. Test the autoexecute macro by retrieving LOTUS28.

As you use worksheets, you will naturally find many places where macros can be quickly written, used, and discarded, and other places where you will want to make a spreadsheet friendly for another person to use. It takes much practice to learn when and how to enter macros, but as you progress, it becomes easier to do so.

END OF LESSON 14

- Type **/QY**, and then **E** to exit to DOS.
- Remove the disks from the disk drive.
- Turn off the monitor, computer, and printer.

SUMMARY

In this lesson, many of the terms and concepts needed to use advanced macro commands are discussed:

- Advanced macro commands can only be used in macros. They are keywords enclosed in curly braces {}, and are of the format {keyword} or {keyword argument1,argument2,...}.

- Advanced macro commands are grouped into five types: data-manipulation, flow-of-control, interactive, screen, and file-manipulation. The last two types are not discussed in this lesson.

- The following macro commands were discussed:

{LET location,entry}	Places the data in the location specified.
{BLANK location}	Erases the contents of the specified location.
{BRANCH location}	Specifies the location of the next macro instruction.
{IF condition} command	If the condition specified is true, the command is executed; otherwise, the instruction in the next cell down is executed.
{QUIT}	Stops the macro's execution.
{RETURN}	Returns the program flow to the calling macro.
{macro-name}	Calls the named macro as a subroutine.
{?}	Suspends macro execution to allow the user to move the cell pointer or to make an entry, and resumes execution when the user presses the (ENTER) key.
{GETNUMBER prompt, location}	Displays the prompt and enters the value input in the specified location.
{GETLABEL prompt, location}	Displays the prompt and enters the label input in the specified location.
{MENUBRANCH location}	The menu block at the location specified is invoked.
{MENUCALL location}	The menu block at the location specified is invoked like a subroutine.
{WAIT time-number}	Suspends macro execution until time-number is reached.

- @CELLPOINTER("address") is used to obtain the address of the current cell.

- Autoexecute macros are executed as soon as their associated spreadsheet is retrieved. These macros are named \0 (zero).

REVIEW QUESTIONS

1. What are advanced macro commands? When are they used?

2. Give and explain the general advanced macro command format.

3. Give an example of a data-manipulation macro command.

4. Give an example of a flow-of-control macro command.

5. Give an example of an interactive macro command.

6. What is the difference between {GOTO} and {BRANCH}? Explain.

7. How do you store user input (from {GETNUMBER} and {GETLABEL} commands) in a current cell?

8. Explain how a menu block is set up, such as how many rows and how many columns it should have and what goes into each row.

9. Explain the difference between {MENUCALL} and {MENUBRANCH}.

10. What is an autoexecute macro? How do you create it? How do you execute it?

EXERCISES

1. a) Retrieve the spreadsheet EX6_1.

   b) Create a menu macro with the following options:

Menu option	Description	Action taken
ASort	Sorts, using total amount owed	Invokes macro that sorts range A3.I12, using total amount owed, in ascending order.
NSort	Sorts, using names	Invokes macro that sorts range A3.I12, using names, alphabetically.
Print	Prints spreadsheet	Invokes macro that prints the entire worksheet (A1.I15).

   c) Test the macro and save the worksheet as EX14_1.

   d) Print the worksheet.

2. a) Retrieve the spreadsheet EX6_2.

   b) Erase the entries in cell range A3 through D11.

   c) You are teaching a programming course in a computer lab which has nine computer terminals for student use. Create a macro \D that prompts the user to enter data on students. Keep count so that you do not enter more than 9 student names.

   d) Create a macro \S that sorts the student records by name, alphabetically.

   e) Create a macro \P that prints the worksheet range A1.G13.

   f) Test the macros. You must always enter nine students.

   g) When you are satisfied, save the worksheet as EX14_2A.

   h) Print the whole worksheet.

i) Create a menu macro whose options are the three macros created in (c), (d), and (e).

j) Test the menu. Remember, you must always enter nine students.

k) When you are satisfied, save the worksheet as EX14_2B.

l) Print the whole worksheet.

LESSON 15
ADD-IN PROGRAMS

OBJECTIVES

Upon completion of the material presented in this lesson, you should be able to:

- Understand the usage of add-in programs with Lotus 1–2–3 Release 2.2
- Attach and detach add-in programs
- Use the Macro Library Manager to save and use macro libraries
- Use the Allways add-in program to enhance printouts of worksheets

Note: The Allways add-in program requires a hard disk and 512K of computer memory. If you are using Lotus 1–2–3 on floppy diskettes, you will not be able to complete the last part of this lesson.

STARTING OFF

Start Lotus 1–2–3 so that a blank spreadsheet is displayed on the screen. Also, insert the data disk in drive B and change the file directory to B.

ADD-IN PROGRAMS

One new feature of Lotus 1–2–3 Release 2.2 is the convenience of attaching add-in programs. An *add-in* program is a computer program designed to be used within 1–2–3, to provide additional features. Add-ins are initially stored on disk, but when they are *attached* to 1–2–3, they are loaded in RAM memory as though they were part of the spreadsheet program.

Note: Add-ins take up RAM memory and reduce the amount of memory available for the worksheet.

When an add-in is loaded into RAM memory from disk, it is said to be *attached*. It remains attached until the end of the Lotus 1–2–3 session, or until you *detach* it, or remove it from RAM memory. Up to ten add-ins can be attached at any time. When an add-in is attached, it can be *invoked,* or executed, by the user.

Although add-ins are available from other vendors, Lotus supplies two add-ins with Lotus 1–2–3 Release 2.2. These are the Macro Library Manager, by Lotus Development Corporation, and Allways, by Funk Software, Incorporated. These add-ins are used later in this lesson to demonstrate the concepts behind, and the use of, add-ins.

ADD-IN COMMAND (/A)

The Add-In command is used to attach and detach add-ins. You will begin by attaching the Macro Library Manager.

- Enter **/A** for Add-In.

    ➤ The Add-In submenu appears:

Attach	Loads an add-in from disk into memory.
Detach	Removes an attached add-in from memory.
Invoke	Activates an add-in that is in memory.
Clear	Removes all attached add-ins from memory.
Quit	Returns to the Ready mode.

- Select Attach.

    ➤ The message prompts you to enter the name of the add-in to attach.
    ➤ On the third line of the control panel, the filenames of add-ins in the 1–2–3 directory are displayed. ALLWAYS.ADN and MACROMGR.ADN should appear on this line.

Note: Add-ins have .ADN extensions, and are stored in the Lotus 1–2–3 directory. Some, like Allways, also have files in a subdirectory, as indicated by the presence of ALLWAYS\ in the menu.

- Select MACROMGR.ADN.

    ➤ The submenu shown on the next page appears for you to select a keystroke for invoking the add-in.

358 USING LOTUS 1-2-3

No-Key	Add-in must be invoked using the / Add-In Invoke command.
7	The ALT-F7 keystroke invokes the add-in.
8	The ALT-F8 keystroke invokes the add-in.
9	The ALT-F9 keystroke invokes the add-in.
10	The ALT-F10 keystroke invokes the add in.

The four ALT-function keys can be used for quickly invoking add-ins. All add-ins can be invoked through the / Add-In Invoke command.

■ Select 7 to be able to invoke the add-in with ALT-F7.

➤ The Add-In submenu reappears.

■ Select Quit.

You have now attached the Macro Library Manager to the spreadsheet program. That means that the Macro Library Manager has been loaded into memory where it will not interfere with the worksheet you have in memory, and can be invoked by pressing ALT-F7. Sometimes you may need to release one or more add-ins because you need the memory space for your current worksheet. You can release one add-in by using the / Add-In Detach command, and all add-ins by using the / Add-In Clear command.

■ **PRACTICE TIME**

1. Release the Macro Library Manager add-in, using the detach option.

2. Attach the Macro Library Manager add-in, so that it can be invoked with the ALT-F9 keystroke.

3. Return to the Ready mode.

MACRO LIBRARY MANAGER

In the previous two lessons, you learned what Lotus 1–2–3 macros are and how to create and use them. While macros have many uses, that they are located in the worksheet sometimes causes problems. If you are working on data, deleting rows and columns may accidentally delete macros and thus interfere with or prevent macro execution. In the last lesson, it was suggested that macros should occupy different rows and columns than those used for the worksheet. Also, if you have created several general-purpose macros, you may need to reenter them or combine them from another worksheet, and then name them, in order to use them in another worksheet. One way to protect and have macros readily available for use in different worksheets is to use the Macro Library Manager add-in. For example, in the last lesson, you created several macros and menu macros for data entry. If you entered several dozen entries in the worksheet, and then decided to delete an entry by deleting a row, you could inadvertently delete a macro cell, which would cause problems. To avoid this problem, you will move the range that contains these macros into the macro library. The macros will still be *invocable* but will reside in memory apart from the worksheet. As an additional benefit, this block of macros will be given a library name and stored on disk; thus, it can later used with any worksheet.

■ Retrieve file LOTUS26.

The worksheet in LOTUS26 has the macros you created for real-estate data entry. To save a block of macros in the macro library, you invoke the add-in and then you follow the prompts and menus.

■ Press (ALT)-(F9) to invoke the Macro Library Manager.

➤ The Macro Library Manager menu appears:

Load	Reads a macro library from disk.
Save	Saves a worksheet range in a macro library.
Edit	Copies the contents of a macro library into the worksheet.
Remove	Erases macro library from memory.
Name-List	Lists the range names contained in a macro library in memory.
Quit	Returns to 1–2–3 Ready mode.

■ Select Save.

➤ You are prompted to enter a macro library name for the block you will save.

The Macro Library Manager will save the block as a macro library, with the .MLB extension, on your data disk.

- Enter **PROPERTY**.

    ➤ The message prompts you to specify the range to move to the macro library.

The data-entry macro block is columns M through T, rows 1 through 30. This range includes the macro names and the macros from columns M through S, plus a blank column (T) after the menu.

- Enter **M1.T30**.

    ➤ A message asks whether you want to use a password to lock the library.

Libraries may be locked with passwords to prevent modification, but passwords are not used to restrict their use. If you use a password, you may enter a password of up to 80 characters. The password is case-sensitive, so the *exact combination* of uppercase and lowercase letters needs to be entered. This time, you will not create a password.

- Select No.

    ➤ The specified range is removed from the worksheet, along with the range names associated with the cells in that range. They now exist in the macro library PROPERTY, which is currently loaded in memory and saved on your data disk as PROPERTY.MLB.

- Move the cell pointer to cell M1.

    ➤ The range M1..T30 is blank. The contents of the range were moved to the macro library.

- Press (ALT)-**D**.

    ➤ The data-entry macro has been invoked.

- Enter information on one piece of property and quit the macro.

- Erase the worksheet.

- Invoke the property menu macro again with ALT-D.
  - ➤ The library (and hence the macro) remained in memory even though the worksheet was erased.
- Add an entry and quit the macro.
  - ➤ The column widths need to be adjusted for appropriate display of the data, but do not worry about this now.
- Invoke the Macro Library Manager (ALT-F9) and remove PROPERTY from memory. The macro library file PROPERTY.MLB remains on disk.

PRACTICE TIME

1. Try to invoke the \d macro. It no longer works.

2. Invoke the Macro Library Manager and load PROPERTY into memory.

3. Again, invoke \d and check that it performs correctly.

4. When you are finished, exit the macro.

When the Macro Library Manager is attached, you can save, load, and remove macro libraries. Each library contains a range of up to 16,376 cells and may contain several macros. Up to ten macro libraries may be loaded at a time.

Note, however, that if you have a macro named \m in the worksheet, you cannot access a macro named \m in a library. Also, if you have several macros with the same name in libraries that are loaded, the Macro Library Manager will select *one* of them when you invoke the name but it may not be the macro you wanted. Thus, it is important to plan ahead when you name macros.

EDITING MACRO LIBRARIES

Sometimes a macro needs to be edited. A macro contained in a macro library can be edited by moving it back into a worksheet. When it has been edited, it can be saved again in the macro library.

To illustrate the ability to edit part of a macro library, you will edit PROPERTY to change it slightly.

- Erase the worksheet.
- Press (ALT)-(F9) to invoke the Macro Library Manager.
- Select Edit.
    ➤ The screen displays a menu of the libraries in memory.
- Select PROPERTY.
    ➤ A menu presents the options Ignore and Overwrite.

If a range name in PROPERTY is the same as a range name in the current worksheet, this menu selection will decide which range name will be kept: Ignore means that the range names in the library will be ignored in the event of a conflict, while Overwrite means that the range names in the library will overwrite current worksheet range-name assignments. When you edit a library in a blank worksheet, as in this case, it does not matter which selection you make.

- Select Overwrite.
    ➤ You are prompted to specify the range in the worksheet to which to retrieve the library.

You only need to select the upper left-corner cell of the range to load the library into. You should use care to ensure that the library will not overwrite any information in your worksheet.

- Enter **A1**.
    ➤ The library PROPERTY is placed into the worksheet with its upper left corner at cell A1.

ADD-IN PROGRAMS **363**

■
PRACTICE TIME

You want to split apartment and condominium listings, currently in column F, into two categories—apartments in column F and condominiums in column G.

1. Move the range G1..G3 to H1..H3, in order to open column G for condominiums.

2. Edit the contents of cell F2 to read **Apartment unit**.

3. In G1 to G3, enter the following:

   G1:   Condo
   G2:   Condominium unit
   G3:   CONDOMINIUM~

- Press (ALT)-(F9) to invoke the Macro Library Manager.
- Select Save and then specify the library name, PROPERTY, the range, A1..I30, and to Replace the existing library. Do not use a password.

■
PRACTICE TIME

Test the \d macro.

Note: The Macro Library Manager can also be used to transfer a template to worksheets; that is, you can compose a template, complete with range names and formulas, and save the range as a library. When you want to place it into another worksheet, you invoke the macro library manager and select the Edit option. This is the same as File Combine, except that the range names are preserved.

364   USING LOTUS 1-2-3

ALLWAYS

In Lesson 11, the various printer options were described. Use of printer options gives you better control of the printout. The Allways add-in has several features that can greatly improve the appearance of printouts.

Allways prints text and numbers in bold or underline, in any of several available fonts. It can draw lines and boxes, double underlines, and shadings. It can include graphs in the printout of the worksheet, and it can print in color, if you have that capability on your printer. Allways also lets you change the screen display colors, if you choose.

Note: Allways requires a hard-disk system with at least 512K of RAM memory; 640K is better. If your system does not meet these requirements, you cannot use the Allways add-in. This lesson assumes that you have already performed the Allways setup.

The exercises in this lesson were tested on DOS 3.1 with 640K RAM memory and on DOS version 3.3, with 1M RAM, in both cases without other RAM-resident programs. If you have difficulties because of insufficient memory, you may be using a version of DOS that uses more memory or you may have another program resident in memory (one that is invoked with a 'hot-key').

When the Allways program is attached, it creates in memory a second worksheet with the printer formatting specifications. When you save a worksheet with Allways attached, the Lotus 1–2–3 worksheet is saved with a .WK1 extension and the Allways worksheet of printer specifications is saved with the same name as the worksheet but with a .ALL extension.

To illustrate some of the Allways features, you will use the LOTUS8 worksheet you previously prepared.

PRACTICE TIME

1. Detach the Macro Library Manager add-in, using / Add-In Detach.

2. Retrieve file LOTUS8.

3. Attach the Allways add-in, assigning the (ALT)-(F8) keystroke to invoke it.

4. Return to the Ready mode.

INVOKING AND USING ALLWAYS

Allways lets you customize the printing of worksheets. It improves their appearance and lets you use printing features that would be difficult to use otherwise.

To recall: When you invoked the Macro Library Manager, a menu appeared. The menu allowed you to load or save libraries. In contrast, when you invoke Allways, the Allways screen appears, which is very similar to the 1–2–3 screen. Within the Allways screen, the / (slash) commands are different: They allow you to access specific Allways features. You can freely toggle between Allways and 1–2–3 by repeatedly invoking Allways.

- Press ALT-F8 to invoke Allways.
  - ▶ The Allways screen, in graphic mode, appears similar to that shown in Screen Display 15–1. Since the display depends on the type of monitor you are using, your screen may have a different number of rows or columns displayed on it.

The Allways screen can display in either text or graphic mode. In text mode, the display is updated more rapidly, but in graphic mode, you have a "What you see is what you get," or WYSIWYG, display, meaning that the display shows what will be printed. You will next switch the screen between the two modes. (Descriptions of the Allways menus are given later.)

- Press **/DMT** for Display Mode Text to change the display to text.
- Press **Q** to quit the Allways menu.
  - ▶ The Allways text display is similar to the Lotus 1–2–3 display.
- Press **/DMG** for Display Mode Graphics to change the display to graphics.
- Press **Q** to quit the menu.
  - ▶ The Allways graphics display is WYSIWYG.

The mode indicator in the upper right-hand corner of the screen shows ALLWAYS, which is the same as the Ready mode in 1–2–3. The top line displays the printing information (font, shading, etc.)

```
FONT(1) Triumvirate 10 pt                                           ALLWAYS
A1: ^PART
        A       B         C             D       E         F        G       H
   1  PART    TYPE    DESCRIPTION     WEIGHT   COST      PRICE   QUANTITY LOCATION
   2  L1003   UPS    200 watt capacity  18.75  195.00    389.00     325   A-8
   3  L1011   UPS    325 watt capacity  36     240.00    479.00      72   C-1
   4  L1029   UPS    450 watt capacity  38.5   315.00    625.00      46   B-1
   5  L1037   UPS   1000 watt capacity  80     625.00   1249.00      12   A-2
   6  L0005   SSS    modem surge protector  1   30.00     59.90     880   A-6
   7  L1045   UPS    200 watt capacity  15     185.00    369.00     470   C-8
   8  L1052   UPS    325 watt capacity  32     230.00    459.00     112   B-3
   9  L1060   UPS    450 watt capacity  33     300.00    599.00      35   A-3
  10  L1078   UPS    675 watt capacity  68     450.00    899.00      60   B-6
  11  L0013   UPS   1800 watt capacity  14     150.00    299.00       0   A-5
  12  L0047   SSS    2-outlet box        1      25.00     49.95    1480   C-4
  13  L0054   SSS    4-outlet strip      3      29.00     57.95    2257   A-7
  14  L0062   SSS    6-outlet strip      3      33.00     65.95    1326   B-7
06-Dec-89   07:55 PM
```

Screen Display 15–1   Allways screen with worksheet.

for the current cell, and the second line in the control panel displays the entry for the current cell or the Allways menu options. The pointer-movement keys work identically as they do in 1–2–3, but you cannot make entries or edit data in the worksheet while you are in Allways.

You can toggle between Allways and 1–2–3 by pressing (ALT)-(F8) when you need to enter or edit data.

- Press (ALT)-(F8) to switch to 1–2–3.
- Press (ALT)-(F8) again to return to Allways.

The initial Allways graphic display may not be very clear on some monitors, but the display can be enlarged in order to display text and numbers more clearly on the screen. You will now enlarge the screen display. This gives you a chance to notice the Allways menu features.

- Enter / (do not press (ENTER)).

- ➤ Allways has a different command menu than 1–2–3. Its main menu has the following options:

Worksheet	Commands that affect column widths, row heights, or the placement of page breaks (printer form-feed commands).
Format	Commands that affect how characters are printed.
Graph	Commands to add or modify graphs (using .PIC files) in the printout.
Layout	Page layout parameters (margins, width, etc.).
Print	Range, go, and align commands; similar to those in 1–2–3.
Display	Commands that affect the screen display.
Special	Copy, move, justify, and import commands.
Quit	Returns to the 1–2–3 Ready mode.

- ■ Select Display.

  - ➤ The display setting window appears, as shown in Screen Display 15–2. The following submenu options are shown in the control panel:

Mode	Text or graphics display mode.
Zoom	Five sizes from 60% to 140% of default (normal) size.
Graphs	Turns graph display on or off.
Colors	Specifies foreground, background, and cell pointer colors.
Quit	Returns to the Allways mode.

- ■ Select Zoom.

  - ➤ The following submenu appears:

Tiny	Reduces cells to 60% normal size.
Small	Reduces cells to 84% normal size.
Normal	Displays cells at normal size.
Large	Enlarges cells to 120% normal size.
Huge	Enlarges cells to 140% normal size.

Screen Display 15–2 Allways/Display menu with settings box.

- Select Large.
- Select Quit to return to the Allways mode.
  ➤ As shown in Screen Display 15–3, the characters are enlarged.
- Press the (HOME) key.

■ FONTS AND BOLDFACE

Allways displays several typefaces in different sizes. A *typeface* is the design of the characters. Examples of typefaces include Times and Helvetica. *Size* is a specific measure of the height of the type. Sizes are specified in *points*, where a point equals 1/72-inch. A *font* is a specified typeface and size, such as Times 10 point, which is the Times typeface of a size (10/72-inch) slightly less than 1/6-inch high.

The titles on the first row could use some emphasis.

ADD-IN PROGRAMS **369**

```
FONT(1) Triumvirate 10 pt                                          ALLWAYS
A1: ^PART
         A     B         C              D        E        F         G
   1   PART  TYPE    DESCRIPTION      WEIGHT   COST     PRICE    QUANTI
   2   L1003  UPS   200 watt capacity  18.75   195.00   389.00      3:
   3   L1011  UPS   325 watt capacity  36      240.00   479.00
   4   L1029  UPS   450 watt capacity  38.5    315.00   625.00
   5   L1037  UPS   1000 watt capacity 80      625.00  1249.00
   6   L0005  SSS   modem surge protector 1     30.00    59.90      8!
   7   L1045  UPS   200 watt capacity  15      185.00   369.00      4:
   8   L1052  UPS   325 watt capacity  32      230.00   459.00      1
   9   L1060  UPS   450 watt capacity  33      300.00   599.00
  10   L1078  UPS   675 watt capacity  68      450.00   899.00
  11   L0013  UPS   1800 watt capacity 14      150.00   299.00
  12   L0047  SSS   2-outlet box        1       25.00    49.95     14!
 06-Dec-89  08:00 PM
```

Screen Display 15–3   Enlarged Allways graphic display.

■ Enter **/F** for Format.

▶ The following submenu appears:

Font	Selects a font for a worksheet range.
Bold	Adds or removes boldface for a range.
Underline	Adds or removes single or double underlining.
Color	Selects a color for printing a range (for color printers only).
Lines	Draws lines, outlines, and boxes around each cell.
Shades	Gives light, medium, black, or no-shading options for a range.
Reset	Removes all user-specified formats from a range and restores default values.
Quit	Returns to the Allways mode.

Screen Display 15–4   Allways font selection menu.

- Select Font.

    ► A selection window appears, as shown in Screen Display 15–4. For your printer, the options may be different.

- If 10-point Times font is available, select that option by moving the highlight with the arrow keys and pressing (ENTER) when the option is highlighted. Otherwise, select any 10-point font, if available.

    ► A message appears asking you to indicate a range to format with this font.

- Select the range **A1..H1.**

    ► As Screen Display 15–5 shows, the screen displays a different font for the top row.

ADD-IN PROGRAMS **371**

```
FONT(5) Times 10 pt                                          ALLWAYS
A1: ^PART

         A        B            C              D        E        F
  1   PART     TYPE     DESCRIPTION       WEIGHT    COST    PRICE    C
  2   L1003    UPS      200 watt capacity    18.75   195.00   389.00
  3   L1011    UPS      325 watt capacity    36      240.00   479.00
  4   L1029    UPS      450 watt capacity    38.5    315.00   625.00
  5   L1037    UPS      1000 watt capacity   80      625.00  1249.00
  6   L0005    SSS      modem surge protector  1      30.00    59.90
  7   L1045    UPS      200 watt capacity    15      185.00   369.00
  8   L1052    UPS      325 watt capacity    32      230.00   459.00
  9   L1060    UPS      450 watt capacity    33      300.00   599.00
 10   L1078    UPS      675 watt capacity    68      450.00   899.00
 11   L0013    UPS      1800 watt capacity   14      150.00   299.00
 12   L0047    SSS      2-outlet box          1       25.00    49.95

06-Dec-89   08:12 PM
```

Screen Display 15-5   Different font in row 1.

■ PRACTICE TIME

1. Use the /F menu options to boldface and double underline the row 1 titles.

2. If available, select a 10-point italic font for range C2..C18 (the description range).

When you select a font for printing using Allways, you do not affect the current worksheet. Unlike the /Range Format command in 1-2-3, which changes settings in the worksheet, Allways keeps the printer settings, including font and shading, in its own work area; it does not change any data in your current worksheet. To see the effect of changing the fonts on the worksheet, you can toggle back to 1–2–3.

- Press (ALT)-(F8) to switch to 1–2–3.

  ➤ There is no effect on the worksheet contents, as can be seen in the top line of the control panel.

- Press (ALT)-(F8) again to return to Allways.

SHADING AND LINES

One of your inventory items has a quantity of 0. You will lightly shade that item for emphasis.

- Move the cell pointer to A11.
- Enter **/FS** for Format Shade.

  ➤ The submenu of shading options appears:

Light	Draws light shading in selected range.
Dark	Draws darker shading in selected range.
Solid	Draws black shading in selected range (often used for border effects).
Clear	Draws no shading in selected range.

- Select Light.

  ➤ You are requested to enter the range to shade.

- Enter **A11.H11**.

  ➤ As shown in Screen Display 15–6, the screen depicts the light shading.

Allways allows you to add lines to the printout for emphasis. For example, you could add a vertical line between the columns containing student names and their first test scores in a worksheet of student grades. To see how the line feature is used, you will outline the worksheet range to be printed.

- Press **/FL** for Format Lines.

  ➤ The following menu options are given:

  Outline   Draws a box around the range.

ADD-IN PROGRAMS **373**

```
FONT(1) Triumvirate 10 pt, SHADE:Light                    ALLWAYS
A11: 'L0013
         A         B            C            D        E        F
   1   PART      TYPE      DESCRIPTION     WEIGHT   COST    PRICE    G
   2   L1003     UPS      200 watt capacity  18.75  195.00   389.00
   3   L1011     UPS      325 watt capacity  36     240.00   479.00
   4   L1029     UPS      450 watt capacity  38.5   315.00   625.00
   5   L1037     UPS      1000 watt capacity 80     625.00  1249.00
   6   L0005     SSS      modem surge protector  1   30.00    59.90
   7   L1045     UPS      200 watt capacity  15     185.00   369.00
   8   L1052     UPS      325 watt capacity  32     230.00   459.00
   9   L1060     UPS      450 watt capacity  33     300.00   599.00
  10   L1078     UPS      675 watt capacity  68     450.00   899.00
  11   L0013     UPS      1800 watt capacity 14     150.00   299.00
  12   L0047     SSS      2-outlet box        1      25.00    49.95
06-Dec-89  08:11 PM
```

Screen Display 15–6   Allways light shading in row 11.

Left	Draws a vertical line at the left side of each cell in a range.
Right	Draws a line at the right side of each cell in a range.
Top	Draws a horizontal line at the top of each cell in a range.
Bottom	Draws a line at the bottom of each cell in a range.
All	Draws a box around each cell in a range.
Clear	Removes all lines.

- Select Outline.

    ➤ A message prompts you for the range to outline.

- Enter the range A1.H18.

    ➤ The range is outlined. In graphics mode, you can see the line on the screen if you move the cell-pointer past column H or below row 17.

PRINTING

Allways is used to enhance the printing of a worksheet. When the formatting has been performed, the printing is similar to that in 1–2–3.

- Enter **/P** for Print.

  ➤ The following submenu options appear:

Go	Prints the specified range.
File	Sends the print output to a file on disk.
Range	Specifies or clears the range to print.
Configuration	Specifies the printer and printer interface.
Settings	Specifies which pages and the number of copies to print.
Quit	Returns to the Allways mode.

- Select Range.

  ➤ The menu options which appear are Set and Clear.

- Select Set.

- Indicate the range to print, **A1.H18**.

- Select Go.

  ➤ Depending on your printer, your worksheet may print on two pages.

MARGINS

The margins between the worksheet and the paper edges can be changed in Allways. You may note that the worksheet printout has rather wide margins. You can change the margins to allow the worksheet to fit onto one page.

- Type **/L** for Layout.

  ➤ The page-layout settings appear. They indicate the paper size, margins, borders, and titles.

➤ The following menu options are available:

Page-Size	Selects paper size.
Margins	Specifies page margins.
Titles	Specifies titles; similar to 1–2–3.
Borders	Specifies printed borders; similar to 1–2–3.
Options	Sets/resets line weights and grid.
Default	Restores or updates default values.
Library	Retrieves, saves, or erases page layouts in a library.

The left and right margins are 1 inch each. You can set both margins to 0.5 inch.

■ Select Margins.

➤ The menu options let you select the margin you want to set.

■ PRACTICE TIME

1. Set both the left and right margins to 0.5.

2. Select Quit twice to return to the Allways mode.

3. Print the worksheet again.

4. Return to 1–2–3 using (ALT)-(F8), and save the worksheet as LOTUS29.

When you save a file in 1–2–3, with Allways attached, the file is saved with a .WK1 extension (the Lotus 1–2–3 file) and with an .ALL extension (the Allways printer formatting file). To see the result of saving LOTUS29 above, you can list all files on diskette in drive B.

■ Type **/FLO** for File List Others.

➤ All the files on the diskette in drive B are listed. There is a LOTUS29.ALL file and a LOTUS29.WK1 file.

- Return to the Ready mode.
- Erase the worksheet.

GRAPHS

In addition to improving the presentation of worksheet printouts, Allways lets you print graphs without exiting to the PrintGraph utility. In fact, Allways can print a graph within a worksheet range, so that the worksheet and one or more graphs can be printed on the same page.

Note: The graph-printing capability is memory intensive, and may require more than 640K memory for many applications. Lotus 1-2-3 supports up to 4 megabytes of expanded memory if it is available in your computer.

To print a graph using Allways, you must first save the graph using 1-2-3, so that there is a .PIC file on disk. You should have several .PIC files on your data disk from Lesson 7. You will print the LOTUS5 worksheet and the BAR1S.PIC graph using Allways.

- Retrieve file LOTUS5.WK1.
- Press (ALT)-(F8) to return to Allways.

Suppose you would like the graph to be placed in the range B10 to F21.

- Type **/G** for Graph.

  ➤ The following submenu appears:

Add	Adds a graph to the worksheet.
Remove	Removes a graph from the worksheet.
Goto	Moves the cell pointer to a graph.
Settings	Specifies various graph settings.
Fonts-Directory	Specifies the directory containing the graph fonts.
Quit	Returns to the Allways mode.

- Select Add.

  ➤ A menu displays the filenames of .PIC files on the data disk.

- Select BAR1S.PIC.

    ▶ You are prompted to enter the range for the graph.

Since you will print the graph on the worksheet itself, you need to indicate the worksheet range where it will appear.

- Enter **B10.F21**.

    ▶ The specified range either is crosshatched, or displays the graph you indicated.

You can toggle between the crosshatching and graph display. If you display the graph, you see what will be printed on the paper. However, the crosshatching is often quicker and more convenient to use, since then the program does not need to redraw the graph each time cell pointer movements cause the screen display to scroll.

- Type **/DG** for Display Graphs.

    ▶ A menu appears asking if you want to display graphs.

- Select No, then Quit.

    ▶ The crosshatching appears.

- Type **/DGYQ** for Display Graphs Yes Quit.

    ▶ The graph is drawn on the screen.

PRACTICE TIME

Select the graph display setting that you prefer to work with.

Next, you will print the worksheet with the graph.

- Enter **/PRS** for Print Range Set.
- Enter **A1.F21** for the print range.

- Select Go to print the graph.
    - ➤ It may take time to print the worksheet with the graph.

EDITING GRAPHS

Suppose you want to print the worksheet with the pie chart that you saved in Lesson 7. You will change things around a bit in order to see the flexibility that Allways permits; for example, the several graph-settings commands in Allways that let you select how the graph will be printed.

- Press (ALT)-(F8) to return to 1–2–3.

The pie chart you created had only one data range. You do not need to display the last two data ranges in the worksheet.

PRACTICE TIME

1. In 1–2–3, erase the range C1..D7.

2. Move the range A1..B7 to the range C1..D7.

3. Return to Allways.

- Type **/GS** for Graph Settings.
    - ➤ A window opens with the names of the PIC files selected for printing.
- Select BAR1S.PIC (the only PIC file in the menu).
- Select PIC-File.
    - ➤ A message appears requesting the name of the new PIC file.
- Enter **PIE1S**.
    - ➤ The PIE1S.PIC file is loaded into memory, replacing BAR1S.PIC.

The pie-chart labels need to be enlarged so they will be able to be read on the printout. You will change several settings to improve the printing of the graph. In the settings, fonts 1 is the font for the first heading and fonts 2 is the font for the remaining text associated with the graph.

- Type **/GS** for Graph Settings.
- Select PIE1S-PIC.
- Select Fonts.
    ➤ A message asks if you want to set fonts 1 or fonts 2.
- Select 1.
    ➤ A window opens with the available fonts.
- Select a font from the list, such as Roman1 or Lotus. (The fonts available will depend on the printer you are using.)
- Select Scale.
    ➤ A message asks if you want to set fonts 1 or fonts 2.
- Select 1.
    ➤ You are asked to indicate the font size.
- Enter **2.00**.

■ PRACTICE TIME

Set the scale for fonts 2 to 2.00 also.

The Allways graphic-display mode (with graph display on) shows that some of the labels of the pie chart sections extend beyond the specified range and will be clipped. You want to adjust the graph size so that the labels are printed correctly. You can do this by specifying margins from within Graph Settings.

- Type **/GS** for Graph Settings.

380 USING LOTUS 1-2-3

- Select PIE1S-PIC.
- Select Margins.

PRACTICE TIME

1. Change the left and right margins to 0.2 and return to the Allways mode.

2. Print the worksheet range that was previously specified.

3. Return to 1–2–3 and save the worksheet as LOTUS30.

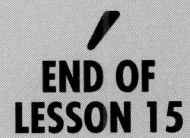

END OF LESSON 15

- Type **/QY**, then press **E** to exit to DOS.
- Remove the disks from the disk drive.
- Turn off the monitor, computer, and printer.

SUMMARY

In this lesson, the use of add-in programs within Lotus 1–2–3 is discussed:

- The / Add-In command is used to attach, detach, clear, or invoke add-in programs.
- Once attached, an add-in can be invoked with an (ALT)-Function key command ((F7), (F8), (F9), or (F10)).
- The Lotus Macro Library Manager can be used to manage commonly-used macro commands.
- When a range is saved in Macro Library Manager, the macros in the range can be executed with the (ALT)-(F3) (Run) command.
- Up to ten libraries can be loaded into memory simultaneously.

ADD-IN PROGRAMS

- Libraries managed by the Macro Library Manager can be in memory, but they do not occupy worksheet cells.
- Allways is used to select fonts and the printing format.
- Allways prints graphs in specified ranges within a worksheet.
- Allways can be used to change the graph to print and to adjust the graph size.
- Allways can be used to change the graph fonts and their sizes.

REVIEW QUESTIONS

1. What is an add-in, and why are add-ins important with 1–2–3?

2. What two steps are necessary to do in order to use an add-in with 1–2–3?

3. By what two ways can you invoke add-ins?

4. How do you make a library from a single-line macro using the Macro Library Manager?

5. What steps do you need to follow in order to use a macro in a library on disk?

6. What are some advantages in using the Macro Library Manager?

7. How do you change the contents of a macro in an existing library?

8. What is the Allways add-in used for?

9. How do you add graphs to a worksheet printout?

10. If you terminate a session when using Allways, how is your work saved for the next Allways session?

EXERCISES

1. a) Retrieve the spreadsheet EX14_1.
   b) Attach and invoke the Macro Library Manager.
   c) Save the menu macro in a library.
   d) Test all the menu options.
   e) Save as EX15_1.

2. a) Retrieve the spreadsheet EX10_2.
   b) Use Allways to format the worksheet for printing. Add the title "HISTORY 11-B" and outline the worksheet. Make the column titles bold and double underlined, and change the font to a typeface other than the default.
   c) Print the worksheet.
   d) Save as EX15_2.

GLOSSARY

@function—See function.

Absolute formula—A formula containing addresses or ranges preceded by $, such as $TABLE or $A$3, to indicate that those addresses do not vary when they are copied to another range.

Access System—A screen and menu that appears when you first start Lotus; allows you to select 1–2–3, PrintGraph, Translate, Install, or Exit.

Add-in—A program designed for use within 1–2–3, to provide additional special features.

Add-in Manager—Feature of Release 2.2 that easily allows add-ins to be attached, detached, or invoked.

Address—A letter-and-number combination that identifies a cell location in a worksheet.

Advanced macro command—A command used within macros that affects execution of the macro or allows manipulation of data within the worksheet.

Align—In 1–2–3, the command that resets the line count to the top line on a page; usually issued after the user has made sure the printer head is aligned at the top of the page.

Allways—An add-in by Funk Software, Incorporated that lets you format worksheets for printing with different fonts, bold and underlining, shading, and outlining, and that allows printing graphs (.PIC files) within 1–2–3.

Argument—The component of functions contained between parentheses, consisting of a cell, a range of cells, a range name, numbers, and formulas, or any combination of these.

Attach—Load into memory. An add-in program needs to be loaded into memory, or attached to 1-2-3, before it can be used.

Autoexecute macro—A macro, named \0, that is automatically executed when a worksheet is retrieved from disk.

Bar chart—A graph that indicates how some quantity varies between units or with time.

Bins—Cells used to display arbitrarily chosen categories and the quantities in them.

Border—The optional display of columns, rows, or both, of worksheet labels on all printed pages.

Built-in function—See function.

Cell—A single location in a worksheet.

Cell pointer—The highlight that indicates the current cell, the cell where your entry will be placed.

Context-sensitive help—A feature where the help screen which is displayed relates to the function you are performing when you press the (F1) (Help) function key.

Control panel—The top three lines of the screen, which indicate the current cell contents, the mode, display menus, and prompts.

Criteria—Formulas or cell entries used to determine records to be extracted, found, or deleted from a database.

Crosshatching—Shading of different portions of a pie chart.

Current cell—The cell presently highlighted by the cell pointer.

Cursor—The blinking character that indicates where your entry will be displayed on the screen.

Data distribution—A feature that allows the user to display how a quantity is distributed around various user-defined values.

Data management—The ability to store, sort, and retrieve data.

Data-manipulation macro command—An advanced macro command that changes the content or format of data in a cell or range.

Database—A range of a worksheet used to manage useful data.

Database functions—Statistical functions that can be used with a database.

Date/Time functions—Functions used for manipulating dates and time.

Default option—A highlighted option that is preselected; the option you can select by simply pressing (ENTER).

Delimited labels—Labels in an ASCII file must be delimited, or enclosed in quotes, for the /File Import Numbers command to read them into a worksheet.

Delimiter—A period or comma that serves to delimit, or separate, the various parts of a function.

Detach—Remove from memory. An attached add-in program can be detached, or removed from memory, to make more memory available for the worksheet or for other add-in programs.

DIF file—A Data Interchange Format file that has a .DIF extension, used by other applications programs.

Disk file—A way to save worksheets for future sessions and graphs for printing; each disk file has a filename, which is used to identify it.

Electronic spreadsheet—Computer software that allows a user to perform the operations of a spreadsheet.

Exploding pie chart—A pie chart with one or more pieces offset from the rest, like a cut-out piece of pie.

Expression—A formula.

Extension—One- to three-character end-part of the filename, preceded by a period; typically used to identify the type of file.

Field—A type of data within a record. A customer record might contain fields for name, account number, address, balance, and credit rating.

Field names—Identifying column labels of database fields.

File combining—Reading a .WK1 file from disk into the current worksheet, combining the two.

File importing—Reading an ASCII file (.PRN extension) from disk into memory.

File linking—Feature of Release 2.2 that allows one worksheet to reference by filename and address (location or range name) the contents of another worksheet.

File-manipulation macro command—An advanced macro command that performs operations on disk files.

File retrieval—Reading a .WK1 file from disk into memory and replacing any existing worksheet.

Filename—A name that identifies a disk file. It consists of one to eight letters, numbers, or the underscore (_) and a period, followed by an optional one- to three-character extension.

Financial functions—Functions that calculate payment on a loan, net present value, and future value of an investment.

Flow-of-control macro command—An advanced macro command that controls the order in which macro commands are carried out.

Font—A specified typeface and size.

Footer—A title, defined in the /Printer Option footer command, printed at the bottom of each page.

Format—The way that data is displayed on a monitor or printer.

Format line—A line inserted by the /Data Parse command to indicate how data in subsequent lines are to be separated into columns.

Formula—A cell entry evaluated to return a result, which is displayed in the cell.

Formula condition—The method of specifying criteria for numeric data.

Formula printout—The printout style that displays the exact cell entries, one cell per line.

Freeze titles—The ability to keep a row or column containing worksheet titles displayed, even if the screen displays parts of the worksheet that are otherwise off-screen.

Function—A built-in formula that produces, or returns, a numerical, logical, or alphameric result, beginning with an @ sign and often containing arguments within parentheses.

Giving a command—The action of accessing the 1–2–3 menu system or pressing a function key or ALT-function-keystroke combination.

Graph settings—The options used in printing graphs.

Header—A title, defined in the /Printer Option Header command, that is printed at the top of each page.

Histogram—A type of graph where the height of each bar represents the magnitudes of various items.

Inserting data—The action of typing an entry into a cell.

Interactive macro command—An advanced macro command that allows the macro, during its execution, to accept input from the user.

Invoke—To cause a macro or add-in to run.

Label—A cell entry consisting of alphanumeric data (which cannot be used for numeric calculations).

Label-prefix character—The initial character entered in a label, which indicates whether the label is to be left- or right-justified, or centered.

Learn feature—A feature of Release 2.2 that allows user's keystrokes to be recorded in a specified range within the worksheet, for use as a macro.

Legend—Descriptive text that identifies the patterns on a graph.

Library—A macro range saved by the Macro Library Manager and consisting of one or more macros that can be invoked, but existing in memory outside the worksheet and thus not associated with worksheet cells.

Line chart—A graph that displays the trends of one or more quantities.

Linking data—A process by which data in one worksheet file can be accessed in another worksheet file by referring to the filename and data location (address or range name).

Logical functions—Functions that return logical "true" (1) or "false" (0) after evaluating the function.

Macro—A sequence of keystrokes (commands, entries, or pointer movements) that are executed through a single keystroke command.

Macro command—See advanced macro command.

Macro Library Manager—An add-in by Lotus Development Corporation that lets the user create and use macro libraries by saving macro ranges from the current worksheet and loading selected libraries from disk.

Macro subroutine—A macro program called, or invoked, by another macro. When complete, the macro subroutine returns control to the calling macro.

Mathematical functions—Functions that handle algebraic expressions, equations, trigonometric functions, and formulas.

Menu macro—A macro block consisting of two to eight menu items, displayed on the control panel with a description on the second line of the highlighted option.

Mode indicator—The indicator in the top right-hand corner of the screen that indicates the mode that 1-2-3 or Allways is in.

Multiple-line macro—A macro consisting of several lines in the same column.

Numeric data—Values, when used in a database.

Parse—Separation of data elements in a long label (imported from an ASCII file) into columns.

Pie chart—A graph that indicates how some quantity is divided up between several categories.

Point—The unit of type height; 1 point = 1/72-inch.

Pointer-movement keys—The arrow keys, on the numeric keypad, which allow you to position the cell pointer.

Presentation graphics—Software-generated graphs with titles and legends for presentation purposes.

Query—Specify records in a database to view or extract.

Range—A rectangular group of cells defined by the addresses of its upper left-hand and lower right-hand cells.

Range name—A name given to a range for convenient reference.

Record—A collection of information about a specific entity, such as an employee or an item of inventory. A record consists of a row in a worksheet.

Relational operator—A mathematical operator that compares two parts of an expression and returns either logical "true" or "false."

Relative formula—A formula whose addresses are copied to a new range relative to the position of each cell in the range.

Repeating label—A label, input with the \ label prefix character, that is repeated across the cell regardless of cell width.

Run key ([ALT]-[F3])—A Release 2.2 feature; a keystroke that allows the user to run any macro.

Save a graph—The creation of a disk file (.PIC extension) containing the commands necessary for other software to display or print the graph.

Screen macro command—An advanced macro command that affects the appearance of the screen, including menus.

Scrolling—The motion of cells within a window, due to pointer-movement commands.

Setting sheets—A feature of Release 2.2 that allows current print, graph, or data-query settings to be displayed on the screen.

Setup string—Code to be sent to the printer that gives a command to the printer but is not itself printed. The command may set the font or pitch, for example.

Size—A specific measure of height for type, measured in points.

Shading—The superimposing of a light, dark, or solid shading over the contents of a specified range, for emphasis in printing.

Sorting—Arranging records in some predetermined manner according to specific keys in the database.

Special functions—Functions that return information about a cell or about the current cell, and functions that allow looking up items from a table.

Stacked-bar graph—A type of bar graph where the individual components are stacked rather than displayed side-by-side.

Statistical functions—Functions that return statistical results, such as sum, average, and standard deviation.

Status line—The bottom line of a worksheet, which displays mode indicators, indicates the conditions of various toggle keys (CAPS, NUM, OVR, END) and status (CALC, CMD, MEM), and which displays the date and time according to the computer's internal clock.

String data—Labels, when used in a database; also called text data.

String functions—Functions that work on alphameric entries in a worksheet.

Subroutine—See macro subroutine.

Template—A worksheet set up with headings and formulas, but without data, and saved on disk as a pre-written worksheet for later use.

Text data—Labels, when used in a database; also called string data.

Three-dimensionality—A Release 3.0 feature that allows up to 256 worksheets in memory at one time, in order to provide a third dimension to worksheets.

Translation—File conversion from the format of one applications program to the format of another, handled within the 1–2–3 Translate Utility.

Typeface—The design of print or display characters, such as Times or Helvetica.

Undo—A feature of Release 2.2 that allows user to cancel the most recent change in a worksheet.

Value—A cell entry consisting of a number or a formula (or expression) that can be evaluated to yield (return) a number.

Video drivers—Computer codes that allow a spreadsheet to be displayed on different types of video monitors.

Window—The screen display; a window onto a small portion of the available worksheet.

Worksheet area—The middle part of the screen, containing a portion of the worksheet; columns are denoted by letters and rows by numbers.

XY-graph—A type of graph where the X data range, as well as the A–F data ranges consist of values, not labels; used for correlation analysis.

LOTUS 1-2-3 COMMAND SUMMARY

This section is a quick reference for the Lotus 1-2-3 commands. This is not a complete list of all Lotus 1-2-3 commands, but it does include some commands not covered in the lessons which you can try on your own.

LOTUS ACCESS SYSTEM MENU

1-2-3	Enter 1-2-3
PrintGraph	Enters graph printing utility.
Translate	Converts files to and from WK1 format.
Install	Starts the installation procedure.
Exit	Returns to DOS.

CONTROL PANEL

Top line	Displays cursor position and entry in current cell on left, and mode on right.
Second line	Displays what is being entered in Value, Label, Edit, or Point modes and displays menu options in Menu mode.
Third line	Displays information about the highlighted menu item.

CELL POINTER MOVEMENT

1. The arrow keys move the cell pointer one position at a time in the direction of the arrow.

2. The (HOME) key moves the cell pointer to cell A1.

3. The (PGUP) and (PGDN) keys move the cursor one screen up and one screen down, respectively.

4. The (CTRL)-(→) (or (TAB)) and (CTRL)-(←) (or (SHIFT)-(TAB)) move the cursor one screen to the right and to the left, respectively.

5. Pressing the (F5) function key (Goto) followed by an address or range name moves the cell pointer directly to the address specified.

CORRECTING MISTAKES

1. /WEY clears the entire worksheet.

2. /RE (ENTER) erases the current cell.

3. The (F2) function key (Edit) allows you to edit the contents of the current cell.

4. During an entry, (BACKSPACE) erases one character at a time to the left of the cursor.

5. Immediately after an entry, the (ALT)-(F4) function key (Undo) replaces the last entry with the previous contents.

1-2-3 FUNCTION KEYS

(F1) (Help)	Displays 1-2-3 Help screen
(F2) (Edit)	Edits contents of current cell
(ALT)-(F3) (Run)	Runs a macro that is selected from a list of range names

Key	Function
ALT-F4 (Undo)	Cancels the previous changes made in the worksheet
F5 (Goto)	Moves cell pointer directly to the indicated cell
ALT-F5 (Learn)	Turns learn mode on and off
F6 (Window)	Moves cell pointer between windows on screen or toggles setting box on and off
F7 (Query)	Repeats last /Data Query specified
ALT-F7 (APP1)	Runs add-in assigned to this key, if any
F8 (Table)	Repeats last /Data Table specified
ALT-F8 (APP2)	Runs add-in assigned to this key, if any
F9 (Calc)	Recalculates all formulas in worksheet
ALT-F9 (APP3)	Runs add-in assigned to this key, if any
F10 (Graph)	Displays current graph
ALT-F10 (APP4)	Displays add-in menu if no add-ins have been assigned to this key; otherwise runs add-in assigned to this key

1-2-3 MENU COMMANDS

/**W** (Worksheet commands)   Commands that affect the worksheet
   G (Global commands)   Commands that affect the entire worksheet
     F (Format commands)   Set the display format
       F (Fixed)   Set the number of decimal positions
       S (Sci)   Scientific, or exponential, format
       C (Currency)   Leading $
       , (Commas)   Commas inserted, negative values set within parentheses
       G (General)   Standard format
       + (+/−)   Horizontal bar graph
       D (Date)   Date and time formats
       T (Text)   Displays formula instead of the result
       H (Hidden)   Suppresses display
     L (Label-Prefix commands)   Position text in cell
       L   Left align
       R   Right align
       C   Center
     C (Column-Width)   Sets column width for entire worksheet

    R (Recalculation)   Sets conditions for worksheet recalculation
    P (Protection)   Enables or disables protection
    D (Default)   Defines default settings for disk and printer
    Z (Zero)   Turns zero suppression on and off
I (Insert)   Inserts blank rows or columns
    C   Column
    R   Row
D (Delete)   Deletes entire rows or columns
    C   Column
    R   Row
C (Column)   Sets characteristics of columns or column ranges
    S (Set-Width)   Sets column width
    R (Reset-Width)   Returns column width to worksheet default
    H (Hide)   Suppresses display of specified columns
    D (Display)   Re-enables display of specified columns
    C (Column-Range)   Sets widths of a range of columns
E (Erase)   Erases entire worksheet
T (Titles)   Freezes titles on screen
    B (Both)   Horizontal and vertical titles
    H (Horizontal)   Titles in a row
    V (Vertical)   Titles in a column
    C (Clear)   Un-freezes titles
W (Window)   Split-window commands
    H (Horizontal)   Splits window horizontally, just above row at cell pointer
    V (Vertical)   Splits window vertically, just left of cell pointer
    S (Sync)   Scrolls windows synchronously
    U (Unsync)   Scrolls windows independently
    C (Clear)   Returns to single-window display
S (Status)   Displays worksheet settings
P (Page)   Inserts a page break above cell pointer
L (Learn)   Captures keystroke-equivalent macro commands in a range
    R (Range)   Sets range (column) for Learn feature
    C (Cancel)   Cancels range for Learn feature
    E (Erase)   Erases range for Learn feature
/R (Range commands)   Commands that affect part of the worksheet

F (Format)   Commands that change the format of a range (See Worksheet Global Format)
L (Label)   Label alignment in a range (See Worksheet Global Label)
E (Erase)   Erases a range
N (Name)   Commands dealing with naming ranges
   C (Create)   Creates a range name
   D (Delete)   Deletes a range name
   L (Labels)   Creates a number of range names using labels
   R (Reset)   Erases all range names
   T (Table)   Displays range names in worksheet as a table
   J (Justify)   Adjusts alignment of a column of labels
P (Prot)   Protects a range from changes
U (Unprot)   Allows changes to a range
I (Input)   Enters data into unprotected cells in a range
V (Value)   Copies a range, converting formulas to their values
T (Trans)   Copies a range, transposing it (interchanging rows and columns)
S (Search)   Finds or replaces contents of formulas and/or labels
   F   Formulas
   L   Labels
   B   Both
     F (Find)   Locates a specified string
        N (Next)   Searches for other occurrences
        Q (Quit)   Discontinues search
     R (Replace)   Locates a specified string and replaces it
        R (Replace)   Replaces one occurrence of string
        A (All)   Replaces all occurrences of string
        N (Next)   Skips this occurrence, locates next occurrence
        Q (Quit)   Discontinues search and replace
/C (Copy)   Copies a range to a new position in the worksheet
/M (Move)   Moves a range to a new position in the worksheet
/F (File)   Commands that involve access to disk
  R (Retrieve)   Retrieves a .WK1 file
  S (Save)   Saves worksheet as .WK1 file
  C (Combine)   Reads part or all of a .WK1 file into the current worksheet
    C (Copy)   New worksheet overwrites existing worksheet data

      A (Add)   New worksheet values are added to existing worksheet values
      S (Subtract)   New worksheet values are subtracted from existing values
        E (Entire-File)   Reads entire file
        N (Named/Specific-Range)   Reads named range
     X (Xtract)   Saves a range of a worksheet as a .WK1 file
        F (Formulas)   Saves formulas
        V (Values)   Saves values of formulas
     E (Erase)   Erases a file on disk
     L (List)   Lists files in current directory
     I (Import)   Imports an ASCII file (.PRN extension)
        T (Text)   Reads file as long labels into a single column
        N (Numbers)   Reads numbers and delimited labels
     D (Directory)   Changes default directory
     A (Admin)   Used for networks and linked files
/P (Print)   Outputs a range
  P (Printer)   Outputs to printer
  F (File)   Outputs to ASCII file on disk
     R (Range)   Specifies range to output
     L (Line)   Issues a line feed
     P (Page)   Issues a form feed (top of next page)
     O (Options)   Parameters that affect appearance of output
        H (Header)   Printed at top of each page
        F (Footer)   Printed at bottom of each page
        M (Margins)   Left, right, top, bottom, or none
        B (Borders)   Columns or rows
        S (Setup)   Printer control string
        P (Pg-Length)   Length of paper
        O (Other)
           A (As-Displayed)   Outputs the results of formulas
           C (Cell-Formulas)   Outputs the formulas themselves
           F (Formatted)   Includes headers, borders, etc.
           U (Unformatted)   No headers, borders, etc.
        Q (Quit)   Exits the Options menu
     C (Clear)   Erases some or all print parameters
     A (Align)   Sets line counter to top of page
     G (Go)   Sends output to printer or file
     Q (Quit)   Returns to Ready mode
/G (Graph)   Commands to create and save graphs

T (Type)   Selects the graph type
   L Line
   B Bar
   X XY
   S Stacked-Bar
   P Pie
X, A–F   Specifies selected data-range
R (Reset)   Resets some or all graph settings
   G (Graph)   Resets all graph settings
   X, A–F   Resets specified data-range settings
   R (Ranges)   Resets all data-ranges
   O (Options)   Resets options
   Q (Quit)   Returns to Graph menu
V (View)   Displays current graph on screen
S (Save)   Saves current graph on disk as .PIC file
O (Options)   Settings to enhance graph appearance
   L (Legend)   Specifies legends for graph data-ranges
   F (Format)   Creates format for graph data-ranges
   G (Graph)   Specifies format for entire graph
   A–F   Specifies format for specific data-range
      L Lines
      S Symbols
      B Both
      N Neither
   Q (Quit)   Returns to Graph Options menu
T (Titles)   Specifies graph and axis titles
   F (First)   Top title on page
   S (Second)   Second title on page
   X (X-Axis)   Axis title at bottom of graph (x-axis)
   Y (Y-Axis)   Axis title at left of graph (y-axis)
G (Grid)   Selects grid type
   H Horizontal
   V Vertical
   B Both
   C Clear
S (Scale)   Specifies scale for axis
   X (X-Scale) x-axis scale
   Y (Y-Scale) y-axis scale
      A (Automatic)   Determined by Lotus 1–2–3
      M (Manual)   User-selected

        L (Lower)   Lower-bound value
        U (Upper)   Upper-bound value
        F (Format)   Axis-format selection
        I (Indicator)   Specifies whether scale indicator is displayed
        Q (Quit)   Returns to Options menu
    S (Skip)   Displays every *n*th value
C (Color)   Displays graph in color
B (B&W)   Displays graph in monochrome
D (Data-Labels)   Uses contents of a range as labels for data points
    A—F   Selects data range for labels
        C (Center)   Locates data labels at locations of data points
        L (Left)   Locates data labels at left of data points
        A (Above)   Locates data labels above data points
        R (Right)   Locates data labels at right of data points
        B (Below)   Locates data labels below data points
    G (Group)   Assigns data labels from worksheet to all ranges
        C (Columnwise)   Divides data labels into data ranges by columns
        R (Rowwise)   Divides data labels into data ranges by rows
    Q (Quit)   Return to options menu
  Q (Quit)   Returns to Print menu
N (Name)   Works with graph names
  U (Use)   Makes current graph the named graph
  C (Create)   Creates a new named graph
  D (Delete)   Deletes a named graph
  R (Reset)   Deletes all named graphs
  T (Table)   Creates a table of all named graphs in worksheet
G (Group)   Specifies data-ranges by worksheet range
Q (Quit)   Returns to Ready mode

/D Data
  F (Fill)   Fills a range with a sequence of numbers
  T (Table)   Performs what-if analysis
    1   One-way data table
    2   Two-way data table
    R (Reset)   Resets data table type

    S (Sort)   Performs sort of a data range
        D (Data-Range)   Specifies data range to be sorted
        P (Primary-Key)   Specifies the primary key column
        S (Secondary-Key)   Specifies the secondary key column
        R (Reset)   Resets all sort settings
        G (Go)   Performs the sort
        Q (Quit)   Returns to the Graph menu
    Q (Query)   Finds a selected record
        I (Input)   Specifies the input data range
        C (Criteria)   Specifies the criteria data range
        O (Output)   Specifies the output data range (for Extract and Unique)
        F (Find)   Displays on screen the records selected
        E (Extract)   Copies to output area all records that meet criteria
        U (Unique)   Copies all nonduplicated records to output range
        D (Delete)   Deletes records that match criteria
        R (Reset)   Resets all query commands
        Q (Quit)   Returns to Ready mode
    D (Distribution)   Determines frequency distribution of values in a range
    M (Matrix)   Matrix inversion or multiplication
    R (Regression)   Performs regression analysis on a range
    P (Parse)   Converts a column of labels into a range of numbers and labels
        F (Format-Line)   Creates or allows user to edit a format line
        I (Input-Column)   Specifies column of labels to convert
        O (Output-Range)   Specifies range for conversion results
        R (Reset)   Resets data parse settings
        G (Go)   Performs parsing
        Q (Quit)   Returns to Ready mode
/S (System)   Temporarily suspends 1–2–3 and returns to operating system
/A (Add-in)   Lets you use add-in programs
    A (Attach)   Loads an add-in into memory
        N (No-Key)   Does not assign an [ALT]-Fn key to invoke the add-in
        7–10   Assigns an [ALT]-Fn key to invoke the add-in
    D (Detach)   Removes an add-in from memory

I (Invoke)   Activates an add-in that is attached
C (Clear)   Removes all add-ins from memory
Q (Quit)   Returns to Ready mode
/Q Quit   Exits Lotus 1–2–3

PRINTER SETUP STRINGS

Note: You may need to consult your printer manual concerning DIP switch settings and other details. Use of uppercase and lowercase is important in the following setup strings.

Printer Model	Compressed	12 cpi	10 cpi	Master Reset
C. Itoh 8510	\027Q	\027E	\027N	\027Y
Epson FX, MX, or RX	\015	\027M	\027P	\027@
Epson LQ	\027x0\015	\027M	\027P	\027@
HP LaserJet	\027&k2S	\027(s12H	\027&k0S	\027E
IBM Proprinter	\015	\027\058	\018	no code
Okidata Microline	\029	\028	\030	no code
Star Micronics Gemini	\015	\027\066\002	\018	\027\064
TI 850	\027P	\027z	\027y	\027@
Toshiba P351	\027\091	\027*1\027E10	no code	\027\0261

PRINTGRAPH MENU COMMANDS

Image-Select   Selects one or more saved files (.PIC) to print
Settings   Controls how graphs are printed
  Image   Controls graph image on the page
    Size   Specifies size and graph proportions
    Font   Specifies fonts used in graph
    Range-Colors   Assigns colors to graph ranges
    Quit   Returns to settings menu
  Hardware   Specifies printer, interface, paper, and directories
    Graphs-Directory   Specifies where the graph (.PIC) files are located
    Fonts-Directory   Specifies where the font (.FNT) files are located
    Interface   Specifies the interface used by the printer
    Printer   Specifies the printer in use
    Size-Paper   Specifies the paper size

        Quit   Returns to settings menu
      Action   Controls what is done between graphs
        Pause   Controls pause between graphs
        Eject   Controls advancing paper to next page
        Quit   Returns to Settings menu
    Save   Saves current settings in configuration file (PGRAPH.CNF)
    Reset   Replaces settings with those in PGRAPH.CNF
    Quit   Returns to PrintGraph main menu
Go   Starts printing selected graphs
Align   Indicates to PrintGraph that paper is properly aligned in printer
Page   Advances printer paper to top of next page
Exit   Ends PrintGraph session and returns to Lotus Access Menu

ALLWAY'S MENU COMMANDS

/W (Worksheet)   Specifies cell sizes and page breaks
    C (Column)   Specifies width of a column
    R (Row)   Specifies the height of a row
    P (Page)   Inserts or removes page breaks
/F (Format)   Specifies how the worksheet is printed
    F (Font)   Specifies fonts for printing the worksheet
        U (Use)   Applies a font to a range
        R (Replace)   Replaces a font in the current font set
        D (Default)   Restores or specifies the default font set
        L (Library)   Retrieves, saves, or erases a font set library on disk
        Q (Quit)   Returns to Allways mode
    B (Bold)   Specifies whether to use boldface in a range
    U (Underline)   Specifies whether to use underline in a range
    C (Color)   Specifies to print ranges in different colors on color printers
    L (Lines)   Specifies horizontal or vertical lines, boxes, or outlines
    S (Shade)   Specifies three shadings or clear (no shading) in a range
    R (Reset)   Removes any formatting applied to a range
    Q (Quit)   Returns to Allways mode

/G (Graph)   Commands that deal with graphs in Allways
  A (Add)   Lets you add a saved graph (.PIC file) to the worksheet
  R (Remove)   Deletes a graph from the worksheet
  G (Goto)   Moves the cell pointer to a graph on the worksheet
  S (Settings)   Modifies the settings of an individual graph on the worksheet
    P (PIC-File)   Replaces graph with another saved graph (.PIC file)
    F (Fonts)   Sets fonts to be used in printing graph
    S (Scale)   Sets scaling factor for fonts
    C (Colors)   Sets colors for graph data ranges
    R (Range)   Moves graph to a different range or change its size
    M (Margins)   Sets margins for graph (within specified range)
    D (Default)   Restores or updates default graph settings
    Q (Quit)   Returns to Allways mode
  F (Fonts-Directory)   Specifies directory containing graph fonts
  Q (Quit)   Returns to Allways mode
/L (Layout)   Specifies positioning and appearance of printed page
  P (Page-Size)   Specifies page size
  M (Margins)   Sets margins to control position of worksheet on page
  T (Titles)   Creates or removes page header or footer
  B (Borders)   Prints border columns and/or rows
  O (Options)   Sets line thickness and printing of the worksheet grid
    L (Line-Weight)   Sets line weight
    G (Grid)   Specifies whether to print worksheet grid lines
    Q (Quit)   Returns to Layout menu
  D (Default)   Updates or restores a page-layout library file
  L (Library)   Saves and retrieves individual page-layout library files
    R (Retrieve)   Retrieves a previously saved page-layout file
    S (Save)   Saves the current page layout to a library file
    E (Erase)   Deletes a page-layout library file from disk
  Q (Quit)   Returns to Allways mode
/P (Print)   Controls the printing process
  G (Go)   Prints the specified range
  F (File)   Sends print file to an encoded (.ENC) file on disk

    R (Range)   Specifies range to print
    C (Configuration)   Specifies printer, printer interface, and options
    S(Settings)   Specifies various print settings
        B (Begin)   Specifies first page to print
        E (End)   Specifies last page to print
        F (First)   Specifies page number of first printed page
        C (Copies)   Specifies number of copies to print
        W (Wait)   Causes printer to pause after each page
        R (Reset)   Restores standard print settings
        Q (Quit)   Returns to Allways mode
    Q (Quit)   Returns to Allways mode
/D (Display)   Affects the way the worksheet is displayed on monitor
    M (Mode)   Switches screen display mode between text and graphics
    Z (Zoom)   Enlarges or reduces the display size of cells
    G (Graphs)   Turns display of graphs on or off
    C (Colors)   Sets colors for foreground, background, and cell pointer
    Q (Quit)   Returns to Allways mode
/S (Special)   Commands that perform large-scale changes to worksheet
    C (Copy)   Copies formats from one range to another
    M (Move)   Moves formats from one range to another
    J (Justify)   Justifies a range of cells
    I (Import)   Applies format and settings of another worksheet to current one
/Q (Quit)   Returns to 1–2–3 Ready mode

ALLWAYS FUNCTION KEYS

Key		Description
[F1]	(Help)	Displays Allways Help screen
[F4]	(Reduce)	Reduces display size
[ALT]-[F4]	(Enlarge)	Enlarges display size
[F5]	(Goto)	Moves cell pointer directly to cell or named range specified
[F6]	(Display)	Switches screen display between text and graphics modes
[ALT]-**B**	(Boldface)	Set/clear toggle

	ALT-G (Grid lines)	On/off toggle
	ALT-L (Lines)	Outline/all/none toggle
	ALT-S (Shading)	Light/dark/solid/none toggle
	ALT-U (Underlining)	Single/double/none toggle

MACRO LIBRARY MANAGER COMMANDS

Load	Copies contents of a macro library (.MLB) to memory for use
Save	Moves contents of a range to a macro library in memory and on disk
Edit	Copies contents of a loaded macro library to worksheet for editing
Remove	Erases a macro library from memory
Name-List	Enters a list in worksheet of range names in a macro library
Quit	Returns to 1–2–3

INDEX

A

@ABS function, 237
Absolute cell reference, 168
Absolute formula, 106
Absolute range name, 256
Access System, 72
@ACOS function, 238
Ascending order sort, 192
Add-in programs, 357
Adding another worksheet's values (/FCA), 287
Address, 75
Allways add-in program, 365
    boldface, 370, 372
    attaching, 365
    display modes, 366
    editing graphs, 379
    fonts, 369
    graphs, 377
    invoking, 365
    lines, 373
    margins, 375
    menu features, 367, 368
    printing, 375
    shading, 373
ALT key, 17
ALT-F3 command (Run), 311
ALT-F4 command (Undo), 100
ALT-F5 command (Learn), 316
#AND# operator, 243
Arguments for functions, 113
ASCII files,
    exporting, 293
    importing, 293
    parsing imported, 297
@ASIN function, 238
@ATAN function, 238
Attaching add-ins, 357, 358
AUTOEXEC.BAT file (DOS), 57
Autoexecute macros, 350
@AVG function, 239

B

Backspace key, 19
Backup, 118
Bar chart, 150
Batch files (DOS), 54
BEEP macro command, 336
Bin range, 213
BLANK macro command, 331
Booting the system
    cold start, 14
    warm start, 14
Borders (/PPOB), 272
BRANCH macro command, 331
Built-in functions, 235

C

Calc command (F9), 238
Call subroutine macro command, 335
Cell
    copying, 105
    current cell, 78
    definition in worksheet, 75
    moving contents of, 135
    specifying a range, 93, 105
    too long for column width, 109
@CELL function, 253
@CELLPOINTER function, 254, 337
Cell pointer, 76
    moving 78
CGA (Color Graphics Adaptor), 8
CHDIR command (DOS), 45
CHKDSK command (DOS), 36
@CHOOSE function, 257
CLS command (DOS), 58
Cold start, 14
@COLS function, 254
Column,
    as title (/WTV), 128
    hiding (/WCH), 133

Column width
    resetting to default (/WCR), 108
    setting a single column (/WCS), 108
    setting a range (/WC), 109
Combining worksheets (/FC), 281
Comma format, 116
Commands
    giving, 79
        for macros, 322, 329
        slash, 79
COMP command (DOS), 42
CONFIG.SYS file (DOS), 60
Context-sensitive help, 100
Control Characters, 17
Control panel, 73, 74
COPY command (DOS), 39
Copy command (/C), 105
Copying formulas, 105
    absolute/relative cell references, 106
Copying values from stored worksheet (/FCC), 281
Correcting errors, 84
@COS function, 238
@COUNT function, 240
Creating a data table (/DT), 220
[CTRL] key, 17
Currency format, 116
Current cell, 76, 78
Current date (@TODAY), 249
Current time (@NOW), 256
Cursor, 86
Cut and paste, 284

D

Data distribution (/DD), 211
Data fill (/DF), 212, 220
Data label (graph), 174, 175
Data management, 187
Data manipulation macro commands, 331
Data parsing, 297
Data Query (/DQ), 193
    absolute cell reference, 200
    Criteria Range, 195, 196
    delete option, 206
    extract, 198
    find, 196
    formula conditions, 200
    Input Range, 195
    multiple selection criteria, 203
    Output Range, 197
    relational operators, 201
    selection criteria, 195
    settings, 193
    unique option, 205
    wild card characters, 199
Data range for graphs
    resetting, 160
Data Sort (/DS)
    primary key, 192
    secondary key, 192
    ascending order, 192
Data Table (/DT), 220
    clear(/DTC), 225
    using one-way data table (/DT1), 221
    using two-way data table (/DT2), 224
Database, 187
Database statistical functions, 250
DATE command (DOS), 58
Date format, 116
@DATE function, 248
Date (printing), 272
@DAY function, 249
DBF file extension, 281
Defaults
    printer, 265
    selecting data drive default (/FD), 90
[DEL] key, 19
Deleting row or column (/WDR, /WDC), 136, 137
Delimiters, 113
Destination range, 105
Detaching add-ins, 358, 359
DIF file extension, 280, 281
DIR command (DOS), 37
Disks, 20
    care and handling, 23
    formatting, 34
    hard disk, 25
Disk drive
    identifying, 26
    default, 32
Disk Operating System (DOS), 31
    AUTOEXEC.BAT file, 57
    CONFIG.SYS file, 60
    creating text files using COPY, 54
    directories/subdirectories, 44
    filename, 38, 91
    path, 56
    wild card character, 39
DISKCOMP command (DOS), 43
DISKCOPY command (DOS), 42
Display format
    menu options, 116
    range (/RF), 117
    setting (/WGF), 114
    text (/WGFT), 139

zero suppression (/WGZ), 118
Displaying a graph (/GV, [F10]), 154, 157
Distribution table, 213
DOS commands, 33
    CHDIR, 45
    CHKDSK, 36
    CLS, 58
    COMP, 42
    COPY, 39
    DATE, 58
    DIR, 37
    DISKCOMP, 43
    DISKCOPY, 42
    ECHO, 58
    ERASE, 41
    executing programs, 48
    FORMAT, 34
    MKDIR, 44
    MODE, 60
    PATH, 56
    PROMPT, 59
    RENAME, 41
    RMDIR, 47
    running programs, 48
    TIME, 58
    TREE, 47
    TYPE, 42
    VER, 34
DOS prompt, 14
@DSUM function, 250

E

ECHO command (DOS), 58
Edit command ([F2]), 86, 138
Edit Mode, 74, 86
EGA (Enhanced Graphics Adaptor), 8
Electronic spreadsheet, 65
[ENTER] key, 17
Entering 123, 73
Entering formulas, 86
Entering labels, 83
Entering selection criteria, 196, 202
Entering values, 84
ERASE command (DOS), 41
Erasing entries (/RE), 80
Erasing the whole worksheet (/WEY), 82
ERR message, 137, 138
ERROR mode, 313
[ESC] key, 18, 341
Executing programs, 48
Exiting LOTUS, 72

Expansion slots, 7
Exporting ASCII files, 293
Extracting a range to a file (/FX), 284
Extracting database records (/DQE), 198

F

[F1] command (Help), 99
[F10] command (Graph), 157
[F2] command (Edit), 86
[F5] command (Goto), 77
[F6] command (Window), 91
[F9] command (Calc), 238
@FALSE function, 244
Field names, 188
Fields (database), 187
File commands (/F), 89
    combining files (/FC), 281
    erasing files (/FE), 90
    extract range (/FX), 284
    display/change directory (/FD), 90
    importing a print/text file (/FI), 293
    retrieving a worksheet (/FR), 101
    saving a worksheet (/FS), 90, 118
File Combine command (/FC), 281
File conversion, 302
File copying (DOS), 39
File importing (/FI), 293
File manipulation macro commands, 330
Filling a range with numbers (/DF), 212, 220
Financial functions, 246
@FIND function, 251
Find Mode, 74
Finding database records (/DQF), 196
Fixed format, 116
Flow of control macro commands, 331
Footer (/PPOF), 271
FORMAT command (DOS), 34
Format line, 297
Formatting disk, 34
Formatting a range (/RF), 117
Formulas
    absolute, 106
    copying, 105
    entering into worksheet, 86
    mathematical operators for, 86
    printout, 140
    relative, 106
Frequency distribution (/DD), 211
Function keys, 17
Functions, 113, 235
    arguments, 236

database statistical, 250
date, 248
ERR, 245
financial, 246
logical, 242
lookup, 254
mathematical, 237
statistical, 239
string, 251
special, 253
time, 248
trigonometric, 238
@FV function, 247

G

General format, 116
GETLABEL macro command, 337
GETNUMBER macro command, 337
Giving commands, 79
    function keys, 77, 84, 91
    slash key (/), 79
Global display format (/WGF), 114
Global settings (/WG), 114
GoTo command ((F5)), 77
Graph commands
    adding grid lines (/GOG), 178
    adding symbols and lines to XY graph
        (/GOFG), 173. 174
    bar graph (/GTB), 160
    creating (/G), 151
    crosshatching, 156
    data labels (/GOD), 174, 175
    displaying ((F10)), 157
    exploding pie, 157
    group (setting multiple data ranges), 163
    legends (/GOL), 164, 165, 170
    line graph (/GTL), 167
    manual scaling (/GOSM), 175, 177
    naming (/GN), 158, 162
    format (/GOF), 174
    grids, 178
    options (/GO), 154, 155
    pie chart (/GTP), 151
    printing, 178
    resetting graph settings (/GR), 160
    saving graphs to disk (/GS), 159
    scaling axes, 175
    selecting graph type (/GT), 154, 160
    setting data range (/GA, /GB, etc.), 154
    setting horizontal (X-axis) (/GX), 154, 160
    setting scale limits (/GOSX, /GOSY), 177, 178
    settings, 154
    stacked bar (/GTS), 166
    titles (/GOT), 155
    viewing (/GV), 154
    XY graph (/GTX), 172
Graph display command key ((F10)), 157
Graph name
    creating, 159
    using, 162
Grid lines, adding to graph (/GOG), 178

H

Hard disk, 25
Headers, 271
Help key ((F1)), 99
Help system, 99
Hidden column, 133
Hidden format, 116
@HLOOKUP function, 254
(HOME) key, 76
@HOUR function, 250

I

@IF function, 244
IF macro command, 334
Importing a print/text file (/FI), 293
@INDEX function, 258
Input commands for macros, 337
Input components, 4, 11
(INS) key, 19
Inserting data, 78
Inserting row or column (/WIR, /WIC), 103
@INT function, 237
Interactive macro commands, 337
    {?} macro, 337
Invoking add-ins, 358, 360
@ISERR function, 245

J

Jumping between windows ((F6)), 132

K

Keyboard, 11, 15

L

Label input command for macros ([GETLABEL]), 337
Label Mode, 74
Label prefix
    characters, 83
    global, 83
    repeating, 107
    setting text alignment in a range, 83
    for data parse format line, 297
Labels, 82
    alignment in a cell, 83
    characters designating labels, 83
    default position, 83
@LEFT function, 251
Legends, adding to a graph (/GOL), 165
@LENGTH function, 251
LET macro command, 331
Line chart, 173
Linking data between files, 289, 291
Logical functions, 242
Logical operators, 242
Lookup functions, 254
@LOWER function, 252

M

Macro Library Manager, 359
    detaching, 365
    editing a library, 363
    invoking macros in library, 361
    removing a library from memory, 362
    saving a library, 360
Macros, 309
    autoexecute macros, 350
    commands, 322, 329
    creating, 310
    editing, 313
    keystroke representations, 318
    Learn feature, 315, 323
    multiple line, 321
    naming, 310, 312
    using [ALT] key, 310
    using tilde, 311
Main memory, 6

Main menu options, 79
Margins
    overriding default (/PPOM), 269
Matching selection criteria, 196, 199, 200
Mathematical functions, 237
Mathematical operators, 86
@MAX function, 240
Menu block for macros, 342
MENUBRANCH macro command, 338, 340
MENUCALL macro command, 338
Menu Mode, 74
Microprocessing unit (MPU), 5
@MID function, 252
@MIN function, 240
@MINUTE function, 250
MKDIR command (DOS), 44
@MOD function, 237
Mode, 74
MODE command (DOS), 60
Mode indicator, 74
Modem, 10
Modular spreadsheets, 284
Monitor, 8
@MONTH function, 249
Motherboard, 5
Mouse, 11
Move command (/M), 135

N

Naming a graph parameters (/GNC), 158, 162
Naming ranges (/RN), 119, 214
#NOT# operator, 243
@NOW function, 250
@NPV function, 247
Numeric data (database), 188
Numeric keyboard, 17
Numerical format
    options, 116
    in graphs (/GOF), 177
    setting in a range (/RF), 117

O

One-Way data table (/DT1), 221
Opening a worksheet file (/FR), 101
Operators
    logical, 242
    mathematical, 86
    relational, 242, 243
#OR# operator, 243

Output Components, 4, 8
Output Range, 197

P

Page length when printing (/PPOP), 269
Page number, 272
Parsing data, 297
PATH command (DOS), 56
Percent format, 116
@PI function, 238
Pie chart, 149
@PMT function, 218, 246
Point Mode, 74
    entering formulas, 87, 88
    entering ranges, 105
Presentation graphics, 149
Print command (/P), 91, 119
Print file,
    creating (/PF), 293
    importing into worksheet (/FI), 293
Print Options (/PPO), 269
Print settings, 267
Print-time commands
    form feed (/PPP), 92, 93
    line feed (/PPL), 92
    set top of page (/PPA), 92, 93
PrintGraph utility, 179
    printing graph, 182
    selecting graph to print, 181
    setting graph directory, 180
Printer
    advancing to top of next page, 93
    default settings (/PPS), 265
    dot matrix, 9
    giving special instructions, 270
    laser, 9
    letter quality, 9
    using, in LOTUS, 71
Printing (/P), 91
    begin (/PPG), 94
    border (/PPOB), 272
    cell formulas, 274
    current date, 272
    footer, 271
    formula (/PPOC), 140
    header, 271
    line, 268
    margin settings (/PPOM), 269
    options (/PPO), 267
    page numbers, 272
    ranges (/PPR), 93, 119

    setup string, 270
    to a disk file, 293
    unformatted, 274
    worksheet formulas, 140, 274
PRN file extension, 280
Processing components, 4, 5
PROMPT command (DOS), 59
Protecting cell values, 115
PRTSC key, 18

Q

Quit macro command, 335
Quitting the worksheet (/WQ), 94

R

RAM (Random Access Memory), 6
@RAND function, 238
Range commands (/R), 80
Range name, 119, 214
    creating, 215
    label (/RNL), 216
    table (/RNT), 217
Ranges
    adjusting column width (/RC), 108
    copying (/C), 105
    erasing (/RE), 80
    filling with a number sequence (/DF), 212, 220
    inserting into current worksheet (/FC), 281
    moving (/M), 135
    naming (/RN), 119
    printing (/PPR), 93, 119
    saving as a worksheet file (/FX), 284
    setting numerical format (/RF), 117
    specifying, 93, 105, 119
    text alignment (/RL), 81
    text justification (/RJ), 81
Ready Mode, 74
Recalculation (/WGR, F9), 115
Records (database), 187
Relational operators, 242, 243
Relative formula, 106
RENAME command (DOS), 41
Repeating labels (\), 107
@REPLACE function, 253
Replacing text (/RS), 142
Retrieving a worksheet file (/FR), 101
RETURN macro command, 335
@RIGHT function, 251
RMDIR command (DOS), 47

ROM (Read Only Memory), 7
@ROUND function, 237
Row
    as title (/WTH), 129
    delete (/WTR), 136
    insert (/WIR), 103
@ROWS function, 254
Running programs, 48

S

Saving a graph (/GS), 159
Saving a range as a worksheet file (/FX), 284
Saving a worksheet file (/FS), 118
Scale, in graphs (/GOSX, /GOSY), 177, 178
SCROLL LOCK key, 77
Scrolling, 77
Scientific format, 116
Screen macro commands, 330,
Searching a database (/DQ), 193
Searching a range (/RS), 142
@SECOND function, 250
Selecting option from menu, 80
Selection criteria in worksheet database, 195, 196, 202
Setup string (/PPOS), 270
@SIN function, 238
Sorting (/DS), 189
    keys, 191
        ascending/descending, 192
        settings, 191
Source cell, 105
Source file (DOS), 54
Space bar, 16
Special functions, 253
Specifying a range
    pointing with the cell pointer, 105
    typing cell address, 93
    using a range name, 119
Specifying selection criteria, 196, 202
Spreadsheet, 65
Split screen (window) (/WW), 130
@SQRT function, 237
Starting LOTUS 1–2–3, 69
Starting the computer, 12
Statistical functions
    for a database, 250
Status indicators, 75
Status line, 73, 75
@STD function, 240
Step Mode, 74
String data (database), 188

@STRING function, 253
@SUM function, 113
Subroutine call macro command, 335
Subtracting another worksheet's values (/FCS), 289
Suppressing zero display (/WGZ), 118
Synchronized windows (/WWS), 132

T

TAB key, 18
Table, creating (/DT), 220
@TAN function, 238
Target file (DOS), 54
Template, 110
Text data (database), 188
Text file, inserting in worksheet (/FI), 293
Text format option, 116
TIME command (DOS), 58
Titles,
    in graphs (/GOT), 155
    moving cell pointer to, 128
    setting worksheet (/WT), 128
@TODAY function, 249
Translate utility, 300
TREE command (DOS), 47
Trigonometric functions, 238
@TRUE function, 244
Two-Way data table, 226
TYPE command (DOS), 42

U

Undo Command ((ALT)-(F4)), 100
@UPPER function, 252

V

@VALUE function, 253
Value Mode, 74
Values, 82
    characters designating values, 82
@VAR function, 240
VER command (DOS), 34
VGA (Video Graphics Array), 8
Viewing a graph (/GV, (F10)), 154, 157
@VLOOKUP function, 254

INDEX **415**

W

WAIT macro command, 338
Warm start (DOS), 14
Width of a column, 108
Window into worksheet, 77
Window command (F6), 91
Windows
   clear (/WWC), 132
   jumping between, 131
   setting (/WW), 130
   synchronization, 132
WK1 file extension, 91, 280
WKS file extension, 280
Worksheet area, 73
Worksheet commands (/W), 103
Worksheets, 65
   cell, 75
   data table, 220
   entries, 83, 86
   erasing an entry (/RE), 80
   erasing the current worksheet (/WEY), 82
   formulas, 86
   GoTo command (F5), 77
   HOME key, 76
   label prefixes, 83
   labels, 82
   modular, 284
   moving the cell pointer, 76
   PGDN PGUP keys, 77
   recalculation (/WGR, F9), 238
   saving worksheet file, 118
   SCROLL LOCK key, 77
   size, 76
   values, 82
   windows, 130
Worksheet Global commands (/WG), 114

X

XY graph, 172

Y

@YEAR function, 249

Z

Zero suppression (/WGZ), 118